Accounting

THIRD CANADIAN EDITION

NANCI LEE American River College

ELAINE HALES Georgian College

Accounting

THIRD CANADIAN EDITION

Prentice
Hall

Toronto

National Library of Canada Cataloguing in Publication Data

Lee, Nanci
     Accounting

3rd Canadian ed.
Includes index.
ISBN 0-13-042972-4

1. Accounting. 2. Accounting—Problems, exercises, etc. I. Hales, Elaine II. Title.

HF5635.A37 2003   657'.042   C2001-903986-7

ISBN 0-13-042972-4

Associate Editor: Rema Tatangelo
Production Editor: Gillian Scobie
Copy Editor: Karen Hunter
Production Coordinator: Deborah Starks
Page Layout: Bill Renaud
Permissions Research: Susan Wallace-Cox
Art Director: Mary Opper
Interior and Cover Design: Lisa Lapointe
Cover Image: PhotoDisc

33 34 35 CP 16 15 14

Printed and bound in Canada.

Contents

CHAPTER THREE

Understanding Debits and Credits and the Trial Balance

CHAPTER FOUR

The General Journal and the General Ledger

CHAPTER SEVEN

The Sales Journal and the Accounts Receivable Subsidiary Ledger

CHAPTER EIGHT

The Purchases Journal and the Accounts Payable Subsidiary Ledger

CHAPTER NINE

The Cash Receipts, Cash Payments, and Combined Cash Journals

CHAPTER TEN

The Bank Account and Cash Funds

CHAPTER ELEVEN

Worksheets, Financial Statements, and Closing Entries for a Merchandising Business

CHAPTER TWELVE

Payroll—Employee Deductions

CHAPTER THIRTEEN # Payroll—Employer Taxes and Other Obligations

CHAPTER FOURTEEN Partnership Accounting

Preface

Welcome to the Third Canadian Edition of *Accounting*! Designed for students with little or no accounting background, this edition makes learning accounting fundamentals as easy as possible. The text also gives students a strong foundation in accounting and a clear understanding of accounting terminology. After completing this first course in accounting, students will be prepared to enter the job market; to understand the usefulness and importance of accounting procedures as business owners, managers, or office workers; and be well-prepared to continue their studies in advanced accounting courses.

From the first edition, we wrote *Accounting* using input from students and instructors. Students at the introductory level find the material easy to understand and instructors find it easy to incorporate into their daily lesson plans. Since then, the text has been thoroughly class tested and refined over several semesters.

The Third Canadian Edition of *Accounting* has been designed to help students feel at ease with the text and subject matter. We have kept the new material in each chapter to a minimum so that readers can absorb the content thoroughly before continuing. Where feasible, we also cover difficult concepts in small segments, so that readers can master the concepts a little at a time. Extensive classroom testing has proved that students respond well when presented with realistic situations; therefore, we continue to illustrate concepts using true-to-life characters and examples of common small business situations.

While *Accounting*, Third Canadian Edition, makes every attempt to communicate clearly with students, it is also designed with instructors in mind. The text is writtten to eliminate questions before they occur, making the job of teaching the class much easier. You will see how easily students respond to the friendly writing style and how the text stimulates class discussion.

Chapter Organization and Features

Accounting offers several special features that reinforce students' learning:

- **Learning objectives** are listed at the beginning of each chapter. They clearly delineate for the reader what skills and concepts are to be gained from the chapter.

- A list of accounting-related **Vocabulary** appears at the beginning of each chapter. Students will notice **bold-face terms,** with those words defined again in the body of the text. This approach reinforces learning and helps students both augment their understanding of the English language and communicate effectively as accountants. Students can really hone their comprehension of accounting terms by reading the **Vocabulary Review** and completing the related **vocabulary exercises** (fill-in-the-blank and word matching) at the end of each chapter.

- Numerous **illustrations** follow the discussion material. We use T accounts, ledgers, journal entries, financial statements, and worksheets throughout the text to help the reader to visually comprehend the written material.

- **Chapter Summaries** provide a concise review of the material presented in the chapter.

- Approximately 10 end-of-chapter **Exercises** follow the vocabulary review. Exercises are relatively short and generally review one specific topic covered in the preceding material.

- **Problems** follow the exercises; they are more comprehensive and progress from easy to more difficult. Like the exercises, the problems review all the major points discussed in the chapters.

- There are three **Comprehensive Problems** in the text. These are similar to a practice set; all the working papers needed to solve the problems are included in the student's packet of working papers. The first problem reviews the concepts presented in Chapters One to Six (the accounting cycle for a service business). The second comprehensive problem appears after Chapter Eleven and covers the material presented in chapters Seven to Eleven (special journals, bank statement reconciliation, and financial statements for a merchandising business). The third comprehensive problem reviews the preparation of the payroll and the related tasks (completing individual employee earnings records; making payments for union dues, federal and provincial income taxes, Canada Pension Plan contributions, employment insurance, workers' compensation insurance, employer's health tax, etc.; and the preparation of the T4 summary for the Canada Customs and Revenue Agency.

Highlights of the Third Canadian Edition

Here are some key enhancements we made to *Accounting* that make it even more readable and informative:

- A fresh new design that will appeal to students who are new to accounting;

- Thorough updates to theory and examples;

- Rewrites of two chapters on payroll now reflect recent changes in the law relating to federal and provincial income tax withholding. This chapter also provides updated rates for employee and employer taxes;

- Expanded material regarding purchases and sales now includes information about the Goods and Services Tax, Provincial Sales Tax, and Harmonized Sales Tax;

- A new chapter on partnership accounting gives students essential knowledge about partnership characteristics, formation, division of net income and loss, adding or withdrawing a partner, and liquidation; and

- New and updated exercises and problems to reflect the improvements to the text.

Supplements

The Working Papers that accompany *Accounting*, Third Canadian Edition, include answer spaces and forms for completing all the exercises, problems, and comprehensive problems in the text. Repetitive use of the forms provides a convenient and realistic link to real-world accounting and reinforces the students' confidence by means of practical application. For the benefit of both instructors and students, we have designed the working papers to correspond exactly with the solutions manual. The Instructor's Solutions Manual contains complete solutions for all exercises, problems and comprehensive problems in the book.

Acknowledgements

We would like to thank all reviewers, whose invaluable comments and suggestions helped to improve the Third Canadian Edition of this textbook.

Mel Sparks	Lambton College
Paul Berry	Mount Allison University
Augusta Ford	College of the North Atlantic
Dianne Girard	Sprott Shaw College
Doug Ringrose	Grant MacEwan College

We also extend our special thanks to acquisitions editor, Samantha Scully; associate editor, Veronica Tomaiuolo; production editor, Gillian Scobie; and designer, Lisa Lapointe.

CHAPTER 1

Starting a Business and the Balance Sheet

LEARNING OBJECTIVES

When you have completed this chapter, you should

1. **have an increased understanding of accounting terminology, particularly as it relates to the balance sheet.**

2. **know how management and accountants work together to make business decisions.**

3. **have a basic knowledge of the fundamental accounting equation.**

4. **be able to analyze transactions that relate to assets, liabilities, and owner's equity.**

5. **be able to prepare a balance sheet.**

VOCABULARY

account	an individual record for assets, liabilities, owner's equity, revenue, cost of goods sold, and expense
accounts payable	a liability of the business; a promise to pay a creditor for services or merchandise received
appreciate	to increase in value
assets	items of value, including cash, equipment, land, buildings, furniture owned by a business
balance sheet	a financial statement that lists the balances of the assets, liabilities, and owner's equity of a business on a particular date; also called statement of financial position when used for not-for-profit organizations
Canada Customs and Revenue Agency (CCRA)	the federal agency that is responsible for collecting income taxes
capital account	a summary of the owner's investments, withdrawals, and net income or loss of a proprietorship or partnership
capital assets	assets that are held for an extended time and that are used to facilitate the production of goods and services
creditor	a person or business to whom a debt is owed
current assets	assets that are cash, that are expected to be converted to cash, or to be used up within a year's time or within the normal operating cycle

current liabilities	debts that are expected to be paid within a year or within the normal operating cycle
discrepancy	difference or disagreement
fundamental accounting equation	Assets = Liabilities + Owner's Equity
liabilities	debts
long-term liabilities	debts that fall due more than one year beyond the balance sheet date, or debts that are not expected to be paid out of current assets
monetary	of or relating to money
owner's equity	the portion of the business assets to which the owner has direct claim
service business	a business that sells a service; examples include accountants, lawyers, doctors, veterinarians
shift in assets	occurs when individual asset values change but the total assets figure does not change
solvent	able to meet financial obligations
transaction	the act of transacting; examples include purchasing merchandise, selling services, paying or receiving cash

Introduction

Many people have dreamed of opening their own business—maybe a restaurant, a riding school, an auto repair shop, or a consulting firm. While starting a business is relatively easy, keeping the business alive and healthy is much more difficult.

The accountant and the accounting records play a very important role in the life of any business. Accounting provides financial information about an economic entity (a business enterprise, a church, a club, a government organization, and so on). The daily **transactions**, such as buying or selling goods and services, making a payment on a loan, or borrowing money—in short, anything that can be measured objectively in **monetary** terms—are recorded and classified. To make the information more usable, it is summarized in accounting reports, which are the basic tools for financial decision making.

Accounting is called the "language of business" because owners, managers, investors, creditors, bankers, and so on communicate with each other using terms such as *cost of goods sold, book value, net income, operating expenses, return on net assets,* and *inventory turnover.* They read financial statements and other detailed accounting data to make intelligent decisions, such as: What price shall be charged? Shall we expand our hours? Hire new people? Take on new products? Offer new services? Borrow money? Cut back? Open another store? Take on a partner? Get out of the business altogether?

Without good records, a business would have difficulty remaining **solvent**, or would not maintain enough cash to pay its bills when they became due. Many new businesses close their doors in failure before the first year has passed, and poor management is frequently cited as the reason. Management must work hand in hand with accountants in analyzing the records in order to make the daily decisions that keep a business successful.

In addition, many persons outside the business are interested in the accounting records. The various government taxing agencies may want to see a firm's books on a regular basis to audit, for example, payroll tax and sales tax records.

At the beginning of every year accountants are called upon to calculate the income taxes for millions of Canadians. They are hired regularly to prepare payroll and sales tax returns for businesses. Accountants may work for **Canada Customs and Revenue Agency (CCRA)**. Their work there might include the auditing of income tax returns for businesses and for individuals. Accountants may be hired to tell you how best to invest your money, how to pay the least amount of income taxes, or how to plan for retirement. Accountants are a very important segment of our society; their services are constantly in demand.

The job of the accountant is normally one where she or he interprets the data in the accounting records, perhaps to help management make decisions or to project future business trends or to suggest several plans of action designed to give the best tax options. The job of a bookkeeper, on the other hand, is one of record keeping. Record keeping entails recording on a regular basis all the transactions of a business, classifying that information, and summarizing the data for presentation to the accountant, who will then interpret the results.

Types of Business Organization

The three main categories of business organization are the: (1) sole proprietorship; (2) partnership; and (3) corporation. A brief description of each follows:

Sole Proprietorship

A sole proprietorship is a business owned by an individual who usually manages the business and makes the business decisions. The net income of the business belongs to the owner, as do the net losses. The owner is personally liable for the debts of the business. A sole proprietorship is easy to form and ends when the owner dies or if the business closes for some other reason. This text will concentrate mainly on sole proprietorships.

Partnership

A partnership has two or more owners who share both the risks and the decision-making; the partners pool their talents and their assets. If the partnership incurs debt that can not be paid out of business funds, the partners are personally liable for paying the creditors. A partnership, like a proprietorship, is easy to form and ends when a partner withdraws or dies.

Corporation

A corporation is owned by its shareholders, but they are not personally liable for the business debts nor are they involved in business decision-making. A corporation may have just a few shareholders, or it may have a large number. A corporation is more difficult to start than a proprietorship or partnership, and it can exist indefinitely. It is not dependent upon the lives of its shareholders.

Starting a Business

Lupe Gomez decides, after attending college and working for several years, to form her own business. She plans to buy the necessary furniture and equipment, hire an assistant, do the necessary advertising, and then open her own computer repair shop. She will be selling no product, but will be providing a service to her clients, thus her business, Computer Wizards, is a **service business**.

The Fundamental Accounting Equation

The **fundamental accounting equation** governs how transactions are recorded. The equation is this:

$$\text{Assets} = \text{Liabilities} + \text{Owner's Equity}.$$

Assets are items of value owned by the business (whether or not they are fully paid for). They may be tangible; that is, have a definite physical form such as office equipment, buildings, land, furniture, supplies, or cash—or they may be intangible, such as an investment in stocks or bonds, a copyright or patent, or amounts due from customers (accounts receivable).

Liabilities are debts owed by the business to various **creditors**.

Owner's equity is the difference between the assets and the liabilities. Therefore, the fundamental accounting equation may be stated as:

$$\text{Assets} - \text{Liabilities} = \text{Owner's Equity}$$

The assets of a business are supplied either by the owner or by another person or business. That portion of the assets to which the owner has a claim is called **owner's equity** and the portion to which creditors have a claim is called liabilities. If, for example, a business owner purchases new equipment that costs $10,000 by making a $6,000 cash down payment, the equipment is owned by both the owner and the creditor until the debt is paid in full.

Transactions of a New Business

Now let's trace the transactions for Computer Wizards to see how Lupe went about getting ready to begin this business venture. We will see how every transaction affects the fundamental accounting equation. It is important to note here that Lupe complies with the mandatory practice of keeping all of her personal records separate from her business records. She owns her own home, a car, furniture, appliances, and cameras, and has personal debts. However, these personal assets and liabilities do not appear on the books of the business, where there is a separate record called an **account** kept for each asset and liability and for the owner's equity.

TRANSACTION 1

Establishing a Business Bank Account   Lupe withdraws $10,000 from her personal savings account, deposits the money in a business account, and orders personalized cheques for Computer Wizards. The fundamental accounting equation looks like this after the deposit:

| Assets | = | Liabilities + Owner's Equity |
Cash	=	Lupe Gomez, Capital
(1) $10,000	=	$10,000

The original investment, additional investments at a later date, and all profits and losses of the business are recorded in a separate account called the **capital account**, or simply Capital, which is an owner's equity account. After this initial deposit, you will note that Assets = Owner's Equity because at this point there are no debts.

TRANSACTION 2

Purchasing Office Equipment and Paying Cash   Lupe purchases a desktop computer with word processing software from Business Equipment Company (BECO) at a total cost of $3,500. She writes a cheque for the equipment. The equation now looks like this:

	Assets			=	Liabilities	+	Owner's Equity
	Cash	+	Equipment	=			Lupe Gomez, Capital
Previous Balances	$10,000						$10,000
(2)	−3,500		+3,500				
New Balances	$ 6,500		+3,500	=			$10,000

Note that assets are still equal to owner's equity because there are no liabilities.

TRANSACTION 3

Purchasing Office Equipment on Account   Lupe purchases additional computer equipment, monitors, and printers from BECO at a total cost of $12,500. Lupe does not pay for the equipment now, but agrees to pay the full amount within 12 months. Amounts owed to creditors are recorded in the liability account entitled **Accounts Payable**. The equation after this transaction looks like this:

	Assets			=	Liabilities	+	Owner's Equity
	Cash	+	Equipment	=	Accounts Payable	+	Lupe Gomez, Capital
Previous Balances	$6,500		$ 3,500	=			$10,000
(3)			+12,500		+ 12,500		
New Balances	$6,500	+	$16,000	=	$12,500	+	$10,000

Notice that liabilities are now $12,500. This means that of the total assets of $22,500 ($6,500 + $16,000), the owner's share is $10,000.

At any time after a transaction has been recorded, total assets will equal total liabilities and owner's equity. You can always check the accuracy of your work by simply adding.

Assets		=	Liabilities + Owner's Equity	
Cash	$ 6,500		Accounts Payable	$12,500
Equipment	16,000		Lupe Gomez, Capital	10,000
Total	$22,500		Total	$22,500

TRANSACTION 4

Purchasing Office Furniture, Making a Cash Down Payment   Lupe buys $4,500 worth of furniture from Prince Andrew Office Furniture Company. She pays $2,500 down and agrees to pay the rest in six months' time. The equation now looks like this:

	Assets						=	Liabilities	+	Owner's Equity
	Cash	+	Equipment	+	Furniture		=	Accounts Payable	+	Lupe Gomez, Capital
Previous Balances	$6,500		$16,000				=	$12,500		$10,000
(4)	−2,500				+4,500			+2,000		
New Balances	$4,000	+	$16,000	+	$4,500		=	$14,500	+	$10,000

Again, a quick check proves the accuracy of the work, because total assets must always equal total liabilities and owner's equity.

Assets		=	Liabilities + Owner's Equity	
Cash	$ 4,000		Accounts Payable	$14,500
Equipment	16,000		Lupe Gomez, Capital	10,000
Furniture	4,500			
Total	$24,500		Total	$24,500

TRANSACTION 5

Purchasing Office Supplies for Cash   Lupe writes a cheque for $800 for supplies. The equation after that transaction looks like this:

	Assets							=	Liabilities	+	Owner's Equity
	Cash	+ Equipment	+	Furniture	+	Supplies		=	Accounts Payable	+	Lupe Gomez, Capital
Previous Balances	$4,000 +	$16,000	+	$4,500				=	$14,500	+	$10,000
(5)	−800					+800					
New Balances	$3,200 +	$16,000	+	$4,500	+	$800		=	$14,500	+	$10,000

TRANSACTION 6

Contributing Personal Assets to the Business   Lupe has several software and office procedures manuals, and other reference books that she contributes to the business. Since these books come from her personal library, their value increases the owner's capital account. Lupe estimates the value of the books to be $200.

	Assets									=	Liabilities	+	Owner's Equity
	Cash	+	Equipment	+	Furniture	+	Supplies	+	Library	=	Accounts Payable	+	Lupe Gomez, Capital
Previous Balances	$3,200 +		$16,000	+	$4,500	+	$800			=	$14,500	+	$10,000
(6)									+200				+200
New Balances	$3,200 +		$16,000	+	$4,500	+	$800	+	$200	=	$14,500	+	$10,200

At this point, do total assets equal total liabilities and owner's equity? This question should be asked after each transaction.

TRANSACTION 7

Paying Money to a Creditor   Lupe pays $500 to BECO as partial payment of the $12,500 owed for the purchase of office equipment (see Transaction 3). Now the equation appears as follows:

	Assets									=	Liabilities	+	Owner's Equity
	Cash	+	Equipment	+	Furniture	+	Supplies	+	Library	=	Accounts Payable	+	Lupe Gomez, Capital
Previous Balances	$3,200 +		$16,000	+	$4,500	+	$800		+200	=	$14,500	+	$10,200
(7)	−500										−500		
New Balances	$2,700 +		$16,000	+	$4,500	+	$800	+	$200	=	$14,000	+	$10,200

Manipulating the Fundamental Accounting Equation

You can see from the transaction that total Assets are $24,200, total Liabilities are $14,000, and Owner's Equity is $10,200. The equation looks like this:

Assets	=	Liabilities	+	Owner's Equity
$24,200	=	$14,000	+	$10,200

Note that if any two parts of the equation are known, the missing part can easily be found.

ILLUSTRATION 1

Assets = Liabilities + Owner's Equity (A = L + OE)   Liabilities are $14,000 and Owner's Equity is $10,200. What is the amount of the Assets?

Liabilities	+	Owner's Equity	=	Assets
$14,000	+	$10,200	=	$24,200

ILLUSTRATION 2

Assets – Liabilities = Owner's Equity (A – L = OE)   Assets are $24,200 and Liabilities are $14,000. What is the amount of the Owner's Equity?

Assets	–	Liabilities	=	Owner's Equity
$24,200	–	$14,000	=	$10,200

ILLUSTRATION 3

Assets – Owner's Equity = Liabilities (A – OE = L)   Assets are $24,200 and Owner's Equity is $10,200. What is the amount of the Liabilities?

Assets	–	Owner's Equity	=	Liabilities
$24,200	–	$10,200	=	$14,000

Total assets must always equal total liabilities plus owner's equity. If, for some reason, the equation is not in balance, a mistake in recording has occurred and the **discrepancy** or difference must be located before continuing.

If total assets increase, the total liabilities and owner's equity must also increase by the same amount (see Transactions 1, 3, 4, and 6). If total assets decrease, the total liabilities and owner's equity must decrease by the same amount (see Transaction 7). It is possible, too, for one asset to increase and another to decrease by the same amount, thus causing no change in total assets or in the fundamental accounting equation. This is called a **shift in assets**. (see Transactions 2 and 5).

The Balance Sheet

Lupe has purchased most of what she needs to begin her business and is ready to prepare her first financial statement, the **balance sheet**, which lists all asset, liability, and owner's equity accounts and proves that the fundamental accounting equation is in balance.

Assets are recorded on the balance sheet at their original, or historic, cost. This is significant because many assets are worth an amount quite different from the one reflected on the balance sheet; such assets as land and buildings often **appreciate**, or become more valuable, over the years. Because assets are economic resources that are expected to benefit future operations, such assets as land, buildings, and equipment are for use and are not for sale. Most assets could not be sold without disrupting normal business activity.

Lupe can see that by the use of her own $10,200 capital contribution plus the $14,000 credit extended to her, she now owns and controls a business that has assets costing $24,200. It is often said that the balance sheet is like a snapshot that shows the

Computer Wizards Balance Sheet January 31, 20XX															
Assets															
Cash		$		2	7	0	0	00							
Supplies					8	0	0	00							
Equipment			1	6	0	0	0	00							
Furniture				4	5	0	0	00							
Library					2	0	0	00							
Total Assets										$	2	4	2	0	0	00
Liabilities															
Accounts Payable		$	1	4	0	0	0	00							
Total Liabilities										$	1	4	0	0	0	00
Owner's Equity															
Lupe Gomez, Capital, January 31, 20XX											1	0	2	0	0	00
Total Liabilities and Owner's Equity										$	2	4	2	0	0	00

financial position or condition of the business at a moment in time. The balance sheet for Computer Wizards on January 31 appears above.

The Heading The balance sheet has a three-part heading that is centred and always includes, in this order: (1) the name of the business; (2) the name of the financial statement; and (3) the day for which the statement is prepared.

Assets With this form of the balance sheet, called the *report form*, assets are listed first. The word *Assets* is centred over the actual listing of accounts. The listing of accounts begins with current assets, which are cash or assets that will be used up or converted to cash within a year's time. (Supplies is an example of an asset that will be used up.) The first asset listed is Cash, followed by Accounts Receivable and Notes Receivable. Receivables represent amounts owed to the business. The other current assets are listed following the receivables, in no particular order.

The **capital assets** titles are listed after the current assets and are those tangible assets that have a useful life of more than one accounting period and that are used in the operations of the business. If there is an account for land, it will be listed first, followed by buildings, equipment, furniture, fixtures, etc. Capital assets are often listed according to how long the assets will last, with the longest-lived capital assets listed first.

Account titles are written next to the vertical line, amounts to be added are listed in the left-hand column and totals are entered in the right-hand column. To indicate addition (or subtraction), a *single* line is drawn all the way across the column from vertical line to vertical line. *Total Assets* is written opposite the total amounts.

Liabilities Leave one blank line before centring the word *Liabilities* over the listing of account titles. There will be, in later chapters, more than one liability. Other account titles might be Taxes Payable, Notes Payable, Mortgage Payable, and so on. Those debts that are due within a year's time are listed first and are called **current liabilities**. In this category, the first listing is usually Accounts Payable, followed by Notes Payable. Notes Payable represent debt evidenced by the signing of a formal document in which the borrower promises to pay back a certain amount of money by a certain time and usually with interest. Other current liabilities are listed in any order after Accounts Payable. **Long-term liabilities** are listed next and are those debts that fall due more than one year beyond the balance sheet date.

Amounts to be added are written in the left-hand column and totals are entered in the right-hand column. In this case, where there is only one account, the amount could have been entered directly into the right-hand column because it is not necessary to find a column total.

Owner's Equity   Again, leave one blank line before centring the words *Owner's Equity* over this last section. The capital account title is listed at the left-hand margin beneath the heading and the amount is listed in the right-hand column. A single line is drawn beneath the amount, which is added to the total liabilities figure. Write *Total Liabilities and Owner's Equity* opposite the sum obtained.

When totals for the assets, the liabilities, and owner's equity have been determined and assets equal liabilities plus owner's equity, a double horizontal line is drawn beneath the total assets and the total liabilities and owners' equity amounts to indicate that the work is in balance and complete.

Dollar Signs and Lines   A dollar sign appears at the beginning of each column and at totals. A line (ruling) must extend all the way across a column. A single line indicates addition or subtraction and a double line indicates that work is complete and in balance. Always use a ruler for drawing lines. Neatness is very important in accounting.

Cents   When money amounts are in even dollars, write two zeros to represent cents. *Do not use XXs.* You may, however, choose to use a straight line or to omit the zeros to indicate even money amounts. For example, seven hundred forty-eight dollars may be written as $748.00, or $748—, or $748.

Summary

Accounting is the language of business and is used by owners, managers, investors, bankers—in short, nearly everyone concerned with business—to communicate vital information to one another. Daily transactions of economic units must be recorded, classified, and summarized into useful reports for management to make intelligent business decisions. Good accounting records help an organization to be profitable and remain solvent.

The fundamental accounting equation states that assets equal liabilities plus owner's equity; this relationship is shown on the balance sheet, which is prepared to show the financial picture of a business on a particular date. Assets are properties owned by a business; liabilities are the debts incurred by the business; and owner's equity is the owner's share in the assets, or that portion of the total asset value to which she or he has a direct claim. A business owner must always keep her or his personal assets and liabilities separate from those of the business.

On the balance sheet, current assets are listed first, followed by items of plant and equipment and land. In the liabilities section, current liabilities are listed first, followed by those due after a year's time.

Vocabulary Review

Here is a list of the words and terms for this chapter:

account	discrepancy
accounts payable	fundamental accounting equation
appreciate	liabilities
assets	long-term liabilities
balance sheet	monetary
Canada Customs and Revenue Agency (CCRA)	owner's equity
capital account	service business
capital assets	shift in assets
creditor	solvent
current assets	transaction
current liabilities	

Fill in the blank with the correct word or term from the list.

1. A financial statement that proves the fundamental accounting equation is the _____.

2. The word _____ means pertaining to money.

3. _____ are items owned by the business.

4. Debts owed by the business are called _____.

5. A business that is able to pay its bills when they become due is said to be _____.

6. A purchase or a sale, receipt or payment of cash, or any other business occurrence that can be measured in dollars and cents is called a/an _____.

7. A/An _____ exists when facts are not in agreement.

8. _____ are debts due within one year.

9. One to whom money is owed is called a/an _____.

10. The owner's investment, net income, and net loss are recorded in the _____.

11. A = L + OE is called the _____.

12. The federal agency responsible for collecting income taxes is the _____.

13. An accounting firm is an example of a/an _____.

14. Assets that are cash or that will be converted to cash or used up in a year's time are called _____.

15. To increase in value is to _____.

16. The owner's claim on the assets of the business is called _____.

17. The separate record for each asset and liability and the owner's capital is called a/an _____.

18. A/an _____ results when the business purchases a service or merchandise and agrees to pay later.

19. Assets that will be held for an extended time and are used to facilitate the production of goods and services for customers are called _____.

20. _____ are those debts that fall due more than one year beyond the balance sheet date.

21. A/An _____ occurs when individual asset values change but there is no change in total assets.

Match the words and terms on the left with the definitions on the right.

22. account
23. accounts payable
24. appreciate
25. assets
26. balance sheet
27. Canada Customs and Revenue Agency (CCRA)
28. capital account
29. capital assets
30. creditor
31. current assets
32. current liabilities
33. discrepancy
34. fundamental accounting equation
35. liabilities
36. long-term liabilities
37. monetary
38. owner's equity
39. service business
40. shift in assets
41. solvent
42. transaction

a. when individual asset values change but total assets do not change
b. things owned
c. one to whom money is owed
d. federal income tax collecting agency
e. the owner's share of the assets
f. disagreement between figures
g. able to pay bills when due
h. debts
i. an individual record for assets, liabilities, and capital
j. an asset that is cash or that will be used up or converted to cash within a year's time
k. a liability account
l. a business occurrence that can be measured in monetary terms and that is recorded on the books
m. an account that summarizes the owner's investments and the business net income and loss
n. to increase in value
o. pertaining to money
p. an accountant, a lawyer, a masseuse
q. A = L + OE
r. a debt due within a year's time
s. assets used to facilitate the production of goods and services and that will be held for an extended period of time.
t. debts that fall due more than one year beyond the balance sheet date
u. statement of financial position

Exercises

EXERCISE 1.1

Complete the following equations:

a. Assets = Liabilities + _____

b. Liabilities + Owner's Equity = _____

c. A – L = _____   g. A – _____ = L

d. A – OE = _____   h. A = L + _____

e. OE + L = _____   i. _____ – L = OE

f. A – _____ = OE   j. _____ – OE = L

EXERCISE 1.2

Use the fundamental accounting equation to find the missing element in each of the following:

a. A = ?   d. A = $7,500

    L = $4,200   L = ?

    OE = $7,100   OE = $4,000

b. A = $18,000   e. A = ?

    L = $6,600   L = $5,800

    OE = ?   OE = $9,470

c. A = $21,000   f. A = $17,600

    L = $8,000   L = ?

    OE = ?   OE = $12,000

EXERCISE 1.3

Identify the following as an asset (A), a liability (L), or an owner's equity (OE) account:

_____ a. Cash   _____ f. Building

_____ b. Accounts Payable _____ g. Equipment

_____ c. Jean Martin, Capital _____ h. Wages Payable

_____ d. Supplies   _____ i. Library

_____ e. Furniture   _____ j. Payroll Taxes Payable

EXERCISE 1.4

Supply the missing figure in the following equations:

	Assets	=	Liabilities	+	Owner's Equity
a.	$_____	=	$2,500	+	$6,700
b.	14,700	=	7,400	+	_____
c.	12,600	=	_____	+	8,400
d.	_____	=	4,100	+	6,300
e.	4,800	=	0	+	_____

EXERCISE 1.5

Study the individual transactions within the equation and describe briefly what has occurred in each. Then determine the dollar value of the total assets and the dollar value of the total liabilities and owner's equity.

		Assets						=	Liabilities + Owner's Equity		
		Cash	+	Equipment	+	Furniture	=	Accounts Payable	+	Capital
a.		$15,000					=			$15,000
b.		–4,000		+4,000						
		11,000	+	4,000			=			15,000
c.						+500		+500		
		11,000	+	4,000	+	500	=	500	+	15,000
d.		–2,000		+6,000				+4,000		
		9,000	+	10,000	+	500	=	4,500	+	15,000
e.		–1,000						–1,000		
		$ 8,000	+	$10,000	+	$500	=	$3,500	+	$15,000

EXERCISE 1.6

Using the following account balances, determine the dollar amount of (a) total assets, (b) total liabilities, and (c) total owner's equity.

Cash	$3,500
Accounts Payable	2,400
Library	700
Equipment	2,850
Capital	7,800
Supplies	1,400
Taxes Payable	350
Furniture	2,100

EXERCISE 1.7

Following is a balance sheet for Jane Wade's Accounting Services. Calculate the dollar amount of the missing figures.

Jane Wade's Accounting Services
Balance Sheet
December 31, 20XX

Assets		
Cash	$3,400	
Supplies	600	
Equipment	(a)	
Furniture	4,000	
Library	1,800	
Total Assets		$ (b)
Liabilities		
Accounts Payable	$2,100	
Notes Payable	(c)	
Total Liabilities		$ 3,400
Owner's Equity		
Jane Wade, Capital, December 31, 20XX		(d)
Total Liabilities and Owner's Equity		$10,200

EXERCISE 1.8

For each of the following indicate whether the transaction will cause total assets to increase (+), decrease (−), or not change (NC):

a. purchased office equipment for cash

b. purchased office equipment on account

c. owner invested cash into the business

d. purchased supplies for cash

e. purchased furniture on account

f. purchased a computer; made a cash down payment, and agreed to pay the balance in six months

g. paid money on account

h. owner contributed personal assets to the business.

EXERCISE 1.9

Describe the effect of each transaction on the total assets, total liabilities, and owner's equity. Indicate an increase by (+), a decrease by (−), and no change by (NC). The first transaction has been completed for you.

	Transaction	Total Assets	Total Liabilities	Owner's Equity
a.	owner invested money from personal funds into the business	+	NC	+
b.	purchased office equipment for cash	_____	_____	_____
c.	purchased furniture for cash	_____	_____	_____
d.	purchased equipment on account	_____	_____	_____
e.	paid money on account	_____	_____	_____
f.	owner donated personal library to the business	_____	_____	_____
g.	purchased equipment; made a cash down payment and agreed to pay the balance in three months	_____	_____	_____

EXERCISE 1.10

Find answers for the following:

a. The assets of the Lake Louise Riding School were $510,000 and the owner's equity was $275,000. What was the total amount of the liabilities?

b. The liabilities of the Queen's Music School were $35,000. This amounted to one-fourth of the total assets. What was the amount of the owner's equity?

c. On December 31 of Year 1, the assets of the Oxford Counselling Centre were $180,000. At the end of Year 2, they had increased by $32,000. The owner's equity at the end of Year 1 was one-third the value of the assets. The liabilities increased by $15,000 from Year I to Year 2. What is the value of the owner's equity at the end of Year 2?

Problems

PROBLEM 1.1

Darlene Shear began a pet-grooming business on May 1, 20XX. She completed the first transactions of the business as follows:

a. withdrew $7,500 from her personal savings account and deposited it in a business bank account

b. purchased grooming supplies for cash at a total cost of $1,400

c. purchased office furniture at a total cost of $2,300, paying $1,000 down and agreeing to pay the balance within 90 days

d. purchased office equipment at a total cost of $3,200, paying no money down but agreeing to pay the full amount within 90 days

e. transferred her complete library of pet-grooming books worth $450 to the business

f. purchased additional supplies for cash at a total cost of $800

g. purchased additional equipment for cash at a total cost of $1,100.

Instructions

1. Record the transactions in equation form showing the increases, decreases, and the balance for each account after each transaction. The asset account titles used in this problem are Cash, Grooming Supplies, Office Furniture, Office Equipment, and Library; the liability account is Accounts Payable; and the owner's equity account is Darlene Shear, Capital.

2. Prove the accuracy of your work by showing that total assets are equal to the total of liabilities and owner's equity.

PROBLEM 1.2

The following is a listing of the accounts and their balances for Sharon Christensen, public accountant:

Cash	$8,000
Supplies	500
Office Furniture	3,500
Office Machines	4,700
Accounts Payable	4,500
Sharon Christensen, Capital	12,200

Instructions

1. Prepare a balance sheet as of February 28, 20XX. Before you begin, review the form and rules for preparing the balance sheet that are explained in this chapter.

2. After completing the balance sheet, check the following:

    a. Is the heading centred?

    b. Does the heading contain three lines?

    c. Is the word *Assets* centred over the asset accounts?

    d. Does a dollar sign appear at the beginning of each column and at totals?

    e. Are the account titles for assets and for liabilities and owner's equity listed right next to the vertical lines?

f. Is there a single rule that extends all the way, across the column beneath the last asset listed and beneath the capital account amount?

g. Is there a double rule beneath the total assets figure and beneath the total liabilities and owner's equity figure?

h. Did you leave one blank line before you centred the words *Owner's Equity* over the capital account?

PROBLEM 1.3

Brian Jardin, a lawyer, opened a business on March 1, 20XX. Brian has done the following:

a. deposited $18,000 into a business bank account

b. bought $4,500 worth of books for the law library; paid cash

c. bought office furniture for a total cost of $4,500; paid $2,500 cash down and agreed to pay the balance in six months

d. purchased computer equipment costing $4,800; paid $2,500 cash down and agreed to pay the balance within six months

e. contributed his personal library worth $3,500 to the business

f. made a $1,000 cash payment on the computer equipment purchased in Transaction d

g. made an $800 cash payment on the furniture purchased in Transaction c.

Instructions

1. Record the transactions in equation form, showing the increases, decreases, and the account balances after each transaction. Asset account titles used in this problem are: Cash, Library, Equipment, and Furniture; the liability account is Accounts Payable; and the owner's equity account is Brian Jardin, Capital.

2. Prove the accuracy of your work by showing that total assets is equal to the total of liabilities and owner's equity.

3. Prepare a balance sheet for Brian Jardin, Lawyer, as of March 31, 20XX.

PROBLEM 1.4

Nancy Samuels just opened an exercise salon called "No Weighting." The value of her exercise equipment is $9,500; the exercise mats cost $2,200; the stereo system cost $3,500; furniture cost $1,800; and the special lighting fixtures cost $875. Nancy owes $5,000 on the exercise equipment and $2,000 on the stereo system. Both of these amounts are due within one year. She has $2,700 cash in the bank.

Instructions

1. Calculate the amount of Nancy's capital account, following this procedure:

    a. List the asset amounts and their balances.

    b. Determine the dollar value of the total assets.

    c. Determine the total accounts payable.

    d. Subtract the total liabilities from the total assets.

2. Prepare a balance sheet for No Weighting as of March 31, 20XX.

PROBLEM 1.5

Pete Fredericks is getting ready to open a math-tutoring business called "Numbers Unlimited." During the month of April 20XX, Pete

    a.   withdraws $2,500 from his personal chequing account and deposits the money in the business account

    b.   buys a tape recorder and a computer (equipment) for $1,400 cash

    c.   buys supplies for $200 cash

    d.   purchases several desks, chairs, and tables for $2,000; pays $500 cash down and agrees to pay the balance in six months

    e.   buys a couch and a chair for the waiting room for $870; pays no money down but agrees to pay the full amount due within one year

    f.   invests another $1,000 cash from personal savings into the business.

Instructions

1.   Record the transactions in equation form showing the increases, decreases, and the balance for each account after each transaction. The asset account titles used in this problem are Cash, Supplies, Equipment, and Furniture; the liability account is Accounts Payable; and the owner's equity account is Pete Fredericks, Capital.

2.   Prove the accuracy of your work by showing that total assets is equal to total liabilities and owner's equity.

3.   Prepare a balance sheet for Numbers Unlimited as of April 30, 20XX.

CHAPTER 2

Profitability and the Income Statement

LEARNING OBJECTIVES

When you have completed this chapter, you should

1. **have an increased understanding of accounting terminology, particularly as it relates to the income statement.**
2. **understand how owner's equity is increased or decreased.**
3. **understand how revenue and expenses affect owner's equity.**
4. **be able to prepare an income statement after analyzing certain transactions.**
5. **be able to prepare a statement of owner's equity detailing the changes that have occurred.**

VOCABULARY

accounting period	a designated time period (for example, a month, quarter, or year) for which a company's net income or net loss is calculated
accounts receivable	debts owed to the business, usually by customers who have received services or merchandise and who have agreed to pay at some future date
accrual method of accounting	an accounting method where revenue is recognized when it is earned and expenses are recorded when they are incurred
accrue	to increase or accumulate
cash method of accounting	an accounting method where revenue is recognized when the cash is received and expenses are recorded when cash is paid
drawing account	an owner's equity account that reflects all cash and/or other assets taken from the business for the owner's personal use
entity	something that exists independently
entity concept	the accounting principle that maintains that a firm's transactions be kept separate from the transactions of the owner or of other firms
expenses	the costs incurred in earning revenue
incur	to become subject to
net income	net profit, or the amount remaining when expenses are deducted from revenue
net loss	the amount by which expenses exceed revenue
proprietor	owner
revenue	the inflow of cash and other assets for goods sold and services performed

Introduction

In Chapter One we learned that Lupe Gomez was willing to invest $10,000 into a business venture called Computer Wizards. People are willing to take such risks partly because they feel their business will be profitable; if it is, all profits accrue to the owner. A **proprietor** (owner) may like the idea of setting his or her own work hours or of providing a service to the community.

In order for a business to be profitable, the revenue must be greater than the expenses. If, however, expenses exceed revenue, the proprietor must **incur** the loss. If cash on hand becomes too low, the business may not remain solvent.

Revenue

Lupe begins her business employing only one full-time person. She has advertised the services of Computer Wizards in local newspapers and receives calls for repairs from local businesses right away. Revenue for Computer Wizards results when services are performed and cash is received for those services, or when services are performed and an account receivable results. Thus, **revenue** is the inflow of cash and other assets for goods sold and services performed.

An **account receivable** is a promise by a customer to pay at some future date. The company selling the service stipulates when the account receivable must be paid. Lupe requires that all accounts receivable be paid within 30 days.

It is important not to confuse cash and revenue, for not all cash coming into a business is revenue. Revenue results for Lupe's business only when services are sold, but cash may come into the business from many other sources. For example, Lupe may withdraw additional cash from her personal savings account and deposit that money into the business account. That would certainly not be considered revenue. The business may borrow money from a bank. Again, this is cash coming into the business, but it is not revenue. There are other examples, of course, and you will learn about them later.

Note that revenue is recorded on the books when it is earned, not necessarily when the cash is received. For example, Lupe may perform services in the amount of $500 for a company on May 3, and may agree to accept payment for the services in June. Lupe will record $500 revenue for May, along with an account receivable for $500. When the cash is received in June, it will not be revenue at that time, but will be reducing the amount of the account receivable.

Revenue increases owner's equity, but it is recorded in a separate revenue account.

Expenses

Expenses are the necessary costs that relate to the earning of revenue. Examples are salaries for employees, payroll taxes, utilities, advertising, and delivery charges. Expenses may be paid in cash as they are incurred, or the business may promise to pay at a later date which results in an account payable.

Not all payments of cash are considered to be expenses. Paying back a loan, for example, is not an expense but a reduction in the liability, Notes Payable. Cash paid for the purchase of equipment is not an expense; it causes an increase in one asset and a decrease in another.

An expense is recorded on the books when it is *incurred*, not necessarily when it is paid. For example, assume that Lupe contracts for $1,000 in radio advertising to be done in May but will not pay for the advertising until July. Lupe will record the $1,000 expense in May along with a $1,000 increase in Accounts Payable. When the bill is paid in July, it is not recorded as an expense again; rather it is a reduction in cash and Accounts Payable.

Expenses decrease owner's equity and are recorded in separate accounts.

Net Income

One of the most important reasons people start their own business is because they expect it to be profitable. The accounting term we will use to describe profits is net income. **Net income** is the excess of revenue over expenses, or, net income is revenue minus expenses.

Net income must be measured for a specific time period in order for the figure to be meaningful. If, for example, you were to say, "I earned $5,000," it would not be particularly significant until you stated that it took one year, one month, or one week to earn the $5,000.

Net Loss

If a business has a period when the expenses are greater than revenue, it is said to have incurred a **net loss**, which is defined simply as the excess of expenses over revenue.

Owner's Withdrawals

With a sole proprietorship, the owner is not considered to be an employee of the business. The salaries of employees are business expenses and income taxes and payroll taxes are deducted from their paycheques. A proprietor of a small business, in contrast, pays income taxes based on the net income of the business for the year.

When the owner decides to withdraw cash or other assets from the business, which he or she may do at any time, that withdrawal is recorded in a separate account called a drawing account and is not considered to be an expense but a reduction in owner's equity. Amounts withdrawn from the business by the owner decrease owner's equity just as amounts invested into the business increase owner's equity.

The **drawing account** will be used to record: (1) cash or other assets taken from the business for the owner's personal use; and (2) the payment of personal bills from the business cheque book.

Accounting Principles

Though the practice of paying personal bills from the business cheque book is a common one, it violates an important accounting principle. There are many accounting principles, or rules, that determine what are acceptable accounting practices. The result is that financial statements of different companies may be compared as the same principles govern how transactions are handled. These principles are called Generally Accepted Accounting Principles, or GAAP. The Accounting Standards Board (AcSB) is responsible for setting the principles, but it receives feedback from many interested groups such as government agencies, unions, lenders, investors, and so on.

The first accounting principle that we will discuss is the **entity concept** which requires that business transactions be kept separate on the books from the owner's personal transactions so that an accurate picture of the firm's earning power can be measured. The entity concept requires also that the accounting records contain only the transactions of one organization. Lupe will have a personal chequing account as well as a business account under the name of Computer Wizards. If she writes a business cheque to pay a personal bill, the transaction will be recorded as an increase in the drawing account and a decrease in cash. Computer Wizards is an accounting **entity** separate from its owner.

Owner's Equity

The owner's equity account, Capital, may be affected by the following:

Increases in Capital:

1. The owner invests cash or other assets into the business.
2. The business earns a net income.

Decreases in Capital:

1. The owner withdraws cash or other assets from the business.
2. The business incurs a net loss.

The Fundamental Accounting Equation with Revenue, Expense, and Drawing

It has already been noted that revenue increases owner's equity, that expenses and withdrawals decrease owner's equity, and that revenue, expenses, and withdrawals are recorded in separate accounts. Because revenue, expenses, and drawing directly affect the owner's equity, the fundamental accounting equation still looks like this:

$$\text{Assets} = \text{Liabilities} + \text{Owner's Equity}$$

but owner's equity must be regarded as being:

$$\text{Owner's Equity} = \text{Owner's Investment} + \text{Revenue} - \text{Expenses} - \text{Withdrawals}$$

Let's look at some typical transactions for Computer Wizards.

TRANSACTION 1

Selling Services for Cash   Lupe agrees to do some repairs for another local business. The work is completed in three days, and the charge for the service is $150. The customer pays cash. The fundamental accounting equation is shown with the previous balances taken from Chapter One. This particular transaction increases cash and increases revenue and affects the equation as follows:

	Assets						=	Liabilities + Owner's Equity				
	Cash	+ Acc. Rec. +	Equip. +	Furn. +	Supp. +	Lib.	=	Acc. Pay.	+ Capital +	Rev. –	Exp. –	Draw.
Previous Balances	$2,700 +	0 +	$16,000 +	$4,500 +	$800 +	$200	= $14,000 +		$10,200			
(1)	+150									+150		
New Balances	$2,850 +	0 +	$16,000 +	$4,500 +	$800 +	$200	= $14,000 +		$10,200 +	$150		

TRANSACTION 2

Selling Services on Account   Computer Wizards agrees to do some work for Allen's Engineering Company over a two-week period. The total cost of the services for this job is $750. Allen's pays no money when the work is delivered but agrees to pay within 30 days, thus creating an account receivable for Computer Wizards. The equation looks like this after both Revenue and the asset Accounts Receivable have been increased:

	Assets						=	Liabilities + Owner's Equity				
	Cash	+ Acc. Rec. +	Equip. +	Furn. +	Supp. +	Lib.	=	Acc. Pay.	+ Capital +	Rev. –	Exp. –	Draw.
Previous Balances	$2,850 +	0 +	$16,000 +	$4,500 +	$800 +	$200	= $14,000 +		$10,200 +	$150		
(2)		+ 750								+750		
New Balances	$2,850 +	$750 +	$16,000 +	$4,500 +	$800 +	$200	= $14,000 +		$10,200 +	$900		

Note that the work performed is recorded as revenue earned even though the cash has not yet been collected for the service.

TRANSACTION 3

Paying Cash for an Expense   Lupe pays a $60 phone bill for Computer Wizards. The equation now looks like this:

	Assets						=	Liabilities + Owner's Equity				
	Cash	+ Acc. Rec. +	Equip. +	Furn. +	Supp. +	Lib.	=	Acc. Pay.	+ Capital +	Rev. –	Exp. –	Draw.
Previous Balances	$2,850 +	$750 +	$16,000 +	$4,500 +	$800 +	$200	= $14,000 +		$10,200 +	$900		
(3)	–60										–60	
New Balances	$2,790 +	$750 +	$16,000 +	$4,500 +	$800 +	$200	= $14,000 +		$10,200 +	$900 –	$60	

TRANSACTION 4

Paying Cash for an Expense   Lupe pays a $100 bill for equipment rental. The equation now looks like this:

	Cash	+ Acc. Rec.	+ Equip.	+ Furn.	+ Supp.	+ Lib.	= Acc. Pay.	+ Capital	+ Rev.	− Exp.	− Draw.
				Assets			=		**Liabilities + Owner's Equity**		
Previous Balances	$2,790	+ $750	+ $16,000	+ $4,500	+ $800	+ $200	= $14,000	+ $10,200	+ $900	− $60	
(4)	−100									−100	
New Balances	$2,690	+ $750	+ $16,000	+ $4,500	+ $800	+ $200	= $14,000	+ $10,200	+ $900	− $160	

If you look carefully at the equation, you will see that Expenses are added together and the total is subtracted from Revenue to keep the equation in balance. Total Assets are now equal to Total Liabilities plus Capital plus Revenue minus Expenses. The equation now looks like this:

Assets	=	Liabilities	+	Capital	+	Revenue	−	Expenses
$24,940	=	$14,000	+	$10,200	+	$900	−	$160
	=				$24,940			

TRANSACTION 5

Withdrawing Cash for Personal Use   Lupe withdraws $250 cash for her personal use. Remember that owner's withdrawals are not considered to be an expense of the business and are recorded in a separate account called *Drawing* or *Owner's Withdrawals*. The equation now looks like this:

	Cash	+ Acc. Rec.	+ Equip.	+ Furn.	+ Supp.	+ Lib.	= Acc. Pay.	+ Capital	+ Rev.	− Exp.	− Draw.
				Assets			=		**Liabilities + Owner's Equity**		
Previous Balances	$2,690	+ $750	+ $16,000	+ $4,500	+ $800	+ $200	= $14,000	+ $10,200	+ $900	− $160	
(5)	−250										−250
New Balances	$2,440	+ $750	+ $16,000	+ $4,500	+ $800	+ $200	= $14,000	+ $10,200	+ $900	− $160	− $250

TRANSACTION 6

Paying Money to a Creditor   Lupe pays $400 to a creditor, BECO, as partial payment for office equipment purchased earlier (see Chapter One, Transaction 3). The equation now looks like this:

	Assets						=	Liabilities + Owner's Equity				
	Cash	**+ Acc. Rec.**	**+ Equip.**	**+ Furn.**	**+ Supp.**	**+ Lib.**	**=**	**Acc. Pay.**	**+ Capital**	**+ Rev.**	**− Exp.**	**− Draw.**
Previous Balances (6)	$2,440 −400	+ $750	+ $16,000	+ $4,500	+ $800	+ $200	=	$14,000 −400	+ $10,200	+ $900	− $160	− $250
New Balances	$2,040	+ $750	+ $16,000	+ $4,500	+ $800	+ $200	=	$13,600	+ $10,200	+ $900	− $160	− $250

Remember, cash paid on account is not an expense. Rather, it is a reduction in the liability, Accounts Payable.

TRANSACTION 7

Incurring an Expense but Delaying Payment   Lupe has some radio advertising done for $375 and agrees to pay the bill within 60 days. Notice that this transaction does not affect assets at all. On the Liabilities and Owner's Equity side of the equation, the $375 is added as a Liability and will be subtracted as an Expense, thus causing no change in Total Liabilities and Owner's Equity. The equation now looks like this:

	Assets						=	Liabilities + Owner's Equity				
	Cash	**+ Acc. Rec.**	**+ Equip.**	**+ Furn.**	**+ Supp.**	**+ Lib.**	**=**	**Acc. Pay.**	**+ Capital**	**+ Rev.**	**− Exp.**	**− Draw.**
Previous Balances (7)	$2,040	+ $750	+ $16,000	+ $4,500	+ $800	+ $200	=	$13,600 +375	+ $10,200	+ $900	− $160 −375	− $250
New Balances	$2,040	+ $750	+ $16,000	+ $4,500	+ $800	+ $200	=	$13,975	+ $10,200	+ $900	− $535	− $250

Notice that expenses are recorded when they are incurred, not when they are paid.

TRANSACTION 8

Receiving Money on Account   Allen's Engineering Service (see Transaction 2) pays $500 to Computer Wizards in partial settlement of its account. The equation now looks like this:

	Assets						=	Liabilities + Owner's Equity				
	Cash	**+ Acc. Rec.**	**+ Equip.**	**+ Furn.**	**+ Supp.**	**+ Lib.**	**=**	**Acc. Pay.**	**+ Capital**	**+ Rev.**	**− Exp.**	**− Draw.**
Previous Balances (8)	$2,040 +500	+ $750 −500	+ $16,000	+ $4,500	+ $800	+ $200	=	$13,975	+ $10,200	+ $900	− $535	− $250
New Balances	$2,540	+ $250	+ $16,000	+ $4,500	+ $800	+ $200	=	$13,975	+ $10,200	+ $900	− $535	− $250

Note that one asset, Cash, has increased by $500 while another asset, Accounts Receivable, has decreased by $500, thus causing a shift in assets. In addition, remember that when money is received on account, it is not considered to be revenue. It is, rather, a reduction in the asset Accounts Receivable. For this particular transaction, the original entry (see Transaction 2) recorded the $750 revenue. When the customer pays the bill later, as is the case here, it would not be logical to count the money received as revenue again.

TRANSACTION 9

Purchasing Equipment, Cash Down Payment   Lupe purchases additional equipment at a total cost of $1,500. She makes a $300 cash down payment and agrees to make monthly payments of $100 for the next year. The equation is affected in the following way:

| | Assets | | | | | = | Liabilities + Owner's Equity | | | | |
| | Acc. | | | | | = | Acc. | | | | |
Cash	+ Rec. +	Equip. +	Furn. +	Supp. +	Lib. =	Pay.	+ Capital +	Rev. –	Exp. –	Draw.
Previous										
Balances	$2,540 + $250 +	$16,000 +	$4,500 +	$800 +	$200 =	$13,975 +	$10,200 +	$900 –	$535 –	$250
(9)	–300	+1,500				+1,200				
New										
Balances	$2,240 + $250 +	$17,500 +	$4,500 +	$800 +	$200 =	$15,175 +	$10,200 +	$900 –	$535 –	$250

Note that Total Assets have increased by $1,200 and that Total Liabilities have increased by $1,200, keeping the equation in balance.

TRANSACTION 10

Investing Additional Cash   Lupe decides to take an additional $3,000 from her personal savings account and deposit it in the business account.

| | Assets | | | | | = | Liabilities + Owner's Equity | | | | |
| | Acc. | | | | | = | Acc. | | | | |
Cash	+ Rec. +	Equip. +	Furn. +	Supp. +	Lib. =	Pay.	+ Capital +	Rev. –	Exp. –	Draw.
Previous										
Balances	$2,240 + $250 +	$17,500 +	$4,500 +	$800 +	$200 =	$15,175 +	$10,200 +	$900 –	$535 –	$250
(10)	+3,000						+3,000			
New										
Balances	$5,240 + $250 +	$17,500 +	$4,500 +	$800 +	$200 =	$15,175 +	$13,200 +	$900 –	$535 –	$250

Notice that this additional investment of $3,000 increases the Capital account but does not affect Revenue.

The preceding ten transactions are typical of the transactions that occurred during the entire month for Computer Wizards. In addition to those already shown, Computer Wizards performed additional services for cash in the amount of $2,400, thus increasing the Cash account from $5,240 to $7,640 and increasing the revenue earned from $900 to $3,300. Lupe paid cash for wages expense, $800; utilities expense, $90; newspaper advertising, $72; and delivery expense, $18. These expenses, along with the others for the month, follow.

Phone Expense	$ 60
Equipment Rental Expense	100
Radio Advertising	375
Wages Expense	800
Utilities Expense	90
Newspaper Advertising	72
Delivery Expense	18
Total Expenses	$1,515

Note that the owner's withdrawals and the money paid on account are not listed as expenses. Total cash after earning the additional revenue and after paying the additional expenses, is $6,660.

The Income Statement

The income statement is the formal financial statement that is prepared to show total revenue, total expenses, and net income or net loss for a specific time period (a month, a quarter, a year), called an **accounting period**. Lupe has decided to adopt a monthly accounting period for her business.

The income statement for Computer Wizards, showing in detail all the revenue earned and the expenses incurred for the month of February, is as follows:

Computer Wizards Income Statement For Month Ended February 28, 20XX																		
Revenue																	
Revenue from Services												$	3	3	0	0	00
Expenses																	
Telephone Expense				$		6	0	00									
Equipment Rental Expense					1	0	0	00									
Advertising expense*					4	4	7	00									
Wages Expense					8	0	0	00									
Utilities Expense						9	0	00									
Delivery Expense						1	8	00									
Total Expenses													1	5	1	5	00
Net income												$	1	7	8	5	00

*Note that newspaper and radio advertising expenses are combined for the income statement under one account entitled *Advertising Expense*.

Rules for Preparing the Income Statement

The Heading   The income statement has a three-part heading that is centred and always includes, in this order: (1) the name of the business; (2) the name of the financial statement; and (3) the time period or the length of time for which the net income is measured.

Revenue   The word Revenue is written at the left next to the vertical line and, on the next line, the name of the revenue account is indented about half an inch. If there is more than one revenue account, the amounts are listed in the left-hand column. *Total Revenue* is written immediately below the last revenue account listed, and the total amount is written in the right-hand column as illustrated.

Revenue														
Revenue from Consulting	$	1	4	5	0	00							
Revenue from Teaching		2	7	0	0	00							
Total Revenue							$	4	1	5	0	00	

Expenses   Leave one blank line after the revenue accounts before writing the word *Expenses* at the left. Again, indent about half an inch and list the expense accounts. There is no particular order for listing expenses. The amounts are entered in the left-hand column and total expenses is written in the right-hand column.

Net Income   The total of expenses is subtracted from the total revenue to obtain net income. If total expenses are larger than total revenue, there is a net loss. Leave one blank line after total expenses before writing *Net Income* or *Net Loss*.

Dollar Signs and Lines   A dollar sign appears at the beginning of each column and by the net income or net loss figure. A single line appears under the amount for the last expense listed (Delivery Expense $18—) to indicate addition and a single line appears beneath the figure for total expenses to indicate subtraction. A double line appears beneath net income to show that work is completed. Remember, all lines are drawn with a ruler and extend all the way across the column.

Statement of Owner's Equity

Because revenue and expense accounts affect owner's equity, the income statement is normally prepared before the balance sheet so that results of operations (net income or net loss) can be included in the owner's equity section of the balance sheet. Lupe prefers, however, to prepare a statement of owner's equity separate from the balance sheet. The statement of owner's equity for Computer Wizards detailing the changes in owner's equity for February is as follows:

Computer Wizards Statement of Owner's Equity For Month Ended February 28, 20XX													
Lupe Gomez, Capital, February 1, 20XX	$	1	0	2	0	0	00						
Add: Net Income for February			1	7	8	5	00						
Additional Investment			3	0	0	0	00						
Subtotal		1	4	9	8	5	00						
Deduct: Lupe Gomez, Drawing			2	5	0	0	00						
Lupe Gomez, Capital, February 28, 20XX								$	1	4	7	3	5	00

Note that net income and Lupe's additional investment have increased owner's equity, while the withdrawals have caused a decrease. A net loss would also cause a decrease in owner's equity.

The following statement of owner's equity shows how a loss is handled for the B.C. Consulting Service:

B.C. Consulting Services Statement of Owner's Equity For Month Ended July 31, 20XX			
T.A. Adams, Capital, July 1, 20XX		$ 4 2 0 0 0 00	
Add: Additional Investment		3 6 0 0 00	
Subtotal		4 5 6 0 0 00	
Deduct: Net Loss for July	$ 4 2 8 0 00		
T.A. Adams, Drawing	2 7 0 0 00		
Total Deductions		6 9 8 0 00	
T.A. Adams, Capital, July 31, 20XX			$ 3 8 6 2 0 00

The statement of owner's equity has a three-part heading similar to the heading of the balance sheet. It contains (1) the name of the company; (2) the name of the statement; and (3) the time period during which the changes occurred.

Calculations are completed in the left-hand column, and the total capital is entered directly into the right-hand column. Often, a third column is required for calculating, as is the case when the net loss must be added to the withdrawals.

The Balance Sheet—Not Detailing Changes in Owner's Equity

The balance sheet for Computer Wizards is similar to the one in Chapter One. When a separate statement of owner's equity is prepared, those changes are not reflected again on the balance sheet; only the ending capital figure appears in the owner's equity section.

Computer Wizards Balance Sheet February 28, 20XX		
Assets		
Cash	$ 6 6 6 0 00	
Accounts Receivable	2 5 0 00	
Supplies	8 0 0 00	
Equipment	1 7 5 0 0 00	
Furniture	4 5 0 0 00	
Library	2 0 0 00	
Total Assets		$ 2 9 9 1 0 00
Liabilities		
Accounts Payable	$ 1 5 1 7 5 00	
Total Liabilities		1 5 1 7 5 00
Owner's Equity		
Lupe Gomez, Capital, February 28, 20XX		1 4 7 3 5 00
Total Liabilities and Owner's Equity		$ 2 9 9 1 0 00

The Balance Sheet—Detailing Changes in Owner's Equity

If Lupe were to choose not to prepare a separate statement of owner's equity, the balance sheet would reflect all the changes in the owner's capital account. The balance sheet for Computer Wizards showing the changes in owner's equity for February is as follows:

Computer Wizards **Balance Sheet** **February 28, 20XX**				
Assets				
Cash	$ 6 6 6 0 00			
Accounts Receivable	2 5 0 00			
Supplies	8 0 0 00			
Equipment	1 7 5 0 0 00			
Furniture	4 5 0 0 00			
Library	2 0 0 00			
Total Assets		$ 2 9 9 1 0 00		
Liabilities				
Accounts Payable	$ 1 5 1 7 5 00			
Total Liabilities		$ 1 5 1 7 5 00		
Owner's Equity				
Lupe Gomez, Capital, February 1, 20XX	$ 1 0 2 0 0 00			
Add: Net Income for February	1 7 8 5 00			
Additional Investment	3 0 0 0 00			
Subtotal	1 4 9 8 5 00			
Deduct: Lupe Gomez, Drawing	2 5 0 00			
Lupe Gomez, Capital, February 28, 20XX		1 4 7 3 5 00		
Total Liabilities and Owner's Equity		$ 2 9 9 1 0 00		

The Accrual Method and the Cash Method of Measuring Net Income

The **accrual method of accounting** is a method whereby all revenue is recognized in the period in which the services are performed (or in the period in which the revenue is earned), whether or not cash is received. Likewise, expenses are recognized (or recorded) in the period in which they are incurred, whether or not cash is paid right away. Revenue may be included in the total accounts receivable and expenses may show up in accounts payable.

For example, assume that a landscape contractor agrees to do some work for a client and sends the bill for the services after all the work is completed. The job was started on November 1 and completed on February 28 of the following year. The contractor would record a portion of the total revenue earned during each of the four months and would simply record an accounts receivable for amounts to be received after completion of the entire job. By the same token, the contractor would record all expenses related to this job when they were incurred, even if creditors agreed to accept payment at a later date. In short, the **accrual method of accounting** recognizes revenue when the services are performed and recognizes expenses as they are incurred.

The **cash method of accounting**, in contrast, recognizes revenue when cash is actually received and recognizes expenses when cash is paid out. In the preceding example of the landscape contractor, revenue for the particular job would not be recognized until March when the cash was received, and expenses would be recorded when they were paid, not when they were incurred. Using the cash method of accounting in this situation would distort the firm's financial position because the contractor was actually performing landscape services from November through February, yet all the revenue for this job by this method would be recognized in March, making that month's income as greatly overstated as the four preceding months' income was understated. An obvious advantage to the cash method of accounting is its simplicity. However, since the cash method distorts the amounts reported as revenues earned and expenses incurred for a particular time period, the accrual method of accounting will be used exclusively in this text.

Summary

Revenue is the inflow into the business of cash and other assets for services performed; expenses are the necessary costs relating to the earning of revenue. The fundamental accounting equation is now expanded to include revenue, expenses, and the owner's withdrawals. It is as follows:

$$\text{Assets} = \text{Liabilities} + \text{Owner's Capital} + \text{Revenue} - \text{Expenses} - \text{Drawing}$$

To earn a profit, revenue must be greater than related expenses. The proprietor may take all profits but must also sustain all losses. The owner may be required to invest additional sums of money from time to time and may withdraw cash or other assets as needed.

The periodic income statement is the financial statement that shows whether or not the business is operating profitably. It lists the revenue accounts and total revenue, the expense accounts and total expenses, and the net income or net loss for the period.

The balance sheet reflects a firm's financial position on a certain date; it may detail the changes in the owner's capital account, or a separate statement of owner's equity may be prepared. The owner's capital account may be increased by a net income or by an additional investment by the owner. It may be decreased by a net loss or by the owner's withdrawals.

Vocabulary Review

Here is a list of the words and terms for this chapter.

accounting period	entity concept
accounts receivable	expenses
accrual method of accounting	incur
accrue	net income
cash method of accounting	net loss
drawing account	proprietor
entity	revenue

Fill in the blank with the correct word or term from the list.

1. The word meaning to increase or accumulate is _____.

2. An owner of a business is called a/an _____.

3. Money owned to the business by charge customers is called _____.

4. To _____ means to be subject to.

5. The amount by which expenses are greater than revenue is referred to as _____.

6. Recording revenue when cash is received and expenses when bills are paid is called the _____.

7. _____ is defined as the inflow of cash and receivables for services performed.

8. The principle that states that a firm's assets be kept separate on the books from the owner's assets is referred to as the _____.

9. The costs incurred in obtaining revenue are _____.

10. The excess of revenue over expenses is _____.

11. Something that exists independently is called a/an _____.

12. A designated time period for which a company's net income or net loss is calculated is called a/an _____.

13. Cash taken by the owner from the business is recorded in the _____ account.

14. Recording revenue when earned and expenses when incurred is called the _____.

Match the words and terms on the left with the definitions on the right.

15. accounting period
16. accounts receivable
17. accrual method of accounting
18. accrue
19. cash method of accounting
20. drawing
21. entity
22. entity concept
23. expenses
24. incur
25. net income
26. net loss
27. proprietor
28. revenue

a. to increase or accumulate

b. the excess of expenses over revenue

c. money owed to the business by charge customers

d. a separate being

e. inflow of cash and receivables for services performed

f. costs incurred in obtaining revenue

g. recording revenue when earned and expenses when incurred

h. to become subject to

i. net profit

j. a time period of a month, a quarter, a year, etc., for which a company's net income or loss is determined

k. a business owner

l. recording revenue when cash is received and recording expenses when they are paid

m. the accounting rule that states that a firm's assets be kept separate from those of the firm's owner

n. cash taken from the business by the owner for personal use

Exercises

EXERCISE 2.1

Identify the following as asset (A), liability (L), owner's equity (OE), revenue (R), or expense (E) accounts:

a. Accounts Receivable
b. Furniture
c. Don Jones, Capital
d. Accounts Payable
e. Equipment
f. Cash
g. Revenue from Services

h. Utilities Expense
i. Taxes Payable
j. Rent Expense
k. Don Jones, Drawing
l. Salaries Expense
m. Office Machines
n. Consulting Revenue

EXERCISE 2.2

	Cash +	Accounts Receivable +	Equipment =	Accounts Payable +	Capital +	Revenue −	Expenses −	Drawing
a.	$10,000		=		$10,000			
b.	−2,000		+2,000					
	8,000		+ 2,000 =		10,000			
c.	+500					+500		
	8,500		+ 2,000 =		10,000 +	500		
d.		+800				+800		
	8,500 +	800	+ 2,000 =		10,000 +	1,300		
e.	−400						−400	
	8,100 +	800	+ 2,000 =		10,000 +	1,300 −	400	
f.	−600							−600
	7,500 +	800	+ 2,000 =		10,000 +	1,300 −	400 −	600
g.			+900	+900				
	7,500 +	800	+ 2,900 =	900 +	10,000 +	1,300 −	400 −	600
h.				+500			−500	
	7,500 +	800	+ 2,900 =	1,400 +	10,000 +	1,300 −	900 −	600
i.	+100	−100						
	$7,600 +	$700	+ $2,900 =	$1,400 +	$10,000 +	$1,300 −	$900 −	$600

1. Does the left-hand side of the final line of the equation equal the right-hand side? (In other words, is the equation "in balance"? Do Total Assets equal Liabilities plus Capital plus Revenue minus Expenses minus Drawing?)
2. Tell what has occurred for each transaction.
3. What is the amount of net income?
4. What is the amount of the ending capital?

EXERCISE 2.3

Describe a transaction that could cause the following to occur:

a. increase one asset and decrease another asset by the same amount
b. increase an asset and increase revenue by the same amount
c. increase an asset and increase owner's equity by the same amount

d. decrease an asset and increase the drawing account by the same amount

e. decrease an asset and increase an expense by the same amount

f. decrease an asset and decrease a liability by the same amount

g. increase a liability and increase an expense.

EXERCISE 2.4

(a) Income Statement (b)		
(c)		
Revenue from Services	$ 1 2 2 0 0 00	
Revenue from Consulting	(d)	
(e)		$ 1 6 2 0 0 00
(f)		
Wages Expense	3 4 0 0 00	
Advertising Expense	1 5 0 0 00	
Telephone Expense	8 0 0 00	
Utilities Expense	2 1 0 0 00	
(g)		(h)
(i)		(j)

Shown above is a partially completed Income Statement for Eugene Evans, Veterinarian, for the month of June, 20XX. Prepare a corrected income statement and fill in the missing headings or figures.

EXERCISE 2.5

The following are some of the accounts and their balances for The Trend Styling Salon. Using only the revenue and expense accounts, prepare an income statement for the month ended June 30, 20XX.

Cash	$2,900
Accounts Receivable	640
Revenue from Haircutting	4,000
Advertising Expense	800
Furniture	3,000
Wages Expense	2,500
Rent Expense	1,750
Miscellaneous Expense	420
Accounts Payable	970
Revenue from Manicuring	620
Utilities Expense	280

EXERCISE 2.6

During May, Harry Chan, proprietor of Poodle Pruners, carried out the transactions listed below. In each case determine whether the transaction represents revenue for the month of May.

a. obtained a $5,000 business loan for the purchase of equipment and furniture

b. trimmed the fur of 14 poodles on May 10 and received $280 cash for the service

c. invested an additional $2,500 into the business

d. received $750 cash on account from customers whose dogs he had trimmed in April

e. trimmed and bathed eight poodles on May 31 at a total cost to customers of $450; five customers paid cash for the service amounting to $150, and the others agreed to pay within 30 days.

During July, Harry Chan carried out the following transactions. Determine which of the following represent expenses for July.

f. on July 1, wrote a cheque for $1,500 in payment of the rent for July

g. on July 3, wrote a $500 cheque to himself to be deposited in his personal chequing account

h. on July 10, wrote a cheque for $725 in payment of an account payable resulting from radio advertising done in June

i. on July 15, wrote a cheque in payment for a desk for the computer and printer

j. on July 20, wrote a cheque for $1,000 to repay a non-interest-bearing loan obtained in February

k. on July 31, wrote a cheque for $120 for gasoline purchases for the business van for July.

EXERCISE 2.7

	(a) (b) (c)			
(d)	$ 2 3 4 0 0 00			
Add: Net Income	(e)			
Additional Investment	2 0 0 0 00			
Subtotal	3 3 6 8 0 00			
Deduct: Charles St. James, Drawing	(f)			
(g)		$ 3 2 8 8 0 00		

Charles St. James has an accounting practice called St. James Accounting. Above is a partially completed Statement of Owner's Equity for the three-month period ending March 31, 20XX. Calculate the amounts for the missing figures and prepare a complete statement of owner's equity.

EXERCISE 2.8

Heather Bullock runs an accounting service. Heather's capital account on May 1 had a balance of $7,800. During May, Heather invested an additional $2,000 into the business from her personal savings. Revenue for the month was $10,740 and expenses were $8,340. The balance in the drawing account on May 31 was $800. Prepare a statement of owner's equity for Heather's Accounting Service on May 31, 20XX.

EXERCISE 2.9

Roger Lemieux has a small business called "Equine Elegance." Roger grooms horses before their shows and gives advice on the proper care of horses. His capital account on November 1 showed a balance of $2,800. Revenue for November was $4,325 and expenses were $4,885. Roger's drawing account showed a balance on November 30 of $480. Prepare a statement of owner's equity for the month ended November 30, 20XX.

EXERCISE 2.10

Following you will find several different possibilities for the statement of owner's equity. Determine in each case the dollar value of the missing figure.

a.	Capital, February 1	$ 8,000
	Net loss for the month	1,500
	Owner's withdrawals	800
	Capital, February 28	?
b.	Capital, May 1	$ 6,100
	Net income for the month	1,800
	Capital, May 31	7,000
	Owner's withdrawals	?
c.	Capital, October 31	$ 8,700
	Net income for the month	1,650
	Owner's withdrawals	1,000
	Capital, October 1	?
d.	Capital, March 1	$10,600
	Owner's withdrawals	2,300
	Net income for the month	1,700
	Additional investment	1,000
	Capital, March 31	?
e.	Capital, September 1	$ 4,900
	Owner's withdrawals	900
	Capital, September 30	3,200
	Net loss for the month	?

EXERCISE 2.11

The balance sheets for Huronia Legal Service, owned by Ross Victor, at the beginning and the end of January showed the following balances:

	January 1	January 31
Total Assets	$27,600	$32,100
Total Liabilities	16,800	18,400

Determine the net income or loss of Huronia Legal Services for the month of January under the following unrelated assumptions:

a. The owner invested an additional $3,000 into the business.

b. The owner withdrew $1,750 from the business for personal use.

c. The owner invested an additional $3,200 and withdrew $1,800 for personal use.

Problems

PROBLEM 2.1

Albert Mar, a decorator, began his own business on September 1 and completed the following transactions in the first month:

a. deposited $5,500 in a bank account for Mar's Home Decorating

b. bought furniture for the office at a total cost of $3,500; made a $1,000 cash down payment and agreed to pay the rest within six months

c. purchased office equipment for $650 cash

d. paid rent, $450

e. received $800 for services rendered

f. paid cash for supplies for the office, $280

g. paid the salary of a part-time employee, $250

h. received a bill for advertising, $380, and decided to pay it later (remember, expenses are recorded when they are incurred, not necessarily when they are paid)

i. bought a computer, $1,000, and paid no money down; the full amount is due in 90 days

j. performed services for a customer and sent a bill for $1,250; the customer agreed to pay within 90 days

k. paid $100 on account (see Transaction h)

l. Albert withdrew $500 from the business for personal use

m. received a cheque (see Transaction j) for $475 from a customer in partial settlement of the account.

Instructions

1. Using the following headings, record each transaction and the new balances after each:

Accounts					Accounts				
Cash +	Receivable +	Supplies +	Furniture +	Equipment =	Payable +	Capital +	Revenue −	Expenses −	Drawing

2. After recording all the transactions, check to make sure that the equation is in balance.

3. Determine the amount of the net income or net loss for the month.

4. Prepare a statement of owner's equity for the month ended September 30, 20XX.

PROBLEM 2.2

Krista Klein owns Krista's Katering. The accounts and their balances are listed below.

Catering Revenue	$9,500
Advertising Expense	1,400
Utilities Expense	2,200
Cash	2,400
Wages Expense	2,200
Krista Klein, Capital, July 1, 20XX	7,400
Food and Beverage Expense	3,550
Delivery Expense	650
Krista Klein, Drawing	1,000

Instructions

1. Prepare an income statement for the month ended July 31, 20XX.
2. Prepare a statement of owner's equity for the month ended July 31, 20XX.

PROBLEM 2.3

Paul Padilla started his own business called Paul's Parking. He completed the following transactions in the month of September:

a. deposited $6,000 into the business account

b. purchased office equipment from J.R.'s Office Supply Company for $1,800; paid $800 cash down and agreed to pay the balance within 90 days

c. paid rent, $1,000

d. paid $240 cash for supplies

e. paid wages, $300

f. received parking lot revenue, $2,000 cash

g. purchased office furniture from J.R.'s Office Supply Company for $2,000; paid $1,000 cash down and agreed to pay the balance within 60 days

h. paid $350 for advertising

i. paid utilities bill, $60

j. paid phone bill, $85

k. received $500 in cash revenue

l. sent bills totalling $650 to regular customers who have been using the parking lot but have not yet paid

m. paid wages, $300

n. wrote a cheque for $200 in partial settlement of the account owed to J.R.'s Office Supply Company (see Transactions b and g)

o. received a bill for advertising, $35; record it now, to be paid later

p. withdrew $400 for personal use.

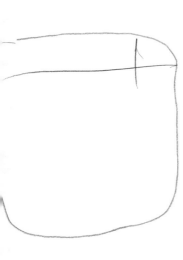

Instructions

1. Using the following headings, record each transaction and the new balance:

Accounts						Accounts				
Cash +	Receivable +	Supplies +	Furniture +	Equipment =		Payable +	Capital +	Revenue –	Expenses –	Drawing

2. After recording all the transactions, check to make sure that the equation is in balance.

3. Determine the amount of net income or net loss for the month.
4. Prepare a balance sheet on September 30, 20XX that shows the changes that have occurred in owner's equity. Do not prepare a separate statement of owner's equity.

PROBLEM 2.4

Following is a list of the accounts and their balances on August 31, 20XX for Tim Hopwell, Child Psychologist.

Cash	$11,800	Accounts Receivable	$2,200
Counselling Revenue	8,600	Insurance Expense	600
Furniture	4,300	Equipment	1,560
Wages Expense	1,200	Utilities Expense	510
Accounts Payable	3,400	Tim Hopwell, Drawing	1,500
Rent Expense	650	Miscellaneous Expense	180
Tim Hopwell, Capital, August 1, 20XX	10,400	Teaching Revenue	2,100

Instructions

1. Prepare an income statement for the month ended August 31, 20XX.
2. Prepare a statement of owner's equity for the month ended August 31, 20XX.
3. Prepare a balance sheet as of August 31, 20XX.

PROBLEM 2.5

Using the figures given for Tim Hopwell, Child Psychologist, in Problem 2.4, prepare a balance sheet on August 31, 20XX that details the changes in the capital account in the owner's equity section,

PROBLEM 2.6

Rita Roth owns the Roth Real Estate Company. The income statement for the month of November shows a net income of $1,762. When the transactions were recorded for the month, however, several errors were made.

a. Rita withdrew $1,200 during the month for personal use. The $1,200 was recorded as a deduction from cash and as an expense.

b. The Roth Real Estate Company performed services amounting to $2,400 for Andy Blake during November, but since he would not be paying for the service until December, the bookkeeper decided to wait until then to record the transaction.

c. A cheque for $700 in payment of an account payable to a local radio station for advertising done in October was recorded as an expense and as a deduction from cash.

d. Rita performed services for E.Z. Agnes Company in November in the amount of $3,700. Agnes paid $2,000 cash and agreed to pay the balance in 60 days. The bookkeeper recorded the transaction by increasing cash by $2,000, increasing accounts payable by $1,700, and increasing revenue by $3,700.

e. Rita made a $250 payment on a non-interest-bearing loan obtained in February. The bookkeeper recorded the payment as an expense and as a deduction from cash.

f. A $375 bill was received for delivery services for the month of November. The bookkeeper decided to put off paying the debt until December, and thus did not record the liability.

g.   Rita donated office equipment valued at $5,000 to the Roth Real Estate Company. The transaction was recorded as an increase to assets and as an increase to revenue.

Instructions

1.   Analyze each incorrect transaction and determine whether the error would cause net income to be overstated (O), understated (U), or not affected (NA).

Example   Rita's original $5,000 investment was recorded as an increase to cash and as an increase to revenue.

Solution   Overstated (revenue is higher than it should be).

CHAPTER 3

Understanding Debits and Credits and the Trial Balance

LEARNING OBJECTIVES

When you have completed this chapter, you should

1. have an increased understanding of accounting terminology.
2. be able to record transactions directly into T accounts, properly identifying the debit and credit amounts.
3. be able to determine account balances.
4. be able to prepare a trial balance from T accounts.
5. be able to prepare from the trial balance an income statement and a balance sheet that details the changes in owner's equity.

VOCABULARY

account balance	the difference between the total debits and the total credits in an account; when the debit total exceeds the credit total, the account has a debit balance; when the credit total exceeds the debit total, the account has a credit balance
chart of accounts	the formal listing, in financial statement order, of a firm's accounts and their numbers
credit	an entry on the right-hand side of an account
debit	an entry on the left-hand side of an account
double-entry bookkeeping	a system of bookkeeping that requires that for every debit entry or set of entries there be a corresponding and equal credit entry or set of entries
normal balance	the type of balance (debit or credit) that an account is normally expected to have
notes payable	liabilities that are evidenced by a formal written promise to pay; often issued when money is borrowed and usually require a payment of interest
note receivable	assets that result when a debtor signs a formal written promise to pay at some future date; may include an interest charge
T account	an informal ledger account drawn to look like a big T; used for illustrative purposes
trial balance	a two-column schedule that lists the accounts in financial statement order along with their balances; used to prove the equality of debits and credits

Introduction

In Chapters One and Two we followed Lupe Gomez and her business, Computer Wizards, through a full month's operations. You studied the fundamental accounting equation and the effects of various transactions on it. You recorded increases and decreases in the accounts by listing the account titles in equation form.

In actual practice, however, increases and decreases are not recorded that way. Transactions are first recorded in a book called a *journal* and then are transferred to individual accounts in a ledger. A *ledger* is a book with a separate page for each asset, liability, owner's equity, revenue, and expense account. The individual accounts summarize everything that has caused an increase or a decrease in them.

It is easier to understand the concepts of debits and credits if the ledger is presented first. You should remember, however, that transactions are recorded first in a journal, which will be presented in Chapter Four.

The T Account

The **T account** is called that because it is drawn to look like a big T. It has three basic parts: (1) the title, (2) a left-hand side, and (3) a right-hand side. The left-hand side of an account is called the **debit** side and the right-hand side is called the **credit** side.

Title of Account	
Left-hand side	Right-hand side
Debit side	Credit side

Rules for Recording Debits and Credits in Balance Sheet Accounts

The debit and credit sides are used for recording increases and decreases in the accounts. When you make an entry on the left-hand side, you are debiting the account; when you make an entry on the right-hand side, you are crediting it. A debit entry sometimes causes an increase in the account and sometimes causes a decrease. The same is true for a credit entry. An easy way to remember the rules for debits and credits is to keep the fundamental accounting equation in mind:

$$\text{Assets} = \text{Liabilities} + \text{Owner's Equity.}$$

Assets appear on the left-hand side of the equation; assets increase by a left-hand, or debit, entry.

Asset Accounts	
Debit side	**Credit** side
for recording	for recording
increases	**decreases**

When a debit increases an account, a credit decreases the same account.

Again, let's look at the fundamental accounting equation:

$$\text{Assets} = \text{Liabilities} + \text{Owner's Equity.}$$

Notice that liabilities and owner's equity appear on the right-hand side of the equation. Note, too, that increases in liabilities and the owner's capital account are recorded on the right-hand, or credit, side.

Asset Accounts		=	Liability Accounts		+	Owner's Capital	
Debit side for recording **increases**	Credit side		Debit side	**Credit** side for recording **increases**		Debit side	**Credit** side for recording **increases**

Again, it is logical that when a credit records an increase in an account, a debit will record a decrease.

Asset Accounts		=	Liability Accounts		+	Owner's Capital	
Debit	Credit		Debit	Credit		Debit	Credit
+	−		−	+		−	+

The **account balance** is determined by subtracting the total of the smaller side from the total of the larger side. If the debit side is larger, the account is said to have a debit balance; if the credit side is larger, the account has a credit balance.

Let's look in detail at the asset account Cash. All the left-hand or debit entries in the account represent increases, or, in this case, deposits of cash into the bank. The ledger account does not show the source of the cash; the journal (discussed in detail in Chapter Four) must be consulted for that information. All the right-hand or credit entries represent cheques written or cash withdrawn. By a quick glance at the cash account, you can easily determine how much cash is on hand, or, in other words, the balance of the account.

The cash account looks like this at the end of October:

Cash

	10/1	Balance	25,000	10/5	4,000
	10/7		3,000	10/10	2,200
Debit	10/14		3,500	10/14	500	Credit
entries	10/21		2,800	10/19	1,000	entries
	10/28		3,900	10/26	1,400
				10/31	300
			38,200		*9,400*
			28,800		

The account balance is determined as follows:

1. Total the debit entries.
2. Total the credit entries.
3. Subtract the smaller total from the larger.
4. Enter the balance on the side of the account with the larger total.

In manual accounting systems, bookkeepers use a pen and write very neatly when making entries in formal accounting records. They do make occasional errors but they do not erase or obliterate them; they simply draw a neat line through the incorrect figure and rewrite the figure above, below, or beside it, wherever it is most convenient.

The debit balance of $28,800 in the cash account represents cash in the bank. Asset accounts have a **normal balance** that is a debit. A credit balance in the cash account would indicate that more cash had been spent than deposited, a situation that could not continue for long. It would be difficult to imagine a situation, though, where an account for land would have a credit balance. Asset accounts have normal debit balances, and liabilities and the owner's capital account have normal credit balances.

The following reviews the relationship between the fundamental accounting equation and the rules for debit and credit in the accounts. Remember, assets appear on the left-hand side of the equation and increase on the left-hand, or debit, side of the account. Liabilities and owner's capital appear on the right-hand side of the equation and increase on the right-hand, or credit, side of the account. Carefully study the following T accounts:

| Assets | = | Liabilities | + | Owner's Equity |

Cash		**Notes Payable**		**Owner's Capital**
Debit	Credit	Debit	Credit	Debit	Credit
+	−	−	+	−	+

Accounts Receivable		**Accounts Payable**
Debit	Credit	Debit	Credit
+	−	−	+

Office Supplies		**Taxes Payable**
Debit	Credit	Debit	Credit
+	−	−	+

Equipment		**Mortgage Payable**
Debit	Credit	Debit	Credit
+	−	−	+

Land	
Debit	Credit
+	−

Recording Transactions in the Accounts

Before the debit and credit amounts can be entered, the following questions must be answered:

1.   Which accounts are affected?

2.   What is the account classification for each account?

3.   Which account(s) will be debited and which will be credited?

4.   Do the debit entries equal the credit entries?

The **double-entry system of bookkeeping** requires that for every debit entry or set of entries there be a corresponding credit entry or set of entries that will be equal in amount. Debits always equal credits (unless a mistake has been made).

Transactions Affecting the Balance Sheet

TRANSACTION 1

On November 1, 20XX, Ben Moore opens a janitorial service by depositing $15,000 from his personal funds into a business account entitled "A-1 Janitorial."

Analysis   The entry increases Cash and increases Owner's Capital. An increase to Cash requires a debit to the account and an increase to Owner's Capital requires a credit.

Cash		110	Ben Moore, Capital		310
+		–	–		+
11/1 15,000					11/1 15,000
(Debit increase)					(Credit increase)

TRANSACTION 2

On November 2, Ben purchases cleaning equipment for $5,000 cash.

Analysis   This entry must increase the asset account Equipment; therefore, a debit to that account is required. To decrease the asset Cash, that account must be credited.

Equipment		150	Cash		110
+		–	+		–
11/2 5,000			11/1 15,000		11/2 5,000
(Debit increase)					(Credit decrease)

Remember that double-entry bookkeeping requires that for every debit entry there be a corresponding and equal credit entry.

TRANSACTION 3

On November 5, Ben purchases $1,200 worth of cleaning supplies on account and agrees to pay within 60 days.

Analysis   This entry will increase the asset account Supplies by a debit and will increase the liability Accounts Payable by a credit.

Supplies		130	Accounts Payable		210
+		–	–		+
11/5 1,200					11/5 1,200
(Debit increase)					(Credit increase)

TRANSACTION 4

On November 6, Ben agrees to sell an unneeded vacuum cleaner to a friend for $650, the vacuum's original cost. The friend signs a non-interest-bearing, six-month **note receivable**.

Analysis   The Equipment account must be decreased, or credited, for $650. Notes Receivable must be increased, or debited, for $650.

Notes Receivable			125	Equipment			150
+		–		+		–	
11/6	**650**			**11/2**	**5,000**	**11/6**	**650**
(Debits increase assets)						(Credits decrease assets)	

TRANSACTION 5

On November 6, Ben purchases a pickup truck costing $15,000. He pays $5,000 down and signs a **note payable** for the remainder.

Analysis   This entry increases the asset account Truck, decreases the asset account Cash, and increases the liability account Notes Payable. *Total* assets will increase by $10,000 and total liabilities will increase by $10,000, thus ensuring that the debits equal the credits.

Truck			140	Cash			110	Notes Payable			220
+		–		+		–		–		+	
11/6	**15,000**			11/1	15,000	11/2	5,000			**11/6**	**10,000**
						11/6	5,000				

Assets	**Liabilities**
Net Increase $10,000	**Net Increase $10,000**

On any individual entry, there may be one or more debits and one or more credits as long as the total debits equal the total credits. A note payable is similar to an account payable except that a note is a formal instrument that is signed by the buyer; it usually stipulates an interest rate, when payments on the note and the interest must be made, and a due date.

TRANSACTION 6

On November 9, Ben makes a $300 payment on the cleaning supplies purchased in Transaction 3.

Analysis   The Cash account must be decreased (requiring a credit entry) and the Accounts Payable must be decreased (requiring a debit entry).

Accounts Payable			210	Cash			110
–		+		+		–	
11/9	**300**	11/5	1,200	11/1	15,000	11/2	5,000
						11/6	5,000
						11/9	**300**
(Debit increase)						(Credit decrease)	

TRANSACTION 7

On November 10, Ben withdraws $800 from the business for his personal use.

Analysis   Remember that in the fundamental accounting equation, drawing is subtracted from the liabilities and owner's equity side. In addition, in the statement of owner's equity, drawing is subtracted from the balance in the capital account. Since credit entries increase the capital account and debit entries decrease the capital account, it is logical that entries to the drawing account be debits, because drawing indirectly causes a decrease in capital.

Ben Moore, Drawing		320	**Cash**		110
+		–	+		–
11/10 800			11/1 15,000	11/2	5,000
				11/6	5,000
				11/9	300
				11/10	**800**
(Debit increases drawing)			(Credit decreases cash)		

TRANSACTION 8

On November 10, Ben receives a cheque for $65 in partial payment of the note that resulted from selling the vacuum cleaner (see Transaction 4).

Analysis The asset Cash must be increased by recording a debit entry and the asset Notes Receivable must be decreased by recording a credit.

Cash		110	**Notes Receivable**		125
+		–	+		–
11/1 15,000	11/2	5,000	11/6 650	**11/10**	**65**
11/10 65	11/6	5,000			
	11/9	300			
	11/10	800			
(Debit increases cash)			(Credit decreases notes receivable)		

Rules for Recording Debits and Credits in Income Statement Accounts

A quick look at the Cash account for A-I Janitorial will reveal that the only debits are the $15,000 original investment and the deposit that Ben made for the $65 received from the sale of an extra vacuum cleaner. Once the business has been established and the necessary items of equipment and supplies have been purchased, the source for additional cash will be the selling of the service or product. Let's review briefly the fundamental accounting equation to refresh our memories as to how revenue and expenses are handled.

Assets = Liabilities + Owner's Equity + Revenue – Expenses – Drawing.

Revenue is added in the equation because it causes an increase in the owner's capital account, and expenses are subtracted because they cause a decrease. The rules for debiting and crediting these accounts directly relate to how they affect owner's capital.

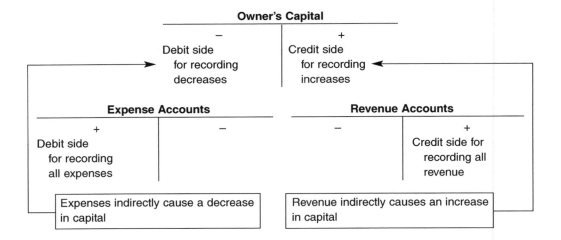

Think of revenue as indirectly causing an increase to the owner's capital account, thus requiring credit entries. In contrast, expenses indirectly cause a decrease in the capital account, thus requiring debit entries. While you are actually increasing the expenses by debits to the account, you will be indirectly decreasing the owner's capital. An actual change in the owner's capital account will take place at the end of the month when a net income or net loss is calculated. Transactions affecting the income statement follow.

TRANSACTION 9

On November 12, Ben advertises the services of his business in the local newspaper. He pays $95 cash for the advertising.

Analysis   Expenses are recorded as debit entries because they indirectly cause a decrease in owner's capital. Cash is decreased by a credit entry.

Advertising Expense			610	Cash				110
+		−			+		−	
11/12	95			11/1	15,000	11/2		5,000
				11/10	65	11/6		5,000
						11/9		300
						11/10		800
						11/12		**95**
(Expenses are recorded as debits)						(Credits decrease cash)		

TRANSACTION 10

On November 14, Ben receives a call from a local business and agrees to shampoo its carpets for $350 cash.

Analysis   An increase of $350 must be recorded in the asset account Cash; therefore, cash must be debited. An increase in revenue is recorded by a credit.

Cash				110
+			−	
11/1	15,000	11/2		5,000
11/10	65	11/6		5,000
11/14	**350**	11/9		300
		11/10		800
		11/12		95
(Cash is				
increased				
by debits)				

Cleaning Revenue			410
−		+	
	11/14		**350**
	(Revenue		
	is recorded		
	as a credit)		

TRANSACTION 11

On November 14, Ben purchases gas and oil for the delivery truck and pays $38 cash.

Analysis   Increases in expenses are recorded as debits and decreases in assets are recorded as credits.

Gas and Oil Expense			620
+		−	
11/14	**38**		
(Expenses			
are recorded			
as debits)			

Cash				110
+			−	
11/1	15,000	11/2		5,000
11/10	65	11/6		5,000
11/14	350	11/9		300
		11/10		800
		11/12		95
		11/14		**38**
		(Assets		
		decreased		
		by credits)		

TRANSACTION 12

On November 15, Ben agrees to clean the floors of a local clinic for $150. The clinic will pay on the fifteenth of the following month.

Analysis   Because we are using the accrual method of accounting, the revenue account is increased by a credit entry even though the cash will be received at a later time. The accrual method recognizes revenue as earned when the services are performed. The corresponding debit entry is to the asset Accounts Receivable.

Accounts Receivable			120
+		−	
11/15	**150**		
(Debits			
increase			
assets)			

Cleaning Revenue			410
−		+	
	11/14		**350**
	11/15		**150**
	(Credits		
	increase		
	revenue)		

TRANSACTION 13

On November 18, Ben decides to advertise the services of his business on a local radio station for a $425 fee, agreeing to pay in 30 days.

Analysis   Increases in expenses are recorded as debits and increases in Accounts Payable are recorded as credits. Again, the accrual method requires that expenses be recorded when incurred, not necessarily when paid.

Advertising Expense		610		Accounts Payable			210
+		−		−		+	
11/12	95			11/9	300	11/5	1,200
11/18	**425**					**11/18**	**425**
(Expenses increase by debits)				(Liabilities increase by credits)			

TRANSACTION 14

On November 19, Ben makes a $492 payment on the note payable for the truck (see Transaction 5). Of the total payment, $295 applies toward the reduction of the amount borrowed and the rest, $197, is payment for interest. Interest is the charge to the borrower for the use of money. It will be discussed in more detail later.

Analysis   This transaction represents a compound entry because more than two accounts are involved. The increase in Interest Expense will be recorded as a debit; the reduction of the liability Notes Payable will be recorded as a debit; and the reduction in the asset Cash will be recorded as a credit.

Interest Expense		650	Notes Payable				220	Cash				110
+		−	−		+			+		−		
11/19	197		11/19	295	11/6	10,000		11/1	15,000	11/2	5,000	
								11/10	65	11/6	5,000	
								11/14	350	11/9	300	
										11/10	800	
										11/14	38	
										11/19	**492**	
(Expenses increase by debits)			(Liabilities decrease by debits)					Assets decrease by credits)				

A Summary of the Rules for Debit and Credit

It is not customary for accountants to refer to accounts as either increasing or decreasing. They know automatically that a credit to cash is a decrease, a credit to accounts payable is an increase, and so on. This information is second nature to them, as it will be to you shortly.

Study the chart that follows to help you memorize the debit-credit rules.

Accounts that Increase by Debits			Accounts that Increase by Credits	
Assets			**Liabilities**	
Debit side	Credit side		Debit side	Credit side
+				+

Owner's Withdrawals			**Owner's Capital**	
Debit side	Credit side		Debit side	Credit side
+				+

Expense Accounts			**Revenue**	
Debit side	Credit side		Debit side	Credit side
+				+

The Chart of Accounts

Each business has its own set of accounts. In this text, eac tification number and a specific name that is used when t accounts are arranged in financial statement order with tl ed first, followed by the income statement accounts. N accounts in family groups with, say, all the assets number ties in the 200s, the owner's equity accounts in the 300s, revenue in the 400s, and expenses in the 600s. Account numbers in the 500s will be assigned to a category of accounts entitled *cost of goods sold*, which will be discussed in a later chapter. Some numbers in each family group are left unassigned to allow for adding new accounts. Following is the **chart of accounts** for A-1 Janitorial. (Some accounts have been added to the ones mentioned earlier in this chapter.)

Chart of Accounts

Account Title	Account Number
Cash	110
Accounts Receivable	120
Notes Receivable	125
Supplies	130
Truck	140
Equipment	150
Accounts Payable	210
Notes Payable	220
Ben Moore, Capital	310
Ben Moore, Drawing	320
Cleaning Revenue	410
Advertising Expense	610
Gas and Oil Expense	620
Wages Expense	630
Utilities Expense	640
Interest Expense	650

The Trial Balance

The bookkeeper makes sure that for each transaction recorded during the accounting period the debits equal the credits. It logically follows that at the end of the accounting period, the total of all the debit entries will equal the total of all the credit entries. If they do not, a mistake has been made.

The **trial balance** is the device that accountants use to determine whether or not total debits equal total credits. The trial balance is prepared directly from the ledger on a two-column schedule. The steps in preparing the trial balance are:

1. Determine the balance of each ledger account.
2. Centre on the two-column schedule the three-part heading, which consists of the company name on the first line, the words Trial Balance on the second line, and the day for which the trial balance is being prepared on the third line.
3. In chart of accounts order, list the account titles and their balances. Debit balances are entered in the left-hand column and credit balances in the right-hand column.
4. Total both columns and compare the totals to determine if they are equal.
5. If the debit column equals the credit column, draw a double line across both columns to indicate they are in balance.

The ledger accounts for A-1 Janitorial follow. Some transactions have been added to the original ones so that the entire month's transactions can be shown.

Cash			110
11/1	15,000	11/2	5,000
11/10	65	11/6	5,000
11/14	350	11/9	300
11/20	5,000	11/10	800
11/21	80	11/12	95
11/30	245	11/14	38
		11/19	492
		11/20	250
		11/21	46
		11/24	40
		11/28	315
		11/29	140
		11/30	45
	20,740		*12,561*
	8,179		

Accounts Receivable			120
11/15	150		
11/27	70		
	220		

Notes Receivable			125
11/6	650	11/10	65
	585		

Supplies			130
11/5	1,200		

Truck			140
11/6	15,000		

Equipment			150
11/2	5,000	11/6	650
	4,350		

Accounts Payable			210
11/9	300	11/5	1,200
		11/18	425
			1,625
			1,325

Notes Payable			220
11/19	295	11/6	10,000
			9,705

Ben Moore, Capital			310
		11/1	15,000
		11/20	5,000
			20,000

Ben Moore, Drawing			320
11/10	800		

Cleaning Revenue			410
		11/14	350
		11/15	150
		11/21	80
		11/27	70
		11/30	245
			895

Advertising Expense			610
11/12	95		
11/18	425		
	520		

Gas and Oil Expense			620
11/14	38		
11/21	46		
11/24	40		
11/30	45		
	169		

Wages Expense			630
11/20	250		
11/28	315		
	565		

Utilities Expense			640
11/29	140		

Interest Expense			650
11/19	197		

The trial balance for A-1 Janitorial, taken directly from the T accounts, follows:

A-1 Janitorial Trial Balance November 30, 20XX																	
Cash		$		8	1	7	9	00									
Accounts Receivable					2	2	0	00									
Notes Receivable					5	8	5	00									
Supplies				1	2	0	0	00									
Truck			1	5	0	0	0	00									
Equipment				4	3	5	0	00									
Accounts Payable										$		1	3	2	5	00	
Notes Payable												9	7	0	5	00	
Ben Moore, Capital											2	0	0	0	0	00	
Ben Moore, Drawing					8	0	0	00									
Cleaning Revenue													8	9	5	00	
Advertising Expense					5	2	0	00									
Gas and Oil Expense					1	6	9	00									
Wages Expense					5	6	5	00									
Utilities Expense					1	4	0	00									
Interest Expense					1	9	7	00									
Totals		$	3	1	9	2	5	00		$	3	1	9	2	5	00	

Trial Balance Limitations

The trial balance may prove that debit entries equal credit entries but may not show other errors that have been made. For example, if an entry is omitted from the ledger, the trial balance will not reveal that. Or the bookkeeper may debit office equipment rather than the furniture account. The trial balance won't show that either. Or the same wrong figure may be entered as a debit and a credit in the ledger. In short, the trial balance is very useful but only for proving that debits equal credits in the ledger.

Trial Balance Errors

If, when the trial balance is complete, the debits and credits are not equal, follow this procedure for locating your error. Working backward,

1. Check to make sure that accounts with debit balances are correctly entered in the debit (left-hand) column of the trial balance and that accounts with credit balances are correctly entered in the credit (right-hand) column.
2. Re-add the debit and credit columns.
3. Check to make sure that the balance of each account has been transferred correctly from the ledger account to the trial balance.
4. Recalculate the balances in the individual accounts.
5. Check to make sure that the correct debits and credits from the journal are entered in the accounts for each transaction.

The Income Statement and the Balance Sheet

Once the trial balance has been completed and is in balance, the income statement and the balance sheet may be prepared directly from it. The financial statements follow:

A-1 Janitorial Income Statement For Month Ended November 30, 20XX		
Revenue		
Cleaning Revenue		$ 8 9 5 00
Expenses		
Advertising Expense	$ 5 2 0 00	
Gas and Oil Expense	1 6 9 00	
Wages Expense	5 6 5 00	
Utilities Expense	1 4 0 00	
Interest Expense	1 9 7 00	
Total Expenses		1 5 9 1 00
Net Loss		$ 6 9 6 00

A-1 Janitorial Balance Sheet November 30, 20XX		
Assets		
Cash	$ 8 1 7 9 00	
Accounts Receivable	2 2 0 00	
Notes Receivable	5 8 5 00	
Supplies	1 2 0 0 00	
Truck	1 5 0 0 0 00	
Equipment	4 3 5 0 00	
Total Assets		$ 2 9 5 3 4 00
Liabilities		
Accounts Payable	$ 1 3 2 5 00	
Notes Payable	9 7 0 5 00	
Total Liabilities		1 1 0 3 0 00
Owner's Equity		
Ben Moore, Capital, November 1, 20XX	1 5 0 0 0 00	
Add: Additional Investment	5 0 0 0 00	
Subtotal	2 0 0 0 0 00	
Deduct: Drawing	$ 8 0 0 00	
Net Loss	6 9 6 00	
Total Deductions	1 4 9 6 00	
Ben Moore, Capital, November 30, 20XX		1 8 5 0 4 00
Total Liabilities and Owner's Equity		$ 2 9 5 3 4 00

Note that a third column has been added to the balance sheet so that drawing and net loss can be added together before the total deductions figures is subtracted from the beginning capital and additional investments total. If there is a net income rather than a net loss, this third column is not necessary.

Summary

A separate record is kept for each asset, liability, owner's equity, revenue, and expense account. The T account is the simplest form of an account; it has a title, a left-hand (debit) side, and a right-hand (credit) side. Debits and credits are used for recording increases and decreases in the accounts.

Transactions are entered first in a journal and then are transferred to the ledger. Double-entry bookkeeping requires that for every debit entry or set of entries there be a corresponding and equal credit entry or set of entries. The fundamental accounting equation may be used to help remember the rules for recording increases and decreases in the accounts.

1. Assets, which appear on the left-hand side of the equation, increase on the left-hand, or debit, side of the account.
2. Liabilities and owner's equity, which appear on the right-hand side of the equation, increase on the right-hand, or credit, side of the account.
3. Revenue, which indirectly increases capital, increases on the same side as the capital account, the credit side.
4. Expenses and owner's withdrawals, which indirectly decrease the owner's capital account, are recorded as debits, just as decreases to the capital account are recorded as debits.

The chart of accounts lists all the accounts in financial statement order and assigns a number to each. The trial balance lists all the accounts and their balances in financial statement order, and it proves the equality of debits and credits.

Vocabulary Review

Here is a list of the words and terms for this chapter:

account balance	normal balance
chart of accounts	notes payable
credit	notes receivable
debit	T account
double-entry bookkeeping	trial balance

Fill in the blank with the correct word or term from the list.

1. An entry on the right-hand side of an account is called a/an _____.
2. An account that is drawn to look like the letter T is called a/an _____.
3. The formal listing of a company's accounts and their numbers is called a/an _____.
4. A system of bookkeeping that requires a corresponding and equal credit entry for every debit entry is called _____.

5. An entry on the left-hand side of an account is a/an _____.

6. The type of balance (debit or credit) that an account is usually expected to have is referred to as its _____.

7. Liabilities that are evidenced by formal written promises to pay are referred to as _____.

8. The figure that is obtained when the smaller side of an account is subtracted from the larger side is called the _____.

9. A schedule that lists all the accounts in financial statement order and their balances and that proves the equality of debits and credits is called a/an _____.

10. Assets that result when debtors sign formal written promises to pay at some future date are called _____.

Match the words and terms on the left with the definitions on the right.

11. debit
12. credit
13. double-entry bookkeeping
14. trial balance
15. T account
16. account balance
17. normal balance
18. chart of accounts
19. notes payable
20. notes receivable

a. a corresponding and equal credit entry or set of entries is required for every debit entry or set of entries

b. the formal listing of a company's accounts

c. an account that is drawn to look like a T

d. an entry on the right-hand side of an account

e. liabilities evidenced by formal written promises to pay

f. a listing of all the accounts in financial statement order and their balances

g. assets resulting when a debtor signs a formal written promise to pay at a future date

h. an entry on the left-hand side of an account

i. the figure that is obtained when the smaller side of an account is subtracted from the larger side

j. the type of balance (debit or credit) that an account normally has

Exercises

EXERCISE 3.1

The debit and credit sides of the following T accounts are identified. Indicate the correct side for recording increases (+) and the correct side for recording decreases (–) for each T account. The solution to the first one is given as an example.

0. Example:

Cash

Debit	Credit
+	–

1. **Owner, Capital**

Debit	Credit

2. **Accounts Receivable**

Debit	Credit

3. **Notes Payable**

Debit	Credit

4. **Rent Expense**

Debit	Credit

5. **Commission Revenue**

Debit	Credit

6.	Owner, Drawing		9.	Rental Revenue	
	Debit	Credit		Debit	Credit

7.	Supplies		10.	Utilities Expense	
	Debit	Credit		Debit	Credit

8.	Accounts Payable	
	Debit	Credit

EXERCISE 3.2

(A) Tell whether the following would cause an increase (+) or a decrease (−) to the account mentioned:

1. a credit to Accounts Receivable
2. a debit to Drawing
3. a debit to Accounts Payable
4. a debit to Interest Expense
5. a credit to Capital
6. a credit to Cash
7. a debit to Notes Receivable
8. a credit to Accounts Payable
9. a debit to Accounts Receivable
10. a credit to Revenue
11. a debit to Cash
12. a debit to Advertising Expense
13. a credit to Notes Receivable
14. a debit to Capital
15. a debit to Mortgage Payable

(B) For each account listed, indicate whether the account has a normal debit balance or a normal credit balance:

16. Accounts Payable
17. Capital
18. Furniture
19. Drawing
20. Wages Expense
21. Cash
22. Revenue from Sales
23. Taxes Payable
24. Supplies
25. Equipment
26. Gas and Oil Expense
27. Commissions Revenue
28. Accounts Receivable
29. Automobile
30. Advertising Expense

EXERCISE 3.3

Determine the balance for each account listed, then prepare a trial balance for Sandra Samson, dentist, as of October 31, 20XX.

Cash			101	Accounts Receivable			110
a)	15,000	b)	360	g)	950	n)	780
d)	1,100	c)	1,720				
l)	250	e)	640	Supplies			115
n)	780	h)	830	q)	620		
		i)	1,940				
		j)	115				
		k)	4,000	Furniture			120
		m)	830	c)	5,100		
		q)	620	k)	4,000		
		r)	130				

Library				125
o)	2,200			

Automobile				140
p)	28,000			

Accounts Payable				210
h)	830	c)		3,380
		f)		155

Notes Payable			215
		p)	28,000

Sandra Samson, Capital			301
		a)	15,000
		o)	2,200

Sandra Samson, Drawing		305
m)	830	

Dental Revenue			401
	d)		1,100
	g)		950
	l)		250

Salary Expense		601
b)	360	
i)	1,940	

Rent Expense		605
e)	640	

Utilities Expense		610
j)	115	

Advertising Expense		615
f)	155	

Interest Expense		620
r)	130	

EXERCISE 3.4

Using the T accounts for Exercise 3.3, briefly describe what has happened for each lettered transaction. The first one has been completed for you as an example.

Example   Transaction a. This represents the owner's original investment in the business.

EXERCISE 3.5

Following is the trial balance for Susan St. Clair, Stylist, on April 30, 20XX. Susan has a new bookkeeper who is not entirely familiar with the process for preparing a trial balance. She has listed all the accounts in alphabetical order, and has made other errors. Find the errors and prepare a corrected trial balance for April 30, 20XX.

April 30, 20XX
Susan St. Clair, Stylist
Trial Balance

		Debit	Credit
120	Accounts Receivable	$ 3,200	
220	Accounts Payable		$ 7,000
640	Advertising Expense	350	
110	Cash	14,000	
130	Equipment	12,000	
620	Gas and Oil Expense		220
310	Susan St. Clair, Capital		33,000
320	Susan St. Clair, Drawing		600
135	Library	1,950	
225	Notes Payable	2,100	
610	Rent Expense	750	
410	Styling Revenue	3,370	
140	Truck	12,000	
630	Wages Expense	400	

EXERCISE 3.6

Following are the chart of accounts and T accounts for Jack Feder, consultant. Analyze each transaction separately, decide which accounts must be debited and credited, and then title the T accounts and enter the correct amounts. In each case, first enter the accounts to be debited. The first transaction has been completed for you.

Chart of Accounts

Assets
100   Cash
105   Accounts Receivable
109   Supplies
115   Office Equipment
120   Land

Liabilities
205   Accounts Payable
210   Notes Payable

Owner's Equity
301   Jack Feder, Capital
310   Jack Feder, Drawing

Revenue
410   Consulting Revenue

Expenses
610   Insurance Expense
620   Utilities Expense
625   Advertising Expense
630   Automobile Expense
635   Rent Expense
645   Interest Expense

Transaction Number	Cash	Land	Jack Feder, Capital
Example Jack Feder invested $10,000 in cash and contributed a parcel of property worth $75,000 to establish his consulting business.	10,000	75,000	85,000
a. Jack purchased $20,000 in office equipment; he paid $5,000 cash down and signed a three-year interest-bearing note for $15,000.			
b. Jack paid $200 cash for an ad in a local magazine.			
c. Jack bought $1,200 in supplies; he paid $400 cash down and agreed to pay the balance in 30 days.			
d. Jack paid $800 for the first month's rent.			
e. Jack borrowed $10,000 from the bank; he signed a two-year interest-bearing note.			
f. Jack performed consulting services and received $1,400 cash.			
g. Jack wrote a cheque for $105 for the insurance premium for the month.			
h. Jack performed $800 in consulting services for a customer who agreed to pay in 30 days.			
i. Jack paid $500 on the supplies purchased in Transaction 3			

j.   Jack wrote a cheque for $175 for the electricity bill.

k.   Jack paid $625 on the note in Transaction e; $415 is for repayment of principal and the rest is for payment of interest.

l.   Jack performed $1,500 in consulting services for a customer who paid $900 in cash and agreed to pay the rest in 60 days.

m.   Jack received $400 on account from a customer.

n.   Jack wrote a cheque for $250 for gasoline and oil for the car for the month.

o.   Jack withdrew $1,000 for personal use.

p.   Jack wrote a cheque for $730 for the monthly payment on the note (in Transaction a); $417 is for repayment of principal and the rest is for payment of interest.

EXERCISE 3.7

Determine for Lester Douglas, a lawyer, which of the following actions represent revenue (R), expense (E), or neither (N) for the month of July 20XX.

_____   a.   received $500 in the mail from a client whose will he prepared in February

_____   b.   invested an additional $3,000 into his law practice

_____   c.   made a $450 payment on a note; $200 applies to the reduction of principal and $250 is for payment of interest

_____   d.   bought a new couch for the office for $970 cash

_____   e.   advised a client in July and received $200 cash

_____   f.   withdrew $2,200 for personal use in July

_____   g.   paid wages for July, $2,000

_____   h.   donated a law library worth $3,500 to the business in July

_____   i.   paid $300 for radio advertising done in May

_____   j.   performed legal services for a client during the last two weeks in July and sent the client a bill for $600

EXERCISE 3.8

The following transactions were recorded in error by the bookkeeper for the Black Canyon Tour Guide Company in April. Determine how each affects revenue and expense. For each, indicate whether revenue and expense will be overstated (O), understated (U), or not affected (NA).

	Revenue	Expense
a. On April 5, the owner performed $630 in services on account. The bookkeeper debited Cash and credited Revenue.	_____	_____
b. The owner purchased office supplies on account for $320. The bookkeeper debited Office Supplies and credited Accounts Payable for $230.	_____	_____
c. The owner wrote a cheque for $196 for the April phone bill. The bookkeeper debited Rent Expense and credited Cash.	_____	_____
d. On April 30, a bill was received for electricity for the month of April. The bookkeeper did not pay it or record it.	_____	_____
e. The owner invested $6,000 additional cash into the business. The bookkeeper debited Cash and credited Revenue.	_____	_____

EXERCISE 3.9

Assume that a trial balance has been prepared and that the debit column does not equal the credit column. Considering each of the following errors separately indicate whether the error would (1) cause the trial balance totals to be unequal and, if so, (2) which side, debit or credit, would be larger because of the error, and (3) by how much? The first item has been completed as an example.

Error	Will Trial Balance Totals Be Unequal?	If So, Which Column Will Be Larger	How Much Larger Will It Be?
Example A $50 debit to cash was not recorded.	Yes	Credit	$50
a. A $25 debit to Accounts Receivable was recorded as a $25 debit to Cash.	_____	_____	_____
b. A $150 debit to Drawing was not recorded.	_____	_____	_____
c. A $75 credit to Accounts Payable was recorded twice.	_____	_____	_____
d. A $1,000 credit to Capital was recorded as a $100 credit to Capital.	_____	_____	_____
e. A $70 debit to Cash was recorded as a $700 debit to Cash.	_____	_____	_____
f. A $60 credit to Taxes Payable was not recorded.	_____	_____	_____
g. A $600 debit to Equipment was recorded as a $600 credit.	_____	_____	_____
h. A $90 credit to Notes Payable was recorded as a $90 debit.	_____	_____	_____
i. A $200 debit to Accounts Receivable was recorded as a $200 credit.	_____	_____	_____
j. A $10 debit to Accounts Payable was recorded as a $10 credit.	_____	_____	_____

Problems

PROBLEM 3.1

The T accounts and the transactions for November 20XX for the Tree Doctor follow:

Cash			**101**
a)	10,000	b)	6,000
f)	800	c)	2,000
j)	5,000	e)	600
k)	1,200	g)	400
s)	300	h)	150
t)	250	i)	900
		l)	250
		m)	140
		n)	200
		o)	900
		q)	300
		r)	500
		u)	175
		v)	200

Accounts Receivable			**120**
p)	600	t)	250
s)	400		

Supplies			**130**
d)	1,000		

Equipment			**140**
c)	5,000		

Truck			**150**
b)	12,000		

Accounts Payable			**210**
q)	300	d)	1,000
v)	200		

Notes Payable			**220**
o)	500	b)	6,000
		c)	3,000

Jack Pine, Capital			**310**
		a)	10,000
		j)	5,000

Jack Pine, Drawing			**320**
i)	900		
r)	500		

Revenue from Services			**410**
		f)	800
		k)	1,200
		p)	600
		s)	700

Truck Repairs, Expense			**610**
l)	250		

Rent Expense			**620**
e)	600		

Utilities Expense			**630**
m)	140		

Advertising Expense			**640**
g)	400		
n)	200		

Interest Expense			**650**
o)	400		

Gas and Oil Expense			**660**
h)	150		
u)	175		

Instructions

1. Analyze each transaction and write a brief description telling what has occurred.
2. Determine the balance for each account.
3. Prepare a trial balance as of November 30, 20XX.
4. Prepare an income statement for the month ended November 30, 20XX.
5. Prepare a balance sheet on November 30, 20XX that details the changes in owner's equity. Do not prepare a separate statement of owner's equity.

PROBLEM 3.2

The chart of accounts and the transactions for the month of January 20XX for Shawn O'Brien, veterinarian, follow:

Chart of Accounts	
100	Cash
110	Accounts Receivable
120	Medical Supplies
130	Office Supplies
140	Equipment
210	Accounts Payable
220	Notes Payable
310	Shawn O'Brien, Capital
320	Shawn O'Brien, Drawing
410	Revenue
610	Rent Expense
620	Salary Expense
630	Utilities Expense
650	Insurance Expense

Transactions

a. Shawn wrote a personal cheque for $18,000 and deposited it in a business account entitled Shawn O'Brien, veterinarian

b. purchased medical supplies that cost $5,000 cash

c. purchased office supplies that cost $400, to be paid for within 30 days

d. purchased office equipment that cost $19,000; paid $3,000 cash down and signed a three-year non-interest-bearing note for the balance

e. cash revenue for the first week was $1,200

f. paid rent, $1,500

g. paid insurance premium, $800

h. paid office salaries of $375

i. made a $200 payment on office supplies purchased in Transaction c

j. performed $2,000 in services; $1,100 received in cash, and the balance is due in 30 days

k. bought examining room equipment that cost $99,000; paid $5,000 cash down and signed a two-year, non-interest-bearing note for the balance

l. received $450 on account from charge customers

m. performed $2,400 in services; received $1,700 in cash, the balance is due in 30 days

n. bought office supplies, $620, on account

o. paid electricity bill, $210

p. paid office salaries, $375

q. received $500 from charge customers

r. paid $1,063 on the equipment purchased in Transaction k

s. paid $780 on the equipment purchased in Transaction d

t. performed $3,000 in services; received $1,700 cash, the balance is due in 30 days

u. received $470 from charge customers

v. owner withdrew $1,500 for personal use

Instructions

1. Prepare and title the T accounts shown in the chart of accounts. Record a plus (+) or a minus (−) on the debit and credit side of each T account to indicate where the increases and decreases will be recorded.

2. Record the transactions in the T accounts, identifying each by letter.

3. Determine the balance for each account.

4. Prepare a trial balance as of January 31, 20XX.

PROBLEM 3.3

Pierre Legault has operated Pierre's Floral Shoppe for six months. The beginning account balances and transactions for the month of August 20XX follow:

Chart of Accounts		
101	Cash	$10,500
110	Accounts Receivable	4,400
115	Office Supplies	970
120	Delivery Van	25,000
130	Computer Equipment	7,500
140	Office Equipment	11,600
210	Accounts Payable	7,500
215	Notes Payable	33,500
301	Pierre Legault, Capital	18,970
310	Pierre Legault, Drawing	
401	Floral Revenue	
601	Rent Expense	
605	Utilities Expense	
610	Advertising Expense	
615	Interest Expense	
620	Gas and Oil Expense	
625	Repairs Expense	
630	Insurance Expense	
640	Salaries Expense	

Transactions

a. purchased computer equipment at a cost of $5,400; paid $2,000 cash down and agreed to pay the balance in 90 days

b. paid rent, $1,200

c. paid utilities bill, $430

d. received $720 from a customer paying on account

e. made a $1,400 payment on the note payable; $530 of this amount is for interest

f. delivered flowers costing $1,720 to a customer; received $1,000 cash, and the balance is due in 30 days

g. received bill for advertising in the amount of $530 to be paid in 60 days

h. paid $1,620 on accounts payable

i. paid $27 from the business bank account to Cotty Cleaners for the owner's dry cleaning

j.   paid salaries, $640

k.   received $2,190 cash for flowers sold

l.   received $630 from a customer paying on account

m.   paid $220 for a tune-up on the delivery van

n.   withdrew $1,500 for personal use

o.   paid $530 on accounts payable

p.   delivered flowers costing $3,400 to a customer who has agreed to pay in 30 days

q.   paid $615 for gas and oil for the delivery van

r.   paid radio advertising in the amount of $780

s.   received bill for auto repairs for $1,650 to be paid in 30 days

t.   made $1,200 payment on notes payable; $425 of this amount is for interest

u.   paid $420 for insurance

v.   withdrew $2,000 for personal use

Instructions

1. Prepare and title the T accounts as named in the chart of accounts. Record a plus (+) or a minus (−) on the debit and credit side of each T account to indicate where increases and decreases will be recorded.

2. Enter the beginning balances front the chart of accounts into the T accounts.

3. Record the transactions in the T accounts, identifying each by letter.

4. Determine the new balance of each account.

5. Prepare a trial balance as of August 31, 20XX.

6. Prepare an income statement for the month of August 20XX.

7. Prepare a balance sheet as of August 31, 20XX that details the changes in owner's equity. Do not prepare a separate statement of owner's equity.

PROBLEM 3.4

Frances Schultz operates a dog-grooming business called "Pet's Pride." The chart of accounts, beginning account balances, and transactions for September 20XX for Pet's Pride follow:

Chart of Accounts		
100	Cash	$ 2,000
105	Accounts Receivable	1,800
110	Grooming Supplies	600
115	Grooming Equipment	5,700
120	Office Furniture	4,900
125	Van	18,000
201	Accounts Payable	3,000
210	Notes Payable	12,000
305	Frances Schultz, Capital	18,000
310	Frances Schultz, Drawing	
401	Grooming Revenue	
605	Rent Expense	
610	Utilities Expense	
612	Insurance Expense	
615	Advertising Expense	
620	Repairs Expense	
625	Gas and Oil Expense	
630	Interest Expense	

Transactions

a. borrowed $5,000 from a local bank; signed an interest-bearing note, agreeing to repay the money within 24 months

b. paid $550 rent

c. received $200 cash from customers for services performed

d. bought a new couch for the waiting room, paid $400 cash down, and signed a 12-month, non-interest-bearing note for $600 for the balance owed

e. wrote a cheque for $800 to reduce amount owed on account to creditors

f. performed grooming services totalling $350 and received $120 in cash; the balance is due in 30 days

g. paid $95 for electricity for the office

h. bought gasoline for the van, $36

i. received a bill for $480 for radio advertising for September; record it now, to be paid at a later time

j. paid monthly insurance premium of $90

k. performed grooming services totalling $275 and received $175 in cash; the balance is due in 30 days

l. received $400 in the mail from charge customers

m. Frances wrote a cheque for $500 for personal use

n. paid $40 for a newspaper ad

o. paid $300 for repairs to equipment

p. performed grooming services and received $110 cash

q. made a loan payment of $800; $450 is interest, the rest applies to reduce the balance in Notes Payable (see Transaction a)

r. Frances withdrew $600 for personal use

s. paid $120 for phone bill

t. performed grooming services totalling $530 and received $300 in cash; the rest is due in 30 days

u. wrote a cheque for $700 to reduce amount owed on account

v. paid $200 for a tune-up for the van

w. received cheques in the mail totalling $470 from charge customers

x. Frances withdrew $300 for personal use

Instructions

1. Set up and title the necessary T accounts and enter the beginning balances in them.

2. Record September's transactions in the T accounts.

3. Determine the balance of each account.

4. Prepare a trial balance as of September 30, 20XX.

5. Prepare an income statement for the month ended September 30, 20XX.

6. Prepare a statement of owner's equity for the month ended September 30, 20XX.

7. Prepare a balance sheet as of September 30, 20XX.

PROBLEM 3.5

The T accounts and the trial balance for Maria's Appliance Repair follow. The trial balance, however, indicates that one or more mistakes have been made.

Cash			**110**
a)	25,000	b)	4,000
i)	450	d)	5,000
m)	1,050	e)	3,200
q)	520	f)	800
v)	1,500	g)	1,200
		k)	150
		l)	370
		o)	2,500
		r)	1,000
		s)	290
		t)	370
		u)	900

Accounts Receivable			**120**
j)	520	q)	520
p)	750		

Supplies			**130**
c)	4,500		
e)	3,200		

Equipment			**140**
b)	10,000		
d)	8,000		

Accounts Payable			**210**
o)	2,500	c)	4,500
s)	290	h)	600
		n)	290

Notes Payable			**220**
r)	1,000	b)	6,000
		d)	3,000

Maria Fore, Capital			**310**
		a)	25,000

Maria Fore, Drawing			**320**
u)	900		

Repair Revenue			**410**
		i)	450
		j)	520
		m)	1,050
		p)	750
		v)	1,500

Rent Expense			**610**
f)	800		

Utilities Expense			**620**
k)	150		

Salary Expense			**630**
l)	370		
t)	370		

Repair Parts Expense			**640**
n)	290		

Advertising Expense			**650**
g)	1,200		
h)	600		

Maria's Appliance Repair
Trial Balance
November 30, 20XX

	Debit	Credit
Cash	$ 8,470	
Accounts Receivable	850	
Supplies	7,700	
Equipment		$18,000
Accounts Payable		2,600
Notes Payable		8,000
Maria Fore, Capital		25,000
Maria Fore, Drawing		900
Repair Revenue		4,720
Rent Expense	800	
Utilities Expense	150	
Salary Expense	640	
Repair Parts Expense	290	
Advertising Expense	1,800	
Totals	$56,700	$59,220

Instructions

1. Locate the errors in the trial balance by using the following procedure:

   a. Re-add the debit and credit columns of the trial balance

   b. If the trial balance does not balance at this point, check to make sure that the balance of each account has been properly transferred to the trial balance and that the balance is entered in the correct debit or credit column.

   c. If the trial balance does not balance at this point, recalculate the balances in the individual accounts.

   d. If the trial balance still does not balance, check the individual entries to make sure that there is a corresponding and equal credit entry for each debit entry.

2. Prepare a corrected trial balance.

PROBLEM 3.6

An income statement showing a net income of $7,200 was prepared for Seymour Enterprises for the month of April 20XX. When the bookkeeper was recording the transactions, however, some errors were made. The errors are as follows:

a. The owner, Carl Seymour, withdrew $1,000 for his personal use, but the $1,000 was debited to Wages Expense and credited to Cash.

b. Customers sent cheques totalling $2,500 through the mail to apply to their accounts from previous months. The bookkeeper debited Cash for $2,500 and credited Revenue for $2,500.

c. Carl wrote a $300 cheque to pay for utilities for April. The bookkeeper debited Advertising Expense for $300 and credited Cash for $300.

d. Carl wrote a cheque for $900 to a creditor to reduce the amount owed on account. The bookkeeper debited Supplies Expense for $900 and credited Cash for $900.

e. Carl performed services on account in April totalling $3,000. The bookkeeper recorded this transaction by debiting Cash for $3,000 and crediting Accounts Payable for $3,000.

f. A $900 bill for repairs to equipment was recorded as a debit to Repairs Expense for $90 and a credit to Cash for $90.

g. A cheque for $75 was received from a customer who was paying on account. The bookkeeper debited Accounts Receivable for $75 and credited Cash for $75.

Instructions

(Consider each error separately.)

1. If the error made will affect net income, determine whether it causes net income to be overstated or understated.

2. Add or subtract the amounts of errors that affect net income to determine the correct net income figure for April.

CHAPTER 4

The General Journal and the General Ledger

LEARNING OBJECTIVES

When you have completed this chapter, you should

1. have an increased understanding of accounting and accounting-related terminology.
2. be able to analyze and record transactions in a general journal.
3. be able to post general journal entries.
4. be able to prepare a trial balance directly from the general ledger and make an organized search for errors if the columns do not at first balance.

VOCABULARY

accumulate	to gather, pile up, collect
book of original entry	the first place where transactions are recorded; a journal
chronological	arranged in order of time occurrence; in date order
compound journal entry	a journal entry with more than one debit and/or credit entry
corresponding	similar or equivalent (equal)
general journal	a journal that is used to record many different types of transactions
general ledger	a ledger that contains a separate record for each asset, liability, owner's equity, revenue, and expense account
journal	a book of original entry in a double-entry system in which transactions are recorded and the accounts to be debited and credited and their amounts are recorded
journalizing	the process of recording entries into the journal
posting	the process of transferring information from the journal to the ledger
posting reference	a cross-reference from the journal entry to its corresponding record in the ledger
slide	when the position of the decimal point is changed as the number is written down (for example, $62.45 is written as $624.50)
transposition	when the order of the numbers is changed (transposed) as they are written down (for example, 758 is written as 578)
verify	to determine or test the truth or accuracy of, as by comparison, investigation, or reference

Introduction

In Chapter Three you learned how to record transactions into T accounts and how to check the accuracy of your work by preparing a trial balance. You will remember, however, that transactions are not recorded directly into the accounts but are first recorded in a book called a **journal**. The journal is called the **book of original entry** because this is where transactions first appear. The **general journal**, which will be introduced in this chapter, may be used to record all different types of transactions, but there are many other kinds of special journals.

The process of recording transactions in a journal is called **journalizing**. Transactions are recorded **chronologically** (in the order of their time occurrence). We will use the transactions of Eppie Kondos to illustrate journalizing; he started a business for cleaning automobile interiors.

In the first transaction, Eppie deposited $15,000 from his personal account into a business account entitled Klean Kar. A debit to Cash and a credit to Capital were required. The general journal entry follows:

		GENERAL JOURNAL			PAGE 1
DATE		**DESCRIPTION**	**POST REF.**	**DEBIT**	**CREDIT**
20XX					
Nov.	1	Cash		15 0 0 0 00	
		Eppie Kondos, Capital			15 0 0 0 00
		To Record Original Investment			

Analysis of a General Journal Entry

a. The year is written at the top of the date column.

b. The month and day on which the transaction occurred follow. The name of the month may be abbreviated and need be written only once at the top of the page. Transactions are recorded chronologically.

c. The debit entry (or entries) is always entered first and appears all the way to the left of the description column. The account name is written exactly as it appears in the chart of accounts.

d. The dollar amount of the debit entry is entered in the debit column.

e. Dollar signs are not used in the journal.

f. The credit entry follows the debit entry on the next line. The names of the account(s) to be credited are indented about half an inch. Again, the account titles are written exactly as they appear in the chart of accounts.

g. The dollar amount of the credit entry is entered in the credit column.

h. A brief explanation of the transaction is written beneath the credit entry. The explanation is not indented.

i. One blank line is left between entries to make reading easier.

j. An entry with more than one debit and/or credit is called a **compound journal entry**. The debits are entered first (in no particular order) and all appear at the extreme left-hand side of the description column. The credit(s) appear next (again in no particular order) and are all indented about half an inch.

k. The **posting reference** column (which is blank with this entry) is used to record the account number only after the dollar amount is transferred to the **corresponding** account in the ledger.

Look over the general journal entries for November 1–6 for Klean Kar.

GENERAL JOURNAL				PAGE 1	
DATE	DESCRIPTION	POST REF.	DEBIT	CREDIT	
20XX					
Nov. 1	Cash		1 5 0 0 0 00		
	Eppie Kondos, Capital			1 5 0 0 0 00	
	Original Investment				
2	Equipment		5 0 0 0 00		
	Cash			5 0 0 0 00	
	Purchased Cleaning Equipment				
5	Supplies		1 2 0 0 00		
	Accounts Payable			1 2 0 0 00	
	Purchased Cleaning Supplies,				
	Total Due in 60 Days				
6	Notes Receivable		6 5 0 00		
	Equipment			6 5 0 00	
	Received a 6-month non-interest bearing				
	note for equipment				
6	Truck		1 5 0 0 0 00		
	Cash			5 0 0 0 00	
	Notes Payable			1 0 0 0 0 00	
	Bought Truck, $10,000 balance due in				
	24 months				

Posting

The ledger, remember, is a book with a separate page for each account title appearing in the chart of accounts. The journal has all the information about a particular transaction in one place, and the ledger has all the information about a particular account in one place. We **accumulate** all transactions affecting an account in the **general ledger**; for example, everything that happens to cash is shown in the Cash account. The process of transferring information from the journal to the ledger is called **posting**. In the journal, the column headed *Post. Ref.* or *PR* shows the number of the ledger account to which the posting is made; in the ledger, the *Post. Ref.* column shows the journal page number from which the posting came. Sometimes *F* replaces *PR*. *F* stands for folio and is often used as another word for posting reference.

The first transaction for Klean Kar is repeated now; the general journal entry is followed by the ledger accounts that are affected.

GENERAL JOURNAL					PAGE 1
DATE	DESCRIPTION	POST REF.	DEBIT	CREDIT	
20XX					
Nov. 1	Cash	110	15 000 00		
	Eppie Kondos, Capital	310		15 000 00	
	Original Investment				

GENERAL LEDGER

Cash — ACCOUNT NO. 110

DATE	EXPLANATION	POST. REF.	DEBIT	CREDIT	BALANCE
20XX					
Nov. 1		GJ1	15 000 00		15 000 00

Eppie Kondos, Capital — ACCOUNT NO. 310

DATE	EXPLANATION	POST. REF.	DEBIT	CREDIT	BALANCE
20XX					
Nov. 1		GJ1		15 000 00	15 000 00

Analysis of Posting

a. Find the page in the general ledger for the first amount to be posted (in this case, Cash). Enter the year at the top of the date column, and enter the month and day as they appear in the journal. The month may be abbreviated.

b. Enter the dollar amount from the debit column of the journal to the debit column for the cash account. Do not use dollar signs in the ledger.

c. Enter the balance of the account into the balance column. Usually the balance must be calculated; in this case, however, there is only one figure.

d. In the posting reference column (PR) of the cash account, enter the initials GJ (which stand for general journal), and enter the journal page number from which the transaction was taken.

e. Enter the account number for cash in the posting reference column of the journal. This is not done until posting has been completed.

f. Repeat Steps a to e now as the credit entry to Eppie Kondos, Capital is posted.

g. Be especially careful when posting—it may save time later by avoiding errors at this point. It is a good idea to visually check each entry when it has been completed.

The General Ledger after Posting Is Completed

Following is the general ledger for Klean Kar showing all the transactions for November.

Cash					ACCOUNT NO. 110
DATE	EXPLANATION	POST. REF.	DEBIT	CREDIT	BALANCE
20XX					
Nov. 1		GJ1	1 5 0 0 0 00		1 5 0 0 0 00
2		GJ1		5 0 0 0 00	1 0 0 0 0 00
6		GJ1		5 0 0 0 00	5 0 0 0 00
9		GJ1		3 0 0 00	4 7 0 0 00
10		GJ1		8 0 0 00	3 9 0 0 00
10		GJ1		9 5 00	3 8 0 5 00
10		GJ1	6 5 00		3 8 7 0 00
14		GJ2		3 8 00	3 8 3 2 00
14		GJ2	3 5 0 00		4 1 8 2 00
20		GJ2		2 5 0 00	3 9 3 2 00
20		GJ2	5 0 0 0 00		8 9 3 2 00
21		GJ2		4 6 00	8 8 8 6 00
21		GJ2	8 0 00		8 9 6 6 00
24		GJ2		4 0 00	8 9 2 6 00
28		GJ3		3 1 5 00	8 6 1 1 00
29		GJ3		1 4 0 00	8 4 7 1 00
30		GJ3		4 5 00	8 4 2 6 00
30		GJ3	2 4 5 00		8 6 7 1 00

Accounts Receivable					ACCOUNT NO. 120
DATE	EXPLANATION	POST. REF.	DEBIT	CREDIT	BALANCE
20XX					
Nov. 15		GJ2	1 5 0 00		1 5 0 00
27		GJ2	7 0 00		2 2 0 00

Notes Receivable					ACCOUNT NO. 125
DATE	EXPLANATION	POST. REF.	DEBIT	CREDIT	BALANCE
20XX					
Nov. 6		GJ1	6 5 0 00		6 5 0 00
10		GJ1		6 5 00	5 8 5 00

Supplies					ACCOUNT NO. 130	
DATE	**EXPLANATION**	**POST. REF.**	**DEBIT**	**CREDIT**	**BALANCE**	
20XX						
Nov. 5		GJ1	1 2 0 0 00		1 2 0 0 00	

Truck					ACCOUNT NO. 140	
DATE	**EXPLANATION**	**POST. REF.**	**DEBIT**	**CREDIT**	**BALANCE**	
20XX						
Nov. 6		GJ1	1 5 0 0 0 00		1 5 0 0 0 00	

Equipment					ACCOUNT NO. 150	
DATE	**EXPLANATION**	**POST. REF.**	**DEBIT**	**CREDIT**	**BALANCE**	
20XX						
Nov. 2		GJ1	5 0 0 0 00		5 0 0 0 00	
6		GJ1		6 5 0 00	4 3 5 0 00	

Accounts Payable					ACCOUNT NO. 210	
DATE	**EXPLANATION**	**POST. REF.**	**DEBIT**	**CREDIT**	**BALANCE**	
20XX						
Nov. 5		GJ1		1 2 0 0 00	1 2 0 0 00	
9		GJ1	3 0 0 00		9 0 0 00	
18		GJ2		4 2 5 00	1 3 2 5 00	

Notes Payable					ACCOUNT NO. 220	
DATE	**EXPLANATION**	**POST. REF.**	**DEBIT**	**CREDIT**	**BALANCE**	
20XX						
Nov. 6		GJ1		1 0 0 0 0 00	1 0 0 0 0 00	

Eppie Kondos, Capital					ACCOUNT NO. 310	
DATE	**EXPLANATION**	**POST. REF.**	**DEBIT**	**CREDIT**	**BALANCE**	
20XX						
Nov. 1		GJ1		1 5 0 0 0 00	1 5 0 0 0 00	
20		GJ2		5 0 0 0 00	2 0 0 0 0 00	

Eppie Kondos, Drawing   ACCOUNT NO. 320

DATE		EXPLANATION	POST. REF.	DEBIT	CREDIT	BALANCE
20XX						
Nov.	10		GJ1	8 0 0 00		8 0 0 00

Cleaning Revenue   ACCOUNT NO. 410

DATE		EXPLANATION	POST. REF.	DEBIT	CREDIT	BALANCE
20XX						
Nov.	14		GJ2		3 5 0 00	3 5 0 00
	15		GJ2		1 5 0 00	5 0 0 00
	21		GJ2		8 0 00	5 8 0 00
	27		GJ2		7 0 00	6 5 0 00
	30		GJ3		2 4 5 00	8 9 5 00

Advertising Expense   ACCOUNT NO. 610

DATE		EXPLANATION	POST. REF.	DEBIT	CREDIT	BALANCE
20XX						
Nov.	10		GJ1	9 5 00		9 5 00
	18		GJ2	4 2 5 00		5 2 0 00

Gas & Oil Expense   ACCOUNT NO. 620

DATE		EXPLANATION	POST. REF.	DEBIT	CREDIT	BALANCE
20XX						
Nov.	14		GJ2	3 8 00		3 8 00
	21		GJ2	4 6 00		8 4 00
	24		GJ2	4 0 00		1 2 4 00
	30		GJ3	4 5 00		1 6 9 00

Wages Expense   ACCOUNT NO. 630

DATE		EXPLANATION	POST. REF.	DEBIT	CREDIT	BALANCE
20XX						
Nov.	20		GJ2	2 5 0 00		2 5 0 00
	28		GJ3	3 1 5 00		5 6 5 00

Utilities Expense						ACCOUNT NO. 640
DATE	**EXPLANATION**	**POST. REF.**	**DEBIT**	**CREDIT**	**BALANCE**	
20XX						
Nov. 29		GJ3	1 4 0 00		1 4 0 00	

The Trial Balance

Once the journalizing and posting are completed, you are ready to prepare a trial balance that will **verify** that debit entries equal credit entries. The dollar amounts appearing on the trial balance are taken directly from the ledger.

Klean Kar		
Trial Balance		
November 30, 20XX		
ACCOUNT	**DEBIT**	**CREDIT**
Cash	$ 8 6 7 1 00	
Accounts Receivable	2 2 0 00	
Notes Receivable	5 8 5 00	
Supplies	1 2 0 0 00	
Truck	1 5 0 0 0 00	
Equipment	4 3 5 0 00	
Accounts Payable		$ 1 3 2 5 00
Notes Payable		1 0 0 0 0 00
Eppie, Kondos, Capital		2 0 0 0 0 00
Eppie Kondos, Drawing	8 0 0 00	
Cleaning Revenue		8 9 5 00
Advertising Expense	5 2 0 00	
Gas and Oil Expense	1 6 9 00	
Wages Expense	5 6 5 00	
Utilities Expense	1 4 0 00	
Totals	$ 3 2 2 2 0 00	$ 3 2 2 2 0 00

If the columns of the trial balance do not equal each other, subtract the smaller side from the larger side to determine the amount of the difference. If, for example, the debit side totals $8,275 and the credit side totals $8,250, the difference is $25. Look for a $25 figure in the journal to see whether you may have posted only half of the entry to the ledger. Or, you might look for a $12.50 posting (half the amount of the difference), which could occur by posting, say, $12.50 as a credit to accounts receivable when you should have posted a $12.50 debit.

Transpositions and Slides

A **transposition** occurs when you transpose (change the order of) numbers as you write them down. For example, if the number you are supposed to record is 357 and the number you do record is 537, you have transposed the 3 and the 5. When a transposition occurs, the difference between the number as it should be and the transposed number will always be evenly divisible by 9.

Table 1
Transpositions

	Number as It Should Be	Number Transposed	Difference	Divide Difference by 9
a.	357	537	537 − 357 = 180	180 ÷ 9 = 20
b.	978	789	978 − 789 = 189	189 ÷ 9 = 21
c.	1,042	1,024	1,042 − 1,024 = 18	18 ÷ 9 = 2
d.	14	41	41 − 14 = 27	27 ÷ 9 = 3

Always subtract the smaller number from the larger number to avoid negative numbers.

A **slide** occurs when the decimal point is incorrectly placed. Let's assume that the correct figure is $7,125 and $71.25 is the figure recorded. This is a slide. As with a transposition, the difference between the number as it should be and the number as it is recorded will be evenly divisible by 9. Subtract $71.25 from $7,125 and the difference is $7,053.75. That number is evenly divisible by 9 ($7,053.75/9 = $783.75). Other examples:

Table 2
Slides

	Number as It Should Be	Number as It Is Recorded	Difference	Divide Difference by 9
a.	7.85	78.50	78.50 − 7.85 = 70.65	70.65 ÷ 9 = 7.85
b.	204	2.04	204 − 2.04 = 201.96	201.96 ÷ 9 = 22.44
c.	60,469	604.69	60,469 − 604.69 = 59,864.31	59,864.31 ÷ 9 = 6,651.59
d.	10,250	1,025	10,250 − 1,025 = 9,225	9,225 ÷ 9 = 1,025

Always subtract the smaller number from the larger to avoid negative numbers.

This information may be helpful when you have totalled the trial balance columns and find that they are not the same. Assume, for example, that the debit total is $10,072 and that the credit total is $10,108. The difference between those two numbers ($10,108 − $10,072), $36, is evenly divisible by 9 ($36/9 = 4). It may be suspected that the reason for the columns not being equal is a transposed number or a slide.

How Recording Errors Affect Net Income

If an error is made when journalizing or posting a transaction to revenue or expense, the net income may be overstated or understated. For example, assume that the owner withdraws $1,000 for personal use. The bookkeeper journalizes this transaction as a debit to salary expense and a credit to cash. Of course, the debit should have been to drawing, not salary expense. This error causes total expenses to be overstated (or too much) and as a result, net income will be understated. Study the following example where revenue is correctly stated and expenses are either overstated or understated.

Revenue and Expenses Correctly Stated	Revenue Correctly Stated and Expenses Overstated	Revenue Correctly Stated and Expenses Understated
$5,000	$5,000	$5,000
−3,000	−4,000	−2,000
$2,000	$1,000	$3,000

As you can see, net income is $2,000 when revenue and expenses are correctly stated. However, when expenses are overstated by $1,000, net income is understated by the same amount; when expenses are understated by $1,000, then net income is overstated by the same amount.

If an error is made in journalizing or posting a transaction to revenue, again net income may be overstated or understated. Assume that the owner deposits $1,000 from her personal savings into the business bank account and the bookkeeper debits cash and credits revenue. The credit should have been to capital and as a result, revenue is overstated. Study the following chart to see how errors in recording revenue affect net income.

Revenue and Expenses Correctly Stated	Revenue Overstated and Expenses Correctly Stated	Revenue Understated and Expenses Correctly Stated
$10,000	$11,000	$9,000
−7,000	−7,000	−7,000
$ 3,000	$ 4,000	$2,000

Again, as is evident, when revenue is overstated by $1,000, net income will be overstated by the same amount, and when revenue is understated, net income will be understated by the same amount.

It is extremely important to exercise care when journalizing and posting so that errors are few and so that the proprietor has an accurate picture of the business net income or loss.

Errors may be made in recording in assets, liabilities, or owner's equity accounts; however, such errors do not affect net income since only revenue and expenses appear on the income statement. Rather, they affect the accuracy of the balance sheet.

Summary

The journal is called the book of original entry because transactions are first recorded there. After a transaction has occurred, journalizing is the first step in the accounting process. The account(s) to be debited are always entered first and the account(s) to be credited are entered below and indented half an inch. A short explanation is written below the credit entry and one blank line is left between entries.

Posting is the second step in the accounting process and is the transferring of information from the journal to the ledger. Preparing a trial balance is the third step, and it involves listing the account titles and their amounts in the appropriate debit or credit column. If the trial balance columns are not equal, the bookkeeper must check to determine by how much the column totals differ. She or he will look for an entry that equals the amount by which the column totals differ or the figure that is half that amount. If the difference between the debit and credit columns of the trial balance is evenly divisible by 9, the error is very likely to be a transposition or a slide.

Vocabulary Review

Here is a list of the words and terms for this chapter:

accumulate	journal
book of original entry	journalizing
chronological	posting
compound journal entry	posting reference
corresponding	slide
general journal	transposition
general ledger	verify

Fill in the blank with the correct word or term from the list.

1. To determine or test the truth of, by comparison or investigation, is to _____.

2. A cross-reference from the journal to the ledger and vice versa is referred to as a/an _____.

3. A book of original entry is referred to as a/an _____.

4. Another word for to gather or pile up is _____.

5. A word that means arranged in date order is _____.

6. A/An _____ contains a separate record for each asset, liability, owner's equity, revenue, and expense account.

7. _____ is the process of transferring information from the journal to the ledger.

8. _____ occurs when the decimal point changes when the number is written down.

9. Transactions are first recorded in the _____.

10. The number 652 copied as 625 is an example of a/an _____.

11. A journal entry with more than one debit and/or credit entry is a/an _____.

12. A word that means similar or equivalent is _____.

13. A journal that is used to record many different types of transactions is a/an _____.

14. _____ is the process of recording entries into the journal.

Match the words and terms on the left with the definitions on the right.

15. accumulate
16. book of original entry
17. chronological
18. compound journal entry
19. corresponding
20. general journal
21. general ledger
22. journal
23. journalizing

a. when the position of the decimal point is changed as the number is written down

b. in date order

c. similar or equivalent

d. a book of original entry

e. to gather

f. when the order of numbers is changed as they are written down

g. to test the accuracy of

24. posting
25. posting reference
26. slide
27. transposition
28. verify

h. the process of transferring information from the journal to the ledger

i. the process of recording transactions into a journal

j. the first place where transactions are recorded

k. a journal used to record many different kinds of transactions

l. a journal entry with more than one debit and/or credit

m. a ledger with separate accounts for asset, liability, owner's equity, revenue, and expense accounts

n. a cross-reference between the journal and the ledger

Exercises

EXERCISE 4.1

Transfer chronologically the transactions entered in the following T accounts into three-column general ledger accounts in the following manner:

1. Write the account title and number at the top of the account.

2. Write the current year at the top of the date column.

3. Enter the month and day in the date column.

4. Write the amount in the appropriate debit or credit column.

5. Calculate the account balance after each entry.

Cash						101
12/1	GJ1	10,000	12/2	GJ1	5,000	
12/10	GJ2	800	12/3	GJ1	1,000	
12/26	GJ4	700	12/12	GJ2	1,500	
12/27	GJ4	500	12/18	GJ3	85	
			12/20	GJ3	250	
			12/28	GJ4	420	
			12/30	GJ5	1,000	

Accounts Receivable						110
12/5	GJ1	500	12/27	GJ4	500	
12/10	GJ2	300				
12/26	GJ4	900				

Supplies			120
12/3	GJ1	3,000	

Equipment			130
12/2	GJ1	5,000	

Accounts Payable						210
12/30	GJ5	1,000	12/3	GJ1	2,000	

Y. Goldstein, Capital						310
			12/1	GJ1	10,000	

Y. Goldstein, Drawing			320
12/12	GJ2	1,500	

Revenue						405
			12/5	GJ1	500	
			12/10	GJ2	1,100	
			12/26	GJ4	1,600	

Insurance Expense			610
12/28	GJ4	420	

Utilities Expense			620
12/18	GJ3	85	

Advertising Expense			630
12/20	GJ3	250	

EXERCISE 4.2

Post the following journal entries into three-column general ledger accounts, calculating a new balance after each posting. Then enter the page number of the journal into the posting reference column of the ledger. The account titles and numbers are: Cash, 101; Accounts Receivable, 110; Supplies, 120; Equipment, 130; Accounts Payable, 210; Pat O'Henry, Capital, 310; Pat O'Henry, Drawing, 320; Revenue from Services, 410; and Utilities Expense, 610.

GENERAL JOURNAL				PAGE 28
DATE	DESCRIPTION	POST REF.	DEBIT	CREDIT
20XX				
Nov. 1	Cash		8 0 0 0 00	
	Pat O'Henry, Capital			8 0 0 0 00
	Original Investment			
3	Equipment		3 0 0 0 00	
	Cash			1 0 0 0 00
	Accounts Payable			2 0 0 0 00
	Purchased Equipment: Balance Due in			
	90 Days			
5	Supplies		4 0 0 00	
	Accounts Payable			4 0 0 00
	Purchased Supplies on Account			
9	Cash		2 7 0 00	
	Revenue from Services			2 7 0 00
	Performed Services for Cash			
10	Pat O'Henry, Drawing		6 5 0 00	
	Cash			6 5 0 00
	Owner's Withdrawal			
12	Accounts Receivable		4 0 0 00	
	Cash		2 5 0 00	
	Revenue from Services			6 5 0 00
	Performed Services			
14	Utilities Expense		9 0 00	
	Cash			9 0 00
	Paid Bill for Electricity			
18	Accounts Payable		4 0 0 00	
	Cash			4 0 0 00
	Paid Money to Creditor			
20	Cash		1 0 0 00	
	Accounts Receivable			1 0 0 00
	Received Money on Account			

EXERCISE 4.3

Determine the balance for each of the following accounts for Buck Jensen, trail guide. Then prepare a trial balance as of June 30, 20XX. (A check mark in the posting reference column of the ledger accounts indicates that the figure that appears in that column has not been posted from a journal, but, in this case, is a balance.)

Cash   ACCOUNT NO. 101

DATE		EXPLANATION	POST. REF.	DEBIT	CREDIT	BALANCE
20XX						
May	31	Balance Forward	✓			2 0 0 0 00
June	1		GJ20	5 0 00		
	7		GJ20	3 7 5 00		
	8		GJ20		1 3 0 00	
	10		GJ20		4 0 0 00	
	14		GJ20	4 0 0 00		
	15		GJ21		5 0 0 00	
	15		GJ21		3 0 0 00	
	16		GJ21		1 4 0 00	
	18		GJ21		4 0 0 00	
	25		GJ22		3 0 0 00	
	28		GJ22	5 2 0 00		
	29		GJ22		8 5 00	
	30		GJ22	1 0 0 00		

Accounts Receivable   ACCOUNT NO. 105

DATE		EXPLANATION	POST. REF.	DEBIT	CREDIT	BALANCE
20XX						
May	31	Balance Forward	✓			5 0 0 00
June	1		GJ20		5 0 00	
	21		GJ21	2 5 0 00		
	30		GJ22		1 0 0 00	

Supplies   ACCOUNT NO. 108

DATE		EXPLANATION	POST. REF.	DEBIT	CREDIT	BALANCE
20XX						
May	31	Balance Forward	✓			4 0 0 00
June	8		GJ20	1 3 0 00		

Equipment — ACCOUNT NO. 110

DATE		EXPLANATION	POST. REF.	DEBIT	CREDIT	BALANCE
20XX						
May	31	Balance Forward	✓			5 0 0 00

Accounts Payable — ACCOUNT NO. 205

DATE		EXPLANATION	POST. REF.	DEBIT	CREDIT	BALANCE
20XX						
May	31	Balance Forward	✓			2 0 0 00
June	10		GJ20	4 0 0 00		
	18		GJ21	4 0 0 00		

Buck Jensen, Capital — ACCOUNT NO. 310

DATE		EXPLANATION	POST. REF.	DEBIT	CREDIT	BALANCE
20XX						
May	31	Balance Forward	✓			5 9 0 0 00

Buck Jensen, Drawing — ACCOUNT NO. 311

DATE		EXPLANATION	POST. REF.	DEBIT	CREDIT	BALANCE
20XX						
June	15		GJ21	5 0 0 00		
	25		GJ22	3 0 0 00		

Guide Revenue — ACCOUNT NO. 401

DATE		EXPLANATION	POST. REF.	DEBIT	CREDIT	BALANCE
20XX						
June	7		GJ20		3 7 5 00	
	14		GJ20		4 0 0 00	
	21		GJ21		2 5 0 00	
	28		GJ22		5 2 0 00	

Stable Expense					ACCOUNT NO. 610
DATE	EXPLANATION	POST. REF.	DEBIT	CREDIT	BALANCE
20XX					
June 16		GJ21	1 4 0 00		
29		GJ22	8 5 00		

Rent Expense					ACCOUNT NO. 620
DATE	EXPLANATION	POST. REF.	DEBIT	CREDIT	BALANCE
20XX					
June 15		GJ21	3 0 0 00		

EXERCISE 4.4

The chart of accounts for Sylvia Song, photographer, follows. Journalize the transactions for the month of April, 20XX, beginning on journal page 18.

Chart of Accounts

101	Cash
105	Accounts Receivable
110	Supplies
120	Photographic Equipment
215	Accounts Payable
220	Notes Payable
305	Sylvia Song, Capital
310	Sylvia Song, Drawing
410	Photographic Revenue
620	Rent Expense
625	Utilities Expense
630	Insurance Expense
640	Advertising Expense

Transactions

April 1	Sylvia photographed a wedding; $500 fee due within 10 days
April 2	paid $650 rent
April 3	received $420 in the mail from charge customer
April 4	portrait revenue is $500; received $200 in cash; and $300 is due in 30 days
April 5	made a loan payment of $150; the note is non-interest-bearing
April 8	paid $80 to reduce Accounts Payable
April 9	Sylvia withdrew $700 for personal use
April 10	paid a monthly insurance premium of $95
April 12	portrait revenue for the week is $1,200; $500 was received in cash, the rest is due in 30 days
April 14	paid telephone bill, $120

April 18   paid for advertising in high school newspaper, $50

April 20   bought a new lens for $825; paid $200 cash down and agreed to pay the rest in 60 days

April 25   portrait revenue is $1,400; $800 was received in cash, the rest is due in 30 days

April 26   received $500 in the mail from charge customers

April 28   paid bill for electricity, $75

April 29   paid cash for photographic supplies, $250

April 30   Sylvia withdrew $500 for personal use

EXERCISE 4.5

Tell whether the following numbers are evenly divisible by 9 following this procedure:

a. Find the sum of the digits of each number in Lines 1–10.

b. Determine whether or not the sum obtained in Step a is evenly divisible by 9. Answer yes or no in the space provided. If the sum of the digits is evenly divisible by 9, the number itself is evenly divisible by 9. The first one is completed for you.

	Number	Sum of the Digits	Evenly Divisible by 9?
1.	306.42	15	No
2.	7,234.12		
3.	46,728		
4.	416,732.85		
5.	8,334.00		
6.	3,939.93		
7.	423		
8.	5.721		
9.	46,901.30		
10.	74,615.91		

EXERCISE 4.6

For each of the following, find the difference between the number as it should be recorded and the number as it is actually recorded. In each case, divide the difference by 9 to prove that the difference between a transposed number or a slide as it should be recorded and as it is recorded will be evenly divisible by 9. The first one is completed for you.

	Number as It Should Be Recorded	Number as It Is Actually Recorded	Difference	Divide Difference by 9
0.	873	837	36	36 ÷ 9 = 4
1.	749	794		
2.	105.20	1,052.00		
3.	37,654	37,645		
4.	10.97	1.097		
5.	52	25		
6.	1.28	2.18		
7.	204	2,040		
8.	7.39	7.93		
9.	40,639	46,039		
10.	10,828	10,288		

EXERCISE 4.7

The following are trial balance totals where an error has been made and is as yet undiscovered. In each case, determine the difference between the debit and credit columns, find the sum of the digits of the difference, then determine whether or not the error is likely to be a slide or a transposition. (It is likely to be a slide or transposition if the difference is evenly divisible by 9.) The first one is completed for you.

	Debit Column	Credit Column	Difference	Sum of the Digits	Is Error Likely to Be a Slide or Transposition
0.	17,604.21	18,522.48	918.27	27	yes
1.	70,732	70,822			
2.	10,450	10,498			
3.	21,732	22,722			
4.	106,549	105,326			
5.	185,410	176,320			

EXERCISE 4.8

The following transactions were journalized correctly, but errors were made when posting. For each, tell whether the errors will cause the trial balance totals to be unequal and, if so, by how much the columns will differ. Also indicate which column of the trial balance, debit or credit, will be larger.

		Will Trial Balance Totals Be Unequal?	If So, by How Much?	Which Column Will Be Larger?
a.	A journal entry debiting Cash and crediting Accounts Receivable for $670 was posted as a debit to Cash of $760 and a credit to Accounts Receivable of $760.			
b.	A journal entry debiting Cash and crediting Revenue for $200 was posted as a debit to Cash of $200 and a credit to Revenue of $2,000.			
c.	A journal entry debiting Rent Expense and crediting Cash for $1,600 was posted as a debit to Advertising Expense of $1,600 and a credit to Cash of $1,600.			
d.	A journal entry debiting Accounts Payable and crediting Cash for $350 was posted as a debit to Accounts Payable of $350 and a credit to Cash of $530.			
e.	A journal entry debiting Accounts Receivable and crediting Revenue for $340 was posted as a debit to Accounts Receivable of $430 and a credit to Revenue of $430.			
f.	A journal entry debiting Drawing and crediting Cash for $600 was posted as a debit to Drawing of $600 and a debit to Cash of $600.			
g.	A journal entry debiting Equipment and crediting Accounts Payable for $2,400 was posted as a debit to Equipment of $2,400 and as a credit to Accounts Payable of $3,400.			
h.	A journal entry debiting Cash and crediting Furniture for $460 was posted as a debit to Cash of $640 and a credit to Furniture of $460.			

EXERCISE 4.9

The following transactions were journalized and posted in error. Considering each separately, determine whether the error will cause total revenue, total expenses, and net income to be overstated (O), understated (U), or not affected (N/A). (If revenue is overstated, net income will also be overstated; likewise, if revenue is understated, net income will be understated. If expenses are overstated, net income will be understated; and if expenses are understated, net income will be overstated.) The first one has been completed for you.

	Total Revenue	Total Expenses	Total Net Income
Example The owner withdrew $750 for personal use. The bookkeeper debited Wages Expense and credited Cash for $750.	N/A	O	U
a. The owner invested an additional $5,000 into the business. The bookkeeper debited Cash and credited Revenue for $5,000.			
b. A cheque for $950 was written in payment of rent. The bookkeeper debited Repairs Expense and credited Cash for $950.			
c. A cheque for $375 was written in payment of an account. The bookkeeper debited Insurance Expense and credited Cash for $375.			
d. $620 was received from charge customers. The bookkeeper debited Accounts Receivable and credited Revenue for $620.			
e. $840 in services were performed on account. The bookkeeper debited Accounts Receivable and credited Capital for $840.			
f. A cheque was written for $775 in payment of the rent. The bookkeeper debited Building and credited Cash for $775.			
g. Salaries amounting to $415 were paid with cash. The bookkeeper debited Drawing and credited Cash for $415.			
h. A cheque was written for $62 in payment of the current month's phone bill. The bookkeeper debited Utilities Expense and credited Cash for $42.			

Problems

PROBLEM 4.1

The chart of accounts and the transactions for June 20XX for Dizzy's Flying School follow:

Chart of Accounts			
101	Cash	310	Dizzy Dawson, Drawing
105	Accounts Receivable	401	Flying Revenue
110	Supplies	610	Repairs Expense
115	Equipment	615	Insurance Expense
120	Airplane	620	Advertising Expense
220	Accounts Payable	630	Fuel Expense
230	Notes Payable	640	Rent Expense
301	Dizzy Dawson, Capital	650	Interest Expense

Transactions

June 1	Dizzy deposited $150,000 into a business account entitled Dizzy's Flying School
June 2	purchased an airplane for instruction purposes; paid $75,000 cash down and signed a five-year, 8 percent note for $200,000 for the balance
June 3	bought office supplies on account for $350
June 3	paid $3,780 cash for month's fuel for the plane
June 6	bought office equipment for $5,000; paid $2,500 cash down and agreed to pay the balance in 30 days
June 9	paid office rent, $750
June 10	paid monthly insurance premium, $900
June 12	Dizzy withdrew $3,500 for personal use
June 15	flying revenue for the first half of the month is $7,000; $4,300 was received in cash, the rest is due within 30 days
June 19	received in the mail a $265 bill for fuel; record it now, to be paid later
June 20	paid $500 on Accounts Payable
June 24	paid $775 for repairs to the plane
June 26	paid $800 for radio advertising
June 30	paid $1,000 on account for office equipment purchased on June 6
June 30	wrote a cheque for $4,666 for a payment on the note of June 2; of that amount $1,334 is for interest.
June 30	flying revenue for the second half of the month is $4,700; $3,500 was received in cash, the rest is due within 30 days
June 30	received $2,800 from charge customers

Instructions

1. Journalize the transactions in a general journal. Number the journal beginning with page 28.
2. Post the transactions to the general ledger.
3. Prepare a trial balance as of June 30, 20XX.
4. Prepare an income statement for the month of June 20XX.
5. Prepare a balance sheet on June 30, 20XX detailing the changes in owner's equity.

PROBLEM 4.2

The chart of accounts and the account balances as of August 1, 20XX for Kwick Kleaners follows:

	Chart of Accounts				
101	Cash	$ 6,500	320	Nathaniel Emerson, Drawing	
110	Accounts Receivable	2,100	410	Cleaning Revenue	
114	Cleaning Supplies	1,950	601	Rent Expense	
115	Cleaning Equipment	95,000	605	Insurance Expense	
120	Office Equipment	8,000	610	Advertising Expense	
210	Accounts Payable	4,500	620	Salary Expense	
220	Notes Payable	50,000	630	Utilities Expense	
310	Nathaniel Emerson, Capital	59,050	635	Interest Expense	

Transactions

August 1	paid rent for August, $1,500
August 1	bought a computer for the office; paid $500 cash down and agreed to paid the balance of $700 within 30 days
August 4	placed an ad in the newspaper for $100; the amount is due in 30 days
August 8	paid $125 for August insurance premium
August 10	bought $400 in cleaning supplies; will pay within 30 days
August 15	paid semi-monthly salaries, $1,080
August 15	cleaning revenue for the first two weeks is $3,300, of which $1,600 is received in cash
August 17	received $2,225 in the mail from charge customers
August 18	paid $700 owed on the computer purchased August 1
August 22	paid $1,000 to reduce the amount owed on a note; $425 of the amount is for interest expense
August 25	paid the telephone bill, $305
August 28	cleaning revenue for the second two weeks is $3,800, of which $2,300 is received in cash
August 29	paid bill for electricity, $120
August 31	paid semimonthly salaries, $1,090
August 31	Nathaniel withdrew $1,800 for personal use

Instructions

1. Enter the balance from the chart of accounts into the ledger. Write *Balance Forward* in the account explanation column and place a check mark (✓) in the posting reference column of each account for which a balance is entered.

2. Journalize the August transactions in a general journal. Number the journal beginning with page 39.

3. Post the transactions.

4. Prepare a trial balance.

5. Prepare an income statement for the month of August 20XX.

6. Prepare a statement of owner's equity for the month of August 20XX.

7. Prepare a balance sheet as of August 31, 20XX.

PROBLEM 4.3

The bookkeeper for David's Dance Studio was new and made several errors when recording the transactions for the first month of business. The chart of accounts and the general journal for the month of December follow:

Chart of Accounts			
101	Cash	310	David Kowalczyk, Capital
120	Accounts Receivable	320	David Kowalczyk, Drawing
130	Supplies	410	Dance Revenue
140	Equipment	610	Utilities Expense
150	Furniture	620	Wages Expense
210	Accounts Payable	630	Advertising Expense
220	Notes Payable		

GENERAL JOURNAL				PAGE 1	
DATE	**DESCRIPTION**	**POST REF.**	**DEBIT**	**CREDIT**	

DATE	DESCRIPTION	POST REF.	DEBIT	CREDIT
20XX				
Dec. 1	Cash		12000 00	
	David Kowalczyk, Capital			12000 00
	To Record Owner's Investment			
2	Equipment		4000 00	
	Cash			1000 00
	Accounts Receivable			3000 00
	Bought Equipment; Paid $1,000 Down;			
	Balance Due in 90 Days			
4	Furniture		2000 00	
	Notes Payable			2000 00
	Bought Furniture: Signed a 6-month,			
	7% Note for $2,000			
5	Cash		500 00	
	Supplies			500 00
	Paid Cash for Supplies			
6	Cash		400 00	
	Dance Revenue			400 00
	To Record Week's Revenue; $400 Received			
	in Cash; $300 Balance Due within 30 Days			
9	Utilities Expense		105 00	
	Cash			105 00
	Paid Bill for Electricity			
10	Cash		370 00	
	David Kowalczyk, Drawing			370 00
	To Record Owner's Withdrawal			
12	Utilities Expense		75 00	
	Accounts Payable			75 00
	Received Phone Bill; Record Now to Be			
	Paid Later			
15	Wages Expense		1200 00	
	Cash			1200 00
	To Record Wages of $800 and Owner's			
	Withdrawal of $400			

	GENERAL JOURNAL				PAGE 2	
DATE	**DESCRIPTION**	**POST REF.**	**DEBIT**		**CREDIT**	
20XX						
Dec. 18	Utilities Expense		7 5 00			
	Cash				7 5 00	
	Payment of Phone Bill Received and					
	Recorded on December 12					
20	Cash		3 0 0 00			
	David Kowalczyk, Capital				3 0 0 00	
	Cash Received from Charge Customers					
23	Advertising Expense		1 7 5 00			
	Accounts Receivable				1 7 5 00	
	Bill Received for Newspaper Ad in					
	December					
24	Equipment		1 0 0 0 00			
	David Kowalczyk, Capital				1 0 0 0 00	
	Owner Donated a Computer to the Business					
26	Wages Expense		7 0 0 00			
	Cash				7 0 0 00	
	Wages of $700					
28	Cash		5 0 0 00			
	Accounts Payable		6 0 0 00			
	Dance Revenue				1 1 0 0 00	
	Revenue of $1,100; $500 Received in					
	Cash					
30	Accounts Receivable		5 0 0 00			
	Cash				5 0 0 00	
	Payment Made on Equipment Purchased					
	on December 2					

Instructions

1. Look over each transaction carefully, including the description of the entry. If the entry is correct, do nothing. If the entry is incorrect draw a line through the incorrect account title or amount and enter the correct title or amount above it. Use journal pages 1 and 2.

2. After entering the account names and numbers in the general ledger, post all the correct transactions.

3. Prepare a trial balance as of December 31, 20XX.

4. Determine the amount of the net income or the net loss for December. Do not prepare a formal income statement.

5. Prepare a statement of owner's equity for the month of December 20XX.

PROBLEM 4.4

An income statement prepared for the Bowmer Company for the month of February 20XX showed a net income of $2,100. The following errors were made by the bookkeeper in recording the transactions for the month:

1. A $700 withdrawal by Barbara Bowmer was recorded by debiting Salary Expense and crediting Cash.

2. Received a bill for February advertising for $500, but did not pay it or record it on the books.

3. Received $950 in the mail from clients who received services in January and recorded the transaction as a debit to Cash and a credit to Revenue.

4. Recorded rent of $1,200 as a debit to Rent Expense of $120 and a credit to Cash of $120.

5. $1,500 cash received for services performed in February was recorded as a debit to Cash and a credit to Barbara Bowmer, Capital.

6. Services performed on account in February amounting to $1,100 were recorded as a debit to Revenue and a credit to Accounts Receivable.

Instructions

1. In each case, on general journal page 47 record the correct journal entry; write "correct entry" as the explanation. Number the entries 1–6.

2. Determine for each entry whether the error will (a) cause revenue to be overstated; (b) cause revenue to be understated; (c) cause expenses to be overstated; or (d) cause expenses to be understated.

3. If either revenue or expense is affected by the error, determine by how much each is overstated or understated.

4. Determine whether each incorrect entry will cause net income to be overstated or understated.

5. Determine the correct net income for the month. Use the headings listed to record your answers. The first error has been analyzed for you as an example.

Error	Will Revenue Be Overstated? By How Much?	Will Revenue Be Understated? By How Much?	Will Expenses Be Overstated? By How Much?	Will Expenses Be Understated? By How Much?	Will Net Income Be Overstated? By How Much?	Will Net Income Be Understated? By How Much?
1.			yes, $700			yes, $700

CHAPTER 5

Adjustments and the Ten-Column Worksheet

LEARNING OBJECTIVES

When you have completed this chapter, you should

1. have a better understanding of accounting terminology.
2. be able to calculate and record adjustments for supplies used, prepaid rent, insurance expense, amortization, wages payable, and unearned revenue.
3. be able to prepare a ten-column worksheet.
4. be able to prepare financial statements directly from the worksheet.
5. be able to journalize adjusting entries directly from the worksheet.

VOCABULARY

accounting cycle	the step-by-step procedure that begins with a transaction and ends with the closing of the books
acquisition	the act of acquiring possession
adjusting entry	an entry made at the end of the accounting period for which no transaction occurs and which brings certain accounts up to date
amortization	the transferring of the cost of an asset to expense over the asset's useful life; also called depreciation
book value	the cost of an asset minus its accumulated amortization
contra asset	an account with a credit balance that subtracts from its related asset account balance on the balance sheet
prepaid expenses	expenses paid in advance and recorded initially as assets
salvage value	the estimated worth of an asset at the end of its useful life
useful life	the number of years over which an asset is depreciated
worksheet	a ten-column form on which the trial balance is entered, adjustments are prepared, and the necessary information for preparing the income statement and balance sheet is accumulated

Introduction

The **accounting cycle** is a series of steps that are repeated for every accounting period. The accounting cycle begins when the first transaction occurs and ends when the bookkeeper closes the books for the period; the cycle is repeated for each accounting period.

The first steps in the accounting cycle are journalizing, posting, and preparing a trial balance. In this chapter, the trial balance will be placed directly onto a **worksheet**, which is a ten-column form used by the bookkeeper to organize the data necessary for preparing the adjusting and closing entries and the financial statements. After the trial balance has been completed and is in balance, the next steps in the accounting cycle are calculating adjustments and completing a worksheet.

An *accounting period*, which is the time span covered by the income statement, determines when (for example, a month, a quarter, a year) financial statements are prepared. Accounting periods must be equal in length so that comparisons can be made from one period to another. The measurement of net income should be as precise as possible, and the matching principle requires that all expenses incurred during an accounting period be subtracted from the revenue earned for that same period. Past or future revenue or expenses must not be recorded on current financial statements.

To help ensure accuracy in reporting net income, certain adjustments to the accounts are made before the financial statements are prepared. These adjusting entries are recorded first on the worksheet, next in the general journal, and finally are posted to the general ledger.

Prepaid Expenses

Businesses often make expenditures that will benefit more than one accounting period. For example, when supplies are purchased, they are expected to last for several accounting periods; insurance policies are frequently purchased for one-, two-, or three-year periods; and rent is often prepaid for several months. Such expenditures in advance are called **prepaid expenses** and are debited to an asset account at the time of payment; at the end of the accounting period, a portion of the cost will be recognized as an expense for the current period. The *unused* portion will remain on the books as an asset, but will eventually be converted to expense.

Adjusting Entries

Until now, when a transaction has been recorded, something has happened to prompt a journal entry. For example, a customer makes a payment on account, services are sold for cash, the owner withdraws money, or the rent is paid. With an **adjusting entry**, however, nothing external happens. Adjusting entries are made simply to bring certain accounts up to date or to make certain accounts accurately reflect their value. For example, the Office Supplies account is debited whenever supplies are purchased, but *no credit to the account is made when supplies are used up* until an adjusting entry is recorded. At the time a one-, two-, or three-year insurance policy is purchased, the total cost is debited to an asset account called Prepaid Insurance, but *no credits are recorded* to the account until an adjusting entry is made. Adjustments to the accounts are made at the end of the accounting period, which may be one month, three months, a year, or some other time period.

Adjustment for Supplies Expense

Assume that on January 1, the Supplies account for Mary Tyus, M.D., has a balance of $255. Assume also that two purchases of supplies are made in January: one on January 14 for $60 and one on January 26 for $35. The general journal entries to record the purchases of supplies are as follows:

DATE		DESCRIPTION	POST REF.	DEBIT	CREDIT
GENERAL JOURNAL					**PAGE 5**
20XX					
Jan.	14	Supplies		6 0 00	
		Cash			6 0 00
		To Record Purchase of Supplies			
	26	Supplies		3 5 00	
		Cash			3 5 00
		To Record Purchase of Supplies			

At the end of January, the Supplies account looks like this.

```
Supplies                                    130

1/1   Balance      255
1/14  GJ5           60
1/26  GJ8           35
                   350
```

On January 31, a physical count of the supplies on hand shows their dollar balance to be $260, yet it appears from the account that $350 worth of supplies is on hand; this is not the case, because some of the supplies have been used. To reflect the accurate value ($260) of the account on January 31, an adjusting entry is made, transferring the used-up portion to the Supplies Expense account. The entry is as follows:

DATE		DESCRIPTION	POST REF.	DEBIT	CREDIT
GENERAL JOURNAL					**PAGE 14**
20XX		Adjusting Entries			
Jan.	31	Supplies Expense		9 0 00	
		Supplies			9 0 00
		To Record Supplies Used for the Month			

The $90 figure used in the adjusting entry was determined by subtracting the ending value of supplies from the balance in the account ($350 − $260 = $90). The Supplies account should reflect the value of the ending inventory after the adjusting entry has been journalized and posted.

Supplies 130

1/1 Balance	255	1/31 Adjusting GJ14	90
1/14 GJ5	60		
1/26 GJ8	35		
	260		

Supplies Expense 605

1/31 Adjusting GJ14	90

The Supplies account is an asset and will appear on the balance sheet; Supplies Expense is an expense and will appear on the income statement. Every adjusting entry will involve both a balance sheet account and an income statement account.

Adjustment for Prepaid Insurance

Assume that on January 2, 20XX Mary Tyus, M.D., purchases a 12-month fire insurance policy for $360. The entry in the general journal is as follows:

GENERAL JOURNAL						PAGE 1	
DATE		DESCRIPTION	POST REF.	DEBIT		CREDIT	
20XX							
Jan.	2	Prepaid Insurance		3 6 0 00			
		Cash				3 6 0 00	
		To Record Purchase of 12-Month Fire					
		Insurance Policy					

The Prepaid Insurance account is an asset and will appear on the balance sheet. Insurance expense should not be debited at the time the policy is purchased, because the expense should logically be spread out over the 12-month period for which the policy is in force.

At the end of the month (or the accounting period), the adjusting entry for insurance is calculated as follows:

$$\$360 \div 12 \text{ Months} = \$30 \text{ Cost per Month.}$$

The general journal entry to transfer a portion of the asset Prepaid Insurance to Insurance Expense is as follows:

GENERAL JOURNAL						PAGE 14	
DATE		DESCRIPTION	POST REF.	DEBIT		CREDIT	
20XX		Adjusting Entries					
Jan.	31	Insurance Expense		3 0 00			
		Prepaid Insurance				3 0 00	
		To Record Insurance Expense for Month					

After the entry has been posted, the T accounts look like this:

Prepaid Insurance   **120**

1/2 GJ1   360 | 1/31 Adjusting GJ14 30

Insurance Expense   **660**

1/31 Adjusting GJ14   30 |

Twelve $30 credits will be journalized and posted, one each month, until the entire $360 has been transferred to Insurance Expense.

Adjustment for Amortization

Assets are divided into two main categories called *current assets* and *capital assets.* Capital assets include buildings, furniture, office or store equipment, cars, and trucks, and are used in the production of other assets (for example, cash or accounts receivable) and generally are not for sale.

When an asset is purchased for use in the business, an asset account is debited. By recording **amortization**, the cost of these assets is converted to expense over time. Assume, for example, that Mary Tyus purchases office equipment costing $10,600 on January 2. It is expected to have a **useful life** of four years and then have a **salvage value** of $1,000. In the general journal, the entry to record the acquisition of the asset is as follows:

GENERAL JOURNAL					PAGE 1	
DATE	**DESCRIPTION**	**POST REF.**	**DEBIT**		**CREDIT**	
20XX						
Jan. 2	Office Equipment		10 6 0 0 00			
	Cash				3 0 0 0 00	
	Notes Payable				7 6 0 0 00	
	To Record Purchase of Office Equipment;					
	Signed a 12-Month, 7% Note					

Accountants may use several methods to determine how much amortization expense will be recognized for an accounting period. The straight-line amortization method recognizes the same amount of expense each accounting period. The bookkeeper must know three things to calculate the straight-line amortization expense: (1) the cost of the asset, (2) the useful life of the asset, and (3) the estimated salvage value. Amortization is calculated as follows:

1. Subtract the salvage value from the cost to determine the amount to be amortized:

$$\$10,600 - \$1,000 = \$9,600.$$

2. Divide the amount to be amortized by the number of years in the useful life to determine the annual amortization:

$$\$9,600 \div 4 = \$2,400.$$

3. If the accounting period is one month, divide yearly amortization by 12 to determine monthly amortization:

$$\$2{,}400 \div 12 = \$200.$$

The adjusting entry to record the amortization is as follows:

		GENERAL JOURNAL												PAGE 14				
DATE		DESCRIPTION	POST REF.				DEBIT							CREDIT				
20XX		Adjusting Entries																
Jan.	31	Amortization Expense					2	0	0	00								
		Accumulated Amortization, Office Equip.												2	0	0	00	
		To Record Amortization on Office Equipment																

When amortization is recorded, credits are not entered directly into the asset account because accounts for assets that are amortized reflect the historical cost. Amortization amounts are recorded in an account called Accumulated Amortization; it is a **contra asset** because it subtracts from its related asset on the balance sheet.

After the adjusting entry for amortization has been posted, the T accounts look like this:

Office Equipment   **150**

1/2   GJ1   10,600 |

Accumulated Amortization: Office Equipment   **151**

| 1/31 Adjusting GJ14   200

Amortization Expense   **670**

1/31 Adjusting GJ14   200 |

The Accumulated Amortization account accumulates the amortization for its related asset. The Office Equipment account and the contra asset account, Accumulated Amortization, look like this six months after the purchase of the equipment:

Office Equipment   **150**

1/2   GJ1   10,600 |

Accumulated Amortization: Office Equipment   **151**

| 1/31 Adjusting GJ14   200
| 2/28 Adjusting GJ18   200
| 3/31 Adjusting GJ22   200
| 4/30 Adjusting GJ27   200
| 5/31 Adjusting GJ32   200
| 6/30 Adjusting GJ37   200

The cost of an asset minus its accumulated amortization is called the asset's **book value.** The balance sheet will show cost, accumulated amortization, and book value for every asset that is amortized. A portion of the balance sheet on June 30 for the preceding purchase and six months' amortization appears as follows:

Mary Tyus, M.D. Balance Sheet June 30, 20XX		
Assets		
Cash		$ 8 1 0 0 00
∿∿∿		
Office Equipment	$ 1 0 6 0 0 00	
Less Accumulated Amortization: Office Equipment	1 2 0 0 00	$ 9 4 0 0 00

Adjustment for Wages Payable

Assume that Mary Tyus incurs $150 in wages every day, Monday through Friday, and that paydays fall on Friday of each week. The end of the accounting period, however, falls on Tuesday, which is January 31, the end of the month. For January expenses to be properly recorded, two days of wages expense (Monday and Tuesday, January 30 and 31) must be recorded for January.

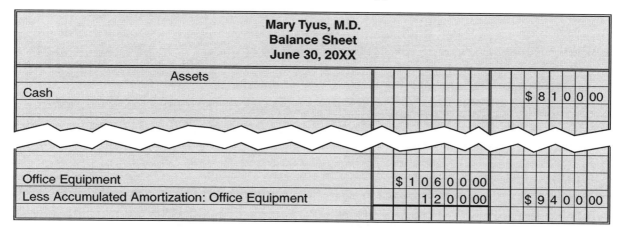

The adjusting entry to record this is as follows:

GENERAL JOURNAL					PAGE 14	
DATE	**DESCRIPTION**	**POST REF.**	**DEBIT**		**CREDIT**	
20XX	Adjusting Entries					
Jan. 31	Wages Expense		3 0 0 00			
	Wages Payable				3 0 0 00	
	To Record Wages Expense for					
	January 30 and 31					

Wages Payable is credited because the wages will not actually be paid until Friday, thus creating a short-term liability. After the adjusting entry is posted, the T accounts look like this:

Wages Expense		640
1/6 GJ2	750	
1/13 GJ5	750	
1/20 GJ7	750	
1/27 GJ9	750	
1/31 Adjusting GJ14	300	

Wages Payable		230
	1/31 Adjusting GJ14	300

On Friday, when the wages are actually paid, the balance from the Wages Payable account must be removed and three days' wages expense must be recognized for February. The entry to record payment of the wages is as follows:

GENERAL JOURNAL				PAGE 15	
DATE	DESCRIPTION	POST REF.	DEBIT	CREDIT	
20XX					
Feb. 3	Wages Expense		450 00		
	Wages Payable		300 00		
	Cash			750 00	
	To Record Payment of Wages for Period				
	January 30–February 3				

After the entry for payment of the wages is posted, the T accounts for Wages Payable and Wages Expense look like this:

Wages Payable			230
2/3 GJ15	300	1/31 Adjusting GJ14	300

Wages Expense		640
1/6 GJ2	750	
1/13 GJ5	750	
1/20 GJ7	750	
1/27 GJ9	750	
1/31 Adjusting GJ14	300	
2/3 GJ15	450	

The Wages Expense account now accurately reflects $450 for the first week in February, and $300 of that week's total wages of $750 has been allocated to January.

Adjustment for Unearned Revenue

Often, a business receives money in advance for services it plans to deliver later. For example, magazine subscriptions are paid in advance, theatres sell season tickets, and dormitories collect room and board at the beginning of the quarter or semester. Cash received in advance of performing the services should not be recognized as revenue.

Assume that Mary Tyus receives $1,000 from Jorge Sanders on January 3 for consulting services that she will perform in the future. The entry to record the $1,000 received is as follows:

GENERAL JOURNAL					PAGE 2	
DATE	DESCRIPTION	POST REF.	DEBIT		CREDIT	
20XX						
Jan. 3	Cash		1 0 0 0 00			
	Unearned Consulting Revenue				1 0 0 0 00	
	Cash Received for Services to be					
	Performed in the Future					

The Unearned Revenue account is a liability, because Mary owes the services to the customer and the $1,000 will not be recognized as revenue until the services are performed.

Assume that by the end of January Mary performs $600 of consulting services for Jorge Sanders. Through an adjusting entry, the $600 will be transferred from the Unearned Revenue account to Earned Revenue.

GENERAL JOURNAL					PAGE 14	
DATE	DESCRIPTION	POST REF.	DEBIT		CREDIT	
20XX	Adjusting Entries					
Jan. 31	Unearned Consulting Revenue		6 0 0 00			
	Consulting Revenue				6 0 0 00	
	To Transfer $600 into Consulting Revenue					

After the adjusting entry has been posted, the T accounts appear as follows:

Unearned Consulting Revenue　　　　　　　**230**

1/31 Adjusting GJ14	600	1/3 GJ2	1,000
			400

Consulting Revenue　　　　　　　**230**

	1/15 GJ11	900
	1/31 Adjusting GJ14	600
		1500

The balance in the Unearned Consulting Revenue account on January 31 is $400. When Mary performs the remainder of the consulting services, that balance, too, will be transferred to Consulting Revenue.

Adjustment for the Accrual of Revenue

In the previous example, Mary Tyus was paid for consulting before the services were performed. A more common occurrence would be one in which Mary performs services but does not receive payment by the end of the accounting period in which the financial statements are prepared. Assume that in January Mary performs medical services for a customer amounting to $2,000. At the end of the month, a bill is sent to the customer and the following adjusting entry to recognize the revenue earned is prepared.

GENERAL JOURNAL				PAGE 14	
DATE	DESCRIPTION	POST REF.	DEBIT	CREDIT	
20XX					
Jan. 31	Accounts Receivable		2 0 0 0 00		
	Medical Revenue			2 0 0 0 00	
	To Record Services Performed and Bills				
	Sent to Customers				

The T accounts look as follows after the adjusting entry is prepared:

Accounts Receivable   **110**

1/1   Balance   400
1/15 GJ7   700
1/31 Adjusting GJ14   2,000

Medical Revenue   **401**

                    1/8   GJ5   2,700
                    1/15 GJ6   3,100
                    1/22 GJ8   3,300
                    1/29 GJ10   2,500
                    1/31 Adjusting GJ14   2,000

Effects of Failing to Record Adjusting Entries

Every adjusting entry involves both an income statement account and a balance sheet account. Failing to record an adjustment causes an overstatement or an understatement of either expenses or revenue and a corresponding overstatement or an understatement of net income.

For example, failing to record an adjustment for an expense (such as the entry that debits Insurance Expense and credits Prepaid Insurance) would cause an understatement of expenses and a resulting overstatement of net income, while failing to record an adjustment for accrued revenue (such as the entry debiting Accounts Receivable and crediting Revenue) would cause an understatement of revenue and an understatement of net income.

Failing to record an adjustment will affect net income. It will also affect owner's equity because net income is added to the owner's capital account at the end of the accounting period. If net income is overstated, owner's capital will also be overstated; and if net income is understated, owner's capital will be understated.

Other accounts, too, will be affected. For example, failing to record the adjustment for supplies used (a debit to Supplies Expense and a credit to Supplies) causes an overstatement of total assets (Supplies), an understatement of total expenses (Supplies Expense), and an overstatement of net income.

The Ten-Column Worksheet

The worksheet is a ten-column form on which the trial balance, the adjustments, an adjusted trial balance, the income statement, and the balance sheet are first prepared. It is prepared in pencil because it is not a formal statement; rather, it is the bookkeeper's tool. It proves that the general ledger is in balance, and it accumulates the information for the adjustments and for the income statement and balance sheet before the adjustments are journalized and the formal statements are prepared in ink.

Trial Balance Columns of the Worksheet

The ten-column worksheet that follows is for Mary Tyus, M.D. The first two columns of the worksheet are for preparing the trial balance. The figures are taken directly from the ledger after all the posting for the period has been completed. The trial balance must be complete and in balance before continuing on to the adjustments columns of the worksheet. A single line to indicate addition is drawn across the debit and credit columns beneath the last item listed, and a double line extends across the debit and credit columns beneath the trial balance totals.

	Mary Tyus, M.D. Worksheet For Month Ended January 31, 20XX		
ACCT. NO.	**ACCOUNT TITLES**	**UNADJUSTED TRIAL BALANCE**	
		DEBIT	**CREDIT**
101	Cash	12 500 00	
105	Accounts Receivable	1 100 00	
110	Notes Receivable	4 700 00	
120	Prepaid Insurance	3 600 00	
130	Supplies	3 500 00	
150	Office Equipment	10 600 00	
151	Accumulated Amort.: OE		
201	Accounts Payable		2 950 00
210	Notes Payable		7 600 00
215	Payroll Taxes Payable		210 00
220	Unearned Consulting Rev.		1 000 00
301	Mary Tyus, Capital		21 692 00
310	Mary Tyus, Drawing	4 800 00	
401	Medical Revenue		11 600 00
405	Consulting Revenue		900 00
601	Rent Expense	3 900 00	
610	Interest Expense	76 00	
615	Utilities Expense	1 420 00	
620	Repairs Expense	2 416 00	
630	Uniforms Expense	500 00	
640	Wages Expense	3 000 00	
650	Payroll Tax Expense	230 00	
	Totals	45 952 00	45 952 00

Adjustments Columns of the Worksheet

Once the trial balance is complete and in balance, the data for the adjustments are entered directly in the adjustments columns opposite their account titles. If the account title does not appear on the original trial balance, it may be added at the bottom of the worksheet.

The letter *a* is written next to the debit and credit amounts for the first adjustment, the letter *b* beside the next adjustment, and so on. The letters identify the adjustments and make them easier to journalize after the worksheet is complete.

The adjustment data for Mary Tyus, M,D., are as follows:

a. The Supplies Expense account is debited and Supplies is credited for $90 to recognize supplies used in January.

b. The Insurance Expense account is debited and Prepaid Insurance is credited for $30 to recognize insurance expense for January.

c. Amortization Expense is debited and Accumulated Amortization is credited for $200 to record amortization expense for January.

d. Wages Expense is debited and Wages Payable is credited for $300 to record accrued wages expense.

e. The liability account Unearned Consulting Revenue is debited and Consulting Revenue is credited for $600 to recognize that portion of the consulting revenue that has been earned in January.

f. Accounts Receivable has been debited and Medical Revenue has been credited for $2,000 to recognize services performed but for which payment has not been received.

The worksheet on page 105 shows the trial balance and the adjustments columns.

Mary Tyus, M.D.
Worksheet
For Month Ended January 31, 20XX

ACCT. NO.	ACCOUNT TITLES	UNADJUSTED TRIAL BALANCE DEBIT	UNADJUSTED TRIAL BALANCE CREDIT	ADJUSTMENTS DEBIT	ADJUSTMENTS CREDIT
101	Cash	12500.00			
105	Accounts Receivable	1100.00		f. 2000.00	
110	Notes Receivable	4700.00			
120	Prepaid Insurance	360.00			b. 30.00
130	Supplies	350.00			a. 90.00
150	Office Equipment	10600.00			
151	Accumulated Amort.: OE				c. 200.00
201	Accounts Payable		2950.00		
210	Notes Payable		7600.00		
215	Payroll Taxes Payable		210.00		
220	Unearned Consulting Rev.		1000.00	e. 600.00	
301	Mary Tyus, Capital		21692.00		
310	Mary Tyus, Drawing	4800.00			
401	Medical Revenue		11600.00		f. 2000.00
405	Consulting Revenue		900.00		e. 600.00
601	Rent Expense	3900.00			
610	Interest Expense	76.00			
615	Utilities Expense	1420.00			
620	Repairs Expense	2416.00			
630	Uniforms Expense	500.00			
640	Wages Expense	3000.00		d. 300.00	
650	Payroll Tax Expense	230.00			
	Totals	45952.00	45952.00		
605	Supplies Expense			a. 90.00	
660	Insurance Expense			b. 30.00	
670	Amortization Expense			c. 200.00	
230	Wages Payable				d. 300.00
				3220.00	3220.00

Adjusted Trial Balance Columns of the Worksheet

The figures in the adjusted trial balance columns, not the ones on the original trial balance, are the ones that will be used by the accountant for preparing the financial statements. The correct procedure for completing the adjusted trial balance is to start with the first account, Cash, and if there is no adjustment, simply extend the balance to its correct debit or credit column of the adjusted trial balance. All accounts without adjustments are treated in the same fashion.

Accounts with adjustments are handled in one of four ways:

1. If the original account has a debit balance and the adjustment is also a debit, add the amounts together and extend the total to the adjusted trial balance as a debit. The adjustment to the Accounts Receivable account (f) is an example.

2. If the original account has a credit balance and the adjustment is also a credit, add the figures and extend the total to the adjusted trial balance as a credit. The adjustment to Medical Revenue (f) is an example.

3. If the account on the original trial balance has a debit balance and the adjustment is a credit, subtract and enter the new but smaller debit balance onto the adjusted trial balance. The adjustment to Supplies (a) is an example.

4. If the account on the original trial balance has a credit balance and the adjustment is a debit, subtract and extend the smaller credit balance to the credit side of the adjusted trial balance. The adjustment to Unearned Consulting Revenue (e) is an example.

The adjusted trial balance appears in the worksheet on page 107.

Mary Tyus, M.D.
Worksheet
For Month Ended January 31, 20XX

ACCT. NO.	ACCOUNT TITLES	UNADJUSTED TRIAL BALANCE DEBIT	CREDIT	ADJUSTMENTS DEBIT	CREDIT	ADJUSTED TRIAL BALANCE DEBIT	CREDIT
101	Cash	125000 00				125000 00	
105	Accounts Receivable	1100 00		f. 2000 00		3100 00	
110	Notes Receivable	4700 00				4700 00	
120	Prepaid Insurance	360 00			b. 30 00	330 00	
130	Supplies	350 00			a. 90 00	260 00	
150	Office Equipment	10600 00				10600 00	
151	Accumulated Amort.: OE				c. 2000 00		2000 00
201	Accounts Payable		2950 00				2950 00
210	Notes Payable		7600 00				7600 00
215	Payroll Taxes Payable		2100 00				2100 00
220	Unearned Consulting Rev.		10000 00	e. 6000 00			4000 00
301	Mary Tyus, Capital		21692 00				21692 00
310	Mary Tyus, Drawing	4800 00				4800 00	
401	Medical Revenue		11600 00		f. 2000 00		13600 00
405	Consulting Revenue		9000 00		e. 6000 00		15000 00
601	Rent Expense	3900 00				3900 00	
610	Interest Expense	76 00				76 00	
615	Utilities Expense	1420 00				1420 00	
620	Repairs Expense	2416 00				2416 00	
630	Uniforms Expense	500 00				500 00	
640	Wages Expense	3000 00		d. 300 00		3300 00	
650	Payroll Tax Expense	230 00				230 00	
	Totals	45952 00	45952 00				
605	Supplies Expense			a. 90 00		90 00	
660	Insurance Expense			b. 30 00		30 00	
670	Amortization Expense			c. 2000 00		2000 00	
230	Wages Payable				d. 300 00		300 00
				3220 00	3220 00	48452 00	48452 00

Income Statement and Balance Sheet Columns of the Worksheet

Once the adjusted trial balance is complete and in balance, each figure is extended to the columns for either the balance sheet or the income statement. The procedure for extending the figures is as follows:

1. Starting at the top with Cash, extend the figures to their correct debit or credit column of the balance sheet. Repeat this procedure for each asset, liability, and owner's equity account that appears on the adjusted trial balance.

2. Beginning with the first revenue account, extend that balance into the credit column of the income statement, and extend all expense account balances into the debit column of the income statement.

Mary Tyus, M.D.
Worksheet
For Month Ended January 31, 20XX

ACCT. NO.	ACCOUNT TITLES	UNADJUSTED TRIAL BALANCE DEBIT	UNADJUSTED TRIAL BALANCE CREDIT	ADJUSTMENTS DEBIT		ADJUSTMENTS CREDIT	
101	Cash	12500 00					
105	Accounts Receivable	1100 00		f.	200 00		
110	Notes Receivable	4700 00					
120	Prepaid Insurance	360 00				b.	30 00
130	Supplies	350 00				a.	90 00
150	Office Equipment	10600 00					
151	Accumulated Amort.: OE					c.	200 00
201	Accounts Payable		2950 00				
210	Notes Payable		7600 00				
215	Payroll Taxes Payable		210 00				
220	Unearned Consulting Rev.		1000 00	e.	600 00		
301	Mary Tyus, Capital		21692 00				
310	Mary Tyus, Drawing	4800 00					
401	Medical Revenue		11600 00			f.	200 00
405	Consulting Revenue		900 00			e.	600 00
601	Rent Expense	3900 00					
610	Interest Expense	76 00					
615	Utilities Expense	1420 00					
620	Repairs Expense	2416 00					
630	Uniforms Expense	500 00					
640	Wages Expense	3000 00		d.	300 00		
650	Payroll Tax Expense	230 00					
	Totals	45952 00	45952 00				
605	Supplies Expense			a.	90 00		
660	Insurance Expense			b.	30 00		
670	Amortization Expense			c.	200 00		
230	Wages Payable					d.	300 00
					3220 00		3220 00

3. Do not omit any of the accounts with adjustments that appear at the bottom of the original trial balance. Some are income statement accounts and others are balance sheet accounts. Supplies Expense, Insurance Expense, and Amortization Expense are extended to the debit column of the income statement, while Wages Payable is a liability and must be extended to the credit column of the balance sheet.

4. Total the four columns of the income statement and the balance sheet and enter totals on the worksheet beneath a single ruled line.

Carefully study the worksheet as it appears after all figures have been extended from the adjusted trial balance columns to the balance sheet and income statement columns.

Mary Tyus, M.D.
Worksheet
For Month Ended January 31, 20XX

ADJUSTED TRIAL BALANCE		INCOME STATEMENT		BALANCE SHEET	
DEBIT	CREDIT	DEBIT	CREDIT	DEBIT	CREDIT
12500 00				12500 00	
3100 00				3100 00	
4700 00				4700 00	
	330 00				330 00
	260 00				260 00
10600 00				10600 00	
	200 00				200 00
	2950 00				2950 00
	7600 00				7600 00
	210 00				210 00
	400 00				400 00
	21692 00				21692 00
4800 00				4800 00	
	13600 00		13600 00		
	1500 00		1500 00		
3900 00		3900 00			
76 00		76 00			
1420 00		1420 00			
2416 00		2416 00			
500 00		500 00			
3300 00		3300 00			
230 00		230 00			
90 00		90 00			
30 00		30 00			
200 00		200 00			
	300 00				300 00
48452 00	48452 00	12162 00	15100 00	36290 00	33352 00

Net Income on the Worksheet

The next steps will verify the accuracy of the bookkeeper's work and will complete the worksheet:

5. Determine the difference between the income statement debit and credit columns. If the credit total (revenue) is larger than the debit total (expenses), a net income has been earned. Enter the net income figure beneath the total on the debit side of the income statement and write the words *Net Income* in the Account Titles column of the worksheet on the same line.

6. Enter the net income figure obtained in Step 5 beneath the credit column total on the balance sheet. This is required because the net income is added to the owner's capital account (which has a credit balance) in the owner's equity section of the balance sheet.

7. Draw a single ruled line beneath the four columns of the income statement and the balance sheet beneath the net income figure.

8. Total the balance sheet columns. At this point, they must equal each other. If they do not, a mistake has been made and the bookkeeper must find it before continuing.

Mary Tyus, M.D.
Worksheet
For Month Ended January 31, 20XX

ACCT. NO.	ACCOUNT TITLES	UNADJUSTED TRIAL BALANCE DEBIT	UNADJUSTED TRIAL BALANCE CREDIT	ADJUSTMENTS DEBIT	ADJUSTMENTS CREDIT
101	Cash	12 500 00			
105	Accounts Receivable	1 100 00		f. 2 000 00	
110	Notes Receivable	4 700 00			
120	Prepaid Insurance	3 60 00			b. 3 0 00
130	Supplies	3 50 00			a. 9 0 00
150	Office Equipment	10 600 00			
151	Accumulated Amort.: OE				c. 2 0 0 00
201	Accounts Payable		2 950 00		
210	Notes Payable		7 600 00		
215	Payroll Taxes Payable		2 10 00		
220	Unearned Consulting Rev.		1 000 00	e. 6 0 0 00	
301	Mary Tyus, Capital		21 692 00		
310	Mary Tyus, Drawing	4 800 00			
401	Medical Revenue		11 600 00		f. 2 0 0 0 00
405	Consulting Revenue		9 00 00		e. 6 0 0 00
601	Rent Expense	3 900 00			
610	Interest Expense	7 60 00			
615	Utilities Expense	1 420 00			
620	Repairs Expense	2 416 00			
630	Uniforms Expense	5 00 00			
640	Wages Expense	3 000 00		d. 3 0 0 00	
650	Payroll Tax Expense	2 30 00			
	Totals	45 952 00	45 952 00		
605	Supplies Expense			a. 9 0 00	
660	Insurance Expense			b. 3 0 00	
670	Amortization Expense			c. 2 0 0 00	
230	Wages Payable				d. 3 0 0 00
				3 2 2 0 00	3 2 2 0 00

9. Total the income statement columns and draw a double ruled line across the income statement and balance sheet columns.

The debit column equals the credit column on the income statement, and the debit column equals the credit column on the balance sheet, but *the columns of the income statement do not equal the columns of the balance sheet.*

Net Loss on the Worksheet

A net *income* figure is added to the credit column of the balance sheet because net income is added to capital when the statement of owner's equity is prepared (credits increase the capital account). If, however, after totalling the income statement columns of the worksheet, the debit column (expenses) is larger than the credit column (revenue), a net loss has occurred; the amount of the net loss is entered beneath the debit column total on the balance sheet to complete the worksheet. A net loss will be subtracted from the owner's capital account when the statement of owner's equity is prepared. Study the partial worksheet for Paul's Preschool for March 20XX on page 112.

Mary Tyus, M.D.
Worksheet
For Month Ended January 31, 20XX

ADJUSTED TRIAL BALANCE		INCOME STATEMENT		BALANCE SHEET	
DEBIT	CREDIT	DEBIT	CREDIT	DEBIT	CREDIT
12500 00				12500 00	
3100 00				3100 00	
4700 00				4700 00	
330 00				330 00	
260 00				260 00	
10600 00				10600 00	
	200 00				200 00
	2950 00				2950 00
	7600 00				7600 00
	210 00				210 00
	400 00				400 00
	21692 00				21692 00
4800 00				4800 00	
	1360 00		1360 00		
	150 00		150 00		
3900 00		3900 00			
76 00		76 00			
1420 00		1420 00			
2416 00		2416 00			
500 00		500 00			
3300 00		3300 00			
230 00		230 00			
90 00		90 00			
30 00		30 00			
200 00		200 00			
	300 00				300 00
48452 00	48452 00	12162 00	15100 00	36290 00	33352 00
		2938 00			2938 00
		15100 00	15100 00	36290 00	36290 00

Paul's Preschool
Worksheet
For Month Ended March 31, 20XX

ACCT. NO.	ACCOUNT TITLES	ADJUSTED TRIAL BALANCE DEBIT	ADJUSTED TRIAL BALANCE CREDIT	INCOME STATEMENT DEBIT	INCOME STATEMENT CREDIT	BALANCE SHEET DEBIT	BALANCE SHEET CREDIT
110	Cash	6720.00				6720.00	
115	Accounts Receivable	1200.00				1200.00	
120	Notes Receivable	905.00				905.00	
130	Prepaid Insurance	600.00				600.00	
140	Supplies	400.00				400.00	
145	Playground Equipment	16190.00				16190.00	
146	Accumulated Amort.: PE		900.00				900.00
200	Accounts Payable		860.00				860.00
201	Notes Payable		9600.00				9600.00
210	Unearned Revenue		250.00				250.00
220	Wages Payable		220.00				220.00
301	Paul Pinchen, Capital		14334.00				14334.00
310	Paul Pinchen, Drawing	1560.00				1560.00	
410	Revenue		2780.00		2780.00		
601	Advertising Expense	105.00		105.00			
610	Rent Expense	800.00		800.00			
615	Utilities Expense	150.00		150.00			
620	Repairs Expense	235.00		235.00			
630	Amortization Expense	300.00		300.00			
640	Wages Expense	1700.00		1700.00			
660	Payroll Tax Expense	102.00		102.00			
670	Interest Expense	127.00		127.00			
680	Supplies Expense	60.00		60.00			
690	Insurance Expense	40.00		40.00			
	Totals	31194.00	31194.00	3619.00	2780.00	27575.00	28414.00
	Net Loss				839.00	839.00	
				3619.00	3619.00	28414.00	28414.00

Preparing the Financial Statements from the Worksheet

Once the worksheet is complete, the accountant can prepare the income statement and the balance sheet directly from the information already there. All the necessary figures, including the totals and the net income or loss, have already been calculated on the worksheet. The necessary figures for the preparation of the statement of owner's equity appear in the balance sheet columns as well as the figures required for the preparation of the balance sheet. There is only one exception: if the owner has made an additional investment during the period, the amount of that investment will be included in the balance of the capital account that appears on the trial balance. The bookkeeper must refer to the capital account in the ledger to determine whether such an additional investment has occurred during the period.

The Income Statement

Because the necessary figures for preparing the income statement are contained in the income statement columns of the worksheet, the bookkeeper simply copies the account names and balances onto the proper income statement form, and then determines the section totals and the net income. The income statement for Mary Tyus, M.D., follows. To check the accuracy of the statement, the net income figure should be checked to be sure that it is the same figure that appears on the worksheet.

Mary Tyus, M.D. Income Statement For Month Ended January 31, 20XX		
Revenue		
Medical Revenue	$ 13 6 0 0 00	
Consulting Revenue	1 5 0 0 00	
Total Revenue		$ 1 5 1 0 0 00
Expenses		
Rent Expense	$ 3 9 0 0 00	
Supplies Expense	9 0 00	
Interest Expense	7 6 00	
Utilities Expense	1 4 2 0 00	
Repairs Expense	2 4 1 6 00	
Uniforms Expense	5 0 0 00	
Wages Expense	3 3 0 0 00	
Payroll Tax Expense	2 3 0 00	
Insurance Expense	3 0 00	
Amortization Expense	2 0 0 00	
Total Expenses		1 2 1 6 2 00
Net Income		2 9 3 8 00

Statement of Owner's Equity

Again, all the necessary figures for the preparation of the statement of owner's equity are contained within the balance sheet columns of the worksheet. The capital at the beginning of the period is that figure which appears on the adjusted trial balance and is extended to the balance sheet credit column. The statement of owner's equity for Mary Tyus, M.D., follows:

Mary Tyus, M.D. Statement of Owner's Equity For Month Ended January 31, 20XX		
Mary Tyus, Capital, January 1, 20XX	$ 2 1 6 9 2 00	
Add: Net Income for January	2 9 3 8 00	
Subtotal	2 4 6 3 0 00	
Deduct: Mary Tyus, Drawing	4 8 0 0 00	
Mary Tyus, Capital, January 31, 20XX		$ 1 9 8 3 0 00

The Balance Sheet

The balance of all the asset and liability accounts appears in the worksheet columns for the balance sheet, and the ending balance for the capital account has been calculated in the statement of owner's equity. If there is no separate statement of owner's equity, of course, those calculations will be made in the owner's equity section of the balance sheet. The balance sheet for Mary Tyus, M.D., follows:

Mary Tyus, M.D. Balance Sheet January 31, 20XX			
Assets			
Cash		$ 1 2 5 0 0 00	
Accounts Receivable		3 1 0 0 00	
Notes Receivable		4 7 0 0 00	
Prepaid Insurance		3 3 0 00	
Supplies		2 6 0 00	
Office Equipment	$ 1 0 6 0 0 00		
Less: Accumulated Amortization	2 0 0 00	1 0 4 0 0 00	
Total Assets			$ 3 1 2 9 0 00
Liabilities			
Accounts Payable		$ 2 9 5 0 00	
Notes Payable		7 6 0 0 00	
Payroll Taxes Payable		2 1 0 00	
Unearned Consulting Revenue		4 0 0 00	
Wages Payable		3 0 0 00	
Total Liabilities			$ 1 1 4 6 0 00
Owner's Equity			
Mary Tyus, Capital, January 31, 20XX			1 9 8 3 0 00
Total Liabilities and Owner's Equity			$ 3 1 2 9 0 00

Finding Errors in the Income Statement and Balance Sheet Columns

Totalling the columns of the income statement and determining the net income or net loss will not show whether an error has been made. Only after the balance sheet columns are totalled and the net income or loss is added to the appropriate column will a mistake become apparent. If, for example, the credit column of the balance sheet does not equal the debit column after the net income is added to the credit column of the balance sheet, a mistake has been made. The error probably is *not* on the adjusted trial balance, because it was in balance before any figures were extended to the balance sheet and income statement. (The adjusted trial balance does not reveal all errors; it only proves the equality of debits and credits.) You can use the following procedure to locate errors on the worksheet:

1. Quickly look at each account on the adjusted trial balance to make sure that each has been extended to the correct financial statement column and in the appropriate debit or credit column. For example, the balance of the Drawing account may have been extended to the credit column of the balance sheet rather than to the debit column.

2. Check also to make sure that the amounts as extended are correct. A number can easily be transposed or a decimal point misplaced when numbers are transferred from one column to another.

3. Check the accounts at the bottom of the original trial balance to make sure that their balances have been extended to the correct income statement or balance sheet column.

4. Re-add the income statement columns.

5. Recalculate the net income or net loss figure.

6. Re-add the balance sheet columns.

7. Make sure that a net income figure appears in the credit column of the balance sheet and that a net loss figure appears in the debit column.

8. Finally, re-add the net income or loss figure to its correct balance sheet column total.

Journalizing the Adjusting Entries

Once the worksheet is complete, the bookkeeper must journalize and post the adjusting entries, because the adjustments will not appear in the ledger until these steps have been completed. The worksheet is used simply to accumulate the information needed to journalize the adjusting entries and to prepare the financial statements.

To begin, centre the words *Adjusting Entries* in the description column of the general journal. To journalize the adjustments, refer to the adjustments columns of the worksheet and, starting with the first adjustment a, copy the debit account title and amount and the credit account title and amount into the general journal. After entering a concise explanation, continue with adjustments b, c, and so on. The general journal entries for the adjustments of Mary Tyus, M.D. follow. The general ledger after the adjustments have been posted appears in the next chapter.

		GENERAL JOURNAL												PAGE 14						
DATE		**DESCRIPTION**	**POST REF.**				**DEBIT**								**CREDIT**				
20XX		Adjusting Entries																		
Jan.	31	Supplies Expense					9	0	00										
		Supplies												9	0	00			
		To Record Supplies Used for the Month																	
	31	Insurance Expense					3	0	00										
		Prepaid Insurance												3	0	00			
		To Record Insurance Expense for the Month																	
	31	Amortization Expense				2	0	0	00										
		Accumulated Amortization: Office Equip.											2	0	0	00			
		To Record Amort. Expenses for the Month																	
	31	Wages Expense				3	0	0	00										
		Wages Payable											3	0	0	00			
		To Record Wages Expense for Jan. 30 & 31																	
	31	Unearned Consulting Revenue				6	0	0	00										
		Consulting Revenue											6	0	0	00			
		To Transfer $600 into Consulting Revenue																	
	31	Accounts Receivable			2	0	0	0	00										
		Medical Revenue										2	0	0	0	00			
		To Record Services Performed and																	
		Bill Sent to Customer																	

Summary

The accounting cycle is a series of steps that are completed each accounting period. The steps covered so far include journalizing, posting, preparing the worksheet with adjustments, preparing the financial statements, and journalizing and posting the adjustments.

The worksheet is the ten-column form used by accountants to accumulate data for the adjusting entries and the financial statements. The following are examples of adjustments:

1. When supplies are purchased, the amount is debited to the asset account Supplies. As supplies are used up, however, no credit entries are made to the account to indicate this. An adjusting entry is required to record the supplies expense; it is recorded as a debit to the Supplies Expense account and a credit to the asset account Supplies.

2. When an insurance policy is purchased, the amount is debited to the asset account Prepaid Insurance. A portion of the cost of the policy is transferred to expense at the end of each accounting period by an adjustment that debits Insurance Expense and credits Prepaid Insurance.

3. When a capital asset such as equipment, furniture, a building, an automobile, or a truck is purchased, its historical cost is recorded in the asset account. At the end of each accounting period, a portion of the cost of each capital asset is transferred to expense by a debit to Amortization Expense and a credit to the contra-asset account Accumulated Amortization. Accumulated Amortization subtracts from the balance of its related asset account on the balance sheet; the balance sheet shows the cost of each asset, its accumulated amortization, and the difference between the two, the book value.

4. When a customer pays in advance for services, the bookkeeper does not recognize the payment as revenue until the services are actually performed. To achieve this, the original entry debits Cash and credits a liability account (the services are owed to the customer) called Unearned Revenue. When the services are actually performed, the cash value of the work done is removed from the Unearned Revenue account by a debit and is entered into an Earned Revenue account by a credit.

5. At the end of the accounting period, the bookkeeper must record services that have been performed, even if they have not yet been paid for. This is accomplished by an adjusting entry that debits the asset Accounts Receivable and credits Revenue.

6. As a bookkeeper, you must record any liabilities that have accrued during the period but do not show on the books as adjustments. The entry to record accrued wages is typical; Wages Expense is debited and Wages Payable is credited.

    You must first enter the adjusting entries in the adjustments columns of the worksheet. Combine the amounts with the figures on the original trial balance to produce an adjusted trial balance. The adjusted trial balance amounts are then extended to two columns for the income statement and two columns for the balance sheet. These are used to calculate the net income or net loss. From these last four columns you will be able to prepare the income statement, statement of owner's equity, and balance sheet.

Vocabulary Review

Here is a list of the words and terms for this chapter:

accounting cycle	contra asset
acquisition	prepaid expenses
adjusting entry	salvage value
amortization	useful life
book value	worksheet

Fill in the blank with the correct word or term from the list.

1. The number of years over which an asset is amortized is the asset's _____.

2. _____ is an account that subtracts from its related asset account on the balance sheet.

3. A/an _____ is the act of acquiring possession.

4. The cost of an asset minus its accumulated amortization is the asset's _____.

5. The periodic transferring of capital asset cost to expense is called _____.

6. The step-by-step procedure that begins with recording transactions and is repeated for each accounting period is the _____.

7. The ten-column form used to organize the data necessary for journalizing the adjustments and preparing the financial statements is the _____.

8. A journal entry made at the end of an accounting period for which no transaction occurs and which brings the ledger up to date is a/an _____.

9. _____ are expense items that are paid for prior to their use.

10. The expected worth of an asset at the end of its useful life is its _____.

Match the words and terms on the left with the definitions on the right.

11. accounting cycle
12. acquisition
13. adjusting entry
14. book value
15. contra asset
16. amortization
17. prepaid expenses
18. salvage value
19. useful life
20. worksheet

a. the act of acquiring

b. the number of years over which an asset is amortized

c. an account that subtracts from its related asset on the balance sheet

d. the accounting procedure that is repeated for each accounting period

e. the form on which the data for adjustments and the financial statements are first accumulated

f. the transferring of capital asset cost to expense

g. the value of an asset at the end of its useful life

h. a journal entry made at the end of the accounting period to bring accounts up to date and for which no transaction occurs

i. the cost minus the accumulated amortization of an asset

j. expense items that are paid for before they are incurred

Exercises

EXERCISE 5.1

On January 2, Phil's Automotive Engineering Company purchased a 12-month insurance policy for $540 cash.

1. Prepare the general journal entry required on January 2 to record the purchase of the policy.

2. Prepare the adjusting entry required on January 31 to record January's insurance expense.

EXERCISE 5.2

Every Friday, Acme Personnel pays its employees weekly salaries amounting to $25,000 ($5,000 per day, Monday through Friday).

1. Prepare the necessary entry on Wednesday, September 30 to record the wages expense for the last three days of September.

2. Prepare the general journal entry required on Friday, October 2 to record payment of the week's wages.

EXERCISE 5.3

On July 1, Andy's Delivery Service received a cheque for $1,500 from Pete's Laundry for delivery services to be performed in July, August, and September.

1. Record the journal entry required on July 1 to record the liability for the services and the receipt of the cash.

2. Prepare the required adjusting entry on July 31, assuming that Andy performs $400 of delivery services for Pete in July.

EXERCISE 5.4

The balance in the Supplies account for The Queen's Limos on September 1 was $235. Purchases of supplies for cash were recorded on September 5 for $110 and on September 19 for $185. The supplies inventory on September 30 as determined by a physical count was $215.

1. Prepare the two journal entries to record supplies purchased on September 5 and 19.

2. Prepare the adjusting entry required on September 30 to record the supplies used during September.

EXERCISE 5.5

Sandra Smythe, public accountant, purchased a laptop computer, printer, and scanner costing $12,000 for her office on January 3. The equipment has a useful life of four years and no salvage value. Sandra paid $5,000 cash down and signed a 24-month, non-interest-bearing note for the remainder.

1. Prepare the general journal entry necessary to record the acquisition of the asset.

2. Prepare the adjusting entry on January 31 to record the amortization on the computer equipment.

3. Assuming that Sandra's accounting period is one year instead of one month, prepare the adjusting entry required on December 31 to record the amortization.

EXERCISE 5.6

Mac's Repair Service performed $2,500 in services for T.A. Luong during the month of December for which no cash was received. On December 31, Mac sent a bill to Luong for $2,500 for the services performed; the bill stipulated that payment should be made within 30 days. Prepare the adjusting entry necessary on December 31 to record earning the revenue.

EXERCISE 5.7

Page 120 shows a portion of a worksheet for Ron Lee, Educational Consultant, on August 31, 20XX. The worksheet has been completed except for calculating the net income or net loss for the month and the final ruling.

1. Calculate the net income or net loss, label it in the account titles column, and enter the amount in the appropriate income statement and balance sheet columns.

2. Total and rule the worksheet.

EXERCISE 5.8

Page 120 shows a portion of a worksheet for Juanita Barbosa, Accountant, on November 30, 20XX. The worksheet has been completed except for calculating the net income or net loss for the month and the final ruling.

1. Calculate the net income or net loss, label it in the account titles column, and enter the amount in the appropriate income statement and balance sheet columns.

2. Total and rule the worksheet.

Ron Lee, Educational Consultant
Worksheet
For Month Ended August 31, 20XX

ACCT. NO.	ACCOUNT TITLES	ADJUSTED TRIAL BALANCE DEBIT	ADJUSTED TRIAL BALANCE CREDIT	INCOME STATEMENT DEBIT	INCOME STATEMENT CREDIT	BALANCE SHEET DEBIT	BALANCE SHEET CREDIT
101	Cash	1980 00				1980 00	
110	Accounts Receivable	970 00				970 00	
120	Notes Receivable	500 00				500 00	
640	Wages Expense	1110 00		1110 00			
650	Supplies Expense	70 00		70 00			
660	Insurance Expense	40 00		40 00			
670	Advertising Expense	150 00		150 00			
	Totals	24620 00	24620 00	4205 00	7811 00	3905 00	3544 00

Juanita Barbosa, Accountant
Worksheet
For Month Ended November 30, 20XX

ACCT. NO.	ACCOUNT TITLES	ADJUSTED TRIAL BALANCE DEBIT	ADJUSTED TRIAL BALANCE CREDIT	INCOME STATEMENT DEBIT	INCOME STATEMENT CREDIT	BALANCE SHEET DEBIT	BALANCE SHEET CREDIT
101	Cash	2305 00				2305 00	
120	Accounts Receivable	1700 00				1700 00	
130	Prepaid Insurance	490 00				490 00	
140	Prepaid Advertising	30 00				30 00	
670	Supplies Expense	85 00		85 00			
680	Advertising Expense	100 00		100 00			
690	Insurance Expense	32 00		32 00			
	Totals	63710 00	63710 00	3810 00	3160 00	5864 00	5929 00

EXERCISE 5.9

Identify the following accounts as asset (A), contra asset (CA), liability (L), owner's equity (OE), revenue (R), or expense (E). Indicate whether the account has a normal debit or credit balance, and tell on which financial statement, the balance sheet (BS) or income statement (IS), each account will appear.

	Account Classification	Normal Debit or Credit Balance	Which Financial Statement?
Example Accounts Receivable	A	debit	BS
a. Notes Payable			
b. Rent Expense			
c. Revenue from Consulting			
d. Office Equipment			
e. Supplies			
f. Supplies Expense			
g. Accumulated Amortization			
h. Prepaid Advertising			
i. Owner's Drawing			
j. Delivery Revenue			
k. Unearned Delivery Revenue			
l. Prepaid Rent			
m. Automobile			
n. Wages Payable			
o. Unearned Consulting Revenue			

EXERCISE 5.10

Following are the trial balance and adjustments columns of the worksheet for George Atkinson, Consultant, for the month of September 20XX. Recopy the information onto a ten-column worksheet and complete it.

George Atkinson, Consultant
Worksheet
For Month Ended September 30, 20XX

ACCT. NO.	ACCOUNT TITLES	Unadjusted Trial Balance Debit	Credit	Adjustments Debit	Credit
101	Cash	12000 00			
105	Accounts Receivable	8500 00		e. 1250 00	
110	Notes Receivable	14000 00			
115	Office Supplies	1500 00			a. 400 00
120	Prepaid Insurance	1290 00			b. 100 00
128	Office Equipment	22000 00			
129	Accumulated Amort.: OE		5520 00		d. 460 00
201	Accounts Payable		1750 00		
205	Notes Payable		9800 00		
206	Payroll Taxes Payable		520 00		
210	Unearned Consulting Rev.		1500 00	f. 900 00	
301	George Atkinson, Capital		42260 00		
310	George Atkinson, Drawing	5000 00			
401	Revenue from Teaching		8500 00		e. 1250 00
405	Revenue from Consulting		1500 00		f. 900 00
601	Rent Expense	2200 00			
603	Utilities Expense	470 00			
620	Advertising Expense	500 00			
630	Wages Expense	3800 00		c. 350 00	
640	Interest Expense	90 00			
	Totals	71350 00	71350 00		
650	Office Supplies Expense			a. 400 00	
615	Insurance Expense			b. 100 00	
220	Wages Payable				c. 350 00
660	Amortization Expense			d. 460 00	
				3460 00	3460 00

EXERCISE 5.11

Following are several circumstances in which the accountant failed to correctly record adjusting entries. For each, tell whether the error in the adjustment would cause an overstatement of expenses and by how much; an understatement of expenses and by how much; an overstatement of revenue and by how much; an understatement of revenue and by how much; an overstatement of net income and by how much; or an understatement of net income and by how much. The first one has been completed as an example.

	Overstatement of Expenses	Understatement of Expenses	Overstatement of Revenue	Understatement of Revenue	Overstatement of Net Income	Understatement of Net Income
Example Accountant did not record adjusting entry for amortization of $1,000		$1,000			$1,000	
a. Accountant did not record supplies used for the period for $500.						
b. Accountant transferred $1,000 from Prepaid Advertising to Advertising Expense when the amount transferred should have been $100.						
c. Accountant did not record accrued wages of $700.						
d. Accountant did not record revenue performed for which cash had not yet been received, and for which bills had not been sent for $5,000.						
e. Accountant did not record amortization of $850 on the equipment.						
f. Accountant did not transfer $150 from Prepaid Insurance to Insurance Expense.						
g. Accountant debited Accounts Receivable and credited Revenue for $650 at the end of the month when a cheque for $650 was received from a customer who was paying on account.						

Problems

PROBLEM 5.1

Following on page 125 are the trial balance and adjustments columns of the worksheet prepared on May 31, 20XX for the Linowitz Trucking Company, owned by Paula Linowitz. The accounting period covers one month.

Instructions

1. Copy the trial balance and adjustments columns onto a ten-column worksheet.

2. Extend the figures to the adjusted trial balance and add the debit and credit columns. If they are equal, place the correct totals on the worksheet and rule the adjusted trial balance. In adjustments e, the three amounts for Accumulated Amortization are combined into one amount for Amortization Expense. The two credits to Trucking Revenue (g and h) are written on one line in the adjustments credit column. When extending, add both credit amounts to Trucking Revenue.

3. Starting with Cash, extend the asset, liability, and owner's equity account balances to the balance sheet columns of the worksheet.

4. Starting with Trucking Revenue, extend the revenue and expense account balances to the income statement columns of the worksheet.

5. Total the income statement columns of the worksheet, determine the net income, and total the balance sheet columns.

6. Enter the net income beneath the debit column total of the income statement and beneath the credit column total of the balance sheet. Add the column totals to the net income. The balance sheet debit and credit totals should be the same, as should the income statement debit and credit totals. If they are not, look for the error.

7. When the worksheet is complete and in balance, draw the correct rulings across the income statement and balance sheet columns.

8. Journalize the adjusting entries on page 30 in the general journal.

Linowitz Trucking Company

Worksheet

For Month Ended May 31, 20XX

ACCT. NO.	ACCOUNT TITLES	UNADJUSTED TRIAL BALANCE DEBIT	CREDIT	ADJUSTMENTS DEBIT	CREDIT
110	Cash	28000 00			
115	Accounts Receivable	4320 00		g. 4900 00	
120	Notes Receivable	7600 00			
125	Office Supplies	1490 00			a. 560 00
130	Trucking Supplies	7130 00			b. 1840 00
140	Prepaid Insurance	4700 00			c. 300 00
150	Prepaid Advertising	6900 00			d. 2300 00
160	Equipment	142000 00			
161	Accumulated Amort.: Equip.		37760 00		e. 2360 00
170	Trucks	732000 00			
171	Accumulated Amort.: Trucks		195200 00		e. 12200 00
180	Office Furniture	3970 00			
181	Accumulated Amort.: OF		1120 00		e. 70 00
200	Accounts Payable		6900 00		
210	Notes Payable		416500 00		
220	Payroll Taxes Payable		800 00		
230	Unearned Revenue		4250 00	h. 2000 00	
300	Paul Linowitz, Capital		264101 00		
310	Paul Linowitz, Drawing	3250 00			
400	Trucking Revenue		37650 00		g. 4900 00
					h. 2000 00
610	Interest Expense	6247 00			
620	Rent Expense	1800 00			
630	Repairs Expense	2404 00			
640	Gas and Oil Expense	3170 00			
650	Utilities Expense	1200 00			
660	Wages Expense	8100 00		f. 950 00	
	Totals	964281 00	964281 00		
605	Office Supplies Expense			a. 560 00	
615	Trucking Supplies Expense			b. 1840 00	
625	Insurance Expense			c. 300 00	
635	Advertising Expense			d. 2300 00	
645	Amortization Expense			e. 14630 00	
240	Wages Payable				f. 950 00
				27480 00	27480 00

PROBLEM 5.2

Following is the trial balance for Carol's Exercise Clinic on June 30, 20XX. The business is owned by Carol Goren, and the accounting period covers one month.

Carol's Exercise Clinic
Trial Balance
June 30, 20XX

Acct. No.	Account Titles	Debit	Credit
101	Cash	$ 4,250	
105	Accounts Receivable	1,535	
110	Notes Receivable	1,690	
120	Supplies	615	
130	Prepaid Insurance	500	
140	Van	23,600	
141	Accumulated Amortization: Van		$10,200
150	Equipment	48,000	
151	Accumulated Amortization: Equipment		2,000
201	Accounts Payable		400
205	Notes Payable		10,000
210	Unearned Revenue		1,000
220	Mortgage Payable		43,000
305	Carol Goren, Capital		14,590
310	Carol Goren, Drawing	2,600	
401	Revenue from Teaching		750
410	Revenue from Exercise Clinic		6,200
602	Utilities Expense	195	
604	Advertising Expense	250	
610	Interest Expense	760	
620	Wages Expense	2,800	
630	Payroll Tax Expense	170	
635	Gas and Oil Expense	130	
650	Repairs Expense	225	
660	Insurance Expense	820	
	Totals	$88,140	$88,140

Instructions

1. Copy the trial balance onto a ten-column worksheet.

2. Calculate the adjustments from the following data and enter them in the adjustments columns of the worksheet. Label the adjustments a, b, c, and so on. Additional account titles and numbers that will be required in this problem are: Supplies Expense, 670; Amortization Expense, 685; and Wages Payable, 230.

   a. The beginning inventory of supplies was $475. A purchase of supplies was made on June 21 for $140, and the ending inventory of supplies was $270.

   b. The insurance policy was purchased for $600 on April 1 of this year. It prepaid the insurance for one year.

   c. The van was purchased last year. It has a useful life of five years and a salvage value of $2,000. The equipment was purchased on February 5 of this year. It is expected to last eight years and will have no salvage value.

   d. June 30 falls on a Thursday. Wages of $100 a day are paid on each Friday. Record the wages expense for Monday through Thursday, June 27 through 30.

   e. On June 1, Carol received a cheque for $1,000 from a local exercise firm to give ten aerobics lessons to its new instructors. Carol taught five of the lessons in June.

f. On June 30, services had been performed in the clinic totalling $1,200 for which no payment had been received and no bills had been sent.

3. Complete the worksheet.

4. Journalize the adjusting entries on page 42 of the general journal.

PROBLEM 5.3

Following is the trial balance for Dancing Dynamics on March 31, 20XX. The business is owned by Jon Phillips, and the accounting period covers three months.

Dancing Dynamics
Trial Balance
March 31, 20XX

Acct. No.	Account Titles	Debit	Credit
101	Cash	$ 1,950	
105	Accounts Receivable	2,700	
110	Supplies	560	
115	Prepaid Insurance	400	
120	Office Equipment	11,500	
121	Accumulated Amortization: OE		
145	Van	18,000	
146	Accumulated Amortization: Van		
201	Accounts Payable		$ 3,520
210	Notes Payable		15,500
215	Payroll Taxes Payable		145
220	Interest Payable		335
230	Unearned Lecturing Revenue		1,500
301	Jon Phillips, Capital		16,370
310	Jon Phillips, Drawing	4,000	
401	Revenue from Dancing		10,520
410	Revenue from Lecturing		840
601	Rent Expense	2,400	
610	Utilities Expense	600	
615	Advertising Expense	450	
620	Repairs Expense	420	
630	Gas and Oil Expense	550	
640	Interest Expense	1,000	
650	Wages Expense	4,200	
	Totals	$48,730	$48,730

Instructions

1. Copy the trial balance onto a ten-column worksheet.

2. Calculate the adjustments for a three-month period from the following data and enter them onto the adjustments columns of the worksheet. Label the adjustments a, b, c, and so on. Additional account titles and numbers required in this problem are: Supplies Expense, 660; Insurance Expense, 670; Amortization Expense, 680; and Wages Payable, 240.

   a. The beginning inventory of supplies on January 1 was $400. One purchase of supplies was made on February 27 for $160. The ending inventory of supplies on March 31, determined by a physical count, was $355.

   b. The insurance policy was purchased on January 2 of this year. Its cost was $400, and it prepaid the insurance for six months.

c. Wages for Dancing Dynamics are $85 a day and are paid every Friday. March 31 falls on a Tuesday.

d. The office equipment was purchased on January 2 of this year. It has an expected useful life of four years and a salvage value of $1,500. The van was purchased on January 4 of this year and has an expected useful life of four years and a salvage value of $2,000.

e. Maybelle Johnson paid Jon $1,500 for five lectures he would be delivering during February, March, and April. Jon has delivered three of the lectures by the end of March.

f. On March 31, $2,100 in dancing revenue services have been performed for which no cash has been received and no bills have been sent.

3. Complete the worksheet.

4. Prepare a statement of owner's equity for the three-month period January 1 through March 31.

5. Journalize the adjusting entries on general journal page 66.

PROBLEM 5.4

The trial balance columns of the worksheet for Marie's Bookkeeping Service for the third quarter of 20XX follow.

Marie's Bookkeeping Service
Trial Balance
September 30, 20XX

Acct. No.	Account Titles	Debit	Credit
101	Cash	$ 4,120	
110	Accounts Receivable	1,780	
115	Office Supplies	920	
120	Prepaid Insurance	300	
125	Prepaid Advertising	600	
130	Office Equipment	18,050	
131	Accumulated Amortization: OE		$ 3,000
150	Automobile	14,800	
151	Accumulated Amortization: Automobile		4,500
201	Accounts Payable		1,100
210	Notes Payable		12,000
215	Payroll Taxes Payable		144
230	Unearned Consulting Revenue		900
301	Marie Himler, Capital		15,066
310	Marie Himler, Drawing	3,600	
401	Revenue from Bookkeeping		8,950
410	Revenue from Consulting		4,750
601	Rent Expense	1,800	
610	Repairs Expense	475	
620	Utilities Expense	450	
630	Advertising Expense	600	
640	Insurance Expense	305	
650	Gas and Oil Expense	210	
660	Wages Expense	2,400	
	Totals	$50,410	$50,410

Instructions

1. Copy the trial balance onto a ten-column worksheet.
2. Record the adjustments from the following data. Label the adjustments a, b, c, and so on. The accounting period covers three months. Additional account titles and numbers required in the problem are: Supplies Expense, 670; Amortization Expense, 680; and Wages Payable, 250.

   a. The inventory of office supplies on September 30 is $520.
   b. The advertising was prepaid on July 1 for a six-month period. (Remember that the adjustment period is three months.)
   c. The $300 figure in Prepaid Insurance represents a six-month policy purchased on July 1.
   d. The auto was purchased on January 1 of the previous year. It has a useful life of four years and a salvage value of $2,800. The office equipment was purchased on July 1 of the previous year. It has a useful life of five years and a salvage value of $3,050.
   e. $700 of the unearned consulting revenue has been earned this period.
   f. Bookkeeping services for $2,200 have been performed but no cash has been received and no bills have been sent to customers.
   g. Wages totalling $75 per day are paid every Friday. September 30 falls on a Thursday.

3. Complete the worksheet for the three-month period.
4. Prepare an income statement for the third quarter.
5. Prepare a statement of owner's equity for the third quarter.
6. Prepare a balance sheet for the third quarter.
7. Journalize the adjusting entries on general journal page 39.

PROBLEM 5.5

The worksheet for Lori's Landscape Service for the month of April 20XX appears on pages 130–131. The trial balance and adjustments columns are without error, but the bookkeeper made several mistakes when extending the figures to the adjusted trial balance. The bookkeeper did not total the adjusted trial balance, but continued on, again making errors when extending figures to the income statement and balance sheet columns. As a result, when the net income was added to the credit column of the balance sheet, it did not balance.

Instructions

1. Look over the worksheet carefully. Check to make sure that the adjusted trial balance is correct. Look for transpositions as well as miscalculations and omissions. Write in all your corrections.
2. Re-add the adjusted trial balance. Do not continue until it is in balance.
3. Check extensions to the balance sheet and income statement columns. Carry forward all corrections made on the adjusted trial balance and check for other errors in these columns.
4. Re-add the balance sheet and income statement columns, write in correct figures, and rule the worksheet.

Lori's Landscape Service
Worksheet
For Month Ended April 30, 20XX

ACCT. NO.	ACCOUNT TITLES	UNADJUSTED TRIAL BALANCE DEBIT	CREDIT	ADJUSTMENTS DEBIT	CREDIT
101	Cash	3050 00			
105	Accounts Receivable	1605 00		g. 500 00	
115	Office Supplies	495 00			b. 205 00
120	Garden Supplies	1840 00			a. 720 00
130	Prepaid Insurance	900 00			c. 100 00
140	Prepaid Advertising	800 00			d. 200 00
150	Office Equipment	8500 00			
151	Accumulated Amort.: OE		2300 00		e. 150 00
160	Garden Equipment	10000 00			
161	Accumulated Amort.: GE		4900 00		e. 230 00
170	Truck	25500 00			
171	Accumulated Amort.: Truck		1060 00		e. 400 00
201	Accounts Payable		1400 00		
210	Notes Payable		15200 00		
215	Payroll Taxes Payable		160 00		
220	Unearned Landscape Rev.		1000 00	h. 600 00	
301	Lori Salzman, Capital		17970 00		
310	Lori Salzman, Drawing	2000 00			
401	Landscape Revenue		4750 00		g. 500 00
					h. 600 00
601	Truck Expense	760 00			
610	Repairs Expense	290 00			
620	Rent Expense	550 00			
630	Wages Expense	1600 00		f. 340 00	
640	Utilities Expense	390 00			
	Totals	58280 00	58280 00		
650	Garden Supplies Expense			a. 720 00	
660	Office Supplies Expense			b. 205 00	
670	Insurance Expense			c. 100 00	
680	Advertising Expense			d. 200 00	
690	Amortization Expense			e. 780 00	
230	Wages Payable				f. 340 00
				3445 00	3445 00

ADJUSTED TRIAL BALANCE		INCOME STATEMENT		BALANCE SHEET	
DEBIT	CREDIT	DEBIT	CREDIT	DEBIT	CREDIT
3050 00				3050 00	
1105 00				1105 00	
290 00				290 00	
1130 00				1310 00	
800 00				800 00	
1000 00				1000 00	
8500 00				8500 00	
	2450 00				2450 00
10000 00				10000 00	
	5220 00				5220 00
25500 00				25500 00	
	1100 00				1100 00
	1400 00				1400 00
	15200 00				15200 00
	160 00				160 00
	1600 00				1600 00
	19790 00				19970 00
2000 00					
	4750 00		4750 00		
670 00		670 00			
290 00		290 00			
550 00		550 00			
1600 00		1600 00			
390 00		390 00			
720 00		720 00			
250 00		250 00			
100 00		100 00			
200 00		200 00			
780 00		780 00			
	340 00	340 00			

PROBLEM 5.6

Before preparing adjusting entries, Jon Smythe, Flight Trainer, calculated his net income for November to be $5,700. His accountant, however, calculated the following necessary adjustments to the accounts:

a.   amortization on the airplane, $3,500

b.   services performed for which payment had not been received and for which no bills had yet been sent, $1,400

c.   accrued wages expense, $425

d.   supplies used in November, $190

e.   insurance expense, $1,500

f. $500 of the balance of $1,300 in unearned revenue had been earned in November.

Instructions

Consider the effect each adjusting entry will have on net income. Determine whether the adjustment will cause net income to be decreased (and by how much) or whether the adjustment will cause net income to be increased (and by how much). The first transaction has been recorded as an example.

Adjustment	Decreases Net Income by This Amount	Increases Net Income by This Amount
a.	$3,500	

2.   Considering the effect the adjusting entries will have, determine the correct amount of net income or loss for the month.

CHAPTER 6

Correcting and Closing Entries

LEARNING OBJECTIVES

When you have completed this chapter, you should

1. **have a better understanding of accounting terminology.**
2. **be able to analyze an incorrect journal entry and determine how to correct it.**
3. **be able to journalize and post the closing entries.**
4. **be able to prepare a post-closing trial balance.**

VOCABULARY

calendar year	January 1 through December 31
closing entries	journal entries that, when posted, bring the account balances of revenue and expense accounts and the drawing account to zero and update the capital account
counteract	to reverse the effects of a previous act
erroneous	wrong or inaccurate
fiscal year	any 12-month period used by a business for determining net income or loss; it may or may not be a calendar year
nominal accounts	all the temporary accounts that will be closed at the end of the accounting period; revenue, expense, and drawing accounts
post-closing	after closing
real accounts	assets, liabilities, and the owner's capital account
temporary proprietorship accounts	another term for nominal accounts

Introduction

If an error is made when journalizing and that incorrect journal entry is posted, the bookkeeper must prepare a new journal entry that will **counteract** the effects of the first entry. Once the correcting entry is posted, the general ledger will be correct.

Chapter Five showed how bookkeepers have developed the worksheet to help them sort out and organize the information required for the adjusting entries and financial statements. The worksheet is also used to help in one of the last steps in the accounting cycle—journalizing the closing entries. The closing entries bring all revenue and expense account balances and the owner's drawing account balance to zero and update the capital account.

Correcting Entries

When an error is made in a journal entry and it is discovered before it is posted, it may be corrected by drawing a line through the incorrect account title(s) and/or amount(s) and writing the correct title(s) and/or amount(s) in small letters and figures immediately above the incorrect entry. It is not acceptable in actual practice to erase in the journal or ledger.

GENERAL JOURNAL					PAGE 25	
DATE	DESCRIPTION	POST REF.	DEBIT		CREDIT	
20XX						
Jan. 11	Cash		1 6 0 00			
	Accounts ~~Payable~~ Receivable				1 6 0 00	
	Received Cash on Account					

Often, however, the error is not discovered right away and the incorrect amounts are posted. When this happens, the easiest way to correct the entry is to prepare a new entry that will **counteract** the effects of the first entry. For example, assume that on January 4 a firm pays $250 cash for office supplies. The bookkeeper debits Medical Supplies and credits Cash for $250. The entry is posted to the ledger. Before the accounting cycle has been completed, the wrong entry is discovered and corrected by debiting Office Supplies and crediting Medical Supplies for $250 in the general journal. Once this entry has been posted, the general ledger will be correct. The entry looks like this:

GENERAL JOURNAL					PAGE 25	
DATE	DESCRIPTION	POST REF.	DEBIT		CREDIT	
20XX	Correcting Entry					
Jan. 28	Office Supplies		2 5 0 00			
	Medical Supplies				2 5 0 00	
	To Correct Entry of January 4					

Debiting Office Supplies for $250 puts the correct amount in that account for the first time, and crediting Medical Supplies for $250 removes the incorrect amount from that account. Another example might be when a customer sends in a cheque for $500 on February 10 to apply to his or her account, and the bookkeeper debits Accounts Receivable and credits Cash for $500 and posts the figures. This error, when discovered on February 28, will be corrected in the following manner:

GENERAL JOURNAL					PAGE 25	
DATE	DESCRIPTION	POST REF.	DEBIT		CREDIT	
20XX	Correcting Entry					
Feb. 28	Cash		1 0 0 0 00			
	Accounts Receivable				1 0 0 0 00	
	To Correct Entry of February 10					

By debiting Cash for $1,000, the effects of the incorrect entry will have been counteracted: a $500 debit is required to reverse the effects of the incorrect $500 credit to Cash and another $500 debit is required for the correct entry. The same logic holds true for the error in Accounts Receivable.

Incorrect amounts, as well as incorrect account titles, may be recorded in error. For example, on March 3, $1,100 is spent on a computer for the office. The bookkeeper **erroneously** records a debit to Office Equipment of $1,000 and a credit to Cash of $1,000 and posts the incorrect amounts. When the error is discovered at the end of the month, it will be handled this way:

GENERAL JOURNAL					PAGE 25	
DATE		DESCRIPTION	POST REF.	DEBIT	CREDIT	
20XX		Correcting Entry				
Mar.	31	Office Equipment		1 0 0 00		
		Cash			1 0 0 00	
		To Correct Entry of March 3				

Correcting entries may occur at any time, and they vary a great deal. Both what was done and what should have been done must be considered before journalizing. Each incorrect entry must be carefully analyzed to determine its effects on the accounts involved; using T accounts may be helpful in the analysis. In each case, the words *Correcting Entry* must be centred in the description column of the general journal before the entry.

Closing Entries

Closing an account means bringing it to a zero balance, and the journal entries that accomplish this are called **closing entries**. All the revenue and expense accounts are closed and the net income or net loss is transferred to the owner's capital account by closing entries; for this reason, revenue and expense accounts are called **temporary proprietorship accounts** or **nominal accounts.**

By bringing the revenue and expense account balances to zero at the end of each accounting period, a new net income or loss figure can more easily be calculated for the next accounting period. The revenue and expense figures of one accounting period should not be confused with those of the next.

Closing entries also update the capital account by crediting it for the amount of the net income and debiting it for the amount of the drawing and net loss. This procedure is repeated in the statement of owner's equity.

The illustrations in this chapter show the closing process at month's end, but many businesses close their books quarterly or at the end of the **fiscal year**. A fiscal year is any 12-month period chosen by a business owner during which the yearly net income or loss is determined and federal and provincial income taxes are calculated, A **calendar year** is the period beginning January 1 and ending December 31. A fiscal year may or may not be a calendar year.

The closing process involves recording the entries in the general journal and posting them to the general ledger. The four closing entries (1) close all revenue accounts; (2) close all expense accounts; (3) close the income summary account by transferring the net income or net loss to the owner's capital account; and (4) close the drawing account by transferring the balance of the drawing account to the owner's capital account.

The Income Summary Account

The Income Summary account is a special account used only in the closing process. Though it is given an account number in the owner's equity category, this account does not appear on the trial balance or on the balance sheet. It is both opened and closed in the closing process and is not used again until the end of the next accounting period.

The Worksheet and the Closing Process

Because the worksheet accumulates all the revenue and expense accounts and the net income in one place, it may be used when journalizing the closing entries. The bookkeeper uses the debit and credit columns of the income statement to determine the account titles and amounts to be used in the closing process. As the closing entries are journalized, check marks (✓) are placed by the amounts in the debit or credit columns. A check mark by each amount in the income statement columns of the worksheet ensures that no accounts have been omitted in the closing process.

Closing the Revenue Accounts

The bookkeeper will close all revenue accounts in the first closing entry. Because revenue accounts have credit balances, debits are required for closing them. The corresponding credit will be to the Income Summary account. Consult the income statement columns of the worksheet to determine the number of revenue accounts, their account titles, and their balances. A portion of the worksheet and the required entry to close the revenue accounts for Mary Tyus, M.D., follows on the next page

ACCT. NO.	ACCOUNT TITLES	ADJUSTED TRIAL BALANCE DEBIT	ADJUSTED TRIAL BALANCE CREDIT	INCOME STATEMENT DEBIT	INCOME STATEMENT CREDIT	
	Mary Tyus, M.D.					
	Worksheet					
	For Month Ended January 31, 20XX					
101	Cash	1 2 5 0 0 00				
105	Accounts Receivable	3 1 0 0 00				
110	Notes Receivable	4 7 0 0 00				
120	Prepaid Insurance	3 3 0 00				
130	Supplies	2 6 0 00				
150	Office Equipment	1 0 6 0 0 00				
151	Accumulated Amort.: OE		2 0 0 00			
201	Accounts Payable		2 9 5 0 00			
210	Notes Payable		7 6 0 0 00			
215	Payroll Taxes Payable		2 1 0 00			
220	Unearned Consulting Rev.		4 0 0 00			
301	Mary Tyus, Capital		2 1 6 9 2 00			
310	Mary Tyus, Drawing	4 8 0 0 00				
401	Medical Revenue		1 3 6 0 0 00		1 3 6 0 0 00	✓
405	Consulting Revenue		1 5 0 0 00		1 5 0 0 00	✓
601	Rent Expense	3 9 0 0 00		3 9 0 0 00		
610	Interest Expense	7 6 00		7 6 00		
615	Utilities Expense	1 4 2 0 00		1 4 2 0 00		
620	Repairs Expense	2 4 1 6 00		2 4 1 6 00		
630	Uniforms Expense	5 0 0 00		5 0 0 00		
640	Wages Expense	3 3 0 0 00		3 3 0 0 00		
650	Payroll Tax Expense	2 3 0 00		2 3 0 00		
	Totals					
605	Supplies Expense	9 0 00		9 0 00		
660	Insurance Expense	3 0 00		3 0 00		
670	Amortization Expense	2 0 0 00		2 0 0 00		
230	Wages Payable		3 0 0 00			
		4 8 4 5 2 00	4 8 4 5 2 00	1 2 1 6 2 00	1 5 1 0 0 00	✓
	Net Income			2 9 3 8 00		
				1 5 1 0 0 00	1 5 1 0 0 00	

		GENERAL JOURNAL															PAGE 15				
DATE		DESCRIPTION	POST REF.	DEBIT								CREDIT									
20XX		Closing Entries																			
Jan.	1	Medical Revenue	401		1	3	6	0	0	00											
		Consulting Revenue	405			1	5	0	0	00											
		Income Summary	315										1	5	1	0	0	00			
		To Close Revenue Accounts																			

As the first closing entry is journalized, check marks (✓) are placed by the revenue amounts on the worksheet to indicate that those accounts have been closed. The following T accounts for Medical Revenue, Consulting Revenue, and Income Summary look like this after the first closing entry is posted:

Medical Revenue   **401**   **Income Summary**   **315**

1/31 Closing 13,600	1/3 Balance 11,600		1/3 Closing 15,100
	1/31 Adjusting 2,000		

Total revenue on
credit side of
Income Summary

Consulting Revenue   **405**

1/31 Closing 1,500	1/31 Balance 900
	1/31 Adjusting 600

The debit and credit sides of the revenue accounts are now equal, and the accounts have a zero balance. The Income Summary account contains on its credit side a total of all the revenue for the period.

Closing the Expense Accounts

The account titles and amounts necessary for preparing the second closing entry may be taken directly from the income statement debit column of the worksheet. The journal entry to close the expense accounts is as follows:

GENERAL JOURNAL				PAGE 15		
DATE	DESCRIPTION	POST REF.	DEBIT		CREDIT	
20XX	Closing Entries					
Jan. 31	Income Summary		1 2 1 6 2 00			
	Rent Expense				3 9 0 0 00	
	Interest Expense				7 6 00	
	Utilities Expense				1 4 2 0 00	
	Repairs Expense				2 4 1 6 00	
	Uniforms Expense				5 0 0 00	
	Wages Expense				3 3 0 0 00	
	Payroll Tax Expense				2 3 0 00	
	Supplies Expense				9 0 00	
	Insurance Expense				3 0 00	
	Amortization Expense				2 0 0 00	
	To Close Expense Accounts					

As the entry is journalized, check marks (✓) are placed by the expense amounts on the worksheet to indicate that the accounts have been closed.

The adjusted trial balance and the income statement columns of the worksheet for Mary Tyus, M.D., follow. Look at it carefully; pay special attention to the check marks that have been entered on the worksheet opposite the revenue and expense amounts. The T accounts also follow to show how they appear after the closing entries have been posted.

Mary Tyus, M.D.
Worksheet
For Month Ended January 31, 20XX

ACCT. NO.	ACCOUNT TITLES	ADJUSTED TRIAL BALANCE DEBIT	ADJUSTED TRIAL BALANCE CREDIT	INCOME STATEMENT DEBIT	INCOME STATEMENT CREDIT
101	Cash	12500 00			
105	Accounts Receivable	3100 00			
110	Notes Receivable	4700 00			
120	Prepaid Insurance	330 00			
130	Supplies	260 00			
150	Office Equipment	10600 00			
151	Accumulated Amort.: OE		200 00		
201	Accounts Payable		2950 00		
210	Notes Payable		7600 00		
215	Payroll Taxes Payable		210 00		
220	Unearned Consulting Rev.		400 00		
301	Mary Tyus, Capital		21692 00		
310	Mary Tyus, Drawing	4800 00			
401	Medical Revenue		13600 00		13600 00 ✓
405	Consulting Revenue		1500 00		1500 00 ✓
601	Rent Expense	3900 00		3900 00 ✓	
610	Interest Expense	76 00		76 00 ✓	
615	Utilities Expense	1420 00		1420 00 ✓	
620	Repairs Expense	2416 00		2416 00 ✓	
630	Uniforms Expense	500 00		500 00 ✓	
640	Wages Expense	3300 00		3300 00 ✓	
650	Payroll Tax Expense	230 00		230 00 ✓	
	Totals				
605	Supplies Expense	90 00		90 00 ✓	
660	Insurance Expense	30 00		30 00 ✓	
670	Amortization Expense	200 00		200 00 ✓	
230	Wages Payable		300 00		
		48452 00	48452 00	12162 00 ✓	15100 00 ✓
	Net Income			2938 00	
				15100 00	15100 00

Rent Expense			601
1/31 Balance 3,900		1/31 Closing	3,900

Supplies Expense			605
1/31 Adjusting 90		1/31 Closing	90

Interest Expense			610
1/31 Balance 76		1/31 Closing	76

Utilities Expense			615
1/31 Balance 1,420		1/31 Closing	1,420

Repairs Expense			620
1/31 Balance 2,416		1/31 Closing	2,416

Uniforms Expense			630
1/31 Balance 500		1/31 Closing	500

Wages Expense			640
1/31 Balance 3,000		1/31 Closing	3,300
1/31 Adjusting 300			

Payroll Tax Expense			650
1/31 Balance 230		1/31 Closing	230

Insurance Expense			660
1/31 Adjusting 30		1/31 Closing	30

Amortization Expense			670
1/31 Adjusting 200		1/31 Closing	200

Income Summary			315
1/31 Closing 12,162		1/31 Closing	15,100
			2,938
Total expenses on debit side		Total revenue on credit side	

After the second closing entry has been posted, the Income Summary account has a credit balance of $2,938, the net income for the period. This is logical, because the total revenue appears on the credit side of the Income Summary account and total expenses appear on the debit side. After the first two closing entries have been posted, the balance in the Income Summary account will always represent the net income or net loss for the period.

Transferring the Net Income (or Loss) to Owner's Capital

The third closing entry begins the process of updating the Capital account in the general ledger by adding to it the net income or subtracting from it the net loss. A net income must be added to capital, which requires a credit to the Capital account; a net loss, on the other hand, requires a debit to capital to reduce the Capital account by the amount of the loss.

The actual dollar amount of the net income or loss is obtained from the income statement columns of the worksheet, where it is first calculated. The third closing entry transferring the net income to capital for Mary Tyus, M.D., follows on the next page.

GENERAL JOURNAL					PAGE 15	
DATE	DESCRIPTION	POST REF.	DEBIT		CREDIT	
20XX	Closing Entries					
Jan. 31	Income Summary		2 9 3 8 00			
	Mary Tyus, Capital				2 9 3 8 00	
	To Transfer Net Income to Capital					

After this third closing entry has been posted, the Income Summary account is closed and the Capital account is increased by the amount of the net income for the period, $2,938.

	Income Summary			**315**	
All expenses	1/31 Closing	12,162	1/31 Closing	15,100	All revenue
and net income	1/31 Closing	2,938			
		15,100		**15,100**	

	Mary Tyus, Capital			**301**	
			1/1 Balance	21,692	
			11/31 Closing	2,938	(Net income)
				24,630	

Transferring Drawing to Capital

The owner's Drawing account is the only *balance sheet* account that is closed. Drawing is subtracted from capital in the statement of owner's equity and in the ledger as one of the steps to determine the ending capital figure. The last closing entry closes the Drawing account and transfers its balance to the Capital account.

GENERAL JOURNAL					PAGE 15	
DATE	DESCRIPTION	POST REF.	DEBIT		CREDIT	
20XX	Closing Entries					
Jan. 31	Mary Tyus, Capital		4 8 0 0 00			
	Mary Tyus, Drawing				4 8 0 0 00	
	To Transfer Balance of Drawing to Capital					

A check mark by the $4,800 Drawing account figure on the worksheet completes the journalizing of the closing entries. After the entry has been posted, the Drawing account and Capital account look like this:

Mary Tyus, Drawing			310
1/31 Balance	4,800	1/31 Closing	4,800

	Mary Tyus, Capital			301	
(Drawing subtracted)	1/31 Closing	4,800	1/1 Balance	21,692	
			1/31 Closing	2,938	(Net income added)
			2/1 Balance	*19,830*	

The new balance of the capital account is $19,830, as revealed when the statement of owner's equity was prepared in Chapter Five.

The financial statements, including the statement of owner's equity, may be prepared before the closing entries are journalized and posted because their source of information is the worksheet.

The Journal and Ledger Illustrated

The closing entries are recorded in the general journal immediately following the adjusting entries. Adjusting entries are always posted before closing entries. Either the word *Adjusting* or the word *Closing* is entered in the explanation column of the ledger account. The closing entries and the general ledger accounts for Mary Tyus, M.D., follow. Those accounts that have not been affected by the adjusting or closing entries are shown with only their January 31 balances.

GENERAL JOURNAL					PAGE 15	
DATE	DESCRIPTION	POST REF.	DEBIT		CREDIT	
20XX	Closing Entries					
Jan. 31	Medical Revenue	401	1 3 6 0 0 00			
	Consulting Revenue	405	1 5 0 0 00			
	Income Summary	315			1 5 1 0 0 00	
	To Close Revenue Accounts					
31	Income Summary	315	1 2 1 6 2 00			
	Rent Expense	601			3 9 0 0 00	
	Interest Expense	610			7 6 00	
	Utilities Expense	615			1 4 2 0 00	
	Repairs Expense	620			2 4 1 6 00	
	Uniforms Expense	630			5 0 0 00	
	Wages Expense	640			3 3 0 0 00	
	Payroll Tax Expense	650			2 3 0 00	
	Supplies Expense	605			9 0 00	
	Insurance Expense	660			3 0 00	
	Amortization Expense	670			2 0 0 00	
	To Close Expense Accounts					
31	Income Summary	315	2 9 3 8 00			
	Mary Tyus, Capital	301			2 9 3 8 00	
	To Transfer Net Income to Capital					
31	Mary Tyus, Capital	301	4 8 0 0 00			
	Mary Tyus, Drawing	310			4 8 0 0 00	
	To Transfer Balance of Drawing to Capital					

Cash					ACCOUNT NO. 101	
DATE	EXPLANATION	POST. REF.	DEBIT	CREDIT	BALANCE	
20XX						
Jan. 31	Balance	✓			1 2 5 0 0 00	

Accounts Receivable					ACCOUNT NO. 105	
DATE	EXPLANATION	POST. REF.	DEBIT	CREDIT	BALANCE	
20XX						
Jan. 31	Balance	✓			1 1 0 0 00	
31	Adjusting	GJ14	2 0 0 0 00		3 1 0 0 00	

Notes Receivable   **ACCOUNT NO. 110**

DATE		EXPLANATION	POST. REF.	DEBIT	CREDIT	BALANCE
20XX						
Jan.	31	Balance	✓			4 7 0 0 00

Prepaid Insurance   **ACCOUNT NO. 120**

DATE		EXPLANATION	POST. REF.	DEBIT	CREDIT	BALANCE
20XX						
Jan.	2		GJ5	3 6 0 00		3 6 0 00
	31	Adjusting	GJ14		3 0 00	3 3 0 00

Supplies   **ACCOUNT NO. 130**

DATE		EXPLANATION	POST. REF.	DEBIT	CREDIT	BALANCE
20XX						
Jan.	1	Balance	✓			2 5 5 00
	14		GJ5	6 0 00		3 1 5 00
	26		GJ8	3 5 00		3 5 0 00
	31	Adjusting	GJ14		9 0 00	2 6 0 00

Office Equipment   **ACCOUNT NO. 150**

DATE		EXPLANATION	POST. REF.	DEBIT	CREDIT	BALANCE
20XX						
Jan.	31	Balance	✓			1 0 6 0 0 00

Accumulated Amortization: Office Equipment   **ACCOUNT NO. 151**

DATE		EXPLANATION	POST. REF.	DEBIT	CREDIT	BALANCE
20XX						
Jan.	31	Adjusting	GJ14		2 0 0 00	2 0 0 00

Accounts Payable   **ACCOUNT NO. 201**

DATE		EXPLANATION	POST. REF.	DEBIT	CREDIT	BALANCE
20XX						
Jan.	31	Balance	✓			2 9 5 0 00

Notes Payable   ACCOUNT NO. 210

DATE		EXPLANATION	POST. REF.	DEBIT	CREDIT	BALANCE
20XX						
Jan.	31	Balance	✓			7 6 0 0 00

Payroll Taxes Payable   ACCOUNT NO. 215

DATE		EXPLANATION	POST. REF.	DEBIT	CREDIT	BALANCE
20XX						
Jan.	31	Balance	✓			2 1 0 00

Unearned Consulting Revenue   ACCOUNT NO. 220

DATE		EXPLANATION	POST. REF.	DEBIT	CREDIT	BALANCE
20XX						
Jan.	3		GJ5		1 0 0 0 00	1 0 0 0 00
	31	Adjusting	GJ14	6 0 0 00		4 0 0 00

Wages Payable   ACCOUNT NO. 230

DATE		EXPLANATION	POST. REF.	DEBIT	CREDIT	BALANCE
20XX						
Jan.	31	Adjusting	GJ14		3 0 0 00	3 0 0 00

Mary Tyus, Capital   ACCOUNT NO. 301

DATE		EXPLANATION	POST. REF.	DEBIT	CREDIT	BALANCE
20XX						
Jan.	31	Balance	✓			2 1 6 9 2 00
	31	Closing	GJ15		2 9 3 8 00	2 4 6 3 0 00
	31	Closing	GJ15	4 8 0 0 00		1 9 8 3 0 00

Mary Tyus, Drawing   ACCOUNT NO. 310

DATE		EXPLANATION	POST. REF.	DEBIT	CREDIT	BALANCE
20XX						
Jan.	31	Balance	✓			4 8 0 0 00
	31	Closing	GJ15		4 8 0 0 00	0

Income Summary — ACCOUNT NO. 315

DATE		EXPLANATION	POST. REF.	DEBIT	CREDIT	BALANCE
20XX						
Jan.	31	Closing	GJ15		15100 00	15100 00
	31	Closing	GJ15	12162 00		2938 00
	31	Closing	GJ15	2938 00		0

Medical Revenue — ACCOUNT NO. 401

DATE		EXPLANATION	POST. REF.	DEBIT	CREDIT	BALANCE
20XX						
Jan.	31	Balance	✓			11600 00
	31	Adjusting	GJ14		2000 00	13600 00
	31	Closing	GJ15	13600 00		0

Consulting Revenue — ACCOUNT NO. 405

DATE		EXPLANATION	POST. REF.	DEBIT	CREDIT	BALANCE
20XX						
Jan.	31	Balance	✓			900 00
	31	Adjusting	GJ14		600 00	1500 00
	31	Closing	GJ15	1500 00		0

Rent Expense — ACCOUNT NO. 601

DATE		EXPLANATION	POST. REF.	DEBIT	CREDIT	BALANCE
20XX						
Jan.	31	Balance	✓			3900 00
	31	Closing	GJ15		3900 00	0

Supplies Expense — ACCOUNT NO. 605

DATE		EXPLANATION	POST. REF.	DEBIT	CREDIT	BALANCE
20XX						
Jan.	31	Adjusting	GJ14	90 00		90 00
	31	Closing	GJ15		90 00	0

Interest Expense   ACCOUNT NO. 610

DATE		EXPLANATION	POST. REF.	DEBIT	CREDIT	BALANCE
20XX						
Jan.	31	Balance	✓			7 6 00
	31	Closing	GJ15		7 6 00	0

Utilities Expense   ACCOUNT NO. 615

DATE		EXPLANATION	POST. REF.	DEBIT	CREDIT	BALANCE
20XX						
Jan.	31	Balance	✓			1 4 2 0 00
	31	Closing	GJ15		1 4 2 0 00	0

Repairs Expense   ACCOUNT NO. 620

DATE		EXPLANATION	POST. REF.	DEBIT	CREDIT	BALANCE
20XX						
Jan.	31	Balance	✓			2 4 1 6 00
	31	Closing	GJ15		2 4 1 6 00	0

Uniforms Expense   ACCOUNT NO. 630

DATE		EXPLANATION	POST. REF.	DEBIT	CREDIT	BALANCE
20XX						
Jan.	31	Balance	✓			5 0 0 00
	31	Closing	GJ15		5 0 0 00	0

Wages Expense   ACCOUNT NO. 640

DATE		EXPLANATION	POST. REF.	DEBIT	CREDIT	BALANCE
20XX						
Jan.	6		GJ2	7 5 0 00		7 5 0 00
	13		GJ6	7 5 0 00		1 5 0 0 00
	20		GJ9	7 5 0 00		2 2 5 0 00
	27		GJ12	7 5 0 00		3 0 0 0 00
	31	Adjusting	GJ14	3 0 0 00		3 3 0 0 00
	31	Closing	GJ15		3 3 0 0 00	0

Payroll Tax Expense — ACCOUNT NO. 650

DATE		EXPLANATION	POST. REF.	DEBIT	CREDIT	BALANCE
20XX						
Jan.	31	Balance	✓			2 3 0 00
	31	Closing	GJ15		2 3 0 00	0

Insurance Expense — ACCOUNT NO. 660

DATE		EXPLANATION	POST. REF.	DEBIT	CREDIT	BALANCE
20XX						
Jan.	31	Adjusting	GJ14	3 0 00		3 0 00
	31	Closing	GJ15		3 0 00	0

Amortization Expense — ACCOUNT NO. 670

DATE		EXPLANATION	POST. REF.	DEBIT	CREDIT	BALANCE
20XX						
Jan.	31	Adjusting	GJ14	2 0 0 00		2 0 0 00
	31	Closing	GJ15		2 0 0 00	0

The Post-Closing Trial Balance

Once the closing entries have been posted, the remaining step in the accounting cycle is to prepare the **post-closing** trial balance. The accounts that appear on the post-closing trial balance are the **real accounts** and include assets, liabilities, and the owner's capital account. The post-closing trial balance is prepared as a last check to ensure that after the adjusting and closing entries have been posted, the ledger is in balance. The post-closing trial balance for Mary Tyus, M.D., follows on the next page.

Mary Tyus, M.D. Post-Closing Trial Balance January 31, 20XX														
Cash	$	1	2	5	0	0	00							
Accounts Receivable			3	1	0	0	00							
Notes Receivable			4	7	0	0	00							
Prepaid Insurance				3	3	0	00							
Supplies				2	6	0	00							
Office Equipment		1	0	6	0	0	00							
Accumulated Amortization: Office Equipment								$			2	0	0	00
Accounts Payable										2	9	5	0	00
Notes Payable										7	6	0	0	00
Payroll Taxes Payable											2	1	0	00
Unearned Consulting Revenue											4	0	0	00
Wages Payable											3	0	0	00
Mary Tyus, Capital										1	9	8	3	0	00
Totals	$	3	1	4	9	0	00	$	3	1	4	9	0	00

Steps in the Accounting Cycle

The accounting cycle begins with recording transactions in the journal and ends with closing the books and preparing the post-closing trial balance. The steps in the accounting cycle are:

1. Journalize the transactions.
2. Post the transactions.
3. Prepare a worksheet, which includes
   a. a trial balance.
   b. the adjustments.
   c. an adjusted trial balance.
   d. figures extended first to the balance sheet and then to the income statement columns.
4. Prepare the financial statements.
5. Journalize the adjusting entries.
6. Post the adjusting entries.
7. Journalize the closing entries.
8. Post the closing entries.
9. Prepare the post-closing trial balance.

Summary

If an error has been made in journalizing and it has not been posted, it may be corrected simply by drawing a line through the incorrect account title(s) and/or amount(s) and entering the correct title(s) and/or amount(s) above. If the journal entry has been posted, however, a new entry must be made that will counteract the effects of the first entry. When the error is discovered, the bookkeeper simply centres the words *Correcting Entry* in the description column of the journal and journalizes a new entry to correct the one in error.

The closing process takes place at the end of the accounting period, which may be at the end of a month, a quarter, or a fiscal year. Closing entries are journalized following the adjusting entries. All the nominal accounts, or the temporary proprietorship accounts, are brought to a zero balance during the closing process, and the owner's capital account is updated. Temporary proprietorship accounts include drawing, revenue, and expense accounts. The four closing entries (1) close all revenue accounts, (2) close all expense accounts, (3) transfer net income or loss to capital, and (4) transfer the balance of drawing to capital.

The Income Summary account is used only in the closing process. The balances of revenue and expense accounts are transferred to it and the net income or loss transferred from it during closing. The Income Summary account is closed after the first three closing entries have been journalized and posted.

The information for the closing entries is available in the income statement and balance sheet columns of the worksheet. Check marks should be placed next to all of the amounts in the income statement columns of the worksheet as they are journalized and next to the drawing account balance as it is closed.

Only the real accounts (assets, liabilities, and owner's capital) remain open after the closing entries have been posted. A post-closing trial balance verifies that the ledger is in balance before the next accounting cycle begins.

Vocabulary Review

Here is a list of the words and terms for this chapter:

calendar year	nominal accounts
closing entries	post-closing
counteract	real accounts
erroneous	temporary proprietorship accounts
fiscal year	

Fill in the blank with the correct word or term from the list.

1. All the revenue and expense accounts are referred to as _____.
2. Journal entries that bring account balances to zero are called _____.
3. All the asset and liability accounts and the owner's capital account are called _____.
4. _____ means "after closing."
5. To perform an act that will reverse the effects of a previous act is to _____.

6. January 1 through December 31 is a/an _____.

7. Something that is wrong or inaccurate is _____.

8. Any 12-month period chosen by a business owner for determining net income is a/an _____.

9. Nominal accounts are also known as _____.

Match the words and terms on the left with the definitions on the right.

10. closing entries
11. counteract
12. erroneous
13. post-closing
14. nominal accounts
15. real accounts
16. fiscal year
17. calendar year
18. temporary proprietorship accounts

a. asset, liability, and the owner's capital account
b. to reverse the effects of a previous act
c. revenue and expense accounts
d. wrong or inaccurate
e. January 1 through December 31
f. after closing
g. journal entries that bring revenue and expense account balances to zero and update the capital account
h. April 1 through March 31
i. the asset, liability, and capital accounts

Exercises

EXERCISE 6.1

Ly Vo owns The Reading School. Following are examples of transactions that have been erroneously journalized and posted by the bookkeeper. Prepare the correcting entry for each. Write the letter of each entry in the date column on page 6 of the general journal. You may omit explanations.

a. Ly Vo wrote a cheque for $220 for office supplies. The bookkeeper debited Office Supplies for $200 and credited Cash for $200.

b. A cheque for $89 was received from a customer of The Reading School who was paying on account. The bookkeeper debited Cash for $89 and credited Accounts Payable for $89.

c. A cheque for $440 was received from a customer of The Reading School who was paying on account. The bookkeeper debited Accounts Payable for $440 and credited Cash for $440.

d. Ly Vo wrote a cheque for $50 to pay an outstanding account. The bookkeeper debited Accounts Receivable for $50 and credited Cash for $50.

e. Ly Vo wrote a cheque for $250 for office furniture. The bookkeeper debited Office Equipment for $250 and credited Accounts Payable for $250.

EXERCISE 6.2

Following are the closing entries on July 31, 20XX for Reliable Answering Service. Post them to accounts with the following titles and account balances.

Chart of Accounts

301	Daniel Black, Capital	$8,750
310	Daniel Black, Drawing	2,400
315	Income Summary	0
401	Revenue	4,000
601	Utilities Expense	190
605	Rent Expense	575
610	Wages Expense	900
615	Advertising Expense	250
620	Payroll Tax Expense	55
630	Supplies Expense	70
640	Amortization Expense	50

GENERAL JOURNAL — PAGE 24

DATE	DESCRIPTION	POST REF.	DEBIT	CREDIT
20XX	**Closing Entries**			
July 31	Revenue		4 0 0 0 00	
	Income Summary			4 0 0 0 00
	To Close Revenue Accounts			
31	Income Summary		2 0 9 0 00	
	Utilities Expense			1 9 0 00
	Rent Expense			5 7 5 00
	Wages Expense			9 0 0 00
	Advertising Expense			2 5 0 00
	Payroll Tax Expense			5 5 00
	Supplies Expense			7 0 00
	Amortization Expense			5 0 00
	To Close Expense Accounts			
31	Income Summary		1 9 1 0 00	
	Daniel Black, Capital			1 9 1 0 00
	To Transfer Net Income to Capital			
31	Daniel Black, Capital		2 4 0 0 00	
	Daniel Black, Drawing			2 4 0 0 00
	To Transfer Balance of Drawing to Capital			

EXERCISE 6.3

Following are the balances of the T accounts for Wayne's Windsurfers on June 30, 20XX. Journalize the closing entries on page 14. The four entries will (1) close all revenue accounts, (2) close all expense accounts, (3) close the income summary account and transfer the profit or loss to the capital account, and (4) close the Drawing account and transfer the balance to the capital account. Post the entries to the T accounts and determine the amount of the ending capital balance.

Wayne Werner, Capital			301
	6/1	Balance	5,250

Insurance Expense			605
6/30	Balance	75	

Wayne Werner, Drawing		310
6/30 Balance	1,000	

Advertising Expense			610
6/30	Balance	250	

Income Summary	315

Repairs Expense			615
6/30	Balance	320	

Revenue			401
	6/30	Balance	2,100

Amortization Expense			650
6/30	Balance	450	

Rent Expense		601
6/30 Balance	400	

Supplies Expense			660
6/30	Balance	30	

EXERCISE 6.4

Tell whether each of the following will cause an increase (+), cause a decrease (–), or have no effect (NE) on net income for March. Assume that adjusting and closing entries are prepared monthly.

_____ a. withdrawals in March by the owner for personal use

_____ b. a purchase of equipment for cash on March 31

_____ c. a bill for electricity for March is received and recorded but not paid

_____ d. an additional investment by the owner on March 9

_____ e. cash paid on an account payable on March 29

_____ f. an adjusting entry on March 31 to record wages payable

_____ g. an adjusting entry on March 31 to record amortization on the automobile

_____ h. a receipt of $3,000 cash on March 1 from a customer who is paying in advance for services to be performed in April, May, and June

_____ i. a $10,000 non-interest-bearing business loan obtained on March 13

_____ j. an adjusting entry on March 31 to record $500 of services performed for which no cash has been received

EXERCISE 6.5

For the following accounts, indicate on which financial statement each will appear (income statement or balance sheet) and whether the account has a normal debit or credit balance. The first one has been completed as an example.

	Which Financial Statement?	Normal Debit or Credit Balance?
Example Capital	balance sheet	credit
a. Equipment		
b. Wages Payable		
c. Supplies Expense		
d. Accumulated Amortization		
e. Unearned Consulting Revenue		
f. Prepaid Advertising		
g. Wages Expense		
h. Supplies		
i. Revenue from Services		
j. Advertising Expense		
k. Prepaid Insurance		
l. Amortization Expense		
m. Unearned Medical Revenue		
n. Insurance Expense		
o. Consulting Revenue		

EXERCISE 6.6

Following are selected ledger accounts for the Tri-More Company on January 31, 20XX. All of the revenue and expense accounts are listed. Journalize the four required closing entries on journal page 27.

230	Unearned Consulting Revenue	$1,000
601	Rent Expense	900
201	Accounts Payable	2,740
310	Sandra Nielsen, Drawing	2,770
401	Revenue	3,055
301	Sandra Nielsen, Capital, January 1, 20XX	6,120
605	Insurance Expense	275
171	Accumulated Amortization: Office Equipment	1,000
610	Advertising Expense	350
615	Wages Expense	1,890
620	Payroll Tax Expense	114
315	income Summary	0
640	Amortization Expense	200
160	Supplies	190
660	Supplies Expense	75

EXERCISE 6.7

Using the information in Exercise 6.6, prepare a statement of owner's equity on January 31, 20XX for the Tri-More Company.

EXERCISE 6.8

Following is the Income Summary account for Kay Song, Consultant, on April 30, 20XX, after the first two closing entries have been posted.

Income Summary   **315**

4/30 Closing 15,820	4/30 Closing 12,485

1. What is the balance of the account before the third closing entry is posted to it?
2. Is the account balance a debit or a credit?
3. After the first two entries have been posted to the Income Summary account, does a debit balance represent a net income or a net loss for the period?
4. After the first two closing entries have been posted, does the credit side of the Income Summary account represent total revenue or total expenses for the period?
5. Will the third closing entry, which transfers net loss to capital, be recorded as a debit or as a credit to Capital? To Income Summary?
6. If there is a net income for the period, will the amount of the net income be recorded as a debit or as a credit to Capital? To Income Summary?

EXERCISE 6.9

Following are the closing entries for Gregory Bronski, Counsellor, on May 31, 20XX. The entries have not been posted. Assuming that the first two entries are correct, determine what is wrong, if anything, with the last two. If you find one or both of them to be incorrect, draw a line through the account title and/or amount and enter the correct account title and/or amount directly above the line. The balance of the Capital account on May 1 was $6,240, and the balance of Drawing on May 31 was $1,800.

GENERAL JOURNAL					PAGE 4	
DATE	DESCRIPTION	POST REF.	DEBIT		CREDIT	
20XX	Closing Entries					
May 31	Revenue from Counselling		1 9 1 6 00			
	Income Summary				1 9 1 6 00	
	To Close Revenue Accounts					
31	Income Summary		2 3 3 4 00			
	Rent Expense				8 9 0 00	
	Utilities Expense				2 2 5 00	
	Wages Expense				8 0 0 00	
	Payroll Tax Expense				7 9 00	
	Supplies Expense				4 5 00	
	Insurance Expense				7 5 00	
	Amortization Expense				2 2 0 00	
	To Close Expense Accounts					
31	Income Summary		3 1 8 00			
	Gregory Bronski, Capital				3 1 8 00	
	To Transfer Net Income to Capital					
31	Gregory Bronski, Drawing		1 8 0 0 00			
	Gregory Bronski, Capital				1 8 0 0 00	
	To Transfer Balance of Drawing to Capital					

EXERCISE 6.10

Following are several examples of incorrect journal entries that have already been posted to the ledger. Tell whether the incorrect entry will affect net income for the month. If so, determine whether it will be overstated (O) or understated (U) and determine by how much the net income will be overstated or understated.

	Will Error Affect Net Income?	If So, Will Net Income Be Overstated or Understated?	By How Much?
a. Services were performed for $500 cash; recorded by a $500 debit to Accounts Receivable and a $500 credit to Revenue.			
b. $100 was received from a customer who was paying on account; recorded by a $110 debit to Cash and a $110 credit to Accounts Receivable.			
c. Owner's withdrawal of $900 was recorded as a $900 debit to Salary Expense and a $900 credit to Cash.			
d. A cheque was written for $175 for payment on account; recorded as a $175 debit to Utilities Expense and a $175 credit to Cash.			
e. $800 in services were performed on account; recorded as an $800 debit to Accounts Receivable and an $800 credit to owner's Capital.			
f. $1,200 in services were performed on account; recorded as a $1,200 debit to Cash and a $1,200 credit to Revenue.			
g. A $168 telephone bill was paid and recorded as a $186 debit to Utilities Expense and a $186 credit to Cash.			
h. The owner invested an additional $1,000 in the business. It was recorded as a $1,000 debit to Cash and a $1,000 credit to Revenue.			
i. A $250 cash payment was made for equipment repairs. It was recorded as a $250 debit to Equipment and a $250 credit to Cash.			
j. A $190 payment was made for gas and oil for a delivery van. Utilities Expense was debited for $190 and Cash was credited for $190.			

Problems

PROBLEM 6.1

Following are several examples of journalizing errors that have been posted.

a. A firm wrote a cheque for $550 for shop supplies. The bookkeeper recorded a debit of $550 to Office Supplies and a Credit of $550 to Cash.

b. A firm wrote a cheque for $550 for shop supplies. The bookkeeper recorded a debit of $505 to Shop Supplies and a credit of $505 to Cash.

c. A firm wrote a cheque for $550 for shop supplies. The bookkeeper recorded a debit of $650 to Shop Supplies and a credit of $650 to Cash.

d. A cheque for $420 was received from a customer paying on account. The bookkeeper recorded a debit to Cash of $402 and a credit to Accounts Receivable for $402.

e. A cheque for $420 was received from a customer paying on account. The bookkeeper recorded a debit to Accounts Receivable for $420 and a credit to Cash for $420.

f. A cheque for $420 was received from a customer paying on account. The bookkeeper recorded a debit to Accounts Receivable for $410 and a credit to Cash for $410.

g. A firm wrote a cheque for $840 to pay an outstanding debt. The bookkeeper recorded a debit to Accounts Payable for $860 and a credit to Cash for $860.

h. A firm wrote a cheque for $840 to pay an outstanding debt. The bookkeeper recorded a debit to Cash of $840 and a credit to Accounts Payable of $840.

i. A firm wrote a cheque for $840 to pay an outstanding debt. The bookkeeper recorded a debit to Accounts Receivable of $840 and a credit to Cash for $840.

j. A firm wrote a cheque for $840 to pay an outstanding debt. The bookkeeper recorded a debit to Accounts Receivable of $480 and a credit to Cash for $480.

Instructions

Prepare correcting entries on page 49 of the general journal. Explanations may be omitted. Enter the letter of the transaction in the date column of the journal.

PROBLEM 6.2

The adjusted trial balance and income statement columns of the worksheet for Dandee Delivery Service for the month of September 20XX follow.

Dandee Delivery Service
Worksheet (Partial)
For Month Ended September 30, 20XX

ACCT. NO.	ACCOUNT TITLES	ADJUSTED TRIAL BALANCE DEBIT	ADJUSTED TRIAL BALANCE CREDIT	INCOME STATEMENT DEBIT	INCOME STATEMENT CREDIT
101	Cash	4 0 2 0 00			
105	Accounts Receivable	8 5 0 00			
110	Supplies	4 9 0 00			
115	Prepaid Insurance	3 0 0 00			
120	Equipment	3 4 6 5 00			
121	Accumulated Amort.: Equip.		1 5 9 0 00		
130	Truck	1 8 5 0 0 00			
131	Accumulated Amort.: Truck		8 2 0 0 00		
201	Accounts Payable		3 0 0 00		
210	Notes Payable		1 0 5 5 0 00		
220	Unearned Delivery Revenue		8 0 0 00		
301	Dee Snyder, Capital		7 8 7 0 00		
310	Dee Snyder, Drawing	3 2 0 0 00			
401	Revenue from Delivery		4 7 2 0 00		4 7 2 0 00
601	Truck Expense	3 1 0 00		3 1 0 00	
610	Rent Expense	9 5 0 00		9 5 0 00	
615	Utilities Expense	2 5 5 00		2 5 5 00	
630	Advertising Expense	5 8 0 00		5 8 0 00	
640	Interest Expense	2 6 0 00		2 6 0 00	
650	Insurance Expense	1 0 0 00		1 0 0 00	
660	Supplies Expense	7 5 00		7 5 00	
670	Amortization Expense	6 7 5 00		6 7 5 00	
	Totals	3 4 0 3 0 00	3 4 0 3 0 00	3 2 0 5 00	4 7 2 0 00
	Net Income			1 5 1 5 00	
				4 7 2 0 00	4 7 2 0 00

Instructions

1. Prepare the four closing entries required on September 30, 20XX on journal page 39. The account number for Income Summary is 315.

2. Post the entries to the general ledger.

3. Prepare a post-closing trial balance.

PROBLEM 6.3

The income statement and balance sheet columns of the worksheet for Softee Diaper Service for the year ended December 31, 20XX follows.

		Softee Diaper Service						
		Worksheet (Partial)						
		For Month Ended December 31, 20XX						
ACCT. NO.	**ACCOUNT TITLES**	**INCOME STATEMENT**				**BALANCE SHEET**		
		DEBIT		**CREDIT**		**DEBIT**		**CREDIT**
101	Cash					7 0 6 4 00		
110	Accounts Receivable					1 5 0 0 00		
115	Notes Receivable					3 0 0 2 00		
120	Supplies					7 7 5 00		
125	Prepaid Insurance					4 0 0 00		
135	Prepaid Advertising					1 5 5 0 00		
136	Equipment					2 4 0 0 0 00		
137	Accumulated Amort.: Equip.							4 5 0 0 00
140	Furniture					4 5 4 0 00		
141	Accumulated Amort.: Furn.							1 6 0 0 00
150	Truck					2 2 0 0 0 00		
151	Accumulated Amort.: Truck							7 0 0 0 00
201	Accounts Payable							1 7 6 5 00
210	Notes Payable							3 0 0 0 0 00
220	Unearned Consulting Rev.							3 5 0 0 00
301	Alex Agnos, Capital							3 7 0 4 1 00
310	Alex Agnos, Drawing					1 2 0 0 0 00		
401	Revenue from Services			4 2 6 2 5 00				
601	Delivery Expense	5 1 0 0 00						
605	Repairs Expense	6 2 0 4 00						
610	Rent Expense	1 2 0 0 0 00						
615	Interest Expense	6 3 9 6 00						
620	Advertising Expense	1 0 0 0 00						
630	Utilities Expense	2 4 0 0 00						
640	Insurance Expense	1 0 0 00						
650	Wages Expense	1 5 0 0 0 00						
660	Payroll Tax Expense	9 0 0 00						
670	Supplies Expense	6 0 0 00						
680	Amortization Expense	1 5 0 0 00						
		5 1 2 0 0 00		4 2 6 2 5 00		7 6 8 3 1 00		8 5 4 0 6 00
	Net Loss			8 5 7 5 00		8 5 7 5 00		
		5 1 2 0 0 00		5 1 2 0 0 00		8 5 4 0 6 00		8 5 4 0 6 00

Instructions

1. Journalize the four closing entries required on December 31, 20XX on journal page 30. The account number for Income Summary is 315.
2. Prepare an income statement for the year ended December 31, 20XX.

3. Prepare a statement of owner's equity for the year ended December 31, 20XX.

4. Prepare a balance sheet as of December 31, 20XX.

PROBLEM 6.4

The worksheet for Robert's Hair Styling for the month of December 20XX is shown on page 162.

Instructions

1. Journalize and post the adjusting entries. Write Adjusting in the explanation column of each ledger account as you post. Use general journal page 27.

2. Journalize and post the closing entries. Write Closing in the explanation column of each ledger account as you post. Use general journal page 28. The account number for Income Summary is 315.

3. Prepare an income statement for the month of December 20XX.

4. Prepare a balance sheet as of December 31. Include the statement of owner's equity on the balance sheet.

5. Prepare a post-closing trial balance.

PROBLEM 6.5

Following is the trial balance for Uncle Ray's Party Service for the third quarter of 20XX.

Uncle Ray's Party Service
Trial Balance
September 30, 20XX

Acct. No.	Account Titles	Debit	Credit
101	Cash	$ 5,214	
110	Accounts Receivable	279	
115	Party Supplies	895	
116	Prepaid Insurance	300	
120	Party Equipment	6,500	
121	Accumulated Amortization Party Equipment		$ 750
130	Van	18,000	
131	Accumulated Amortization: Van		1,250
201	Accounts Payable		756
205	Notes Payable		11,404
210	Unearned Party Revenue		600
301	Ray Whittier, Capital		19,714
310	Ray Whittier, Drawing	4,500	
401	Revenue from Party Services		8,742
601	Wages Expense	4,046	
610	Repairs Expense	750	
620	Rent Expense	1,500	
630	Payroll Tax Expense	125	
640	Utilities Expense	507	
670	Advertising Expense	600	
	Totals	$43,216	$43,216

ACCT. NO.	ACCOUNT TITLES	Unadjusted Trial Balance Debit	Unadjusted Trial Balance Credit	Adjustments Debit	Adjustments Credit	Adjusted Trial Balance Debit	Adjusted Trial Balance Credit	Income Statement Debit	Income Statement Credit	Balance Sheet Debit	Balance Sheet Credit
101	Cash	6400 00				6400 00				6400 00	
110	Accounts Receivable	1250 00		(f.) 300 00		1550 00				1550 00	
120	Beauty Supplies	2800 00			(a.) 1290 00	1510 00				1510 00	
125	Office Supplies	980 00			(b.) 430 00	550 00				550 00	
130	Prepaid Insurance	1440 00			(c.) 240 00	1200 00				1200 00	
135	Hair Styling Equipment	1800 00				1800 00				1800 00	
136	Accumulated Amort.: HSE		5500 00		(e.) 250 00		5750 00				5750 00
140	Office Equipment	1050 00				1050 00				1050 00	
141	Accumulated Amort.: OE		1837 00		(e.) 167 00		2004 00				2004 00
150	Furniture	6200 00				6200 00				6200 00	
151	Accumulated Amort.: Furn.		1100 00		(e.) 100 00		1200 00				1200 00
160	Automobile	18200 00				18200 00				18200 00	
161	Accumulated Amort.: Auto.		3663 00		(e.) 333 00		3996 00				3996 00
205	Accounts Payble		2940 00				2940 00				2940 00
220	Notes Payable		15600 00				15600 00				15600 00
230	Unearned Hair Styling Rev.		500 00	(g.) 200 00			300 00				300 00
301	Robert Goodwin, Capital		36526 00				36526 00				36526 00
310	Robert Goodwin, Drawing	2500 00				2500 00				2500 00	
401	Hair Styling Revenue		6150 00		(f.) 300 00 (g.) 200 00		6650 00		6650 00		
601	Rent Expense	1800 00				1800 00		1800 00			
610	Advertising Expense	500 00				500 00		500 00			
620	Utilities Expense	470 00				470 00		470 00			
1630	Repairs Expense	220 00				220 00		220 00			
640	Interest Expense	156 00				156 00		156 00			
650	Wages Expense	2200 00		(d.) 330 00		2530 00		2530 00			
655	Payroll Tax Expense	200 00				200 00		200 00			
	Totals	73816 00	73816 00								
615	Beauty Supplies Expense			(a.) 1290 00		1290 00		1290 00			
625	Office Supplies Expense			(b.) 430 00		430 00		430 00			
635	Insurance Expense			(c.) 240 00		240 00		240 00			
240	Wages Payable				(d.) 330 00		330 00				330 00
670	Amortization Expense			(e.) 850 00		850 00		850 00			
				3640 00	3640 00	75296 00	75296 00	8686 00	6650 00	66610 00	68646 00
	Net Loss								2036 00	2036 00	
								8686 00	8686 00	68646 00	68646 00

Instructions

1. Copy the trial balance onto the trial balance columns of a ten-column worksheet.

2. Record the adjustments from the following data for the three-month period ending September 30, 20XX. Account numbers that you will need to complete this problem include: Party Supplies Expense, 680; Insurance Expense, 690; Amortization Expense, 675, Wages Payable, 220; and Income Summary, 320.

   a. The inventory of party supplies on September 30 is $585.

   b. The insurance policy was purchased on July 1 for $300 for a 12-month period.

   c. The party equipment was purchased on January 2 of this year. It has a useful life of four years and a salvage value of $500. The van was purchased on April 1 of this year. It has a useful life of three years and a salvage value of $3,000.

   d. One-half of the balance in the Unearned Party Revenue account has been earned this quarter.

   e. September 30 falls on a Wednesday. Record three days' wages expense at $100 a day for September 28 through 30.

   f. Ray performed services amounting to $900 for which no cash has been received or bills sent.

3. Complete the worksheet.

4. Journalize the adjusting entries. Assign page number 84 to the journal.

5. Journalize the closing entries. Use general journal page 35.

PROBLEM 6.6

Because of errors, the trial balance of the Banff Springs Delivery Service as of November 30, 20XX does not balance.

Banff Springs Delivery Service
Trial Balance
November 30, 20XX

Acct. No.	Account Titles	Debit	Credit
101	Cash	$ 9,280	
110	Accounts Receivable	2,130	
115	Supplies	780	
120	Office Equipment	3,215	
125	Furniture	1,450	
130	Delivery Van	2,500	
210	Accounts Payable		$ 4,990
215	Notes Payable		11,230
301	Dan McNaughton, Capital		14,200
310	Dan McNaughton, Drawing	2,180	
401	Delivery Revenue		6,250
605	Rent Expense	1,120	
610	Salary Expense	2,240	
615	Insurance Expense	1,435	
620	Advertising Expense	820	
630	Interest Expense	1,385	
	Totals	$28,535	$36,670

While looking over the accounting records, the accountant discovers the following errors:

    a.   On November 15, services were performed on account for $815. The entry was recorded as a credit to Delivery Revenue and a credit to Accounts Payable.

    b.   A $900 cash withdrawal on November 29 by the owner was recorded as a debit to Capital and a credit to Cash.

    c.   A $360 bill was received for advertising done in November; it was decided to pay the bill in 60 days. It was recorded as a debit to Advertising Expense and a credit to Accounts Receivable.

    d.   An additional $2,000 investment by the owner on November 30 was correctly posted to the capital account, but the corresponding debit entry was not posted.

    e.   A $1,000 withdrawal by the owner on November 20 was recorded as a debit to Salary Expense and a credit to Cash.

    f.   A receipt of $655 from a customer paying on account was recorded as a $650 debit to Cash and a $655 credit to Accounts Receivable.

    g.   A cheque in the amount of $2,750 in payment of a note payable was recorded as a $2,750 debit to Notes Payable and a $7,250 credit to Cash.

Instructions

1. Individually analyze each error and its effect on the accounts; then calculate new balances for the accounts affected. (It may be helpful to use T accounts for the analysis.)
2. Prepare a corrected trial balance as of November 30, 20XX.

Comprehensive Problem 1 for Review of Chapters One–Six

Following are the chart of accounts and account balances on October 1, Year 3, for *Le Grand Journal*, a newspaper. Also following are the transactions for the month of October, Year 3.

Chart of Accounts			
110	Cash	$ 17,540.63	
120	Accounts Receivable	12,409.15	
130	Supplies	1,962.00	
135	Prepaid Insurance	600.00	
138	Land	36,000.00	
140	Equipment	75,000.00	
141	Accumulated Amortization: Equipment		$ 19,800.00
150	Delivery Van	21,640.00	
151	Accumulated Amortization: Delivery Van		10,800.00
160	Furniture	4,300.00	
161	Accumulated Amortization: Furniture		2,145.00
170	Building	195,000.00	
171	Accumulated Amortization: Building		24,750.00
210	Accounts Payable		4,203.32
220	Notes Payable		31,490.60
225	Unearned Consulting Revenue		
230	Mortgage Payable: Building		122,400.00
240	Wages Payable		
310	Jean Pierre Dubois, Capital		148,862.86
320	Jean Pierre Dubois, Drawing		
330	Income Summary		
410	Revenue from Subscriptions		
420	Consulting Revenue		
610	Utilities Expense		
620	Wages Expense		
630	Advertising Expense		
640	Gasoline and Oil Expense		
650	Building Repairs Expense		
655	Van Repairs Expense		
660	Interest Expense		
670	Supplies Expense		
680	Insurance Expense		
690	Amortization Expense		

Transactions

October 1	wrote cheque #2169 for $2,400 for the personal use of Jean Pierre Dubois
October 2	received $1,000 in cash from the Montréal Magazine for ten hours of consulting services to be provided by J.P. Dubois in the future (credit to Unearned Consulting Revenue)
October 3	wrote cheque #2170 for $375.62 for payment of telephone bill
October 5	wrote cheque #2171 for $147.70 for payment for gasoline for the van
October 6	bought $420 in supplies; agreed to pay within 30 days
October 7	wrote cheque #2172 for $570.61 to pay bill for electricity
October 7	recorded $5,200 in subscription revenue for the week; $4,010 was received in cash and the rest is due within 30 days
October 9	wrote cheque #2173 for $1,760.50 in payment of monthly mortgage on building; $1,240.10 is for payment of interest, and the rest applies toward reduction of the principal (the amount borrowed)
October 10	wrote cheque #2174 for $1,460.82 for repairs to the building
October 12	received cheques totalling $2,060.49 from charge customers
October 13	purchased office supplies costing $1,540.22; wrote cheque #2175 for $850.22 as a cash down payment and agreed to pay the balance in 60 days
October 14	wrote cheque #2176 for $2,100 for personal use of J.P. Dubois
October 14	wrote cheque #2177 for $3,410.77 to pay wages from October 1 through 14
October 15	recorded $6,100 in subscription revenue for the week; $4,650.25 was received in cash, and the rest is due within 30 days
October 16	wrote cheque #2178 for $217.40 to pay for repairs to the van
October 17	wrote cheque #2179 for $168.40 for gasoline and oil for the van
October 19	received cheques from charge customers totalling $1,971.14
October 20	wrote cheque #2180 for $2,462.90 to pay for television advertising
October 21	recorded $4,742.80 in subscription revenue for the week; $3,960.20 was received in cash, and the rest is due within 30 days
October 23	received a bill for radio advertising for $950 (record it now to be paid within 30 days)
October 24	wrote cheque #2181 for $1,500 for personal use of J.P. Dubois
October 25	wrote cheque #2182 for $542.68 for building repairs
October 26	wrote cheque #2183 for $650 to reduce the amount owed on account
October 28	recorded $5,001 in subscription revenue for the week; $4,019.50 was received in cash, and the rest is due within 30 days
October 28	wrote cheque #2184 for $3,410.77 to pay wages from October 15 through 28
October 29	wrote cheque #2185 for $822.86 for payment on note; $640.32 is payment for interest, and the rest applies to reduction of the principal
October 30	wrote cheque #2186 for $260.14 for gasoline and oil for the van
October 31	wrote cheque #2187 for $420 to reduce the amount owed to creditors

Instructions

1. Enter the account names, numbers, and balances into the general ledger.

2. Record October's transactions in a general journal. Begin numbering with page 20.

3. Post the transactions to the general ledger.

4. Prepare a trial balance on the first two columns of a ten-column worksheet.

5. Prepare the adjustments from the following data:

   a. The inventory of supplies on October 31, determined by a physical count, is $1,140.75.

   b. The $600 figure in the Prepaid Insurance account on October 1 represents the remaining balance of a 12-month insurance policy purchased on April 1 of this year for $1,200.

   c. The equipment was purchased in January of Year 1. It has a useful life of 10 years and a salvage value of $3,000.

   d. The delivery van was purchased in July of Year 1. It has a useful life of four years and a salvage value of $2,440.

   e. The furniture was purchased in January of Year 1. It has a useful life of five years and a salvage value of $400.

   f. The building was purchased in January of Year 1. It has a useful life of 20 years and a salvage value of $15,000.

   g. Three hours of consulting (at $100 per hour) were performed by J.P. Dubois during October for the Montréal Magazine. (Refer to October 2 transaction.)

   h. October 31 falls on a Monday. Record one day's wages expense at $341.07.

   i. Unrecorded Subscription Revenue during October (for which customers have not paid) is $2,017.15.

6. Complete the worksheet.

7. Prepare an income statement for the month of October 20XX.

8. Prepare a statement of owner's equity for the month of October 20XX.

9. Prepare a balance sheet as of October 31, 20XX. Include only the ending capital figure in the owner's equity section.

10. Journalize the adjusting entries in the general journal. Continue in the same journal. Centre the words "Adjusting Entries" in the description column of the journal before recording the entries.

11. Post the adjusting entries to the general ledger.

12. Journalize the closing entries in the general journal. Continue in the same journal as before. Centre the words "Closing Entries" in the description column of the journal before recording the entries.

13. Post the closing entries to the general ledger.

14. Prepare a post-closing trial balance.

CHAPTER 7

The Sales Journal and the Accounts Receivable Subsidiary Ledger

LEARNING OBJECTIVES

When you have completed this chapter, you should

1. **have an increased understanding of accounting terminology.**
2. **have an increased understanding of merchandising businesses.**
3. **be able to record entries directly into the special sales journal and perform summary posting.**
4. **be able to post to the accounts receivable subsidiary ledger and prepare a schedule of accounts receivable.**
5. **be able to calculate and account for Provincial Sales Tax.**
6. **be able to account for the Goods and Services Tax (GST).**
7. **have an increased understanding of the Harmonized Sales Tax (HST).**
8. **be able to account for sales returns and allowances and sales discounts.**

VOCABULARY

contra	indicates against or opposing
control accounts	the accounts receivable or accounts payable accounts present in the general ledger with balances representing the total of all customer or creditor balances in the accounts receivable or accounts payable ledger
credit memorandum	a document issued by the seller that informs the buyer that her or his accounts receivable has been credited (reduced) because of a merchandise return or an allowance
crossfooting	totalling the columns of a multicolumn journal and proving that the total of the debit columns equals the total of the credit columns
discount period	a period of time during which a customer may take a cash discount from a credit invoice; terms are specified on the invoice
Goods and Services Tax (GST)	introduced in 1991; a 7 percent tax that applies to services as well as goods, and to retail and wholesale sales

Gross sales	total sales for a period before sales returns, allowances and sales discounts have been deducted
Harmonized Sales Tax (HST)	introduced in 1997; combines the Provincial Sales Tax (PST) and the Goods and Services Tax into one tax. (The HST is currently collected in New Brunswick, Newfoundland, and Nova Scotia.)
merchandise	goods that may be bought and/or sold
merchandising business	a business that buys and/or sells merchandise
merchant	a person who operates a merchandising business
Provincial Sales Tax (PST)	a tax on sales made at the retail level (there is no PST in Alberta). (In this text, we will use 8 percent)
retailer	one who sells goods in small quantities to customers
sales discounts	a cash discount allowed a customer for payment of an invoice within a specified period of time; recorded as a debit in the contra revenue account of Sales Discounts
subsidiary	secondary in importance; subordinate
subsidiary ledger	a ledger subordinate to the general ledger; the accounts receivable subsidiary ledger and/or the accounts payable subsidiary ledger
summary posting	when the journal totals rather than the individual amounts are posted to the general ledger
wholesaler	one who sells goods in large quantities, as to a retailer

Introduction

So far in our study of accounting, we have discussed only service businesses. We are now ready to expand our learning to include merchandising businesses and the special kinds of accounting procedures used by such businesses.

A service business, you will remember, sells the services of its owner and/or employees. A **merchandising business**, in contrast, sells a product, sometimes along with a service.

The product usually has to be bought by the **merchant** before it can be resold. Therefore, when determining at what price to sell, the owner must take into account not only all the related expenses, but also the cost price of the **merchandise** to be sold as well as the amount of profit desired.

In this and the chapters to come, you will become familiar with some new accounts and journals and with two new ledgers.

Special Journals

In addition to the general journal, many firms use special journals. An important advantage of using special journals is the amount of time saved by the bookkeeper when journalizing and posting. In addition, when more than one journal is being used, more than one person may be recording journal entries at the same time.

There are four special journals examined here. Their names and functions are examined as follows:

Journal	Function	Posting Reference
Sales Journal	Used to record all sales of merchandise on account	S
Purchases Journal	Used to record all purchases of merchandise for resale on account	P
Cash Receipts Journal	Used to record all incoming cash	CR
Cash Payments Journal	Used to record all outgoing cash	CP

The special journals may be designed to fit the needs of the individual business. Each one may be a little different from the other, but the principles for recording and posting remain the same.

The Sales Account

When merchandise is sold, the amount is credited to a revenue account called Sales. It is handled in the same way as Revenue from Consulting, Medical Revenue, or any of the other revenue accounts used to record services performed. The Sales account appears as the first item on the income statement under the Revenue from Sales heading.

Sales and Sales Invoices

Frank Phelps owns a **retail** sporting goods store called "Phelps Sporting Goods." A retail store sells to the final consumer. Frank purchases tennis rackets, racquetball shoes, running shorts, exercise bikes, and so on from **wholesalers** who sell in large amounts to retailers. He then calculates how much he wants to mark up each item and adds the amount of the markup to the cost price to determine the selling price.

Frank must consider three things when determining the markup: (1) the cost of the merchandise: (2) the related expenses that will be incurred in selling the item; and (3) the average amount of profit desired on the merchandise sold.

In general journal form, ignoring for now the related taxes, a sale on account to P.R. Collins appears as follows:

GENERAL JOURNAL				PAGE 6	
DATE	DESCRIPTION	POST REF.	DEBIT	CREDIT	
20XX					
June 1	Accounts Receivable—P.R. Collins		1 2 5 00		
	Sales			1 2 5 00	
	To Record Sale on Account; Invoice 507				

Frank does not, however, use a general journal for the recording of sales. His reasons are:

1. For each entry, the words *Accounts Receivable* (or *Cash*) and *Sales* must be laboriously written into the general journal.

2. For each entry, two amounts must be posted to the general ledger from the general journal.

Both of these tasks take up the bookkeeper's valuable time. When using a special sales journal, much of this time is saved.

Before we discuss the sales journal in detail, the provincial sales tax and the goods and services tax will be presented.

Provincial Sales Tax (PST)

In all provinces except Alberta, New Brunswick, Nova Scotia, and Newfoundland, a provincial sales tax must be added on to the total invoice price when a retail sale is made. Not only does the PST rate vary from province to province, the method for calculating and recording it also varies. In this text, we will use 8 percent for the PST. The following are the sales tax rates for each province as of February 20, 2002.

Province	Sales Tax Rate
Alberta	0.0%
British Columbia	7.5%
Manitoba	7.0%
New Brunswick	N/A (replaced by HST)
Newfoundland	N/A (replaced by HST)
Nova Scotia	N/A (replaced by HST)
Ontario	8.0%
Prince Edward Island	10.0%
Quebec	7.5%
Saskatchewan	6.0%

Various items (such as children's clothing and food items) may be exempt from the sales tax, however these items differ from province to province. Each province may also decide what the tax rate will be. Any retailer who sells merchandise that is taxable must register with her or his province and apply for and receive a retail sales tax vendor's permit.

In all provinces where there is a PST, except Quebec, the calculation is done as in the following example. Assume that Phelps Sporting Goods sells two fishing poles on account at $220 each for a total of $440 to a customer. The PST is calculated as follows:

$$\$440 \times .08 = \$35.20$$

The amount of the provincial sales tax will be added to the sales price of the merchandise sold, and the customer will pay the total amount, plus an amount for Goods and Services Tax (GST). In Quebec, the PST is calculated as 7.5% of the total of the cost of the goods plus the GST. Note that Quebec PST, is, like the GST, a multi-level, value-added tax. A new account, Provincial Sales Tax Payable, will be used to record the PST. PST Payable is a liability account, has a credit balance, and will show on the balance sheet with the other liabilities. PST Payable is a liability because it is a debt owed by the business. It is NOT an expense because the customer pays the tax.

The Federal Goods and Services Tax (GST)

Introduced in 1991, the Goods and Services Tax (GST) is a 7 percent mutli-level, value-added tax that applies to most sales of services and merchandise. GST applies to wholesale as well as retail sales, thus it is paid by nearly everybody. For example, a business owner must pay the GST on merchandise purchased for resale and then must collect it when merchandise is resold. The difference between the amount paid to suppliers and the amount collected from customers is the amount that must be remitted to the federal government. It is possible, in fact, for a business owner to receive a refund from the government for GST, though a successful business owner should receive more GST tax money from its customers than it pays to its suppliers.

All businesses in Canada (with the exception of very small ones) must be registered with Canada Customs and Revenue Agency (CCRA). Each business will be assigned a number which must appear on all correspondence with and remittances to the federal government.

A new account, Goods and Services Tax Payable, will be used to record amounts collected from customers. GST Payable is a liability, has a credit balance, and will show on the balance sheet with the other liabilities.

Let us return to the Phelps Sporting Goods Company and the sale on account of two fishing poles sold for $220 each. Tax calculations for the sale are as follows.

Provincial Sales Tax (PST)

$$\$440 \times .08 = \$35.20$$

Goods and Services Tax (GST)

$$\$440 \times .07 = \$30.80$$

Here is the invoice from Phelps Sporting Goods.

INVOICE

Phelps Sporting Goods
806 Humber Drive
London, Ontario N6G 3B5

Sold to:	Jeri Kensington 39 Thistle Street Brockville, Ont. K6V 2A4	**Number:** **Terms:** **Date:**	80557 Net 30 June 1, 20XX

Quantity	Description	Unit Price	Total Price
2	Sportsmaster fishing poles Item #401-78993	$220.00	$440.00
	Subtotal		$440.00
	PST		35.20
	GST		30.80
	Total		$506.00

Multiple copies of prenumbered sales invoices are prepared at the time a sale is made; one copy goes to the customer and another goes to the accounting department. The invoice shows the quantity of the item sold, a brief description of the item, the unit price, the PST, GST, and the total price. The customer's name appears on the invoice, and for credit sales, the customer's address. This sale could be recorded in the general journal as follows. Remember, the exact amount of the sale (excluding taxes) is recorded in the new revenue account, Sales.

Note that the accounts receivable account is debited for the amount of the sale plus the amount of the taxes. Remember, the customer pays the PST and the GST. Phelps Sporting Goods is collecting the tax money to remit at a later time to the federal government.

GENERAL JOURNAL					PAGE 1
DATE	DESCRIPTION	POST. REF.	DEBIT	CREDIT	
20XX					
June 1	Accounts Receivable		5 0 6 00		
	Sales			4 4 0 00	
	Provincial Sales Tax Payable			3 5 20	
	GST Payable			3 0 80	
	To Record Sale on Account; Invoice 80557				

Harmonized Sales Tax

In 1997, the Harmonized Sales Tax went into effect in a few provinces (New Brunswick, Newfoundland, and Nova Scotia). The Harmonized Sales Tax (HST) combines the Provincial Sales Tax and the Goods and Services Tax into one tax. The HST tax rate is less then the PST and GST would be if combined; however, the HST applies to most services as well as to sales of merchandise, whereas the PST does not apply to services. And the HST applies to both retail and wholesale sales.

The provincial and federal governments have agreed to a percentage split of the HST, with 7 percent going to the federal government and 8 percent to the particular province.

For our purposes, it is important to remember that the rules for recording HST are the same as for recording GST.

The Sales Journal

The previous sale is shown recorded in the general journal, but in fact, most businesses would record it in a special journal, the Sales Journal. Sales may be recorded in the Sales Journal directly from the sales invoices.

The special sales journal follows. Note that there are special columns for debits to accounts receivable, credits to PST Payable, credits to GST Payable, and for credits to sales. Because there are special columns, the account titles do not have to be written in the journal for every entry, as they are in the general journal. This of course saves a great deal of time for the bookkeeper. What must be written for each sale, however, is the customer's name. The sale made on June 1 to Jeri Kensington is shown along with other sales for the month.

SALES JOURNAL								PAGE 43
DATE	SALES INVOICE NUMBER	CUSTOMER'S NAME	POST. REF.	ACCOUNTS RECEIVABLE DEBIT	PST PAYABLE CREDIT	GST PAYABLE CREDIT	SALES CREDIT	
20XX								
June 1	80557	J. Kensington		5 0 6 00	3 5 20	3 0 80	4 4 0 00	
1	80558	P. R. Jones		4 6 0 00	3 2 00	2 8 00	4 0 0 00	
4	80559	C. Y. Little		1 7 2 50	1 2 00	1 0 50	1 5 0 00	
9	80560	J. L. King		8 6 2 50	6 0 00	5 2 50	7 5 0 00	
29	80561	J. Cousteau		5 2 9 0 00	3 6 8 00	3 2 2 00	4 6 0 0 00	
		Totals		7 2 9 1 00	5 0 7 20	4 4 3 80	6 3 4 0 00	

The sales journal is used to record only one kind of transaction, the sale of merchandise on account. Cash sales will be recorded in the cash receipts journal.

Totalling and Crossfooting the Sales Journal

Once the entries for the month are complete, it is necessary to total and compare the columns in the sales journal. This is called **crossfooting**. As with all journal entries, the debits must equal the credits. To prove this, simply: (1) add all the debit totals; (2) add all the credit totals; and (3) check to see if the totals are the same. If they are not, an error has been made and must be found before any posting can occur.

(1) Debit totals: $7,291.00

(2) Credit totals: $507.20 + $443.80 + $6,340.00 = $7,291.00

(3) Debit totals equal credit totals

Posting the Multicolumn Sales Journal

Once crossfooting is complete, then posting may also be completed. Simply look at the column headings and post to the related general ledger account. For example, the first column heading reads "Accounts Receivable Debit". The total of the column (rather than individual amounts) is posted as a debit to accounts receivable. This is called **summary posting**. The next column head reads "PST Payable Credit" and this column total is posted as a credit to PST Payable in the general ledger, and so on until all the column totals have been posted. When posting has been completed, place the account number beneath the column total. The sales journal and the T accounts after posting to the general ledger has been completed follow:

					SALES JOURNAL						PAGE 43	
DATE	SALES INVOICE NUMBER	CUSTOMER'S NAME	POST. REF.		ACCOUNTS RECEIVABLE DEBIT		PST PAYABLE CREDIT		GST PAYABLE CREDIT		SALES CREDIT	
20XX												
June 1	80557	J. Kensington			506 00		35 20		30 80		440 00	
1	80558	P. R. Jones			460 00		32 00		28 00		400 00	
4	80559	C. Y. Little			172 50		12 00		10 50		150 00	
9	80560	J. L. King			862 50		60 00		52 50		750 00	
29	80561	J. Cousteau			5290 00		368 00		322 00		4600 00	
		Totals			7291 00		507 20		443 80		6340 00	
					(110)		(225)		(235)		(401)	

General Ledger

Accounts Receivable			110
6/30 S43	7,291.00		

GST Payable			235
		6/30 S43	443.80

PST Payable			225
		6/30 S43	507.20

Sales			401
		6/30 S43	6,340.00

The Accounts Receivable Subsidiary Ledger

The accounts receivable account in the general ledger shows the *total* amount owed by all customers. It does not show amounts owed by *individual* customers. However, a business owner must know how much individual customers have charged and paid on their accounts so that billing can be carried out.

In the accounts receivable subsidiary ledger, each customer has a separate page for the recording of his or her charge purchases, any payments made on the account, and the account balance. The accounts receivable ledger is called a **subsidiary** ledger because it is under the control of the accounts receivable account in the general ledger. The accounts receivable account is called a **control account** because its balance provides a check; the total of all the individual balances that are kept in the accounts receivable subsidiary ledger must equal the balance in the accounts receivable control account in the general ledger.

The accounts receivable subsidiary ledger is not meant to replace the general ledger; rather, it is designed to give specific information that the general ledger does not give.

Posting to the Accounts Receivable Subsidiary Ledger

The postings to the accounts receivable subsidiary ledger come primarily from the sales journal, where the charge sales are first recorded, and from the cash receipts journal, where customers' payments on account are recorded

The sales journal, the general ledger accounts affected, and the accounts receivable subsidiary ledger (arranged in alphabetical order) follow:

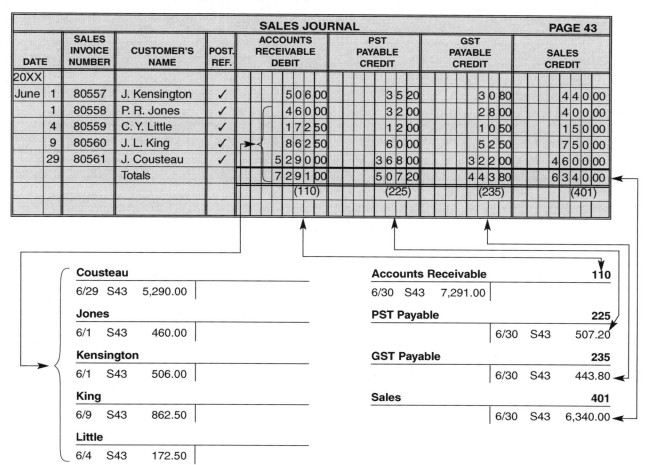

		SALES JOURNAL					PAGE 43
DATE	SALES INVOICE NUMBER	CUSTOMER'S NAME	POST. REF.	ACCOUNTS RECEIVABLE DEBIT	PST PAYABLE CREDIT	GST PAYABLE CREDIT	SALES CREDIT
20XX							
June 1	80557	J. Kensington	✓	506 00	35 20	30 80	440 00
1	80558	P. R. Jones	✓	460 00	32 00	28 00	400 00
4	80559	C. Y. Little	✓	172 50	12 00	10 50	150 00
9	80560	J. L. King	✓	862 50	60 00	52 50	750 00
29	80561	J. Cousteau	✓	5290 00	368 00	322 00	4600 00
		Totals		7291 00	507 20	443 80	6340 00
				(110)	(225)	(235)	(401)

Cousteau

6/29 S43   5,290.00

Jones

6/1   S43   460.00

Kensington

6/1   S43   506.00

King

6/9   S43   862.50

Little

6/4   S43   172.50

Accounts Receivable   110

6/30 S43   7,291.00

PST Payable   225

6/30 S43   507.20

GST Payable   235

6/30 S43   443.80

Sales   401

6/30 S43   6,340.00

Amounts are posted daily to the accounts receivable ledger while column totals are posted only at the end of the month. Account numbers are not used in subsidiary ledgers in this text because the ledgers will be arranged alphabetically. A check mark (✓) is placed in the posting reference column of the sales journal as amounts are posted, and S and the page number are entered in the accounts receivable ledgers.

The Schedule of Accounts Receivable

At the end of the accounting period, a schedule of accounts receivable is prepared directly from the accounts receivable subsidiary ledger. Each customer and her or his balance owed are listed on the schedule. The total owed by customers as shown on the schedule of accounts receivable must equal the balance in the accounts receivable control account in the general ledger, which also, you will remember, shows the total owed by all customers. If the totals do not agree, a mistake has been made.

The accounts receivable subsidiary ledger, the schedule of accounts receivable, and the accounts receivable control account from the general ledger follow:

ACCOUNTS RECEIVABLE SUBSIDIARY LEDGER

J. Cousteau

DATE	EXPLANATION	POST. REF.	DEBIT	CREDIT	BALANCE
20XX					
June 29		S43	5 2 9 0 00		5 2 9 0 00

P.R. Jones

DATE	EXPLANATION	POST. REF.	DEBIT	CREDIT	BALANCE
20XX					
June 1		S43	4 6 0 00		4 6 0 00

J. Kensington

DATE	EXPLANATION	POST. REF.	DEBIT	CREDIT	BALANCE
20XX					
June 1		S43	5 0 6 00		5 0 6 00

J. L. King

DATE	EXPLANATION	POST. REF.	DEBIT	CREDIT	BALANCE
20XX					
June 9		S43	8 6 2 50		8 6 2 50

C.Y. Little						
DATE	**EXPLANATION**	**POST. REF.**	**DEBIT**	**CREDIT**	**BALANCE**	
20XX						
June 4		S43	1 7 2 50		1 7 2 50	

Phelps Sporting Goods **Schedule of Accounts Receivable** **June 30, 20XX**		
Cousteau	$ 5 2 9 0 00	
Jones	4 6 0 0 00	
Kensington	5 0 6 00	
King	8 6 2 50	
Little	1 7 2 50	
Total		$ 7 2 9 1 00

Accounts Receivable					ACCOUNT NO. 110	
DATE	**EXPLANATION**	**POST. REF.**	**DEBIT**	**CREDIT**	**BALANCE**	
20XX						
June 30		S43	7 2 9 1 00		7 2 9 1 00	

Note that the illustration shows only debit entries to accounts receivable. Normally, the accounts receivable account would have credit entries in it also. For example, when a customer pays on account, the debit to cash and the credit to accounts receivable are recorded in the cash receipts journal. The credit to accounts receivable will be posted to both the control account and the subsidiary ledger.

Posting Accounts Receivable from the General Journal

From now on, when any general journal entry is made that involves accounts receivable, double posting will be required. For example, assume that a charge sale was made to Barbara Sanders on September 11 in the amount of $530, plus 8 percent PST and 7 percent GST. The entry in General Journal form is:

GENERAL JOURNAL					**PAGE 9**	
DATE	**DESCRIPTION**	**POST REF.**	**DEBIT**	**CREDIT**		
20XX						
Sept. 11	Accounts Receivable—Barbara Sanders		6 0 9 50			
	Sales			5 3 0 00		
	Provincial Sales Tax Payable			4 2 40		
	GST Payable			3 7 10		
	To Record Sale on Account, Plus Taxes					

The amount charged to accounts receivable must be posted to the accounts receivable control account in the general ledger. In addition, the sales and taxes payable amounts must be posted to the general ledger. The T accounts after posting appear as follows:

General Ledger		Accounts Receivable Subsidiary Ledger	
Accounts Receivable 110		**Barbara Sanders**	
9/11 GJ9 609.50		9/11 GJ9 609.50	
Provincial Sales Tax Payable 225			
	9/11 GJ9 42.40		
GST Payable 235			
	9/11 GJ9 37.10		
Sales 401			
	9/11 GJ9 530.00		

The posting reference column of the general journal after posting has been completed for this transaction looks like this:

GENERAL JOURNAL				PAGE 9	
DATE	DESCRIPTION	POST REF.	DEBIT	CREDIT	
20XX					
Sept. 11	Accounts Receivable—Barbara Sanders	110/✓	6 0 9 50		
	Sales	401		5 3 0 00	
	Provincial Sales Tax Payable	225		4 2 40	
	GST Payable	235		3 7 10	
	To Record Sale on Account, Plus Taxes				

Notice that a diagonal line is placed in the posting reference column of the general journal opposite the debit entry to accounts receivable. When the posting to the accounts receivable control account has been completed, the account number is placed before the diagonal line 110/ . When the amount is posted to Sanders' account in the accounts receivable subsidiary ledger, a check mark is placed after the diagonal line 110/✓.

Sales Returns and Allowances

The Sales Returns and Allowances account is used to record a return of merchandise by the customer or to record an allowance granted by the seller because of inferior, defective, or damaged merchandise. When such returns or allowances occur, a **credit memorandum** is given to the customer. It is called a credit memorandum because it indicates that the customer's accounts receivable will be credited. The credit memorandum is, like the sales invoice, prepared with multiple copies; one copy goes to the customer and one to the accounting department. Although it might be feasible simply to debit the sales account for returns and allowances, it is not desirable because owners and managers prefer to keep track of how many returns there are, who is making the returns, and which merchandise is being returned. Too many returns may indicate customer dissatisfaction with the merchandise and may require considering a new supplier.

A sales return reverses the effects on the books of the original sale. Therefore, the sales returns and allowances account has a debit balance; ultimately, it will be a subtraction from sales on the income statement. For this reason, the sales returns and allowances account is called a **contra** sales account. It is included in the revenue category on the chart of accounts even though its balance is the opposite of that of the sales account.

Assume that on October 3, 20XX, Phelps Sporting Goods sold four tennis rackets on account to Schwartz Company for $110 each. The transaction was recorded in Phelps Sporting Goods' sales journal. On October 10, 20XX, Schwartz Company returned one of the rackets because the strings were faulty. Sales returns, when they relate to credit sales, are recorded in the general journal. The entry to record the return follows:

GENERAL JOURNAL					PAGE 47
DATE	DESCRIPTION	POST REF.	DEBIT	CREDIT	
20XX					
Oct. 10	Sales Returns and Allowances	450	1 1 0 00		
	Accounts Receivable—Schwartz Co.	110/✓		1 1 0 00	
	To Record Return of Faulty Tennis Racket				

Following are the general ledger accounts affected and Schwartz Company's account in the accounts receivable subsidiary ledger after the sale and return have been posted. Normally, the individual sale to Schwartz Company would not appear in the accounts receivable control account because only the total of the sales journal is posted there. It is included here only for the purpose of this illustration.

General Ledger

Accounts Receivable Subsidiary Ledger

Accounts Receivable		110	Schwartz Company
10/3 S29	440	10/10 GJ47 110	10/3 S29 440	10/10 GJ47 110

Sales   **401**

10/3 S29 440

Sales Returns and Allowances   **450**

10/10 GJ47 110

If a customer is charged tax when a sale is made and later returns the merchandise, credit must be given to the customer not only for the merchandise returned, but also for the tax.

For example, assume that on October 4, 20XX Phelps Sporting Goods sold two warm-up suits on account to Arlene Davidson for $70 each plus 8 percent PST and 7 percent GST. The entry, in general journal form, looks like this:

GENERAL JOURNAL					PAGE 47
DATE	DESCRIPTION	POST REF.	DEBIT	CREDIT	
20XX					
Oct. 4	Accounts Receivable—Arlene Davidson		1 6 1 00		
	Sales			1 4 0 00	
	Provincial Sales Tax Payable			1 1 20	
	GST Payable			9 80	
	To Record Sale on Account Plus Taxes				

Assume that on October 6, Arlene returned one of the warm-up suits for credit. The entry to record the return looks like this:

GENERAL JOURNAL						PAGE 47	
DATE	DESCRIPTION	POST REF.		DEBIT		CREDIT	
20XX							
Oct. 6	Sales Returns and Allowances			7 0 00			
	PST Payable			5 60			
	GST Payable			4 90			
	Accounts Receivable—Arlene Davidson					8 0 50	
	To Record Return of Merchandise						

Notice that the sales returns and allowances account is debited for the amount of the original selling price of the returned item and PST payable and GST payable are debited for the amount of the taxes relating to the returned item. PST payable and GST payable must be reduced because when merchandise is returned, a sale has been reversed and no tax is required.

Sales Discounts

When a credit sale is made and no discount is offered for paying early, the terms may be expressed on the invoice as net 30, which means that the full amount of the invoice is due within 30 days. Often, however, a wholesaler will grant discount terms to credit buyers. The terms will indicate that a certain percent of the purchase price will be deducted if the buyer pays the invoice within a certain discount period. Such terms might be 2/10, n/30 (read as two-ten, net-thirty), which means that a 2 percent discount will be allowed if the invoice is paid within 10 days of the invoice date. The discount is applied to the value of merchandise only and not to the taxes charged. If the invoice is not paid within 10 days, the total invoice price must be paid within 30 days of the invoice date.

When the sale is made, the seller does not know whether the buyer will take advantage of credit terms. Therefore, sales are recorded in the sales journal at their full invoice price. It is only when the customer pays that it becomes evident whether a discount has been taken or not. If a discount has been taken, it is recorded in a special account called sales discounts. Sales discounts has a debit balance and, like sales returns and allowances, subtracts from sales on the income statement. The sales discount account is classified as a contra revenue account and is assigned a number in the revenue category.

Assume that on October 3 a credit sale is made by Victoria Plumbing Supplies (a wholesaler) to Joe's Hardware in the amount of $5,000 plus 7 percent GST. The terms are 1/10, n/30. (A 1 percent discount is allowed if the invoice is paid within 10 days of the invoice date, or the net amount is due within 30 days.) The entry is recorded on page 30 of the sales journal as illustrated:

SALES JOURNAL							PAGE 30	
DATE	SALES INVOICE NUMBER	CUSTOMER'S NAME	POST. REF.	ACCOUNTS RECEIVABLE DEBIT		GST PAYABLE CREDIT	SALES CREDIT	
20XX								
Oct. 3	1046	Joe's Hardware	✓	5 3 5 0 00		3 5 0 00	5 0 0 0 00	

You will notice that the sales journal in this example does not have a PST payable column. Since Victoria Plumbing Supplies is a wholesaler, they are not required to collect provincial sales tax.

Joe's Hardware has 10 days from the date of the invoice to pay and receive the 1 percent discount; it has, then, until October 13 (3 + 10). (When calculating a due date, do not count the first day.) Assume that on October 13 a cheque is received by Victoria Plumbing from Joe's Hardware. The cheque is for the amount of the sale of October 3 minus the 1 percent discount. The discount is calculated like this:

1. Change 1 percent to its decimal equivalent (1% = 01. = .01) by moving the decimal point two places to the left.

2. Multiply .01 by $5,000 to get $50, the amount of the discount. (Note that the discount relates only to the sale itself. No discount is allowed on the GST payable.)
   The entry in general journal form looks like this:

GENERAL JOURNAL				PAGE 20	
DATE	DESCRIPTION	POST REF.	DEBIT	CREDIT	
20XX					
Oct. 13	Cash	101	5 3 0 0 00		
	Sales Discount	430	5 0 00		
	Accounts Receivable—Joe's Hardware	110/✓		5 3 5 0 00	
	To Record Payment Received on				
	Invoice 1046, Less 1% Discount				

Notice that Accounts Receivable is credited for the full amount of the sale, $5,350, even though the customer remitted only $5,300. This is necessary so that no balance remains in Accounts Receivable. The customer has paid in full by taking advantage of the sales discount. After posting has been completed, the ledger accounts look like this:

General Ledger

Cash   101
10/13 GJ20   5,300 |

Accounts Receivable   110
10/3 S30   5,350 | 10/13 GJ20   5,350

GST Payable   215
                   | 10/3 S30   350

Sales   401
                   | 10/3 S30   5,000

Sales Discounts   430
10/13 GJ20   50 |

Accounts Receivable Subsidiary Ledger

Joe's Hardware
10/3 S30   5,350 | 10/13 GJ20   5,350

Sales Returns and Allowances and Sales Discounts on the Income Statement

Both sales discounts and sales returns and allowances are contra sales accounts and subtract from sales on the income statement. A portion of the income statement for Victoria Plumbing Supplies is reproduced here.

Victoria Plumbing Supplies Income Statement For Month Ended October 31, 20XX				
Revenue				
Sales			$ 1 2 5 7 0 00	
Less: Sales Returns and Allowances	$ 7 5 00			
Sales Discounts	6 0 00		1 3 5 00	
Net Sales				$ 1 2 4 3 5 00

Note that net sales represents total (or **gross**) **sales** minus all returns, allowances, and discounts.

Paying PST, GST, and HST

The Provincial Sales Tax Payable, Goods and Services Tax Payable, and Harmonized Sales Tax Payable are current liabilities and reflect on the balance sheet with the other liabilities. Remember, these taxes collected by the business are not expenses because the customer pays them. The business collects the money and remits it to the proper government agency at the appropriate time.

The entry to pay the taxes in general journal form is as follows:

GENERAL JOURNAL				PAGE	
DATE	DESCRIPTION	POST REF.	DEBIT	CREDIT	
20XX					
April 15	PST Payable		5 9 0 00		
	Cash			5 9 0 00	
	To Record Payment of Provincial Sales Tax				
April 15	GST Payable		4 3 0 00		
	Cash			4 3 0 00	
	To Record Payment of Goods and Services				
	Tax				

If the payment were for the Harmonized Sales Tax, the debit would be to Harmonized Sales Tax Payable and the credit would be to Cash.

Summary

A merchandising business sells a product, perhaps along with a service; thus, accounting procedures for merchandising firms are different from those for service businesses. In the "5 Journal System," four special journals are used along with the General Journal. They are: (1) the sales journal, for recording sales of merchandise on account; (2) the purchases journal, for recording purchases of merchandise for resale on account; (3) the cash receipts journal, for recording all cash coming into the business; and (4) the cash payments journal, for recording all outgoing cash. These special journals save the bookkeeper a great deal of time because they cut down on the amount of writing required in the journal and on the number of individual postings.

When a credit sale of merchandise is made, that sale is recorded in a special sales journal by entering the date, the invoice number, the customer's name, the taxes, and the amount. The totals of the columns in the sales journal are posted to the related general ledger accounts. In addition, each entry in the sales journal must be posted as a debit to the customer's account in the accounts receivable subsidiary ledger. The total owed by each customer is listed on a schedule of accounts receivable at the end of the accounting period; that total must equal the balance in the accounts receivable control account in the general ledger.

Customer returns of merchandise (or allowances) are recorded as a debit in the contra sales account entitled sales returns and allowances. Another contra sales account, sales discounts, is debited when customers pay within a certain specified time in order to receive a discount.

Businesses will often grant a sales discount to credit customers if those customers pay within a certain time. For example, credit terms of 2/10, n/30 indicate that a 2 percent discount will be granted if the invoice is paid within 10 days of the invoice date. If it is not, the customer has 30 days from the invoice date in which to pay.

Both sales returns and allowances and sales discounts are subtracted from sales on the income statement.

Most firms are required to collect provincial sales taxes and GST or HST from their customers and remit those taxes to the government. Taxes collected are recorded in liability accounts entitled provincial sales tax payable, GST payable, and HST payable. Taxes collected from customers and later remitted to the government are not an expense; rather they appear on the balance sheet as current liabilities.

Vocabulary Review

Here is a list of the words and terms for this chapter:

contra	merchandising business
control accounts	merchant
credit memorandum	Provincial Sales Tax (PST)
crossfooting	retailer
discount period	sales discount
Goods and Services Tax (GST)	subsidiary
gross sales	subsidiary ledger
Harmonized Sales Tax (HST)	summary posting
merchandise	wholesaler

Fill in the blank with the correct word or term from the list.

1. One who operates a merchandising business is a/an _____.

2. The accounts receivable and accounts payable accounts in the general ledger are called _____.

3. The _____ went into effect in 1997 and combines the PST and GST in some provinces.

4. One who sells goods in large quantities, as to a retailer, is a _____.

5. If the terms of an invoice are 2/10, n/30 and the customer pays within 10 days, the 10 days is referred to as the _____.

6. A/an _____ sells in small quantities to the final consumer.

7. The _____ is a tax that was introduced in 1991 and applies to services and goods, to retail and wholesale sales.

8. The sales returns and allowances account is an example of a _____ revenue account.

9. A cash discount given a customer for payment of an invoice within a specified period of time is called a/an _____.

10. When a customer returns merchandise and his or her accounts receivable account is reduced, a _____ is issued.

11. _____ is goods that may be bought or sold.

12. A word that means secondary in importance is _____.

13. A/an _____ is a business that buys and/or sells goods.

14. When journal totals are posted, this is referred to as _____.

15. The _____ is a tax on sales made at the retail level.

16. Sales before returns and discounts are deducted are referred to as _____.

17. The accounts receivable ledger is called a/an _____.

18. When the columns of a multicolumn journal are totalled to ensure that the debit columns equal the credit columns, this is called _____.

Match the words and terms on the left with the definitions on the right.

19. contra	**a.**	the posting of journal totals
20. control accounts	**b.**	a tax that combines PST and GST
21. credit memorandum	**c.**	totalling and proving the columns of a journal
22. crossfooting	**d.**	a cash discount allowed for paying an invoice within a specified period of time
23. discount period		
24. GST	**e.**	a document issued to reduce a customer's accounts receivable
25. gross sales		
26. HST	**f.**	one who sells to the final consumer in small amounts
27. merchandise		
28. merchandising business	**g.**	sales before returns, allowances, and discounts are subtracted
29. merchant	**h.**	goods that may be bought or sold
30. PST	**i.**	a tax on retail sales
31. retailer	**j.**	the accounts receivable and accounts payable accounts
32. sales discounts		

33. subsidiary

34. subsidiary ledger

35. summary posting

36. wholesaler

k. the length of time allowed a customer for payment of a credit invoice at a discount

l. opposing

m. secondary in importance

n. one who sells in large quantities, usually to a retailer

o. a ledger subordinate to the general ledger

p. a person who operates a merchandising business

q. a business that buys and/or sells merchandise

r. a tax on goods and services, on retailers and wholesalers

Exercises

EXERCISE 7.1

In each case, determine the amount of the sales discount and the last day on which the discount may be taken. The months of the year and the number of days in each are included for your reference.

Month	Number of Days	Month	Number of Days
January	31	July	31
February	28	August	31
March	31	September	30
April	30	October	31
May	31	November	30
June	30	December	31

February has 29 days in leap years. An easy way to tell whether or not any particular year is a leap year is to determine whether the year is evenly divisible by 4. For example, 2008 is a leap year because 2008 ÷ 4 = 502. The division comes out even.

	Invoice Amount	Invoice Date	Terms	Amount of Discount	Last Day to Pay and Receive Discount
a.	$ 1,200	January 26	1/15, n/60	_____	_____
b.	3,780	March 22	2/10, n/30	_____	_____
c.	10,460	June 20	2/15, n/30	_____	_____
d.	475	July 29	1/10, n/60	_____	_____
e.	520	August 30	2/15, n/60	_____	_____
f.	1,650	September 30	2/10, n/30	_____	_____
g.	5,720	November 16	1/15, n/60	_____	_____
h.	15,240	October 19	2/15, n/60	_____	_____

EXERCISE 7.2

Claudia Shayne owns a retail shop called "Pick-A-Wick"; she sells unusual candles. Record the following in general journal form and post to the general ledger and the accounts receivable subsidiary ledger. Use journal page 24 and the following account titles and numbers: Cash, 101; Accounts Receivable, 110; Provincial Sales Tax Payable, 210; GST Payable, 230; Sales, 405; and Sales Returns and Allowances, 410.

December 5   sold ten candles to Roger Merino on account; $215 plus 8 percent PST and 7 percent GST; invoice 16432

December 6   issued credit memo 203 to Roger Merino, who returned two candles priced at $15 each plus 8 percent PST and 7 percent GST

December 23   sold candles to Roger Merino for $48 cash plus 8 percent PST and 7 percent GST

December 30   received payment in full from Roger Merino for the balance owed on invoice 16432 less the December 6 return

EXERCISE 7.3

Lee Kawasaki owns a wholesale waterbed store. He sells to retailers and offers credit terms of 2/10, n/30. No PST is collected; however, 7 percent GST must be collected. Record the following entries in general journal form on page 16. Post your entries to the general ledger and to the accounts receivable subsidiary ledger. Use the following account titles and numbers: Cash, 101; Accounts Receivable, 110; GST Payable, 235; Sales, 401; Sales Returns and Allowances, 405; and Sales Discounts, 410.

April 2   sold $4,000 worth of merchandise on account to Waterbeds Galore; terms 2/10, n/30; invoice 2111-40

April 4   Waterbeds Galore reported that three frames from the April 2 purchase were damaged in shipment; Lee issued credit memo 40-32 for $75, plus 7 percent GST

April 12   received a cheque from Waterbeds Galore for the total amount owed minus the April 4 return and the discount

EXERCISE 7.4

Following are T accounts for Carolyn's Candy & Confectioner with a series of transactions related to a sale on account to one customer. The posting reference CR indicates that a payment on account has been received by Carolyn's and has been recorded in the cash receipts journal. The posting reference CP indicates that a payment has been made by Carolyn's and has been recorded in the cash payments journal. Briefly describe what has occurred on (a) June 3, (b) June 6, (c) June 13, and (d) July 12.

Cash   **101**

6/13 CR9	115.00	7/12 CP12	15.00

Accounts Receivable   **110**

6/3	S6	172.50	6/6	GJ8	57.50
			6/13	CR9	115.00

Provincial Sales Tax Payable   **220**

6/6	GJ8	4.00	6/3	S6	12.00
7/12	CP12	8.00			

GST Payable   **225**

6/6	GJ8	3.50	6/3	S6	10.50
7/12	CP12	7.00			

Sales 401

	6/3 S6	150.00

Sales Returns and Allowances 405

6/6 GJ8	50.00	

EXERCISE 7.5

Following is the sales journal for Clay Pots for November 20XX and the general journal entries relating to sales returns and allowances. The terms are 2/10, n/30.

		SALES JOURNAL						PAGE 14	
DATE	SALES INVOICE NUMBER	CUSTOMER'S NAME	POST. REF.	ACCOUNTS RECEIVABLE DEBIT		GST PAYABLE CREDIT		SALES CREDIT	
20XX									
Nov. 1	1762	Barbara Boone		224 70		14 70		210 00	
3	1763	Buster Jayne		363 80		23 80		340 00	
8	1764	Jana Trickle		192 60		12 60		180 00	
10	1765	Barbara Boone		96 30		6 30		90 00	
15	1766	Bud Marengo		481 50		31 50		450 00	
18	1767	John Stamas		235 40		15 40		220 00	
25	1768	Jana Trickle		80 25		5 25		75 00	
30	1769	Barbara Boone		171 20		11 20		160 00	
		Totals		1845 75		120 75		1725 00	

	GENERAL JOURNAL				PAGE 9	
DATE	DESCRIPTION	POST REF.	DEBIT		CREDIT	
20XX						
Nov. 5	Sales Returns and Allowances	405	40 00			
	GST Payable	235	2 80			
	Accounts Receivable—B. Boone	110/✓			42 80	
	To Record Return of Merchandise					
10	Sales Returns and Allowances	405	30 00			
	GST Payable	235	2 10			
	Accounts Receivable—J. Trickle	110/✓			32 10	
	To Record Return of Merchandise					

Answer the following:

a. Where will the totals of the sales journal be posted?

b. Including both the sales and general journals, how many separate postings must be made to the accounts receivable subsidiary ledger? To the accounts receivable control account?

c. If Barbara Boone sends a cheque to Clay Pots on November 11 to cover her total purchases up until that date, how much should she remit?

d. If Jana Trickle sends a cheque to Clay Pots on November 23, how much should she remit?

e.   What is the last day on which Bud Marengo may pay and still receive the discount? How much will be due on that date?

f.   What is the last day on which Barbara Boone may pay and still receive the discount for her November 30 purchase? How much will be due on that date?

EXERCISE 7.6

Pete Agnos owns a retail men's clothing store called "Man's Choice." Pete's total sales for October 20XX were $28,700. Sales returns and allowances were 1 percent of the gross sales, and sales discounts were 2 percent of the credit sales, which were $12,700. Prepare the revenue section of the income statement for Man's Choice for the month of October 20XX.

EXERCISE 7.7

Following is the accounts receivable subsidiary ledger for Marie's Auto Parts. Calculate the balance after each transaction and prepare a schedule of accounts receivable on March 31, 20XX. The balance in the accounts receivable control account on March 31 is $1,480. CR in the posting reference column indicates that a payment on account has been recorded in the cash receipts journal.

ACCOUNTS RECEIVABLE SUBSIDIARY LEDGER

Bug Repair Shop

DATE		EXPLANATION	POST. REF.	DEBIT	CREDIT	BALANCE
20XX						
Mar.	1		S3	8 7 0 00		
	11		CR4		4 0 0 00	
	15		S4	5 5 0 00		
	19		GJ5		1 5 0 00	

Foreign Auto Repair

DATE		EXPLANATION	POST. REF.	DEBIT	CREDIT	BALANCE
20XX						
Mar.	12		S4	6 5 00		
	14		S4	1 7 0 00		
	15		GJ5		4 0 00	

Joanna Grimm

DATE		EXPLANATION	POST. REF.	DEBIT	CREDIT	BALANCE
20XX						
Mar.	15		S4	3 7 5 00		
	25		CR4		3 7 5 00	
	28		S4	4 2 5 00		
	31		GJ6		1 2 5 00	

Kurt Zander

DATE		EXPLANATION	POST. REF.	DEBIT	CREDIT	BALANCE
20XX						
Mar.	20		S4	2 0 6 00		
	24		S4	1 1 5 00		
	25		S4	6 5 00		
	26		GJ6		6 5 00	
	30		CR4		2 0 6 00	

EXERCISE 7.8

Sure Sound Stereos uses a multicolumn sales journal to record its sales on account to customers. It is required to collect 8 percent PST and 7 percent GST on all sales. Following is a partial chart of accounts.

110	Accounts Receivable
230	Provincial Sales Tax Payable
235	GST Payable
405	Sales

Complete the multicolumn sales journal and indicate how it would look after all postings have been completed.

	SALES JOURNAL						PAGE 7
DATE	SALES INVOICE NUMBER	CUSTOMER'S NAME	POST. REF.	ACCOUNTS RECEIVABLE DEBIT	PST PAYABLE CREDIT	GST PAYABLE CREDIT	SALES CREDIT
20XX							
May 3	305	R. Joyce					2 4 0 00
7	306	L. Hemming					7 8 0 00
11	307	T. Ayotte					1 2 1 5 00
15	308	F. Brooks					8 4 00
23	309	L. Lyons					5 3 0 00
29	310	C. Little					1 9 2 0 00
31	311	N. Thomas					2 3 0 00
		Totals					

Problems

PROBLEM 7.1

Roxanne Simas owns a feed store called "R & S Feed and Supplies." Roxanne sells to ranchers and is not required to collect provincial sales tax, but she must collect 7 percent GST. Following are the transactions relating to credit sales for March 20XX:

March 1   sold alfalfa to Bar-D Ranch; $800; invoice 1660

March 3   sold grain to Sleepy River Ranch; $180; invoice 1661

March 5   sold supplies to Oak Hill Ranch; $570; invoice 1662

March 7   sold supplies to Sleepy River Ranch; $270; invoice 1663

March 8   issued credit memorandum 420-D to Oak Hill Ranch for supplies returned; $150

March 11 sold supplies to Bar-D Ranch: $950; invoice 1664

March 15 issued credit memorandum 421-D to Bar-D Ranch for supplies returned; $200

March 20 sold hay to Angus Acres; $1,500; invoice 1665

March 24 sold salt blocks to Sleepy River Ranch; $120; invoice 1666

March 25 issued credit memorandum 422-D to Sleepy River Ranch for merchandise returned; $60

March 29 sold grain to Angus Acres; $550; invoice 1667

Instructions

1. Enter the following account titles, numbers, and March 1 balances into the general ledger and the accounts receivable subsidiary ledger.

	General Ledger		Accounts Receivable Subsidiary Ledger	
110	Accounts Receivable	$1,005	Angus Acres	$250
205	GST Payable		Bar-D Ranch	175
400	Sales		Oak Hill Ranch	460
410	Sales Returns and Allowances		Sleepy River Ranch	120

2. Use page 3 for the sales journal and page 7 for the general journal.

3. Assuming that the terms of sales are net 30, record sales on account in the sales journal (use the one in Exercise 7.5 as a model), and record sales returns and allowances in the general journal.

4. Post to the accounts receivable subsidiary ledger immediately after each transaction.

5. After carefully checking the addition, total and rule the sales journal.

6. Post to the general ledger first from the sales journal and then from the general journal.

7. Prepare a schedule of accounts receivable as of March 31. Compare its total with the balance in the accounts receivable control account.

PROBLEM 7.2

Henry Hicks sells small appliances to retailers. He is not required to collect PST, but he must collect 7 percent GST. Following are the transactions relating to credit sales for June 20XX for Henry's store, H & H Appliances.

June 1   sold irons and hair dryers to Bestco; $850; invoice 1835

June 4   sold toasters and waffle irons to Buy 'N Save; $1,500; invoice 1836

June 6   issued credit memorandum 704-13 to Bestco for merchandise returned; $250

June 10   sold blenders and mixers to Buy 'N Save; $1,475; invoice 1837

June 15   sold crepe makers to Apco; $750; invoice 1838

June 18   issued credit memo 704-14 to Buy 'N Save for merchandise returned; $50

June 20   sold toaster ovens and car vacuums to Bestco; $1,720; invoice 1839

June 26   sold electric knives to Apco; $460; invoice 1840

June 28   issued credit memorandum 704-15 to Bestco for damaged merchandise; $100

June 30   sold electric frying pans to Apco; $625; invoice 1841

Instructions

1. Enter the following account titles, numbers, and June 1 balances into the general ledger and the accounts receivable subsidiary ledger.

	General Ledger		**Accounts Receivable Subsidiary Ledger**	
110	Accounts Receivable	$1,980	Apco	$650
205	GST Payable		Bestco	490
401	Sales		Buy 'N Save	840
410	Sales Returns and Allowances			

2. Use page 6 for the sales journal and page 18 for the general journal.

3. Assuming that the terms of sale are net 30, record sales on account in the sales journal and record sales returns and allowances in the general journal. Use the sales journal in Exercise 7.5 as a model.

4. Post to the accounts receivable subsidiary ledger immediately after each transaction.

5. After carefully checking the addition, total and rule the sales journal.

6. Post to the general ledger first from the sales journal and then from the general journal.

7. Prepare a schedule of accounts receivable as of June 30. Compare its total with the balance in the accounts receivable control account.

PROBLEM 7.3

The transactions relating to credit sales for August 20XX for Wanda's Beauty Supplies follow. Wanda is a retailer who sells directly to consumers and is required to collect 8 percent PST and 7 percent GST on all sales.

August 1   sold supplies to Andy Johnson; $50; invoice 4302

August 4   sold supplies to Georgia Keene; $125; invoice 4303

August 6	sold supplies to Byron Metzinger; $75; invoice 4304
August 8	issued credit memorandum 16032-A to Georgia Keene for supplies returned; $30
August 10	sold supplies to Andy Johnson; $30; invoice 4305
August 14	sold supplies to Joe Nagasaki; $220; invoice 4306
August 18	issued credit memorandum 16033-A to Byron Metzinger for damaged merchandise; $10
August 22	sold supplies to Andy Johnson; $40; invoice 4307
August 24	issued credit memorandum 16034-A to Joe Nagasaki for merchandise returned; $20
August 26	sold supplies to Byron Metzinger; $75; invoice 4308
August 29	sold supplies to Georgia Keene; $165; invoice 4309
August 30	issued credit memorandum 16035-A to Georgia Keene for merchandise returned; $50

Instructions

1. Enter the following account titles, numbers, and August 1 balances into the general ledger and the accounts receivable subsidiary ledger.

General Ledger		Accounts Receivable Subsidiary Ledger	
110 Accounts Receivable	$500	Andy Johnson	$125
210 PST Payable	120	Georgia Keene	80
230 GST Payable	105	Byron Metzinger	240
410 Sales		Joe Nagasaki	55
420 Sales Returns and Allowances			

2. Use page 8 for the sales journal and page 14 for the general journal

3. Assuming that the terms of sale are net 30, record sales plus 8 percent PST and 7 percent GST in the multicolumn sales journal and record sales returns in the general journal.

4. Post to the accounts receivable subsidiary ledger immediately after each transaction.

5. After carefully checking the addition, total and rule the sales journal.

6. Post to the general ledger first from the sales journal and then from the general journal.

7. Prepare a schedule of accounts receivable as of August 31. Compare its total with the balance in the Accounts Receivable control account.

PROBLEM 7.4

Wiley Manual owns a wholesale furniture warehouse called "The House of Wiley." No PST is charged to his customers, but 7 percent GST is collected on all sales. The following transactions relating to credit sales took place during the month of May 20XX. Be sure to read through all the instructions before beginning the problem.

May 1	sold merchandise on account to Mack's Bar Stools: $3,000, terms 2/10, n/30; invoice 2000

May 4	sold merchandise on account to Kitchen Korner; $4,500, terms 2/10, n/30; invoice 2001
May 6	issued credit memorandum 14-280 to grant a $200 allowance to Mack's Bar Stools on the May 1 purchase because of damage to several stools
May 10	received a cheque from Mack's Bar Stools for the balance owed on May 1 purchase less the return on May 6
May 15	sold merchandise on account to House of Maple; $970, terms 2/10, n/30; invoice 2002
May 16	received a cheque front Kitchen Korner for the balance owed on May 4 purchase
May 19	sold merchandise on account to Mack's Bar Stool; $1,500, terms 2/10, n/30; invoice 2003
May 22	issued credit memorandum 14-281 to House of Maple; it returned $200 of May 15 purchase
May 24	sold merchandise on account to Chairs, Inc.; $1,050, terms 2/10, n/30; invoice 2004
May 25	received a cheque from House of Maple for payment of the balance owed on May 15 invoice less the return on May 22
May 27	sold merchandise on account to Chairs, Inc.; $500, terms 2/10, n/30; invoice 2005
May 30	sold merchandise on account to House of Maple; $700, terms 2/10, n/30; invoice 2006

Instructions

1. Enter the following account titles and numbers into the general ledger and the accounts receivable subsidiary ledger. The accounts receivable control account on May 1 has a zero balance because all customers had paid in full as of that date.

	General Ledger		**Accounts Receivable Subsidiary Ledger**	
101	Cash	$4,620	Chairs, Inc.	0
110	Accounts Receivable	0	House of Maple	0
235	GST Payable		Kitchen Korner	0
401	Sales		Mack's Bar Stools	0
406	Sales Discounts			
411	Sales Returns and Allowances			

2. Use page 5 for the sales journal and page 11 for the general journal.

3. Record sales on account in a sales journal and record sales returns and allowances in the general journal. Record receipt of cash and sales discounts in the general journal. (Later on, you will record all incoming cash in the cash receipts journal.)

4. Post to the accounts receivable subsidiary ledger immediately after each transaction.

5. After carefully checking the addition, total and rule the sales journal.

6. Post to the general ledger first from the sales journal and then from the general journal.

7. Prepare a schedule of accounts receivable as of May 31. Compare its total with the balance in the accounts receivable control account.

PROBLEM 7.5

Following are the transactions for Super Shirts, a retail shirt and sweater store, relating to credit sales for the month of November 20XX. Eight percent PST and 7 percent GST must be collected on all sales. Credit terms for all customers are 3/10, n/30.

November 1	sold merchandise to Gabrielle Ladouceur; $250; invoice 3301
November 3	sold merchandise to Jana Harris; $560; invoice 3302
November 5	sold merchandise to Lynda Bruining; $650; invoice 3303
November 9	issued credit memorandum 4062-A to Jana Harris for damaged merchandise; $30
November 10	received a cheque from Gabrielle Ladouceur for payment of November 1 invoice
November 13	received a cheque from Jana Harris in payment of November 3 invoice less the November 9 return
November 15	sold merchandise to Denise Vernon; $95; invoice 3304
November 18	sold merchandise to Gabrielle Ladouceur; $80; invoice 3305
November 20	sold merchandise to Lynda Bruining; $150; invoice 3306
November 22	received a cheque from Lynda Bruining in payment of November 5 invoice
November 24	issued credit memorandum 4063-A to Denise Vernon for merchandise returned; $20
November 25	received a cheque from Denise Vernon in payment of November 15 invoice less the return of November 24
November 27	issued credit memorandum 4064-A to Lynda Bruining for damaged merchandise, $50
November 29	sold merchandise to Jana Harris; $240; invoice 3307
November 30	received a cheque from Lynda Bruining in payment of November 20 invoice less the return of November 27

Instructions

1. Enter the following account titles and numbers into the general ledger and the accounts receivable subsidiary ledger. The accounts receivable control account on November 1 has a zero balance because all customers had paid in full as of that date.

	General Ledger		Accounts Receivable Subsidiary Ledger
101	Cash	$3,740	Lynda Bruining
110	Accounts Receivable		Jana Harris
210	Provincial Sales Tax Payable		Gabrielle Ladouceur
215	GST Payable		Denise Vernon
401	Sales		
405	Sales Discounts		
410	Sales Returns and Allowances		

2. Use page 11 for the sales journal and page 26 for the general journal.

3. Record sales on account in a sales journal and record sales returns and allowances in the general journal. Record receipts of cash and sales discounts in the general journal. (Later on, you will record all incoming cash in the cash receipts journal.)

4. Post to the accounts receivable ledger immediately after each transaction.

5. After carefully checking the addition, total and rule the sales journal.

6. Post to the general ledger first from the sales journal and then from the general journal.

7. Prepare a schedule of accounts receivable and compare its total with the balance in the accounts receivable control account.

CHAPTER 8

The Purchases Journal and the Accounts Payable Subsidiary Ledger

LEARNING OBJECTIVES

When you have completed this chapter, you should

1. have an increased understanding of accounting terminology.
2. be able to record entries directly into the purchases journal and perform summary posting.
3. be able to record GST paid on merchandise purchased.
4. be able to post to the accounts payable subsidiary ledger and prepare a schedule of accounts payable.
5. be able to account for freight charges.
6. be able to account for purchases returns and allowances.
7. be able to calculate and account for purchases discounts.
8. be able to calculate single trade discounts.
9. recognize several different forms of credit terms.

VOCABULARY

contra liability	an account with a debit balance that subtracts from a related liability account; in this chapter, the contra liability account is GST Refundable which will subtract from the balance in GST Payable to determine the amount owed to CCRA
debit memorandum	a document issued by the buyer that informs the seller that her or his accounts payable has been reduced, or debited, because of a return or allowance
F. O. B.	"free on board"; the seller of merchandise will pay the freight charges to a specified location and then the buyer will pay the freight charges from this location to the final destination
FOB destination	free on board to the destination; the seller pays the freight charges to the destination of the goods where title to the goods passes to the buyer
FOB shipping point	free on board to the shipping point; seller pays for the cost of loading the goods at the point of shipment where title to the goods passes to the buyer; buyer will pay the freight charges

in transit	in the process of being moved from one place to another
list price	the price listed in the seller's catalogue
net price	the list price minus the trade discount
purchases discounts	discounts allowed on purchases; a contra purchases account subtracts from purchases in the Cost of Goods Sold section of the Income Statement
purchase invoice	the invoice that is received by the buyer when the ordered goods are shipped; from the point of view of the seller, the invoice is a sales invoice and is prepared by the seller
purchase order	a form prepared, usually by the purchasing department, giving written authorization to buy merchandise
purchase requisition	a form prepared by a particular department requesting the purchasing department to buy specific merchandise and prepare a formal purchase order
purchases returns and allowances	a contra purchases account that subtracts from purchases in the Cost of Goods Sold section of the Income Statement; the account is used to record returns or reductions in the price of the merchandise purchased
trade discount	a discount given to the buyer at the time of purchase as an incentive; a trade discount is not recorded on the books
vendor	a seller of merchandise

Introduction

In Chapter Seven, we learned how Frank Phelps, owner of Phelps Sporting Goods, dealt with some of the special accounting needs of merchandising businesses. Specifically, the unit dealt with credit sales of merchandise. In this unit, we will see how Frank handles the purchase of merchandise for resale.

Purchases and the Purchase Invoice

In a small firm, a purchase order may be made directly and simply. Often, the sales representative will obtain an order from the owner or manager when he or she makes a regular sales call on the particular business. Or, a purchase order may be placed by phone or fax. When the merchandise is delivered, it is important for the buyer to receive a copy of the seller's invoice and to check carefully the goods received against that invoice.

In larger firms, a more formal approach to purchasing is used. A **purchase requisition** is made by any department and is forwarded to the purchasing department. Purchase requisitions are made with multiple copies; one of the copies is sent to the purchasing department and one is kept by the department that issues the request. No accounting entry is made at this time.

When the proper authority in the purchasing department approves the requisition, a formal **purchase order** is prepared. Purchase orders are numbered consecutively and are carefully accounted for. Multiple copies are usually prepared: the original will be sent to the supplier from whom the merchandise is being purchased; one copy is retained by the purchasing department; one copy goes to the department that placed the order; and one copy goes to the receiving clerk. When the merchandise is received, the receiving clerk will check the packing slip from the **vendor** against the purchase order to make sure that everything ordered was actually delivered and will verify that the terms on the packing slip are the same terms originally agreed upon. It is good practice to send copies of purchase orders to the accounting department, too, so that invoice calculations may be verified and prices checked against the sales invoice.

When the sales invoice arrives, either with the merchandise ordered or separately, a copy of the invoice is sent to the accounting department to be recorded. The sales invoice received from the vendor is, from the point of view of the buyer, a **purchase invoice**. Therefore, at this point in time, the accountant will be recording the purchase of merchandise.

Following is the purchase invoice that arrived with the shipment when Frank Phelps ordered skis and bindings from Cold Weather Sports, Inc.

Cold Weather Sports, Inc. **204 Superior St.** **Sault Ste. Marie, Ontario** **P6B 4K9**			**Invoice No. 5307**	

		Invoice Date	**Your Order No. & Date**	
		June 4	608	June 1

Terms 2/15, n/30	**FOB** Shipping Point	**Shipped Via** Provincial Transport	**Shipped from** Sault Ste. Marie

Sold to: Phelps Sporting Goods 806 Humber Drive London, Ontario N6G 3B5	**Ship to:** Same

Quantity **Shipped**	**Description**	**Unit** **Price**	**Extension**
6	Tuf-Lite, 170 mm, Skis, #S46130	85.00	510.00
10	Tuf-Lite, 190 mm, Skis, #S46t32	85.00	850.00
8	Ski-Rite, 150 mm, Skis, #Q04329	50.00	400.00
20	Eazy-On Bindings, #J46523	40.00	800.00
			2,560.00
	7% GST		179.20
	Total		$2,739.20

When this shipment arrives from Cold Weather Sports, Inc., the person who receives the goods should check the incoming order to make sure that everything that appears on the packing slip is included with the shipment. The receiving person will be asked to sign the packing slip indicating that all the goods are there and are in satisfactory condition. If a careful check is not made at this point, it may be discovered later that a portion of the shipment is missing or that some items have been damaged in transit.

GST Accounts

In Chapter Seven, the GST Payable account was introduced; it was used each time a sale or a sales return and allowance was made. Remember that the GST Payable account is a *liability* because the tax is collected on behalf of the federal government and the money must be remitted to Canada Customs and Revenue Agency (CCRA), at appropriate intervals.

The goods and services tax (GST) is a multi-level tax that applies to most transactions throughout the production and marketing process. The majority of goods and services sold or provided in Canada are taxable under the GST at the rate of 7 percent. Some examples of goods and services taxed at 7 percent include:

- automobiles
- gasoline and car repairs
- soft drinks, candies, and confections
- restaurant meals
- clothing and footwear
- advertising services
- taxi and limousine fares
- legal and accounting fees
- hotel accommodations
- barbers' and hairstylists' services.

A limited number of goods and services, such as sales of basic groceries and prescription drugs, are also taxable, *but at a rate of 0 percent*. Some examples include:

- basic groceries (milk, bread, vegetables)
- agricultural and most fishery products (wheat, grain, raw wool, unprocessed tobacco, fish for human consumption, and farm livestock, with some exceptions such as horses)
- prescription drugs and drug dispensing fees
- medical devices (hearing aids, wheelchairs, eyeglasses, etc.)
- exports.

As you already know, the customers of a business are charged a 7 percent Goods and Services Tax (GST) when a sale is made to them. In addition, the business must pay the 7 percent tax when a purchase is made by them. As discussed in the previous chapter, the account used to record the GST charged to customers is GST Payable. This account is a liability because the amounts collected from customers must be remitted to Canada Customs and Revenue Agency. However, any GST paid by the business on its own purchases may be deducted from the GST Payable balance and the *difference* is then remitted to CCRA at the appropriate time. The GST paid by the business on its own purchases is debited to an account called GST Refundable. The balance in GST Refundable is subtracted from the balance in GST Payable at the end of the period to determine the amount owed to CCRA.

Following are the T accounts for the month of February for GST Payable and GST Refundable.

GST Payable			215	**GST Refundable**			216
	2/8	S81	985.60	2/8	P95	792.50	
	2/15	S82	854.30	2/15	P96	642.90	
	2/21	S83	990.50	2/21	P97	800.70	
	2/28	S84	1,450.90	2/28	P98	590.50	
			4,281.30			**2,826.60**	

GST Payable is a liability; it represents the amount collected from customers.

*GST Refundable is a **contra liability**. It represents the amount paid to suppliers. Its balance is subtracted from the balance in GST Payable to determine amount due CCRA.*

The GST Refundable account and GST Payable account are closed to a third account called GST Owing when the taxes are remitted to the federal government. After closing, if the balance in GST Owing is a credit balance, the amount is paid to CCRA and the cycle starts over again. If, on the other hand, GST Owing shows a debit balance, the business may apply for a refund from CCRA. This would indicate that the business paid more in GST than it collected from customers, though this would be unlikely for a successful business.

Following are the entries to close GST Payable and GST Refundable to GST Owing.

GENERAL JOURNAL					
DATE	DESCRIPTION	POST REF.	DEBIT		CREDIT
20XX					
Mar. 31	GST Payable		4 2 8 1 30		
	GST Owing				4 2 8 1 30
	To Close GST Payable Account				
31	GST Owing		2 8 2 6 60		
	GST Refundable				2 8 2 6 60
	To Close GST Refundable Account				

Once these entries are posted to the general ledger, the GST Payable and the GST Refundable accounts are closed. The GST Owing account has a balance of $1,454.70. This is the amount that will be remitted to the federal government.

The Purchases Account

All merchandise that is purchased for resale is debited to a special account called Purchases; it is assigned a number in the new category, cost of goods sold. Accounts that appear in the cost of goods sold category will be used in calculating the actual cost of the merchandise that is sold. Cost of goods sold will be discussed in detail in Chapter Eleven.

Assume that Phelps Sporting Goods recorded the credit purchase of ski equipment from Cold Weather Sports, Inc. in a general journal. The entry would look like this:

GENERAL JOURNAL					PAGE 11
DATE	DESCRIPTION	POST REF.	DEBIT		CREDIT
20XX					
June 4	Purchases		2 5 6 0 00		
	GST Refundable		1 7 9 20		
	Accounts Pay.—Cold Weather Sports, Inc.				2 7 3 9 20

Remember that the purchases account is debited only for the purchase of merchandise for resale. When merchandise is purchased that is not for resale, it is debited to its appropriate asset account. For example, assume that Frank purchased a small computer on account for use by his bookkeeper. The entry would be a debit to Office Equipment and a credit to Accounts Payable and would be recorded in the general journal rather than the purchases journal.

The Purchases Journal

Phelps Sporting Goods uses special journals to record sales, purchases, cash receipts, and cash payments. The general journal is not used for recording purchases on account because: (1) for each entry, the words *Purchases, GST Refundable,* and *Accounts Payable* would have to be written into the journal; and (2) for each entry, three amounts would have to be posted to the general ledger.

As is true with the sales journal, use of the purchases journal saves the bookkeeper's valuable time. The purchases journal is used only for the recording of credit purchases of merchandise for resale. Because this is the case, every entry in the purchases journal will result in a debit to purchases, a debit to GST Refundable, and a credit to accounts payable. As with the sales journal, it is not necessary to write the words *Purchases, GST Refundable,* and *Accounts Payable* with each entry. It is necessary only to enter the date, the creditor's name, the invoice number, and the correct amounts in the appropriate columns.

Following is the purchases journal for Phelps Sporting Goods for the month of June 20XX:

		PURCHASES JOURNAL					
DATE	SUPPLIER'S NAME	INV. NO.	POST. REF.	PURCHASES DEBIT	GST REFUNDABLE DEBIT	ACCOUNTS PAYABLE CREDIT
20XX						
June 4	Cold Weather Sports, Inc.	5307		2 5 6 0 00	1 7 9 20	2 7 3 9 20
8	Running World	1042		5 7 4 00	4 0 18	6 1 4 18
10	Racquet Warehouse	879		7 4 0 00	5 1 80	7 9 1 80
14	Running World	1078		7 6 0 00	5 3 20	8 1 3 20
19	Sports Supplies	7061		1 4 0 9 00	9 8 63	1 5 0 7 63
21	Cold Weather Sports, Inc.	5390		9 6 2 00	6 7 34	1 0 2 9 34
28	Running World	1091		4 1 6 00	2 9 12	4 4 5 12
	Totals			7 4 2 1 00	5 1 9 47	7 9 4 0 47

After the columns have been totalled, crossfooting must be completed before any posting is performed to ensure that the debit columns equal the credit columns. Again, the steps for crossfooting are:

1) Debit column totals $7,421.00 + $519.47 = $7,940.47
2) Credit column total $7,940.47
3) Debit totals equal Credit totals

Once the proof has been constructed, draw a single line across the amount columns and a double line beneath the totals across all column totals.

Posting the Purchases Journal

The total of the purchases journal must be posted to the general ledger. Following are the general ledger accounts affected.

Accounts Payable																			ACCOUNT NO. 205					
DATE		EXPLANATION	POST. REF.	DEBIT					CREDIT						BALANCE					
20XX																				
June	30		P6							7	9	4	0	47			7	9	4	0	47

GST Refundable																			ACCOUNT NO. 215					
DATE		EXPLANATION	POST. REF.	DEBIT					CREDIT						BALANCE					
20XX																				
June	30		P6		5	1	9	47										5	1	9	47

Purchases																			ACCOUNT NO. 511					
DATE		EXPLANATION	POST. REF.	DEBIT					CREDIT						BALANCE					
20XX																				
June	30		P6	7	4	2	1	00								7	4	2	1	00

If all of Phelps Sporting Goods's credit purchases had been recorded in the general journal, not only would the journalizing have been much more time-consuming, but seven separate postings to the purchases account and seven separate postings to the GST Refundable and accounts payable accounts would have been required. Summary posting (when journal totals are posted) saves a great deal of time.

The Accounts Payable Subsidiary Ledger

The accounts payable subsidiary ledger shows the amounts owed to individual creditors. All charge purchases, purchases returns and allowances, and payments made to creditors appear in this ledger. The accounts payable account in the general ledger is, like the accounts receivable account, a control account. The balance in the accounts payable account represents the total amount owed to all creditors. The accounts payable subsidiary ledger shows the individual amounts owed. Of course, the total of the individual creditors' balances must equal the balance in the control account.

You will be working with three different ledgers from now on. They are:

1. the general ledger, which contains separate records for all assets, liabilities, owner's equity, revenue, cost of goods sold, and expense accounts;

2. the accounts receivable subsidiary ledger, which contains individual accounts for all charge customers showing all credit sales made to them, their sales returns and allowances, and all payments received; and,

3. the accounts payable subsidiary ledger, which contains individual accounts for all creditors showing all credit purchases, purchases returns and allowances, and all payments made.

The accounts receivable and accounts payable subsidiary ledgers are frequently referred to as simply the accounts receivable ledger and the accounts payable ledger.

Posting to the Accounts Payable Subsidiary Ledger

Credit postings to the accounts payable subsidiary ledger come primarily from the purchases journal. Debit entries come mainly from the cash payments journal (when money is paid on account). Debit or credit entries may also come from the general journal; for example, a correcting entry may be made or a purchases return or allowance may be granted.

The purchases journal, the general ledger accounts affected when the total is posted, and the accounts payable ledger (arranged in alphabetical order) follow.

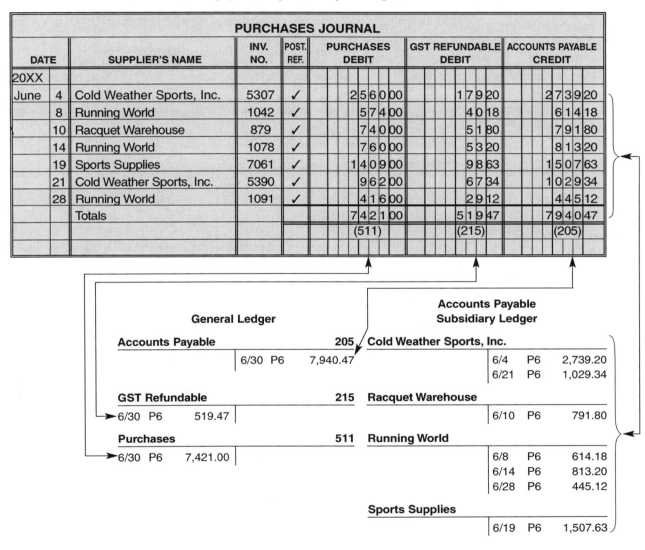

When an amount is posted to the accounts payable ledger, place a check mark (✓) opposite the creditor's name in the posting reference column of the purchases journal and write P and the page number in the creditor's account in the ledger. When the total of the purchases journal is posted, indicate that by writing the account numbers for purchases, GST Refundable, and accounts payable under the column totals.

The Schedule of Accounts Payable

A schedule of accounts payable is prepared at the end of the accounting period and alphabetically lists each creditor and the amount owed. The total of the schedule of accounts payable must be compared with the balance in the accounts payable control account. The two figures must be the same; if they are not, the bookkeeper must search for the error.

The accounts payable subsidiary ledger, the schedule of accounts payable, and the accounts payable control account follow.

Cold Weather Sports, Inc.

DATE		EXPLANATION	POST. REF.	DEBIT	CREDIT	BALANCE
20XX						
June	4		P6		2 7 3 9 20	2 7 3 9 20
	21		P6		1 0 2 9 34	3 7 6 8 54

Racquet Warehouse

DATE		EXPLANATION	POST. REF.	DEBIT	CREDIT	BALANCE
20XX						
June	10		P6		7 9 1 80	7 9 1 80

Running World

DATE		EXPLANATION	POST. REF.	DEBIT	CREDIT	BALANCE
20XX						
June	8		P6		6 1 4 18	6 1 4 18
	14		P6		8 1 3 20	1 4 2 7 38
	28		P6		4 4 5 12	1 8 7 2 50

Sports Supplies

DATE		EXPLANATION	POST. REF.	DEBIT	CREDIT	BALANCE
20XX						
June	19		P6		1 5 0 7 63	1 5 0 7 63

Phelps Sporting Goods Schedule of Accounts Payable June 30, 20XX																
Cold Weather Sports, Inc.			$	3	7	6	8	54								
Racquet Warehouse					7	9	1	80								
Running World				1	8	7	2	50								
Sports Supplies				1	5	0	7	63								
Total										$	7	9	4	0	47	

Accounts Payable   ACCOUNT NO. 205

DATE		EXPLANATION	POST. REF.	DEBIT						CREDIT						BALANCE					
20XX																					
June	30		P6								7	9	4	0	47		7	9	4	0	47

The accounts payable account would normally have more than one entry in it. For example, payments made on account would be posted to it from the cash payments journal (which will be introduced in the next chapter), and purchases returns and allowances would be posted to it from the general journal.

The Freight In Account

Often, freight charges are incurred when merchandise is purchased. Such charges are logically considered to be an added cost of the merchandise purchased, because it is usually the buyer who pays the freight charges, either directly or indirectly through higher prices for the merchandise purchased. For this reason, the cost of freight could be debited directly to the purchases account. Most businesses, however, prefer to keep freight costs separate from the cost of purchases. Knowing exactly how much is spent for various methods of transporting goods is valuable to management in controlling costs. Decisions have to be made concerning which type of transportation (air, truck, rail) to use; keeping careful accounting records of freight costs provides valuable information in making those decisions.

An account called Freight In is debited for freight costs. The journal entry to record the transportation charge on the shipment of skis and bindings from Sault Ste. Marie is as follows:

GENERAL JOURNAL													PAGE 6				
DATE		DESCRIPTION	POST REF.	DEBIT						CREDIT							
20XX																	
June	8	Freight In			1	7	5	00									
		GST Refundable				1	2	25									
		Accounts Payable—Provincial Transport									1	8	7	25			
		To Record Freight Charges on Cold															
		Weather Sports, Inc., Invoice 5307															

Of course, if the freight charges were paid by cash, the entry would appear in the cash payments journal.

The freight in account is, like purchases, a cost of goods sold account, and its balance will be added to net purchases on the income statement as shown:

Net Purchases	$7,421
Add Freight In	175
Cost of Purchases	$7,596

FOB Shipping Point and FOB Destination

Before goods are shipped, there must be an agreement between buyer and seller as to which party will pay the freight charges. The purchase order and the seller's invoice will stipulate either FOB shipping point or FOB destination. **FOB shipping point** means free on board to the shipping point, that is, the seller will pay to have the goods loaded at the point of shipment, but will not pay the transportation costs from the shipping point to the destination. Title to the goods passes to the buyer at the shipping point, and the buyer will pay the freight charges upon arrival of the merchandise.

If the terms are **FOB destination**, that means free on board to the destination agreed upon, and the seller will pay the freight charges. Title to the goods passes to the buyer when the goods arrive.

Whether the freight terms are FOB shipping point or FOB destination, it may be assumed that the buyer will pay the transportation charges, either directly or indirectly.

Debit and Credit Memoranda

When damaged or unsatisfactory merchandise is returned, or when the buyer is given an allowance for such, the buyer issues a **debit memorandum** to the seller indicating that the buyer's account payable has been debited or reduced. When the bookkeeper receives a debit memorandum, she or he records it by crediting an account called purchases returns and allowances and debiting accounts payable in the general journal. This same transaction on the books of the seller would be recorded as a debit to sales returns and allowances and as a credit to accounts receivable. If the seller (instead of the buyer) had issued the memo, it would have been called a credit memorandum, because on the books of the seller, a credit to accounts receivable is being recorded. Thus, a credit memorandum can reduce accounts receivable or increase accounts payable, and a debit memorandum can increase accounts receivable or reduce accounts payable, depending on who (buyer or seller) is issuing it.

Purchases Returns and Allowances

Although it would be possible simply to credit the purchases account for returns and allowances, it is good accounting practice to keep a separate record for them. It may help management to make future decisions about which merchandise to buy or which vendor to contact for a particular product. An excessive number of returns of any product or to any vendor may indicate that the purchasing policy needs revision.

Assume that on June 9 Frank Phelps, owner of Phelps Sporting Goods, contacted Cold Weather Sports by telephone to report that the Eazy-On bindings that it had sent were factory-damaged and had to be adjusted before they could be used. The manager of Cold Weather Sports suggested that if Frank would keep the bindings and make the necessary adjustments, he would give a $10 allowance on each binding ordered. Frank agreed and a $200 debit memorandum was issued by Phelps Sporting Goods on June 9. The general journal entry and the related T accounts for recording of the allowance follow. Note that the original purchase from Cold Weather Sports is shown in the accounts payable control account even though such individual entries are not usually shown in the control account. (Credit purchases, remember, are individually recorded in the purchases journal, but only the totals of the columns are posted to the general ledger.)

Note that accounts payable is debited for the amount of the return plus the amount of the GST taxes. This reduces the amount of money owed to Cold Weather Sports. GST refundable is credited, which reduces the balance of that account, too, since it has a normal debit balance. **Purchases returns and allowances** is credited because it is a contra-purchases account and will subtract from purchases on the income statement in the cost of goods sold section.

GENERAL JOURNAL					PAGE 6
DATE	DESCRIPTION	POST REF.	DEBIT	CREDIT	
20XX					
June 9	Accounts Pay.—Cold Weather Sports, Inc.	205/✓	2 1 4 00		
	GST Refundable	215		1 4 00	
	Purchases Returns and Allowances	512		2 0 0 00	
	To Record Debit Memorandum, Invoice 5307				

General Ledger

Accounts Payable   205

6/9   GJ6   214.00 | 6/4   P6   2,739.20

GST Refundable   215

6/4   P6   179.20 | 6/9   GJ6   14.00

Purchases Returns and Allowances   512

   6/9   GJ6   200.00

Accounts Payable Subsidiary Ledger

Cold Weather Sports, Inc.

6/9   GJ6   214.00 | 6/4   P6   2,739.20

Purchases Discounts

Many times the buyer will be allowed a **purchase discount** if the invoice is paid within a certain number of days. The terms indicated on invoice 5307 from Cold Weather Sports, Inc. are 2/15, n/30. If Phelps Sporting Goods pays within 15 days of the invoice date, a 2 percent discount may be deducted from the total invoice price of the merchandise. Remember, too, that Phelps Sporting Goods received a $200 allowance for damaged merchandise on invoice 5307. The procedure for calculating the amount due if it is paid within the discount period is as follow.

Step 1.   Calculate the last day for payment within the discount period. Terms are 2/15, n/30 and the invoice date is June 4.

     June   4
     +   15   (2/15, n/30)
     June   19   last day for payment within the discount period.

Step 2.   Calculate the balance owed on the merchandise by referring to the
            T account for Cold Weather Sports.

Cold Weather Sports, Inc.

6/9 GJ6	214.00	6/4 P6	2,739.20
			2,525.20

Step 3.   Calculate the cash discount. It must be figured on the original price of
            the merchandise minus the return; do not include GST (refer to the June
            4 entry in the purchases journal on page 201.)

    a.   original price of merchandise $2,560.00

    b.   subtract return of merchandise   −200.00

    c.   invoice amount less return $2,360.00

    d.   multiply by discount rate   × .02

    e.   discount amount $ 47.20

Step 4.   Calculate the final balance due on the invoice. Subtract the discount
            amount from the balance owed in the account. Note that the balance
            owed includes GST.

    a.   balance in account $2,525.20

    b.   subtract discount   − 47.20

    c.   balance due on invoice $2,478.00

The invoice must be paid by June 19 in order to receive the 2 percent discount. On
or before that date, a cheque for $2,478 may be remitted to Cold Weather Sports, Inc.
The discount is recorded as a credit to an account called Purchases Discounts. It, like
Purchases Returns and Allowances, is shown in the cost of goods sold category on the
chart of accounts. **Purchases Discounts** is a contra purchases account and will be subtracted from the balance of purchases on the income statement. The general journal
entry on Phelps Sporting Goods' books to record the payment of Cold Weather Sports'
invoice 5307 looks like this:

GENERAL JOURNAL				PAGE 6
DATE	**DESCRIPTION**	**POST REF.**	**DEBIT**	**CREDIT**
20XX				
June 19	Accounts Pay.—Cold Weather Sports, Inc.	205/✓	2 5 2 5 20	
	Cash	101		2 4 7 8 00
	Purchases Discounts	513		4 7 20
	To Record Payment in Full of Invoice 5307			

Note that accounts payable has been debited for $2,525.20, the balance owed on the
invoice, even though only $2,478 was actually paid. This is necessary to show that Phelps
Sporting Goods has, in effect, saved $47.20 by taking advantage of the discount and does
not owe any more on this particular invoice.

The following T accounts outline the original purchase from Cold Weather Sports,
the purchase allowance, and the payment of the invoice within the discount period.

The entries are outlined as follows:

a.   a debit to Purchases, a debit to GST Refundable, and credits to Accounts Payable
    and Cold Weather Sports to record the original purchase.

b. a debit to Accounts Payable and Cold Weather Sports, a credit to GST Refundable, and a credit to Purchases Returns and Allowances to record the $200 debit memorandum issued by Phelps Sporting Goods.

c. a debit to Accounts Payable and Cold Weather Sports and credits to Purchases Discounts and Cash to record payment of the invoice within the discount period.

General Ledger		Accounts Payable Subsidiary Ledger	

Cash   101

6/1 Balance 10,000.00 | 6/19 GJ6 2,478.00 (c)

Cold Weather Sports, Inc.

(b) 6/9 GJ6   214.00 | 6/4 P6   2,739.20 (a)
(c) 6/19 GJ6 2,525.20 |

Accounts Payable   205

(b) 6/9 GJ6   214.00 | 6/4 P6   2,739.20 (a)
(c) 6/19 GJ6 2,525.20 |

GST Refundable   215

(a) 6/4 P6   179.20 | 6/9 GJ6   14.00 (b)

Purchases   511

(a) 6/4 P6   2,560.00 |

Purchases Returns and Allowances   512

| 6/9 GJ6   200.00 (b)

Purchases Discounts   513

| 6/19 GJ6   47.20 (c)

Purchases discounts and purchases returns and allowances are subtracted from purchases on the income statement. This is logical because a return or an allowance is like a purchase not made, and the purchases discount reduces the cost of the merchandise. The portion of the income statement that shows Purchases and its related accounts looks like this:

Partial Income Statement			
Cost of Goods Sold			
Purchases		$ 45 000 00	
Less: Purchases Returns and Allowances	$ 2 700 00		
Purchases Discounts	2 900 00	5 600 00	
Net Purchases		39 400 00	
Add Freight In		1 200 00	
Cost of Purchases			$ 40 600 00

Single Trade Discounts

Most sellers print catalogues from which buyers may choose their merchandise. The catalogues list the seller's prices, and the catalogue price is thus called the **list price**. Sellers may grant a discount at the time of the sale to the buyer, and that discount is called a

trade discount. The list price minus the trade discount is known as the **net price**. By changing the trade discount offered, the seller may easily change the price charged. It is easier and more economical for the seller to change the discount offered than to change the entire catalogue. In addition, larger trade discounts may be offered to customers who place larger orders.

Trade discounts are not recorded on the books of the seller or the buyer. Only the actual price charged for the merchandise is recorded. It is necessary, though, for the bookkeeper to be able to calculate trade discounts so that invoices may be checked for accuracy.

Assume that on June 21 a sales representative from Running World calls on Frank Phelps of Phelps Sporting Goods. Frank orders 30 pairs of running shoes with a list price of $25 per pair minus a 10 percent trade discount. The total price paid for the shoes is calculated as follows:

Step 1. Calculate the total list price.
30 pairs $\times$ $25 = $750

Step 2. Calculate the trade discount (10 percent).

    a. Move the decimal point two places to the left in 10 percent.
10% = 10. = .10

    b. Multiply the list price by the trade discount.
$750 $\times$ .10 = $75

Step 3. Calculate the net price of the invoice.

Calculate the total purchase price by subtracting the trade discount from the list price. $750 − $75 = $675

Step 4. Calculate the total invoice price.

    a. Multiply the net price of the invoice by 7 percent GST.
$675 $\times$ .07 = $47.25

    b. Add the net price of the invoice to the 7 percent GST.
$675 + $47.25 = $722.25

The net price of the invoice is $675; the total invoice price is $722.25. On the books of Phelps Sporting Goods, the entry will be recorded as a debit to Purchases for the net price of $675, a debit to GST Refundable for $47.25, and a credit to Accounts Payable for the full amount owing of $722.25. On the books of Running World, the entry will be recorded as a debit of $722.25 to Accounts Receivable, a credit to GST Payable of $47.25, and a credit to Sales of $675.

Remember, the amount of the trade discount is not recorded on the books of the buyer or the seller.

Trade Discounts and Credit Terms on the Same Invoice

Frequently, a trade discount will be offered to the buyer along with credit terms to encourage early payment of the invoice.

For example, assume that on July 11 Phelps Sporting Goods purchased merchandise from Racquet Warehouse with a list price of $1,500 minus a trade discount of 5 percent. In addition, credit terms of 2/10, n/30 were offered. The net price for the purchase is:

a. $1,500 $\times$ .05 = $75

b. $1,500 − $75 = $1,425 (net invoice price).

The total invoice price is:

c. $1,425 \times .07 = \$99.75$ (GST)

d. $\$1,425 + \$99.75 = \$1,524.75$ (total invoice price).

The entry will be recorded in the purchases journal as follows:

	PURCHASES JOURNAL				PAGE 7		
DATE	SUPPLIER'S NAME	INV. NO.	POST. REF.	PURCHASES DEBIT	GST REFUNDABLE DEBIT	ACCOUNTS PAYABLE CREDIT	
20XX							
July 11	Racquet Warehouse	956		1 4 2 5 00	9 9 75	1 5 2 4 75	

The last day for payment of the invoice within the discount period is July 21 (July 11 + 10 days). The discount is 2 percent of $1,425, or $28.50. Remember, the discount is figured on the purchase price, not the GST.

The entry in general journal form to record the payment of the invoice is as follows:

	GENERAL JOURNAL			PAGE 8	
DATE	DESCRIPTION	POST REF.	DEBIT	CREDIT	
20XX					
July 21	Accounts Payable—Racquet Warehouse		1 5 2 4 75		
	Cash			1 4 9 6 25	
	Purchases Discounts			2 8 50	
	To Record Payment of Invoice 956				

Note that the trade discount was not recorded on the books. Rather, it was calculated and subtracted from the list price ($1,500 − $75 = $1,425). The purchases discount was calculated on the actual purchase price, $1,425 and recorded in the books.

Credit Terms

There are many different credit terms offered to buyers. Some of the more common ones are listed here.

Terms	
2/10, n/30	A 2 percent discount is offered if the invoice is paid within 10 days of the invoice date; or, if no discount is taken, total invoice amount is due within 30 days of the invoice date.
2/10, EOM	A 2 percent discount is allowed if the invoice is paid within 10 days after the end of the current month; if no discount is taken, total invoice amount is due at the end of the month following the current month.
n/10, EOM	No discount is allowed. The net amount is due within 10 days after the end of the current month.
30 days	No discount is allowed. The net amount is due within 30 days after the date of the invoice.
COD	Cash on delivery or collect on delivery. The amount of the invoice must be paid at the time the goods are delivered.

Summary

In many large firms, the purchasing process requires that a purchase requisition be filled out by the department making the request, and a purchase order be filled out by the purchasing department. The accounting entry is recorded upon receipt of the goods ordered and purchase invoice. All goods bought for resale will be debited to an account called purchases. A new category of accounts called cost of goods sold will include the purchases account, freight in, purchases returns and allowances, and purchases discounts.

A special journal, the purchases journal, is used to record all credit purchases of merchandise for resale. With both the sales and purchases journal, column totals (rather than individual amounts) are posted. This, you will remember, is called summary posting. In addition, each entry in the purchases journal is posted as a credit to the individual creditors' accounts in the accounts payable subsidiary ledger. At the end of the accounting period, a schedule of accounts payable is prepared, and the total is compared with the balance of the accounts payable account in the general ledger. The figures must be the same. If they are not the same, an error has been made that must be located and corrected.

The 7 percent Goods and Services Tax (GST) is charged to customers when merchandise is sold, and it is paid by merchants when goods for resale are bought. GST collected from customers is credited to GST Payable and GST paid for goods bought by merchants is debited to GST Refundable, which is a contra liability account. The GST Payable and GST Refundable accounts are closed out to an account called GST Owing at the end of the accounting period. A credit balance in GST Owing will determine the amount of the cheque to be sent to Canada Customs and Revenue Agency.

Freight charges are considered to be part of the cost of the merchandise purchased and are debited to an account called freight in. The balance of the freight in account is added to the balance of net purchases on the income statement to arrive at the cost of purchases. On the seller's invoice, either FOB shipping point or FOB destination will be indicated. FOB shipping point means free on board to the point of shipment and the buyer will reimburse the carrier; FOB destination means free on board to the destination and the seller will pay the carrier.

When purchased merchandise is returned or is damaged, the buyer will issue a debit memorandum to the seller that indicates that the buyer's accounts payable account is being reduced by a debit. When the seller receives the debit memo, the accounts receivable account on the books of the seller must also be reduced by the same amount if the buyer has a valid claim. The return of merchandise is recorded on the buyer's books as a credit to purchases returns and allowances, a credit to GST Refundable, and a debit to accounts payable (or cash, in case a refund is being made); the same return on the seller's books will be recorded as a debit to sales returns and allowances, a debit to GST Payable, and a credit to accounts receivable (or cash).

A trade discount may be granted to the buyer. If that is the case, the buyer subtracts the amount of the trade discount from the list price of the merchandise and records only the actual purchase price. Trade discounts are not recorded on the books of the buyer or the seller.

In addition to the trade discount, credit terms may be offered on the same invoice by the seller to encourage prompt payment.

Vocabulary Review

Here is a list of the words and terms for this chapter.

contra liability	purchases discounts
debit memorandum	purchase invoice
F.O.B.	purchase order
FOB destination	purchase requisition
FOB shipping point	purchases returns and allowances
in transit	trade discount
list price	vendor
net price	

Fill in the blank with the correct word or term from the list.

1. _____ means in the process of being moved from one place to another.
2. The invoice that is received by the buyer when goods ordered have been shipped is referred to, from the viewpoint of the buyer, as a/an _____.
3. Another term for a seller of merchandise is _____.
4. When the purchasing department prepares a form ordering merchandise, the form is referred to as a/an _____.
5. A form made out by a department that requests the purchasing department to order merchandise is referred to as a/an _____.
6. A discount granted to the buyer at the time of purchase, often for volume buying, is referred to as a/an _____.
7. The price of merchandise that is shown in the seller's catalogue is referred to as the _____.
8. The catalogue price minus the trade discount is referred to as the _____.
9. When the seller pays the freight charges all the way to the buyer's destination, the freight terms are _____.
10. When the seller pays only for loading the merchandise at the point of shipment, the freight terms are _____.
11. A document issued by the buyer to the seller, indicating that the accounts payable account is being reduced on the books of the buyer, is referred to as a/an _____.
12. The contra purchases account that is used to record customers' returns is called _____.
13. _____ means free on board, or, the buyer receives ordered merchandise with no freight charges up to a certain specified location.
14. When a discount is given on merchandise purchased, the discount amount is recorded as a credit in the _____ account.
15. GST Refundable is a/an _____ account with a debit balance that subtracts from GST Payable to determine the amount owed to Canada Customs and Revenue Agency.

Match the words and terms on the left with the definitions on the right.

16. contra liability
17. debit memorandum
18. F.O.B.
19. FOB destination
20. FOB shipping point
21. in transit
22. list price
23. net price
24. purchases discounts
25. purchase invoice
26. purchase order
27. purchases returns and allowances
28. purchase requisition
29. trade discount
30. vendor

a. freight charges paid by the seller to the buyer's destination
b. the GST Refundable account
c. the invoice that is received with the ordered merchandise
d. free on board
e. a request to the purchasing department that merchandise be ordered
f. catalogue price minus trade discount
g. the account that is credited when a return or an allowance is granted to a customer
h. one who sells merchandise
i. a formal order for merchandise made by the purchasing department
j. the catalogue price
k. the cost of loading merchandise at the point of shipment is paid by the seller and buyer pays to the destination
l. a contra purchases account in which discounts are recorded on purchases
m. a document issued by the buyer indicating that the buyer's accounts payable account is being reduced
n. a discount granted to the buyer at the time of purchase
o. in the process of being moved

Exercises

EXERCISE 8.1

In each case, determine (1) the last day on which the invoice may be paid to receive the discount; (2) the last day on which the invoice may be paid after the discount period; and (3) the amount of the discount. For a list of the months and the number of days in each, refer to Chapter Seven, Exercise 7.1.

	Invoice Amount	Invoice Date	Terms	Last Day for Discount	Last Day for Payment after Discount	Amount of Discount
a.	$1,000	January 18	1/15, n/60	_____	_____	_____
b.	4,750	February 20	2/10, EOM	_____	_____	_____
c.	500	April 25	2/10, n/30	_____	_____	_____
d.	8,040	June 27	1/15, n/30	_____	_____	_____
e.	3,000	July 29	60 days	_____	_____	_____
f.	5,500	September 11	2/10, n/60	_____	_____	_____
g.	7,420	November 21	1/15, n/60	_____	_____	_____
h.	9,000	December 14	1/10, EOM	_____	_____	_____

EXERCISE 8.2

Sylvia McMurtry owns Sylvia's Sandwich Shop. Record the following purchase in the purchases journal (page 5) and the return and cash payment in the general journal (page 8).

April 10   Sylvia purchased 40 kg of prime rib for $160 plus 7 percent GST from Restaurant Supplies, Inc.; terms, 2/10, EOM, Invoice 1078.

April 11   Sylvia called the manager of Restaurant Supplies, Inc. to complain about the quality of the prime rib delivered on April 10. She suggested that Restaurant Supplies, Inc. grant a 20 percent allowance. It agreed, and she issued a debit memo for $32 plus 7 percent GST to Restaurant Supplies, Inc.

April 30   Sylvia issued a cheque to Restaurant Supplies, Inc. to pay the balance owed on the April 10 purchase.

EXERCISE 8.3

In Exercise 8.2, you recorded three transactions for Sylvia's Sandwich Shop. They related to a purchase, a return, and a payment. Now record the same transactions for Restaurant Supplies, Inc. as they will relate to the same sale, return, and receipt of payment on April 10, 11, and 30. Use the sales journal (page 5) and the general journal (page 17).

EXERCISE 8.4

Record the following purchase in a purchases journal (page 7) and the cash payments and debit memo in a general journal (page 14).

July 1   Dino purchased 200 kg of whole wheat flour and 75 kg of cracked wheat flour from Nature's Lifestyle Products, an out-of-town vendor. The list price for the whole wheat flour is $50 and the list price for the cracked wheat flour is $26. Nature's Lifestyle allowed a 10 percent trade discount. Seven percent GST is paid on all purchases and the credit terms are 2/15, n/30 Invoice 29420.

July 2   Dino wrote a cheque to United Delivery Service for $15 plus GST for delivering the goods ordered from Nature's Lifestyle Products.

July 2   Dino issued a $50 debit memorandum to Nature's Lifestyle Products because of damaged merchandise.

July 16   Dino sent a cheque to Nature's Lifestyle Products for the amount owed on the July 1 purchase.

EXERCISE 8.5

In Exercise 8.4, you recorded for Dino's Deli four transactions that related to a purchase, a payment for freight, a return, and a payment for the purchase. Now record the same transactions for Nature's Lifestyle Products as they relate to the sale, the return, and the receipt of payment. Use the sales journal (page 7) and a general journal (page 18).

EXERCISE 8.6

Following are T accounts for Plant City that relate to one purchase and the subsequent returns and payment of the invoice. Briefly describe what has occurred on August 10 (two transactions), August 12, and August 20. The posting reference notation CP refers to an entry in the cash payments journal.

Cash			101
	8/10 CP12	53.50	
	8/20 CP12	945.00	

Accounts Payable			210
8/12 GJ9	107.00	8/10 P8	1,070.00
8/20 CP12	963.00		

GST Refundable			220
8/10 P8	70.00	8/12 GJ9	7.00
8/10 CP12	3.50		

Purchases			501
8/10 P8	1,000.00		

Purchases Returns and Allowances			520
		8/12 GJ9	100.00

Purchases Discounts			530
		8/20 CPI2	18.00

Freight In			540
8/10 CP12	50.00		

EXERCISE 8.7

Following is the purchases journal for Plant City for the month of September 20XX and the general journal entries that relate to purchases returns and allowances:

PURCHASES JOURNAL							PAGE 9
DATE	SUPPLIER'S NAME	INV. NO.	POST. REF.	PURCHASES DEBIT	GST REFUNDABLE DEBIT	ACCOUNTS PAYABLE CREDIT	
20XX							
Sept 1	Planters Unlimited	9721		270 00	18 90	288 90	
6	Green Growers	10649		500 00	35 00	535 00	
16	Plant Food, Inc.	4298		190 00	13 30	203 30	
21	Planters Unlimited	9846		940 00	65 80	1005 80	
26	ABC Nursery	17408		1620 00	113 40	1733 40	
30	Green Growers	10841		650 00	45 50	695 50	
	Totals			4170 00	291 90	4461 90	

GENERAL JOURNAL					PAGE 14
DATE	DESCRIPTION	POST REF.	DEBIT	CREDIT	
20XX					
Sept. 2	Accounts Payable—Planters Unlimited		107 00		
	GST Refundable			7 00	
	Purchases Returns and Allowances			100 00	
	To Record Debit Memo 604-C; Invoice 9721				
27	Accounts Payable—ABC Nursery		214 00		
	GST Refundable			14 00	
	Purchases Returns and Allowances			200 00	
	To Record Debit Memo 605-C; Invoice 17408				

Answer the following:

a. Where will the totals of the purchases journal be posted?

b. Including both the purchases journal and the general journal, how many separate postings must be made to the accounts payable subsidiary ledger?

c. How much money must be sent on September 11 to Planters Unlimited in full payment of invoice 9721 (Terms: 1/10, n/30.)

d. What is the last day for payment within the discount period on the September 16 purchase from Plant Food, Inc., invoice 4298? What amount must be remitted to Plant Food, Inc. on that date? (Terms: 1/10, EOM.)

EXERCISE 8.8

In July 20XX, Fashion Jewellery recorded a total of $14,500 in the purchases journal. Purchases returns and allowances for the same period were $275; purchases discounts were $260; and freight charges were $570. Calculate the cost of purchases.

EXERCISE 8.9

Following is the accounts payable subsidiary ledger for Kid's Klothes. Calculate the balance after each transaction and prepare a schedule of accounts payable on August 31, 20XX. In the posting reference column, CP indicates a payment on account recorded in the cash payments journal. The balance in the accounts payable control account on August 31, 20XX is $2,895.

ACCOUNTS PAYABLE SUBSIDIARY LEDGER

All Weather Coats

DATE		EXPLANATION	POST. REF.	DEBIT	CREDIT	BALANCE
20XX						
Aug.	1		P8		500 00	
	3		GJ10	150 00		
	5		P9		700 00	
	11		CP14	350 00		

Canvas Clothes

DATE		EXPLANATION	POST. REF.	DEBIT	CREDIT	BALANCE
20XX						
Aug.	4		P8		250 00	
	9		P8		460 00	
	10		GJ10	100 00		
	14		CP14	150 00		
	20		P8		300 00	

Kiddie Korner

DATE	EXPLANATION	POST. REF.	DEBIT	CREDIT	BALANCE
20XX					
Aug. 7		P8		2 6 0 00	
9		P8		4 1 0 00	
10		P8		5 2 0 00	
17		CP14	2 6 0 00		

Little Men

DATE	EXPLANATION	POST. REF.	DEBIT	CREDIT	BALANCE
20XX					
Aug. 15		P8		3 0 5 00	
16		GJ10	3 0 5 00		
17		P8		4 2 0 00	
27		CP14	4 2 0 00		
31		P8		5 0 5 00	

EXERCISE 8.10

Give the account classification for each of the following accounts. Classifications are asset, contra asset, liability, owner's equity, revenue, contra revenue, cost of goods sold, contra purchases, and expense. Also indicate whether the account has a normal debit or credit balance, and on which financial statement (income statement or balance sheet) the account appears. The first one has been completed as an example.

Account Title	Classification	Normal Debit or Credit Balance	Which Financial Statement?
Example Accumulated Amortization	contra asset	credit	balance sheet
a. Mortgage Payable			
b. Sales			
c. Unearned Revenue			
d. Supplies Expense			
e. GST Payable			
f. Purchases Discounts			
g. Freight In			
h. Amortization Expense			
i. Purchases Returns and Allowances			
j. GST Refundable			
k. Prepaid Advertising			
l. Supplies			
m. Provincial Sales Tax Payable			
n. Merchandise Inventory			
o. Accounts Receivable			
p. Drawing			
q. Sales Returns and Allowances			
r. Prepaid insurance			
s. Sales Discounts			

Problems

PROBLEM 8.1

Carol Ruckle owns a small jewellery store called "Rings 'n Things." Seven percent GST is paid on all purchases. Following are the transactions relating to credit purchases for the month of May 20XX:

May 1	purchased 14K gold chains from M & M Jewellery on invoice 17-420 dated May 1; list price was $3,000 minus a 5 percent trade discount
May 3	purchased 18K rings from Ring Warehouse on invoice 48260 dated May 2; list price was $2,500 minus a trade discount of 10 percent
May 4	issued a $300 debit memo 620-A to Ring Warehouse relating to the May 3 purchase
May 9	purchased pendants from Gold Products Co. on invoice 12411 dated May 7; list price was $1,100 minus a trade discount of 5 percent
May 15	issued a cheque to M & M Jewellery in full payment of the outstanding May 1 balance plus the amount owed on the May 1 invoice 17-420
May 18	purchased earrings from Silver Supplies on invoice 9072-8 dated May 16; list price is $450; no trade discount granted
May 20	issued a $50 debit memo 621-A to Silver Supplies relating to May 18 purchase
May 24	issued a cheque to Ring Warehouse in full payment of the May 3 purchase less the May 4 return
May 26	purchased rings and bracelets from Silver Supplies on invoice 9159-A dated May 25; list price is $570; no trade discount granted
May 28	purchased ankle bracelets from Rich's Supplies on invoice 1049 dated May 27; list price is $400 minus a 10 percent trade discount

Instructions

1. Enter the following account titles, numbers, and May 1 balances into the general ledger and the accounts payable subsidiary ledger.

General Ledger		Accounts Payable Subsidiary Ledger	
101 Cash	$8,700	Gold Products Co.	$ 0
210 Accounts Payable	7,600	M & M Jewellery	2,000
220 GST Refundable	500	Rich's Supplies	4,500
511 Purchases	0	Ring Warehouse	0
515 Purchases Returns and Allowances	0	Silver Supplies	1,100

2. Use page 5 for the purchases journal and page 21 for the general journal.
3. Assuming that the purchase terms are net 30, record purchases on account in the purchases journal, purchases returns and allowances in the general journal, and cash payments in the general journal. (Later on, you will record all payments of cash in the cash payments journal.)
4. Post to the accounts payable ledger immediately after each transaction is journalized.
5. Post to the general ledger first from the purchases journal and then from the general journal.
6. Prepare a schedule of accounts payable and compare the total with the balance in the accounts payable control account on May 31.

PROBLEM 8.2

Curt Nodd owns a western clothing store called "Curt's Country Clothes." Curt pays 7 percent GST on all purchases. Following are the transactions relating to credit purchases for the month of February 20XX.

February 1	purchased jeans from Cowhand Supplies on invoice 7612 dated February 1; list price was $500; terms 2/10, n/30
February 4	purchased leather vests from Leather Products on invoice 1039 dated February 3; list price was $1,200; terms 1/15, n/30
February 8	issued debit memorandum 16-123 to Leather Products in the amount of $300 relating to their invoice 1039
February 9	purchased shirts from Cowhand Supplies on invoice 7690 dated February 7; list price was $490; terms 2/10, n/30
February 11	wrote a cheque to Cowhand Supplies in full payment of February 1 invoice 7612
February 12	purchased coats from Double R Supplies on invoice 6401 dated February 12; list price was $2,500; terms 2/10, EOM
February 13	issued debit memorandum 16-124 to Double R Supplies in the amount of $150 relating to their invoice 6401 dated February 12
February 14	wrote a cheque to Leather Products in full payment of the February 3 invoice 1039, minus the February 8 return
February 24	wrote a cheque to Cowhand Supplies in full payment of invoice 7690 dated February 7
February 26	purchased boots from Ringo Western Wear on invoice 5622 dated February 25; list price was $1,000; terms 1/15, n/60
February 28	wrote a cheque to Double R Supplies in full payment of February 12 invoice 6401, minus the February 13 return

Instructions

1. Enter the following account titles, numbers, and February 1 balances into the general ledger and the accounts payable subsidiary ledger.

	General Ledger		Accounts Payable Subsidiary Ledger	
101	Cash	$7,230	Cowhand Supplies	$3,000
211	Accounts Payable	6,430	Double R Supplies	2,000
220	GST Refundable	420	Leather Products	1,430
511	Purchases	0	Ringo Western Wear	0
515	Purchases Returns and Allowances	0		
520	Purchases Discounts	0		

2. Use page 2 for the purchases journal and page 5 for the general journal.
3. Record purchases on account in the purchases journal, purchases returns and allowances in the general journal, and cash payments (including purchases discounts) in the general journal. (Later on, you will record all payments of cash in the cash payments journal.)
4. Post to the accounts payable ledger immediately after each transaction is journalized.
5. Post to the general ledger first from the purchases journal and then from the general journal.

6. Prepare a schedule of accounts payable and compare the total with the balance in the accounts payable control account on February 28.

PROBLEM 8.3

Following are the transactions relating to credit purchases for Household Supplies for the month of January 20XX. Seven percent GST is paid on all purchases.

January 2   purchased merchandise from A-1 Products on invoice 76403 dated January 2; list price was $5,000 minus a 10 percent trade discount; terms 1/15, n/30

January 2   wrote a cheque to Intra-Province Delivery Co. for $75 plus 7 percent GST relating to A-1 Products' purchase invoice 76403 dated January 2

January 3   purchased merchandise from Zumwalt's on invoice 1240 dated January 3; list price was $4,000; no trade discount allowed; terms 2/10, n/30

January 4   issued debit memo 643-B in the amount of $500 to Zumwalt's relating to its January 3 invoice 1240; merchandise was damaged

January 8   purchased merchandise from Best Products on invoice 6243 dated January 8; list price was $3,500 less trade discount of 10 percent; terms 2/10, EOM

January 8   wrote a cheque to Overnight Delivery Co. for $50 plus 7 percent GST relating to Best Products' invoice 6243

January 12   issued a cheque to Zumwalt's in full payment of its January 3 invoice 1240 less the January 4 return

January 15   purchased merchandise from Klean Homes on invoice 1649 dated January 15; list price was $8,000 less a 5 percent trade discount; terms 1/10, EOM

January 17   issued a cheque to A-1 Products in full payment of its January 2 invoice 76403

January 18   purchased merchandise from Klean Homes on invoice 1701 dated January 18; list price was $2,600 less a 5 percent trade discount; terms 1/10, EOM

January 19   issued debit memo 644-B in the amount of $400 to Klean Homes relating to its January 18 invoice 1701

January 22   purchased merchandise from Zumwalt's on invoice 1322 dated January 22; list price was $3,700; no trade discount allowed; terms 2/10, n/30

January 24   purchased merchandise from Bargain Basement on invoice 16404 dated January 24; list price was $1,500 less a trade discount of 5 percent; terms n/30

January 28   purchased merchandise from A-1 Products on invoice 77106 dated January 28; list price was $4,700 minus a 10 percent trade discount; terms 1/15, n/30

January 28   wrote a cheque to Intra-Province Delivery Co. for $75 plus 7 percent GST relating to A-1 Products' January 28 purchase invoice 77106

Instructions

1. Enter the following account titles, numbers, and January 1 balances into the general ledger and the accounts payable subsidiary ledger:

	General Ledger		Accounts Payable Subsidiary Ledger	
101	Cash	$16,100	A-1 Products	$3,000
211	Accounts Payable	8,900	Bargain Basement	2,500
230	GST Refundable	580	Best Products	0
501	Purchases	0	Klean Homes	2,000
510	Purchases Returns and Allowances	0	Zumwalt's	1,400
520	Purchases Discounts	0		
525	Freight In	0		

2. Use page 31 for the purchases journal and page 49 for the general journal.
3. Record purchases on account in the purchases journal, purchases returns and allowances in the general journal, and cash payments in the general journal. Remember, trade discounts are not recorded on the books of the buyer or the seller.
4. Post to the accounts payable ledger immediately after each transaction is journalized.
5. Post to the general ledger first from the purchases journal and then from the general journal.
6. Prepare a schedule of accounts payable and compare the total with the balance in the accounts payable control account on January 31.

PROBLEM 8.4

Following are the transactions relating to credit sales and credit purchases for Ray's Sewing Centre for the month of October 20XX. Seven percent GST is charged on all sales and paid on all purchases.

October 1	purchased merchandise from Kathy's Sewright Machines on invoice 60213 dated October 1; list price was $5,720; terms n/30
October 1	issued a cheque for $70 plus 7 percent GST to Speedee Delivery Co. for delivering the purchase from Kathy's Sewright Machines
October 5	sold merchandise to B.L. Botham; invoice 8037; list price is $60 plus 8 percent provincial sales tax; terms n/30
October 9	purchased merchandise from G & B Fabrics on invoice 9160 dated October 9; list price was $4,200; terms n/30
October 10	issued debit memorandum 581 in the amount of $1,000 plus 7 percent GST to G & B Fabrics relating to invoice 9160; merchandise was returned
October 14	issued a cheque to Kathy's Sewright Machines in full payment of their October 1 invoice 60213
October 17	sold merchandise to The Sewing Corner; invoice 8038 dated October 17; list price is $980 plus 8 percent provincial sales tax, terms are net 30
October 19	issued credit memorandum 603 for $345 to The Sewing Corner relating to invoice 8038 dated October 17; $300 of the amount relates to the list price of the merchandise, $24 relates to the provincial sales tax, and $21 relates to GST
October 22	received a cheque from B.L. Botham in full payment of invoice 8037 dated October 5
October 25	issued a cheque to G & B Fabrics in full payment of invoice 9160 dated October 9, less the return on October 10

October 27	sold merchandise to The Sewing Corner; invoice 8039; list price is $850 plus 8 percent provincial sales tax; terms n/30
October 28	received a cheque from The Sewing Corner in full payment of invoice 8038 dated October 17, less the return on October 19
October 29	purchased merchandise from Kwik-Sew on invoice 1641 dated October 29; list price was $880; terms n/30
October 29	issued a cheque for $50 plus 7 percent GST to Fast Freight for delivering the purchase from Kwik-Sew on October 29
October 30	issued debit memorandum 582 for $106 plus 7 percent GST to Kwik-Sew related to invoice 1641 of October 29
October 31	received a cheque from The Sewing Corner in full payment of invoice 8039 dated October 27
October 31	issued a cheque to Kwik-Sew in full payment of invoice 1641 dated October 29, less the return on October 30

Instructions

1. Listed below is a partial chart of accounts for Ray's Sewing Centre. In this problem, you are not required to post to the general ledger, but you will use the account titles when journalizing.

Partial Chart of Accounts
101 Cash
110 Accounts Receivable
210 Accounts Payable
220 Provincial Sales Tax Payable
230 GST Payable
240 GST Refundable
405 Sales
410 Sales Returns and Allowances
505 Purchases
520 Purchases Returns and Allowances
525 Freight In

2. Enter the following names into the accounts receivable and accounts payable subsidiary ledgers.

Accounts Receivable Subsidiary Ledger	Accounts Payable Subsidiary Ledger
B.L. Botham	G & B Fabrics
The Sewing Corner	Kathy's Sewright Machines
	Kwik-Sew

3. Record all sales on account in a sales journal designed to account for sales tax; use page 18. Record all purchases on account in a purchases journal; use page 10. Record all other transactions in a general journal; begin numbering with page 28.
   a. Post to the accounts receivable and accounts payable subsidiary ledgers immediately after each transaction.
   b. Total, check that the debit column totals equal the credit column totals, and rule the sales and purchases journals.

PROBLEM 8.5

Following are the transactions relating to credit sales and credit purchases for Wing's Mercantile for the month of June 20XX. On all credit sales, Wing's grants charge customers credit terms of 2/10, n/30. Wing's is not required to collect provincial sales tax, but it must charge 7 percent GST on all sales and pay 7 percent GST on all purchases.

June 1   purchased merchandise from Wilson Supplies on invoice 1643 dated June 1; list price was $500; terms n/30

June 2   sold merchandise to A.G. Rogers, invoice 7029; list price was $120; terms 2/10, n/30

June 3   issued debit memo 603 to Wilson Supplies in the amount of $25 plus 7 percent GST; relates to purchase invoice 1643 of June 1

June 5   sold merchandise on account to B.B. Ulrich, invoice 7030; list price was $250; terms 2/10, n/30

June 6   issued credit memo 804 to B.B. Ulrich in the amount of $50 plus 7 percent GST; relates to sales invoice 7030 of June 5

June 8   purchased merchandise from Moreno's Appliances on invoice 32961 dated June 8; list price was $3,000 less a 5 percent trade discount; terms n/30

June 8   issued a cheque to Van's Delivery for $100 plus 7 percent GST relating to the June 8 purchase invoice 32961 from Moreno's Appliances

June 10   purchased merchandise from Van Riper Wholesale House on invoice 20396 dated June 10; list price was $1,650; terms n/30

June 12   received a cheque from A.G. Rogers in full payment of the June 2 invoice 7029

June 14   sold merchandise on account to P.S. Tolstoy, invoice 7031; list price was $370; terms 2/10, n/30

June 15   received a cheque from B.B. Ulrich in full payment of June 5 invoice 7030, minus the return on June 6

June 18   purchased merchandise from Wilson Supplies on invoice 1699 dated June 18; list price was $800; terms n/30

June 20   issued debit memo 604 to Wilson Supplies in the amount of $100 plus 7 percent GST; relates to purchase invoice 1699 of June 18

June 23   sold merchandise to A.G. Rogers, invoice 7032; list price was $325; terms 2/10, n/30

June 24   issued a cheque to Moreno's Appliances in full payment of June 8 purchase, invoice 32961

June 27   purchased merchandise from Moreno's Appliances on invoice 32998 dated June 27; list price was $1,800 less a 5 percent trade discount; terms n/30

June 27   issued a cheque to Van's Delivery for $75 plus 7 percent GST relating to June 27 purchase from Moreno's Appliances

June 29   received a cheque from P.S. Tolstoy in full payment of June 14 invoice 7031

June 30   paid amount owed to Wilson Supplies for purchases on June 1 invoice 1643 and June 18 invoice 1699 minus the returns on June 3 and June 20

Instructions

1. Following is a partial chart of accounts for Wing's Mercantile. In this problem, you are not required to post to the general ledger, but you may use the account titles when journalizing.

Partial Chart of Accounts

101	Cash
110	Accounts Receivable
210	Accounts Payable
220	GST Payable
230	GST Refundable
405	Sales
410	Sales Discounts
415	Sales Returns and Allowances
545	Purchases
560	Purchases Returns and Allowances
570	Freight In

2. Enter the following names into the accounts receivable and accounts payable subsidiary ledgers.

Accounts Receivable Subsidiary Ledger	Accounts Payable Subsidiary Ledger
A.G. Rogers	Moreno's Appliances
P.S. Tolstoy	Van Riper Wholesale House
B.B. Ulrich	Wilson Supplies

3. Record sales on account in the sales journal; use page 32. Record purchases on account in the purchases journal; use page 19. Record sales returns and allowances, sales discounts, purchases returns and allowances, and cash transactions in the general journal; begin numbering with page 68.
4. Total and rule the sales and purchases journals.
5. Post to the accounts receivable ledger and the accounts payable ledger immediately after each transaction.

CHAPTER 9

The Cash Receipts, Cash Payments, and Combined Cash Journals

LEARNING OBJECTIVES

When you have completed this chapter, you should

1. have a better understanding of accounting terminology.
2. have a basic understanding of internal control.
3. have a basic understanding of cash management.
4. be able to account for credit card sales.
5. be able to record entries directly into the cash receipts, cash payments, and combined cash journals.
6. be able to post from the cash receipts, cash payments, and combined cash journals directly into the general ledger and subsidiary ledgers.
7. be able to calculate and account for interest received and interest paid.

VOCABULARY

collateral	property that is acceptable as security for a loan
combined journal	a journal that combines all special journals into one journal; also called a synoptic journal
expenditure	an amount spent
foreclose	a legal proceeding whereby the lender deprives the borrower of the right to retain ownership of the property pledged as collateral; foreclosure is a legal means available to the lender when the borrower is behind in payments
fraud	a dishonest act in which someone is cheated
interest	a charge for borrowing money
interest formula	the formula used for calculating simple interest: Interest = Principal $\times$ Rate $\times$ Time or $I = P \times R \times T$
justify	to show or prove to be just, right, or fair
maker	the person who borrows money and signs a promissory note
negotiable	capable of being legally transferred from one person to another

payee	the person who lends the money and to whom payments of principal and interest are made
principal	the amount of money borrowed
promissory note	a legal document signed by the borrower (the maker) that specifies the amount borrowed, the interest rate, the time, and the due date of the loan
reimburse	to repay
repossess	to take back possession of
sundry	miscellaneous
valid	sufficiently supported by facts; legally sound

Introduction

The purchases and sales journals and the cash receipts and cash payments journals are designed to meet the needs of the particular company using them and to save the bookkeeper a great deal of time in the journalizing and posting processes. In Chapters Seven and Eight, we learned how Frank Phelps, owner of Phelps Sporting Goods, handled sales and purchases, returns and allowances, Goods and Services Tax, Provincial Sales Tax, freight charges, and discounts. In this chapter, we will see how receipts and payments of cash are handled and how special precautions are taken to safeguard against the theft of cash.

Internal Control

Many management decisions are based in part on data obtained from the accounting records, therefore, accounting information must be accurate. A strong system of internal control will help ensure that this is the case,

Internal control refers to the steps taken by a company to: (1) protect its resources from theft, waste, and inefficiency; (2) ensure that accounting data are accurate; and (3) evaluate employees and departments to determine the level of their performance and whether they are complying with company policy.

One important principle of internal control is that, whenever possible, no one employee should be responsible for handling all phases of a transaction from beginning to end. This is especially true with cash transactions, since cash is particularly susceptible to theft.

Cash Management

Proper management of cash will minimize losses from theft or **fraud** and provide for the accurate accounting of cash. It will ensure that enough cash is on hand for the business to remain solvent and will allow a reserve for emergencies. Proper cash management will also provide for any extra cash to be invested.

For strong internal control of cash, the following guidelines should be observed:

1. Cash receipts should be deposited daily.
2. Cash payments should be made by cheque (not from the cash register or cash on hand unless a petty cash fund has been established).
3. The functions of receiving cash, making cash payments, and accounting for cash should be kept separate.

4. One employee should be designated to verify the amount of every cash payment and to determine whether the payment is **valid**; another employee should be designated to write the cheques. The same person should not be designated to verify the validity and amount of an **expenditure** *and* to write the cheques.

5. Routines for handling cash should be established and carefully followed.

The reasons for these procedures are fairly obvious. When cash is deposited daily, it is not lying around as a temptation. Payments should not be made directly from the cash register, because it may be difficult or too time-consuming to verify amounts and to justify payment; thus, unwarranted cash payments may be made. If more than one person is involved in receiving money at the cash register, the chance of error is greater and the chance of finding the person responsible for the error less likely. The functions of receiving cash should be kept separate from the paying of and the accounting for cash to help prevent employee theft. Such theft is made much more difficult when two or more persons have to be involved. When a specific routine has been established for handling cash, management can more easily check to see that the procedures are being followed.

Sources of Cash Receipts

Cash received is primarily from two sources: (1) cash sales and (2) cash received on account. Retail cash sales are normally recorded on a cash register and should be plainly visible to the customer. If the employee fraudulently records an amount different from that charged the customer, management hopes that the customer will complain and thus provide an outside check on the employees.

The use of prenumbered sales tickets also helps to strengthen internal control. One copy of the sales ticket is given to the customer and one copy is retained at the cash register. All tickets must be accounted for at the end of the day. The total of all the tickets must equal the total cash received that day as verified by the manager or some employee other than the one who received the cash.

Cash Short and Over

Some small errors may be expected in the handling of cash. However, large cash discrepancies, errors made consistently by one employee, or errors that cannot be explained call for immediate attention by management.

Assume that the total amount from the prenumbered sales tickets shows that cash sales on January 11 are $1,240. However, the actual cash in the cash register is only $1,230. (Perhaps the cashier accidentally gave a customer an extra $10 in change.) The general journal entry to record the day's cash sales would be as follows:

GENERAL JOURNAL						PAGE 1	
DATE		DESCRIPTION	POST REF.	DEBIT		CREDIT	
20XX							
Jan.	1	Cash		1 2 3 0 00			
		Cash Short and Over		1 0 00			
		Sales				1 2 4 0 00	
		To Record Cash Sales					

However, if the total of the sales tickets showed sales on January 11 to be $1,240 but the actual cash on hand proved to be $1,250, the general journal entry would appear as follows:

GENERAL JOURNAL					PAGE 1
DATE	DESCRIPTION	POST REF.	DEBIT	CREDIT	
20XX					
Jan. 11	Cash		1 2 5 0 00		
	Cash Short and Over			1 0 00	
	Sales			1 2 4 0 00	
	To Record Cash Sales				

The Cash Short and Over account is debited when cash is short and credited when cash is over. If the Cash Short and Over account has a credit balance at the end of the accounting period, it is shown on the income statement in a special category called "Other Income," which follows the net income from operations section. If Cash Short and Over has a debit balance, it will appear in the category called "Other Expenses."

Credit Card Sales

Credit cards such as MasterCard and Visa are quite common. After credit approval, the customer is issued the card, which may then be used for purchases in most stores. When making a purchase, the customer signs a credit card draft. The customer then owes the money to the company that issued the credit card, not to the store making the sale. The credit card company will reimburse the store owner when she or he deposits the credit card draft in the store's bank account. Eventually, the customer reimburses the credit card company. Some credit card drafts cannot be directly deposited; in these cases, the credit card companies require the store making the sale to mail the sales drafts to them and in return they mail a cheque to the store. When this occurs, the store making the sale debits an account receivable from the credit card company at the time of the sale.

The advantages to the merchant of offering credit card sales are many:

1. Cash from credit sales is received quickly.

2. Costly credit checks are not required, because the customer owes money to the credit card company, not to the store making the sale.

3. No uncollectible accounts expense is incurred with credit card sales.

Bank credit card drafts (such as MasterCard or Visa) may be deposited directly into the merchant's bank account, similar to a deposit of a customer's cheque. At the end of the month, the fee for using the credit card company services is deducted directly from the merchant's chequing account, or it may be deducted when the deposit is made. This fee is debited to an account called Credit Card Discount Expense, which shows on the income statement along with the other expenses.

Assume that Phelps Sporting Goods sells merchandise to Chan Ching on March 1; she presents an Ultra Charge card for payment. The Ultra Charge Company allows the merchant to deposit the sales drafts minus a 4 percent discount directly to the store's bank account. The discount is applied to the sale plus the related taxes. The entry in general journal form to record the sale is:

GENERAL JOURNAL																PAGE 17					
DATE		DESCRIPTION	POST REF.	DEBIT						CREDIT											
20XX																					
Mar.	1	Cash			1	1	0	4	00												
		Credit Card Discount Expense					4	6	00												
		Sales										1	0	0	0	00					
		PST Payable												8	0	00					
		GST Payable												7	0	00					
		To Record Receipt of Cash for Ultra Charge																			
		Sales Less a 4% Discount																			

The Cash Receipts Journal

The cash receipts journal is, like the other special journals, designed to meet the needs of the particular company using it. All cash received by the company is entered in the cash receipts journal, and every entry in it will be a debit to Cash. Thus, the first column (or the last, as the accountant prefers) will be a cash debit column. If the merchant allows nonbank credit card sales, a special debit column for credit card discount expense may be included. A special debit column may also be included to record sales discounts as customers take advantage of credit terms by paying their invoices early. Credit columns may include accounts receivable, sales, GST payable, and PST payable. Other columns may be added if the need arises.

To determine which special columns to use in the cash receipts journal, the accountant must analyze the kinds of transactions that normally occur. For many businesses, the most common examples will be cash received from sales and cash received from customers who are paying on account. These transactions are illustrated in general journal form.

GENERAL JOURNAL																PAGE 1				
DATE		DESCRIPTION	POST REF.	DEBIT						CREDIT										
20XX																				
Jan.	4	Cash				2	3	0	00											
		Sales										2	0	0	00					
		GST Payable											1	4	00					
		PST Payable											1	6	00					
		To Record Cash Sales																		
	5	Cash					5	0	00											
		Accounts Receivable—Jo Suzuki											5	0	00					
		To Record Receipt of Money on Account																		

Less frequent transactions might include a cash investment by the owner, a cash sale of assets, or a receipt of money on an outstanding note.

GENERAL JOURNAL					PAGE 1	
DATE	DESCRIPTION	POST REF.	DEBIT		CREDIT	
20XX						
Jan. 6	Cash		3 0 0 0 00			
	E. LeClair, Capital				3 0 0 0 00	
	To Record Additional Investment					
9	Cash		5 3 5 00			
	GST Payable				3 5 00	
	Office Equipment				5 0 0 00	
	To Record Sale of Equipment at Cost					
11	Cash		7 5 0 00			
	Notes Receivable				7 5 0 00	
	To Record Cash Received as Payment on					
	Note from P. Santos					

As you are aware, each transaction has been recorded separately and must be posted separately, thus occupying a great deal of the bookkeeper's time. Let's look now at how these transactions, and some others as well, would appear in a multicolumn cash receipts journal.

CASH RECEIPTS JOURNAL

DATE		RECEIVED FROM	ACCOUNT CREDITED	POST. REF.	SUNDRY ACCOUNTS CREDIT	ACCOUNTS RECEIVABLE CREDIT	SALES CREDIT	GST PAYABLE CREDIT	PST PAYABLE CREDIT	CREDIT CARD DISCOUNT DEBIT	CASH DEBIT
20XX											
Jan.	4	Cash Sales					20000	1400	1600		23000
Jan.	5	Jo Suzuki		✓		5000					5000
Jan.	6	E. LeClair	E. LeClair, Capital	310	300000						300000
Jan.	9	Sale of OE	Office Equipment	130	50000			3500			53500
Jan.	11	P. Santos	Notes Receivable	120	75000						75000
Jan.	15	Cash Sales					97000	6790	7760	4462	107088
Jan.	17	Cash Sales					55000	3850	4400		63250
Jan.	19	P. Marlborough		✓		8000					8000
Jan.	21	Cash Sales					10000	700	800		11500
Jan.	24	C. Langlois		✓		7500					7500
Jan.	27	Cash Sales					4000	280	320		4600
Jan.	30	Cash Sales					9000	630	720		10350
Jan.	31	Cash Sales					194000	13580	15520	8924	214176
		Totals			425000	20500	389000	30730	31120	13386	882964
					(X)	(110)	(401)	(210)	(215)	(630)	(101)

Analysis of Individual Transactions

January 4   This transaction is to record cash sales plus 7 percent GST and 8 percent PST. Since there are special columns for each of these accounts, only the words *Cash Sales* and the amounts need to be entered. Similar transactions appear on January 15, 17, 21, 27, and 30.

January 5   A $50 cheque was received from Jo Suzuki to apply on her outstanding account. The $50 is entered in the accounts receivable credit column and the cash debit column. Her name is written in the received from column so that the $50 may be posted to the accounts receivable subsidiary ledger. The January 19 and 24 transactions are similar. If the company offers cash discounts for prompt payment, an additional column entitled sales discounts would be added.

January 6   E. LeClair invested an additional $3,000 cash into the business. This entry requires a debit to Cash and a credit to Capital. Because there is no special column for the Capital account, the amount is entered in the **sundry** credit column and in the cash debit column. For all entries in the sundry column, the account title must be written in the account credited column so that the amount can be posted to the correct general ledger account.

January 9   Surplus office equipment was sold at cost plus 7 percent GST. Again, because there is no special column for office equipment, $500 is entered in the sundry credit column, $35 in the GST payable column, and the total of $535 in the cash debit column. The account title, Office Equipment, must be written in the account credited column so that the amount can be posted to the correct general ledger account.

January 11   Paul Santos paid $750 on a non-interest-bearing note. The amount is entered in the sundry credit and the cash debit columns and Notes Receivable is written in the account credited column.

January 15 $1,115.50 (minus a 4 percent credit card discount fee) is received resulting from credit card drafts. Seven percent GST and 8 percent PST were deposited in the bank. The total cash received, $1,070.88, is entered in the cash debit column. The amount of the sale, $970, is entered in the sales credit column, the GST charged of $67.90 is entered in the GST payable credit column, and the sales tax of $77.60 is entered in the PST payable credit column. There is a similar entry on January 31.

Crossfooting the Cash Receipts Journal

When all the entries for the period have been journalized, total each individual column, crossfoot and rule the journal. Crossfooting is shown as follows:

Column	Debit Total	Credit Total
Sundry		$4,250.00
Accounts Receivable		205.00
Sales		3,890.00
GST Payable		307.30
PST Payable		311.20
Credit Card Discount	$ 133.86	
Cash	8,829.64	
Totals	$8,963.50	$8,963.50

Ruling the Cash Receipts Journal

When crossfooting has been completed, a single line is drawn that extends across all account columns beneath the last entry. Beneath the totals, a double line is drawn across the account columns.

Posting the Cash Receipts Journal

At the end of the accounting period, summary posting is performed in three steps:

1. All column totals, except the sundry column total, are posted. As each amount is posted, the account number is written beneath the total in parentheses.

2. Daily postings must be made to the general ledger for the amounts that appear in the sundry column. The account numbers are entered in the posting reference column of the journal after each amount is posted, and CR and the page number are entered in the posting reference column of the general ledger accounts. An X is placed beneath the sundry column total at the end of the period to indicate that the column total is not posted.

3. Daily, each amount entered in the accounts receivable credit column is posted separately to the accounts receivable ledger. A check mark is placed in the posting reference column of the journal after posting has been completed.

The completed journal appears on page 232. T accounts for the general ledger and for the accounts receivable ledger appear as follows:

Partial General Ledger

Cash   101

1/1 Balance 4,500.00	
1/31 CR7 8,829.64	

Accounts Receivable   110

1/1 Balance 6,000.00	1/31 CR7 205.00

Notes Receivable   120

1/1 Balance 2,000.00	1/11 CR7 750.00

Office Equipment   130

1/1 Balance 5,000.00	1/9 CR7 500.00

GST Payable   210

	1/1 Balance 28.00
	1/31 CR7 307.30

PST Payable   215

	1/1 Balance 30.00
	1/31 CR7 311.20

E. LeClair, Capital   310

	1/1 Balance 6,000.00
	1/6 CR7 3,000.00

Sales   401

	1/31 CR7 3,890.00

Credit Card Discount Expense   630

1/31 CR7 133.86	

Partial Accounts Receivable Subsidiary Ledger

P. Marlborough

1/1 Balance 300.00	1/19 CR7 80.00

Jo Suzuki

1/1 Balance 120.00	1/5 CR7 50.00

C. Langlois

1/1 Balance 75.00	1/24 CR7 75.00

Recording Sales Discounts in the Cash Receipts Journal

If it is company policy to allow credit terms, the cash receipts journal should be designed with a special debit column for sales discounts. Assume that on January 10 a sale of $500 plus 7 percent GST and 8 percent PST is made to Joseph Lee and that credit terms are 2/10, n/30. On January 19, Joseph Lee sends a cheque in full payment of the purchase. The transaction is entered in the cash receipts journal shown on page 237.

The Cash Payments Journal

Good internal control of cash requires bills to be paid by cheque, and the cash payments journal is the special journal in which all cheques written are recorded. It may be designed to meet the particular needs of any company; special columns may be added to the journal for those transactions that occur frequently.

In a typical business, cash must be spent in a large number of places, but incoming cash comes from only a few sources. For example, typical transactions where cash is paid out might include payments on account and payments for rent, wages, utilities, advertising, delivery, and phone, while sources of money coming into a business are often limited primarily to cash sales or money received on account.

Some common transactions involving the payment of cash are shown in general journal form on page 236.

If a general journal rather than a cash payments journal is used to record cash transactions, a large number of postings are required. The use of the cash payments journal saves a great deal of time. Transactions involving cash payments are shown in the cash payments journal on page 237.

In the cash payments journal, the cheque number is shown for each transaction. Strong internal control requires that every cheque be accounted for; even when a cheque is voided, it is recorded so that missing cheque numbers can be easily noticed. For every transaction:

1. The date and cheque number are written.
2. The name of the payee is written in the paid to column and the account title to be debited is entered in the account debited column (when there is no special column).
3. The amount to be credited to Cash is entered in the cash credit column.
4. The amount to be debited is entered in the sundry, accounts payable, purchases, or GST refundable columns. The purchases column is used to record cash purchases of merchandise.
5. If a purchase discount is being recorded, it will appear in the column for purchases discounts. Always make sure before you record such a transaction that the two credits (cash and purchases discounts) equal the debit to accounts payable.

Totalling, Crossfooting, and Ruling the Cash Payments Journal

Once all the entries for the period have been completed, each column is totalled and crossfooted. Once the equality of debits and credits has been determined, a single line is drawn across all the amount columns and a double line beneath the last entry is drawn across all columns beneath the totals as shown on page 237.

			GENERAL JOURNAL	POST REF.	DEBIT		CREDIT		PAGE 7
DATE			DESCRIPTION						
20XX									
July	1		Rent Expense		7 5 0 00				
			Cash				7 5 0 00		
			To Record Payment of Rent						
	3		Purchases		8 0 0 00				
			GST Refundable		5 6 00				
			Cash				8 5 6 00		
			To Record Purchase of Merchandise						
	5		Roberta Smith, Drawing		5 0 0 00				
			Cash				5 0 0 00		
			To Record Owner's Withdrawal						
	7		Provincial Sales Tax Payable		1 8 0 00				
			Cash				1 8 0 00		
			To Record Payment of Sales Tax						
	8		Salaries Expense		3 4 0 00				
			Cash				3 4 0 00		
			To Record Payment of Weekly Salaries						
	10		Accounts Payable—Unity Products		1 2 0 0 00				
			Cash				1 1 7 6 00		
			Purchases Discounts				2 4 00		
			To Record Payment in Full of Invoice #76432						

Posting the Cash Payments Journal

The procedure used when posting the cash payments journal is as follows:

1. All debits to Accounts Payable must be posted immediately to the accounts payable ledger. A check mark is placed in the posting reference column of the journal to indicate that posting to the accounts payable ledger has taken place, and CP and the page number are entered in the posting reference column of the ledger.

2. Each entry that is recorded in the sundry column as a debit is posted immediately to the appropriate general ledger account. The ledger account number is written in the posting reference column of the journal, and CP and the page number are written in the posting reference column of the general ledger accounts.

3. The totals of the special columns are posted to the general ledger. The account number in parentheses is placed beneath the column total after posting has taken place, and CP and the page number are written in the posting reference column of the general ledger account. An X must be placed in parentheses beneath the sundry column total to indicate that amounts in that column are posted individually.

CASH RECEIPTS JOURNAL

DATE	RECEIVED FROM	ACCOUNT CREDITED	POST. REF.	SUNDRY ACCOUNTS CREDIT	ACCOUNTS RECEIVABLE CREDIT	SALES CREDIT	GST PAYABLE CREDIT	PST PAYABLE CREDIT	SALES DISCOUNTS DEBIT	CASH DEBIT
20XX										
Jan. 19	Joseph Lee					57500			1000	56500

CASH PAYMENTS JOURNAL

DATE	CHQ. NO.	ACCOUNT DEBITED	POST. REF.	SUNDRY ACCOUNTS DEBIT	ACCOUNTS PAYABLE DEBIT	PURCHASES DEBIT	GST REFUNDABLE DEBIT	PURCHASES DISCOUNT CREDIT	CASH CREDIT
20XX									
July 1	1071	Rent Expense, Star Realty	610	75000					75000
3	1072	Bonland, Ltd.				80000	5600		85600
5	1073	R. Smith, Drawing	310	50000					50000
7	1074	PST Payable	210	18000					18000
8	1075	Salaries Expense	615	34000					34000
10	1076	Unity Products	✓		120000			2400	117600
15	1077	Delivery Expense	630	3000			210		3210
18	1078	Joy Moroni Company	✓		100000			1000	99000
20	1079	R. Smith, Drawing	310	50000					50000
24	1080	Freight In	540	7500			525		8025
27	1081	Kozak Lumber				140000	9800		149800
31	1082	Unity Products	✓		160000			3200	156800
31	1083	Void							
		Totals		237500	380000	220000	16135	6600	847035
				(X)	(201)	(501)	(211)	(511)	(101)

Refer now to the completed cash payments journal on page 237. Pay special attention to the posting reference notations. T accounts for the general ledger and the accounts payable ledger appear as follows:

Partial General Ledger

Cash	101
7/1 Balance 12,500.00	7/31 CP7 8,470.35

Accounts Payable	201
7/31 CP7 3,800.00	7/1 Balance 8,500.00

GST Refundable	211
7/31 CP7 161.35	

Provincial Sales Tax Payable	210
7/7 CP7 180.00	7/1 Balance 180.00

Roberta Smith, Drawing	310
7/5 CP7 500.00	
7/20 CP7 500.00	

Purchases	501
7/31 CP7 2200.00	

Purchases Discount	511
	7/31 CP7 66.00

Freight in	540
7/24 CP7 75.00	

Rent Expense	610
7/1 CP7 750.00	

Salaries Expense	615
7/8 CP7 340.00	

Delivery Expense	630
7/15 CP7 30.00	

Partial Accounts Payable Subsidiary Ledger

Joy Moroni Company	
7/18 CP7 1,000	7/1 Balance 1,000

Unity Products	
7/11 CP7 1,200	7/1 Balance 2,800
7/31 CP7 1,600	

The Combined Cash Journal

Specialized journals like the ones described make it possible for several people to work on the accounting records at the same time and are used by firms that have a relatively large number of repetitive transactions. However, in a small business where all transactions are recorded by one person, a combined journal may be used. The **combined journal** combines all of the special journals into one journal and is sometimes referred to as a synoptic journal.

A combined journal is usually designed to meet the needs of the company using it. The one illustrated in this text has 12 amount columns, but additional columns can be added if there are a sufficient number of each kind of transaction to warrant posting the amounts as a column total.

CASH DEBIT	CASH CREDIT	GST REFUNDABLE DEBIT	GST PAYABLE CREDIT	DATE	CHEQUE NUMBER	ACCOUNT TITLES AND EXPLANATIONS
				COMBINED CASH JOURNAL		
			1 4 00	July 1		Davey Wilkes
			(3 50	3		Sales Returns & Allowances, D. Wilkes
		4 9 00		4		Marlwood Fashions, Inv. 4206, 2/10, n/30
		(1 4 00		6		Purchases Returns & Allowances, Marlwood
	2 8 5 00			8	147	Utilities Expense
1 6 0 50				12		Davey Wilkes
	5 2 5 00			14	148	Marlwood Fashions, Purchases Discounts
8 5 6 00			5 6 00	15		Cash Sales
			3 5 00	17		Davey Wilkes
		4 2 00		18		Marlwood Fashions, Invoice 5309, 2/10, n/30
1 0 1 6 50	8 1 0 00	7 7 00	1 0 1 50			
(101)	(101)	(220)	(215)			

Analysis of Individual Transactions

Following is an explanation of the entries included in the combined cash journal.

July 1   Sold $200 in merchandise plus 7 percent GST on account to Davey Wilkes on sales invoice 307. The sale is recorded by entering the customer's name in the account titles and explanations column and the invoice number in the invoice number column. The amount of the sale, $200, is recorded in the sales credit column, and the GST of $14 ($200 × .07) is recorded in the GST payable column. The full amount owing by the customer is recorded in the accounts receivable debit column ($200 + $14 = $214). The entry on July 17 is similar.

July 3   Issued credit memorandum 02-75 to Davey Wilkes for $50 plus 7 percent GST for merchandise returned. This sales return will be recorded by entering the account title Sales Returns and Allowances and the customer's name in the account titles and explanations column. The amount of the sales return, $50, is entered in the sundry debit column and the 7 percent GST ($3.50) is entered in the GST Payable credit column in brackets to indicate it is a debit to GST Payable. Some students ask why this amount is not entered as a debit to GST Refundable. It is because that account is used to record only GST paid by the merchant when a purchase is made. Note that the amount of the return plus the GST ($53.50) is entered in the accounts receivable credit column.

July 4   Purchased merchandise for resale from Marlwood Fashions for $700 plus 7 percent GST on invoice 4206; terms 2/10, n/30. This purchase of merchandise is recorded by entering the supplier's name, invoice number, and terms in the account titles and explanations column. The amount of the purchase is recorded in the purchases column, and the 7 percent GST is recorded in the GST refundable column. The total amount owing is entered in the accounts payable credit column. The entry on July 18 is similar.

July 6   Issued debit memorandum 123-45 to Marlwood Fashions for $200 plus 7 percent GST for merchandise returned. This purchase return is recorded by entering the account title Purchases Returns and Allowances and the supplier's name in the account titles and explanations column. The amount of the purchase return of $200 is entered in the sundry credit column and

POST. REF.	SUNDRY DEBIT	SUNDRY CREDIT	ACCOUNTS RECEIVABLE		ACCOUNTS PAYABLE		PURCHASES DEBIT	SALES CREDIT	INVOICE NUMBER
			DEBIT	CREDIT	DEBIT	CREDIT			
✓			214 00					200 00	307
410	50 00			53 50					
✓						749 00	700 00		
510		200 00			214 00				
630	285 00								
✓				160 50					
✓/520		10 00			535 00				
								800 00	
✓			535 00					500 00	308
✓						642 00	600 00		
	335 00	210 00	749 00	214 00	749 00	1391 00	1300 00	1500 00	
	(X)	(X)	(110)	(110)	(210)	(210)	(500)	(401)	

PAGE 17

the 7 percent GST ($14) is entered in the GST Refundable column in brackets to indicate it is a credit to GST Refundable. It would not be appropriate to record this amount in the GST Payable column because GST Payable is used to record taxes paid by the customer. Note that the amount of the return plus the GST ($214) is entered in the accounts payable debit column.

July 8   Issued cheque 147 for $285 to Bell Canada in payment of the telephone bill. This transaction is recorded by entering the cheque number in the cheque number column, and then the account title Utilities Expense in the account titles and explanations column. The $285 is recorded in the sundry debit column and in the cash credit column.

July 12   Received a cheque from Davey Wilkes in full payment of his July 1 invoice less the sales return of July 3. The receipt of the cheque will be recorded first by entering the customer's name in the account titles and explanations column and then by entering the amount of the payment, $160.50, in the cash debit column and the accounts receivable credit column.

July 14   Issued cheque 148 for $525 to Marlwood Fashions in full payment of its July 4 invoice less the purchase return of July 6. This transaction is recorded by entering the supplier's name and the account title Purchases Discounts in the account titles and explanations column. The full amount outstanding $535 ($700 – $200 =$500 + $35 GST) will be entered in the accounts payable debit column; the purchase discount of $10 ($500 × .02) will be entered in the sundry credit column; and the amount of the cheque, $525, will be entered in the cash credit column.

July 15   Recorded cash sales for the first half of the month totalling $800 plus 7 percent GST. Cash sales are entered by writing the words "Cash Sales" in the account titles and explanations column. The full amount of cash, $856, is entered in the cash debit column; the amount of the cash sales in entered in the sales column; the 7 percent GST ($800 × .07 = $56) is entered in the GST Payable column.

July 17   Sold merchandise on account to Davey Wilkes on sales invoice 308; $500 plus 7 percent GST.

July 18   Purchased merchandise for resale from Marlwood Fashions for $600 plus 7 percent GST on invoice 5309; terms 2/10, n/30.

Rules for Recording Transactions in the Combined Journal

Note the following rules for recording transactions in and posting from a combined journal:

1. The date is always entered first for every transaction.
2. If an amount is to be entered in the sundry columns, the accounts receivable columns, or the accounts payable columns, the account title or the person's name must be entered in the account titles and explanations column.
3. Any amounts entered in the sundry columns are posted as individual amounts to the accounts named and the column totals are not posted.
4. Any amounts entered in the accounts receivable and accounts payable columns are posted as individual amounts to the subsidiary ledger accounts, and the column totals are posted to the control accounts.
5. All other amounts entered in the journal are posted as column totals.

Crossfooting, Ruling, and Posting the Combined Cash Journal

Total and crossfoot the journal as usual. When a figure is entered in brackets in a column, that figure must be subtracted as it represents a balance opposite the other figures in the column.

Post to the accounts receivable and accounts payable ledgers immediately after each transaction. Also post immediately all amounts entered in the sundry columns. CJ and the page number are entered in the posting reference columns of the ledgers. Post all column totals (except Sundry) and place account numbers beneath the totals.

The T accounts relating to the combined journal after posting has been completed appear as follows:

Partial General Ledger

Cash			101	Purchases		500
7/31 CJ 17	1,016.50	7/31 CJ17	810.00	7/31 CJ17 1,300.00		

Accounts Receivable			110	Purchases Returns and Allowances		510
7/31 CJ17	749.00	7/31 CJ17	214.00		7/6 CJ17	200.00

Accounts Payable			210	Purchases Discounts		520
7/31 CJ17	749.00	7/31 CJ17	1,391.00		7/14 CJ17	10.00

GST Payable			215	Utilities Expense		630
		7/31 CJ17	101.50	7/8 CJ17 285.00		

GST Refundable		220
7/31 CJ17	77.00	

Sales			401
		7/31 CJ17	1,500.00

Sales Returns and Allowances		410
7/3 CJ17	50.00	

Partial Accounts Receivable Subsidiary Ledger			**Partial Accounts Payable Subsidiary Ledger**	

Davey Wilkes

7/1 CJ17	214.00	7/3 CJ17	53.50
7/17 CJ17	535.00	7/12 CJ17	160.50

Marlwood Fashions

7/6 CJ17	214.00	7/4 CJ17	749.00
7/14 CJ17	535.00	7/18 CJ17	642.00

Recording Interest Paid

Major purchases of equipment, inventory, vehicles, or other assets are often paid for partially through the issuance of a note. A note is, like a cheque, a **negotiable** instrument; that is, it can be bought and sold. Usually, when a note is issued by the seller, the item sold is held as **collateral** for the note; in other words, title does not fully pass to the buyer until the note is paid in full. The seller normally retains the option to **repossess** the merchandise sold (or to **foreclose** on property) if the terms of the note are not met.

Assume, for example, that Valley Restaurant Supply sold booths and tables to Tony's Pizza on July 1, 20XX at a total cost of $24,000 plus 7 percent GST. Tony paid $14,000 cash as a down payment and signed a note for the other $11,680. The **interest** rate agreed on was 12 percent per year. Tony agreed to pay the full amount of the note and the interest at the end of one year's time. Tony signed the following **promissory note**.

$11,680.00	Bedford, N.S.	July 1, 20XX

One year after date ___I___ promise to pay

to the order of _____Valley Restaurant Supply_____

_____Eleven Thousand Six Hundred and Eighty -------------- 00/100 dollars

at _____Bank of Nova Scotia, Bedford, N.S._____

Value received. Interest at ___12%___

No. ___502___   Due ___July 1, 20XX___

Tony Agostini

Tony's Pizza

Tony Agostini is the borrower, or the **maker**, of the note; he signs the note and is required to pay back the **principal** plus the interest. Valley Restaurant Supply is referred to as the **payee** of the note and is the firm to which payment will be made. The stated interest rate is always to be regarded as an annual rate unless otherwise specified.

A purchase such as Tony's, with a cash down payment and the signing of a note, could be recorded in the general journal as follows:

GENERAL JOURNAL				PAGE 18	
DATE	DESCRIPTION	POST REF.	DEBIT	CREDIT
20XX					
July 1	Furniture		2 4 0 0 0 00	
	GST Refundable		1 6 8 0 00	
	Cash			1 4 0 0 0 00
	Notes Payable			1 1 6 8 0 00
	To Record Purchase of Booths and Tables			
	from Valley Restaurant Supply; Signed a			
	One-Year, 12% Note			

Because all payments of cash should be recorded in the cash payments journal, the entry would best be recorded as shown below.

CASH PAYMENTS JOURNAL							PAGE 7			
DATE	CHQ. NO.	PAID TO	ACCOUNT DEBITED	POST. REF.	SUNDRY ACCOUNTS DEBIT	ACCOUNTS PAYABLE DEBIT	GST REFUNDABLE DEBIT	PURCHASES DISCOUNT CREDIT	CASH CREDIT
20XX									
July 1	1768	Valley Restaurant Supply	Furniture		24000 00		1680 00		14000 00
			Notes Payable		(11680 00)				

The debit to Furniture for $24,000 is entered as usual in the sundry column; the GST Refundable of $1,680 is entered in the GST Refundable debit column; and the $14,000 credit to Cash is entered in the cash credit column. Since there is no special credit column for Notes Payable or a sundry credit column, the $11,680 credit to Notes Payable is entered in brackets in the sundry debit column. The brackets indicate that the $11,680 is to be posted with a balance opposite the one indicated in the column head, or, in this case, that the $11,680 is a *credit* rather than a *debit*.

Calculation of Interest

At the end of the year, when Tony pays the $11,680 plus interest to Valley Restaurant Supply, the entry will be recorded in the cash payments journal. The ordinary simple interest on the note is calculated as follows:

Interest Formula

$$\text{Interest} = \text{Principal} \times \text{Rate} \times \text{Time}$$
$$I = P \times R \times T$$

$$\text{where principal} = \text{amount borrowed}$$
$$\text{rate} = \text{interest rate}$$
$$\text{time} = \text{length of time for which money is kept}$$

Interest Calculation

1. Change the interest rate into a decimal by moving the decimal point two places to the left:

$$12\% = 12. = .12$$

2. Multiply:

$$I = P \times R \times T$$
$$I = \$11,680 \times .12 \times 1 \ (1 \ year)$$
$$I = \$1,401.60$$

Note: 12 percent means 12 hundredths and may be expressed in decimal form as .12 or in fraction form as 12/100.

Two or more lines may be used when recording an entry in the cash payments journal. Interest Expense is treated like any other expense account, except that it is shown at the bottom of the income statement in a category called Other Expenses. ("Other" refers to expenses not normally classified as regular operating expenses.)

CASH PAYMENTS JOURNAL									PAGE 7
DATE	CHQ. NO.	PAID TO	ACCOUNT DEBITED	POST. REF.	SUNDRY ACCOUNTS DEBIT	ACCOUNTS PAYABLE DEBIT	GST REFUNDABLE DEBIT	PURCHASES DISCOUNT CREDIT	CASH CREDIT
20XX									
July 1	2691	Valley Restaurant Supply	Notes Payable		11680 00				13081 60
			Interest Expense		1401 60				

Recording Interest Received

The transaction between Tony Agostini and Valley Restaurant Supply may be used to illustrate the receipt of interest as well as the payment of interest. The following shows how the transaction would be handled on the books of Valley Restaurant Supply. The original sale of the booths and tables to Tony Agostini could be recorded in the general journal as follows:

GENERAL JOURNAL				PAGE 9
DATE	DESCRIPTION	POST REF.	DEBIT	CREDIT
20XX				
July 1	Notes Receivable		11680 00	
	Cash		1400 00	
	Sales			24000 00
	GST Payable			1680 00
	To Record Sale of Booths and Tables to			
	Tony's Pizza; Issued a One-Year, 12% Note			

However, the transaction should be recorded in a cash receipts journal. Note that there is no special column for provincial sales tax payable because Valley Restaurant Supply is a wholesaler and is not required to charge PST. Also, because there is no sundry debit column in the cash receipts journal, the $11,080 debit to Notes Receivable is entered in brackets in the sundry credit column to indicate that the amount is to be posted as a debit.

CASH RECEIPTS JOURNAL								PAGE 7
DATE	RECEIVED FROM	ACCOUNT CREDITED	POST. REF.	SUNDRY ACCOUNTS CREDIT	ACCOUNTS RECEIVABLE CREDIT	SALES CREDIT	GST PAYABLE CREDIT	CASH DEBIT
20XX								
July 1	Tony Agostini	Notes Receivable		(1 168000)		2400000	168000	1400000

When, one year later, Valley Restaurant Supply receives the cheque from Tony's Pizza, it will be recorded in the cash receipts journal as follows:

CASH RECEIPTS JOURNAL								PAGE 7
DATE	RECEIVED FROM	ACCOUNT CREDITED	POST. REF.	SUNDRY ACCOUNTS CREDIT	ACCOUNTS RECEIVABLE CREDIT	SALES CREDIT	GST PAYABLE CREDIT	CASH DEBIT
20XX								
July 1	Tony Agostini	Notes Receivable		1168000				1308160
		Interest Income		140160				

Again, two or more lines may be used for the entry. Interest Income is a miscellaneous income item and is shown at the bottom of the income statement under Other Income.

Other Income and Other Expense on the Income Statement

The net income figure with which you are already familiar refers to income from operations and is that regular operating income that results from the company's selling its product or service. The net operating income figure is compared and analyzed from period to period, and net income must be compared from the same source. Therefore, income items that are irregular are listed at the bottom of the income statement as an addition after net income from operations has been calculated. Other income might result from interest received, a credit balance in the Cash Short and Over account, Rent income (resulting when the business rents out an unused portion of the premises), or a gain incurred on the sale or disposition of an asset.

Other expense items are those expenses not normally incurred in regular operations and may include interest expense or a debit balance in the Cash Short and Over account. A portion of an income statement, with sections for other income and other expense, is shown here.

Toy Warehouse Income Statement For Month Ended July 31, 20XX					
Revenue					
Sales			$ 7 5 0 0 0 00		
Less: Sales Returns and Allowances	$ 4 0 0 0 00				
Sales Discounts	1 3 0 0 00		5 3 0 0 00		
Net Sales				$ 6 9 7 0 0 00	
Net Income from Operations				$ 7 0 0 0 00	
Other Income					
Interest Income		$ 8 0 0 00			
Miscellaneous Income		2 0 0 00			
Total Other Income		1 0 0 0 00			
Other Expense					
Interest Expense		3 5 0 00		6 5 0 00	
Net Income				$ 7 6 5 0 00	

Miscellaneous Ordinary Interest Calculations

When money is borrowed for a period of time other than one year, the time portion of the interest formula will not be 1 (for one year). If, for example, money is borrowed for two years, the ordinary simple interest will be twice as much as if borrowed for one year.

Example $10,000 is borrowed at 9 percent for two years.

Formula: $I = P \times R \times T$
$I = \$10,000 \times 9\% \times 2$
$I = \$10,000 \times .09 \times 2$
$I = \$1,800$

If money is borrowed for half a year, the ordinary simple interest will be one-half of what it would be for a whole year. When the time is expressed in months, a fraction is used in the formula to express it. The numerator is the number of months for which the money is borrowed and the denominator is 12 (for one year).

Example $10,000 is borrowed at 12 percent for six months.

Formula: $I = P \times R \times T$
$I = \$10,000 \times .12 \times 6/12$
$I = \$600$

or, on a calculator,

$I = P \times R \times T$
$I = \$10,000 \times .12 \times .5$
(.5 is one-half or 6/12 of a year)
$I = \$600$

When money is borrowed for a specific number of days, a fraction is also used in the formula to express the time. The numerator will be the number of days for which the money is borrowed and the denominator will be 365.

Example $10,000 is borrowed at 12 percent for 60 days.

Formula: $I = P \times R \times T$
$I = 10,000 \times .12 \times 60/365$
$I = \$197.26$

Summary

A strong system of internal control will help a business protect its resources from theft, waste, and inefficiency; ensure that accounting data are accurate; and evaluate employees and departments to determine their level of performance. A strong system of internal control also provides a basis for regularly evaluating employees and departments and establishes a routine for the handling and management of cash.

Cash is received primarily from cash sales and from customers who are paying on account. Many stores, in addition, allow credit card sales; the store receives from the bank an amount equal to the total credit card sales minus a fee for the service. The amount of the fee is debited to an account called credit card discount expense.

All cash received is recorded in the cash receipts journal, and all cheques written are recorded in the cash payments journal. Every entry in the cash receipts journal is a debit to Cash, and every entry in the cash payments journal is a credit to Cash. Special columns are included in the journals as required. Immediate postings are required to the accounts receivable and accounts payable subsidiary ledgers, and daily postings are required from the sundry columns of the cash receipts and cash payments journals. At the end of the accounting period, the journals are crossfooted and ruled before summary posting is performed.

The combined cash journal is used primarily by professionals or small business owners. The process for journalizing and posting from the combined cash journal is the same as for the cash receipts and cash payments journals.

Sometimes merchandise or services are sold by accepting a promissory note for a portion or all that is owed. The maker of the note normally agrees to pay back the principal and interest within a certain time. The formula for calculating interest is: Interest = Principal × Rate × Time ($I = P \times R \times T$). Interest rates are normally expressed in terms of a year. Interest paid is recorded in the cash payments journal, and interest received is recorded in the cash receipts journal.

Vocabulary Review

Here is a list of the words and terms for this chapter:

collateral	interest
combined journal	interest formula
expenditure	justify
foreclose	maker
fraud	negotiable

payee

principal

promissory note

reimburse

repossess

sundry

valid

Fill in the blank with the correct word or term from the list.

1. A legal document that shows the amount borrowed, the interest rate, and the due date of the money borrowed and that is signed by the maker is called a/an _____.

2. A person who borrows money and who signs a note is called the _____ of the note.

3. The lender is called the _____ of the note.

4. The amount of money borrowed is called the _____.

5. An amount spent is a/an _____.

6. Security that is given for a loan is called _____.

7. A dishonest act in which someone is cheated is called _____.

8. The _____ is I = P × R × T.

9. To show or prove that something is right is to _____.

10. To take back possession of is to _____.

11. Another word for miscellaneous is _____.

12. When a borrower is behind in payments, the lender may choose to _____ on the property, thus depriving the borrower of ownership rights.

13. A charge made for the use of money is called _____.

14. A document that may be transferred from one party to another is said to be _____.

15. To repay is to _____.

16. Having facts to support something makes it _____.

17. A/An _____ is a journal that combines all special journals into one journal; sometimes called a synoptic journal.

Match the words and terms on the left with the definitions on the right.

18. collateral		**a.**	to take back possession of
19. combined journal		**b.**	the lender
20. expenditure		**c.**	I = P × R × T
21. foreclose		**d.**	a dishonest act to deceive someone
22. fraud		**e.**	the amount borrowed
23. interest		**f.**	miscellaneous
24. interest formula		**g.**	to repay
25. justify		**h.**	transferable from one person or party to another
26. maker		**i.**	the borrower
27. negotiable		**j.**	an amount spent
28. payee		**k.**	security for a loan
29. principal		**l.**	an amount charged for borrowing money

30. promissory note

31. reimburse

32. repossess

33. sundry

34. valid

m. legally sound because of facts or evidence

n. a legal document indicating an amount of money borrowed, the interest rate, and the time; it is signed by the maker

o. a journal that combines all special journals

p. to prove to be right or fair

q. to deprive a borrower of her of his ownership rights

Exercises

EXERCISE 9.1

Record the following in general journal form for Handy Hardware for the month of October 20XX. Handy Hardware is required to collect 8 percent PST and 7 percent GST. Account titles required are Cash, Accounts Receivable, PST Payable, GST Payable, Sales, and Credit Card Discount Expense. Use journal page 14.

October 1   sold merchandise for cash to Rick Trevino, $90 plus 7 percent GST and 8 percent PST; invoice 143-L

October 4   sold merchandise for cash to Sandra Butler for $120 plus 7 percent GST and 8 percent PST; invoice 172-L

October 9 $658.95 is deposited into the bank for sales to customers who used their credit cards; the $658.95 represents charge sales for the first week of October totalling $600 plus 7 percent GST and 8 percent PST, minus a $4^1/_2$ percent fee ($31.05).

EXERCISE 9.2

Record the following in general journal form for Noah's Boat Supplies for the month of May 20XX. Noah is not required to collect provincial sales tax, but he must collect and pay 7 percent GST. Account titles required are Cash, Accounts Receivable, Accounts Payable, GST Payable, GST Refundable, Sales, Sales Returns and Allowances, Sales Discounts, Purchases, Purchases Returns and Allowances, and Purchases Discounts. Use journal page 6.

May 1   sold merchandise for $500 plus 7 percent GST to Flip Olsen; terms 1/10, n/30; invoice 4269-A.

May 2   issued credit memorandum 643 to Flip Olsen in the amount of $50 plus 7 percent GST; relates to invoice 4269-A dated May 1

May 4   purchased merchandise for $850 plus 7 percent GST from Water World; terms 2/10, n/60; invoice 72643

May 5   issued debit memo 916 to Water World in the amount of $100 plus 7 percent GST; relates to invoice 72643 dated May 4

May 11   received a cheque from Flip Olsen in full payment of invoice 4269-A, minus the May 2 return

May 14   sent cheque 1688 to Water World in full payment of its invoice 72643, minus the May 5 return

EXERCISE 9.3

Calculate the ordinary simple interest for the following. Round your answers to the nearest penny where necessary.

	Interest	=	Principal	×	Rate	×	Time
a.	_____	=	$ 5,000	×	14%	×	1 year
b.	_____	=	3,000	×	8	×	3 months
c.	_____	=	8,500	×	10	×	6 months
d.	_____	=	12,000	×	9	×	3 months
e.	_____	=	1,000	×	7	×	60 days
f.	_____	=	2,400	×	11	×	30 days
g.	_____	=	10,000	×	6	×	1 month
h.	_____	=	25,000	×	12	×	5 months
i.	_____	=	50,000	×	10	×	15 days
j.	_____	=	14,000	×	9	×	6 months

EXERCISE 9.4

Following are some of the account balances for Roger's Antiques on June 30, 20XX. Determine (a) the amount of net sales and (b) the cost of purchases.

Sales	$12,000
Purchases	7,500
Purchases Discounts	75
Sales Discounts	180
Freight In	500
Sales Returns and Allowances	370
Purchases Returns and Allowances	180
Delivery Expense	275

EXERCISE 9.5

Prepare the following entries in general journal form for Atlantic Marina. Account titles required are Cash, Notes Payable, and Interest Expense. Use journal page 2.

February 1   borrowed $5,000 from Commonwealth Bank, signed a six-month, 11 percent note payable; record the receipt of the cash

August 1   wrote a cheque to Commonwealth Bank in full payment of the February 1 note plus the 11 percent interest

EXERCISE 9.6

Prepare the following entries in general journal form for Wanda's Wholesale Jewellery. Account titles required are Cash, Notes Receivable, GST Payable, Sales, and Interest Income. Use journal page 2.

September 1   sold merchandise for $7,000 plus 7 percent GST to Gold House; accepted a three-month, 10 percent note in payment

December 1   received a cheque from Gold House in full payment of the September 1 note plus interest

EXERCISE 9.7

At the end of the day on March 18, Geri's Jeans had total cash sales of $590 plus 7 percent GST and 8 percent PST as evidenced by the cash register totals. However, the actual cash on hand was only $673.50. In general journal form, prepare the entry to record the cash sales on March 18. Account titles required are Cash, PST Payable, GST Payable, Sales, and Cash Short and Over. Use journal page 9.

EXERCISE 9.8

1. Record the following cash sales in a general journal (page 10) for Geri's Jeans for the first week in March. (You may omit explanations.)
2. Determine whether the Cash Short and Over account has a debit or credit balance and the amount of the balance.

Date	Sales	Actual Cash on Hand	Cash Short and (Over)
March 1	$2,754	$2,774	($20)
March 2	2,329	2,334	($5)
March 3	1,645	1,635	$10
March 4	1,520	1,519	$1
March 5	2,116	2,166	($50)
March 6	2,904	2,886	$18
March 7	1,592	1,590	$2

EXERCISE 9.9

After looking over the following different kinds of transactions, determine into which journal each should be recorded. Identify the journals by their posting reference notations: sales journal, S; purchases journal, P; cash receipts journal, CR; cash payments journal, CP; and general journal, GJ.

	Type of Transaction	Which Journal?
a.	paid monthly telephone bill	_____
b.	purchase of merchandise for resale on account	_____
c.	receipt of cash from a customer who is paying on account	_____
d.	purchase of furniture on account	_____
e.	sale of merchandise on account	_____
f.	owner withdrew cash for personal use	_____
g.	made payment to a creditor	_____
h.	sold extra item of office equipment; will receive payment within 90 days	_____
i.	owner invested additional cash into the business	_____
j.	adjusting entries	_____
k.	purchase of office equipment for cash	_____
l.	borrowed money from a bank	_____
m.	issued credit memorandum to a customer to whom merchandise was originally sold on account	_____
n.	made payment on a loan, plus interest	_____
o.	cash purchase of merchandise for resale	_____
p.	recorded cash sales plus 6 percent sales tax	_____
q.	received payment less a 2 percent discount from a customer to whom merchandise was sold earlier	_____
r.	owner invested personal property into the business	_____
s.	closing entries	_____
t.	issued a debit memorandum to creditor from whom merchandise was purchased on account	_____

Problems

PROBLEM 9.1

At her retail shop, Suzie Niessen sells gifts for cash and on account. She also allows credit card sales through the Horizon Credit Card Company. Seven percent GST is collected on all sales. Following are a partial chart of accounts and the transactions relating to cash received for the month of October 20XX.

Partial Chart of Accounts	
101	Cash
110	Accounts Receivable
120	Notes Receivable
130	Office Equipment
220	GST Payable
301	Suzie Niessen, Capital
401	Sales
410	Interest Income
610	Credit Card Discount Expense

Transactions

October 1	cash sales, $175 plus 7 percent GST
October 4	received a cheque for $189 from Ron King to apply on his account
October 8	deposited some credit card sales drafts in the bank; the sales totalled $1,500 plus 7 percent GST; the credit card discount charged is $71
October 12	cash sales, $290 plus 7 percent GST
October 15	Suzie Niessen invested an additional $6,000 in the business
October 17	Suzie decided to sell to Al Torino an extra item of office equipment for $5,500 cash, plus 7 percent GST; this was her original cost for the equipment
October 20	received a cheque for $52.50 from Barbara Goode to apply on her account
October 24	deposited some credit card sales drafts in the bank; the sales totalled $2,500 plus 7 percent GST; the credit card discount charged is $118
October 27	cash sales, $700 plus 7 percent GST
October 31	received a cheque from Andrew Pate for $1,200; this represents full payment of his $1,000 outstanding note of a year ago, plus interest

Instructions

1. Journalize the transactions in a cash receipts journal. Use page 10.
2. Total, crossfoot, and rule the journal.

PROBLEM 9.2

Wayne Werner owns a retail store called Artists' Supply Shop. Wayne takes advantage of all purchases discounts offered. Following are a partial chart of accounts and the transactions relating to cash payments for the month of April 20XX.

	Partial Chart of Accounts
101	Cash
220	Accounts Payable
230	Notes Payable
235	GST Refundable
240	Payroll Taxes Payable
320	Wayne Werner, Drawing
501	Purchases
510	Purchases Discount
520	Freight In
605	Rent Expense
610	Utilities Expense
620	Insurance Expense
630	Interest Expense

Transactions

April 1	wrote cheque 5203 to Star Realty for $650 for April rent
April 3	wrote cheque 5204 for $125 plus 7 percent GST to Kwik Delivery when it delivered an out-of-town purchase
April 6	Wayne Werner withdrew $500 for personal use; cheque 5205
April 8	wrote cheque 5206 for $175 to Canada Customs and Revenue Agency for payroll taxes due
April 11	wrote cheque 5207 for $1,890 to Sandberg's Paints in payment of its invoice 1643-2 for $1,800 plus 7 percent GST, less a 2 percent discount
April 12	wrote cheque 5208 to Creative Concepts for $870 plus 7 percent GST for purchase of art supplies for resale. (Note: this is a cash purchase of merchandise for resale.)
April 15	wrote cheque 5209 for $140 to Ontario Hydro for electricity bill
April 19	wrote cheque 5210 for $1,272 to Art Corner in payment of its invoice 469-20 for $1,200 plus 7 percent GST, less a 1 percent discount
April 22	wrote cheque 5211 to Bell Canada for $92 in payment of telephone bill
April 23	wrote cheque 5212 to the Queen's Colours for $580 plus 7 percent GST for purchase of art supplies for resale
April 25	wrote cheque 5213 to Royal Bank for $525 in full payment of a $500 note plus interest
April 28	Wayne Werner withdrew $500 for personal use; cheque 5214
April 30	wrote cheque 5215 for $525 to Sandberg's Paints in payment of its invoice 1740-2 for $500 plus 7 percent GST, less a 2 percent discount
April 30	wrote cheque 5216 to Creative Concepts for $642 plus 7 percent GST for purchase of art supplies for resale (note: this is a cash purchase of merchandise for resale)

Instructions

1. Journalize the transactions in a cash payments journal. Use page 4.
2. Total, crossfoot, and rule the journal.

PROBLEM 9.3

Grace O'Brien owns a retail store called The Book Depot. Grace sells merchandise for cash and on account and also accepts credit card sales through the Wonder Charge Company. Grace takes advantage of all purchases discounts by paying within the discount period. Seven percent GST is charged on each sale and is paid on each purchase. Following are a partial chart of accounts with balances for selected accounts as of December 1, partial schedules of accounts receivable and accounts payable as of December 1, and the cash transactions for December.

Partial Chart of Accounts

101	Cash	$3,800	
110	Accounts Receivable	5,000	
120	Notes Receivable	400	
201	Accounts Payable		$3,000
210	Notes Payable		2,500
220	GST Payable		600
230	GST Refundable	280	
301	Grace O'Brien, Capital		7,500
310	Grace O'Brien, Drawing		
401	Sales		
410	Interest Income		
501	Purchases		
510	Purchases Discounts		
601	Credit Card Discount Expense		
610	Salaries Expense		
620	Utilities Expense		
630	Rent Expense		
640	Interest Expense		

Partial Schedule of Accounts Receivable

Ellen Brown	$ 150.00
Kenneth Kong	150.00
Wonder Charge Company	3,531.00

Partial Schedule of Accounts Payable

Book Wholesalers	$802.50
Paperbacks, Inc.	963.00

Transactions

December 1	cash sales, $320 plus 7 percent GST
December 2	wrote cheque 9013 to East Coast Realty for December rent; $1,500
December 5	received a $70 cheque from Ellen Brown to apply on her account
December 6	wrote cheque 9014 to Book Wholesalers for $787.50 in full payment of its invoice 1620-A for $750 plus 7 percent GST, less a 2 percent discount
December 8	wrote cheque 9015 to Books Unlimited for $630 plus 7 percent GST for purchase of books for resale
December 9	received payment front Wonder Charge Company for sales that totalled $1,100 plus 7 percent GST; the credit card discount charged was $52
December 10	wrote cheque 9016 to Cheryl Stinson for her part-time salary, $220
December 11	wrote cheque 9017 to Bell Canada in payment of telephone bill, $82
December 12	Grace O'Brien invested an additional $4,500 into the business
December 15	cash sales, $570 plus 7 percent GST

December 16	Grace O'Brien withdrew $800 for personal use; cheque 9018
December 17	wrote cheque 9019 to Paperbacks, Inc. for $954, which represents payment in full of its invoice 16204 for $900 plus 7 percent GST, less a 1 percent discount
December 18	received a $50 cheque from Kenneth Kong to apply on his account
December 19	wrote cheque 9020 to Calgary Book Nook for $980 plus 7 percent GST for purchase of books for resale
December 24	received a cheque from Thomas Payne for $440, which represents full payment of his outstanding note for $400 plus interest
December 26	wrote cheque 9021 to Ontario Hydro in payment of electricity bill, $230
December 26	wrote cheque 9022 to Books Unlimited for $520 plus 7 percent GST for purchase of books for resale
December 28	cash sales, $900 plus 7 percent GST
December 29	wrote cheque 9023 for $2,750 to Eastern Savings Company in full payment of outstanding note of $2,500 plus interest
December 30	received cheque from Ellen Brown for $80 to apply on her account
December 31	received payment from Wonder Charge Company for sales that totalled $2,200 plus 7 percent GST; the credit card discount charged is $104

Instructions

1. Transfer the account balances to the general ledger accounts and to the subsidiary ledger accounts.

2. Journalize December's transactions into a cash receipts journal, page 16, and a cash payments journal, page 20.

3. As a transaction is entered in an accounts receivable or accounts payable column, post it immediately to the appropriate subsidiary ledger.

4. As a transaction is entered in a sundry column, post immediately to the general ledger.

5. When journalizing is complete, total, crossfoot and rule the journals.

6. Post the journal totals.

PROBLEM 9.4

J. DeKlerk owns a retail store called Family Cycles. He sells bicycles and parts, both for cash and on account. DeKlerk uses a cash receipts journal, a cash payments journal, sales and purchases journals, and a general journal. DeKlerk is required to collect 7 percent GST on all sales and pay 7 percent GST on all purchases; terms of credit sales are n/30. Following are the partial chart of accounts, partial accounts receivable and accounts payable ledgers, and the transactions for Family Cycles for the month of May 20XX.

Partial Accounts Receivable Subsidiary Ledger		Partial Accounts Payable Subsidiary Ledger	
Bob Dole	$400	Bike World	0
R. Santiago	0	Computer World	0
H. Wiggins	0	Cycle World	0
J. Quesnelle	0	The Cyclery	0

Partial Chart of Accounts

101	Cash	$18,650
110	Accounts Receivable	2,040
130	Office Equipment	0
210	Accounts Payable	1,570
220	GST Payable	2,030
230	GST Refundable	1,460
301	J. DeKlerk, Capital	16,400
310	J. DeKlerk, Drawing	0
401	Sales	0
410	Sales Returns and Allowances	0
501	Purchases	0
510	Purchases Returns and Allowances	0
601	Rent Expense	0
620	Utilities Expense	0
630	Credit Card Discount Expense	0

Transactions

May 1	purchased unassembled bicycles from Bike World on account; $1,750 plus 7 percent GST; invoice 72403 dated May 1; terms n/30
May 2	wrote cheque 4039 to Olympic Realty for $800 for the May rent
May 3	sold a bicycle to Hortense Wiggins on account; $250 plus 7 percent GST; invoice 2031-14.
May 4	wrote cheque 4040 to B.C. Hydro for $180 for electricity bill
May 5	received in the mail a $400 cheque from Bob Dole in payment of his account
May 10	purchased bicycle parts on account from The Cyclery; $800 plus 7 percent GST; invoice 6043-A dated May 10; terms n/30
May 11	sold a bicycle to Doc Smoley for $275 cash plus 7 percent GST; invoice 2031-15
May 12	De Klerk wrote cheque 4041 for $600 for personal use
May 13	wrote cheque 4042 to World Sports for $800 plus 7 percent GST for the purchase of bicycles for resale
May 15	sold bicycle parts on account to R. Santiago; $50 plus 7 percent GST; invoice 2031-16
May 15	deposited credit card sales drafts in the bank; the sales totalled $2,450 plus 7 percent GST; the credit card discount charged is $98
May 16	wrote cheque 4043 to Bike World in full payment of Family Cycles' May 1 purchase; invoice 72403
May 18	sold five bicycles to Riders Anonymous for $1,250 cash plus 7 percent GST; invoice 2031-17
May 19	purchased bicycle parts on account from Cycle World; $570 plus 7 percent GST; invoice 42137 dated May 19; terms n/30
May 20	Family Cycles issued debit memorandum 231-B for $60 plus 7 percent GST to Cycle World relating to its invoice 42137 of May 19; Family Cycles is returning some parts to Cycle World

May 21	wrote cheque 4044 to The Cyclery in full payment of Family Cycles' May 10 purchase, invoice 6043-A
May 21	wrote cheque 4045 to Atlas Cycles for $922 plus 7 percent GST for purchase of bicycle parts for resale
May 23	sold three bicycles to Rose Santiago on account; $950 plus 7 percent GST; invoice 2031-18
May 24	received a $100 cheque in the mail from Hortense Wiggins to apply on her account
May 26	purchased a small computer on account for office use from Computer World; $4,000 plus 7 percent GST; invoice 9034-21 dated May 26; terms n/30
May 27	wrote cheque 4046 to Bell Canada in payment of phone bill, $90
May 28	sold bicycle parts on account to Joe Quesnelle; $160 plus 7 percent GST; invoice 2031-19
May 29	Family Cycles issued credit memorandum 603-C for $10 plus 7 percent GST to Joe Quesnelle relating to May 28 invoice 2031-19; he returned a portion of the parts he had purchased
May 31	purchased bicycle parts on account from The Cyclery; $350 plus 7 percent GST; invoice 30116 dated May 31; terms n/30
May 31	deposited credit card sales drafts in the bank; the sales totalled $3,190 plus 7 percent GST; the credit card discount charged is $127.60

Instructions

1. Enter account titles and balances in the general, accounts receivable, and accounts payable ledgers.
2. Journalize sales of merchandise on account in the sales journal, page 5: purchases of merchandise on account in the purchases journal, page 6; cash receipts in the cash receipts journal, page 7; cash payments in the cash payments journal, page 8; and miscellaneous entries in the general journal, page 15.
2. As a transaction is entered to accounts receivable or accounts payable, post it immediately to the appropriate subsidiary ledger.
3. As a transaction is entered in a sundry column, post immediately to the general ledger.
4. When journalizing is complete, total, crossfoot and rule the special journals.
5. Post the transactions in the general journal and post the special journal totals. Remember to post the sales and purchases journal totals before posting cash receipts and cash payments journal totals.

PROBLEM 9.5

Butler Products sells kitchen cabinets to wholesale outlets. It does not have to collect provincial sales tax, but it must charge and pay 7 percent GST on all sales and purchases. All sales and purchases on account have credit terms of n/30. Following is a partial chart of accounts, the names in the accounts receivable and accounts payable ledgers, and the transactions for the month of March 20XX.

Partial Chart of Accounts

---

101   Cash
110   Accounts Receivable
210   Accounts Payable
215   Notes Payable
220   GST Payable
230   GST Refundable
310   Jack Daniels, Capital
320   Jack Daniels, Drawing
401   Sales
410   Sales Returns and Allowances
510   Purchases
520   Purchases Returns and Allowances
610   Salaries Expense
620   Advertising Expense
630   Rent Expense

**Accounts Receivable
Subsidiary Ledger**

Creative Cookery
Dawson Designs
Krafty Kitchens

**Accounts Payable
Subsidiary Ledger**

Allistar Supplies
International Importers
Kitchen Kupboards

March 1	paid rent of $650, cheque 1101
March 3	paid for advertising in *The Tribune*, $330 plus 7 percent GST, cheque 1102
March 3	purchased unassembled cabinets from International Importers on account, $1,450 plus 7 percent GST, invoice 506
March 5	sold cabinets to Dawson Designs on account, $750 plus 7 percent GST, invoice 107
March 7	purchased products from Kitchen Kupboards on account, $1,240 plus 7 percent GST, invoice 5092
March 9	issued a debit memorandum to Kitchen Kupboards in the amount of $280 plus 7 percent GST for damaged merchandise received on the May 7 invoice 5092 (note: the $19.60 credit to GST refundable will be recorded in parentheses in the GST refundable *debit* column)
March 12	sold cabinets to Krafty Kitchens on account, $2,200 plus 7 percent GST, invoice 108
March 15	Paid semimonthly salaries in the amount of $1,080, cheque 1103
March 18	purchased materials from Allistar Supplies on account, $490 plus 7 percent GST, invoice 6042
March 19	sold cabinets to Dawson Designs on account, $1,480 plus 7 percent GST, invoice 109
March 21	borrowed $2,000 from the Toronto Dominion Bank on a 12-month note payable with interest at 8 percent
March 22	sold cabinets to Creative Cookery on account, $1,750 plus 7 percent GST, invoice 110
March 23	issued credit memorandum to Creative Cookery in the amount of $400 plus 7 percent GST as an allowance for defective merchandise received by

it on invoice 110 dated March 22 (note: the $28 debit to GST payable will be recorded in parentheses in the GST payable credit column)

March 24	received a cheque from Dawson Designs in full payment of March 5 invoice 107
March 25	issued cheque 1104 to International Importers in full payment of its March 3 invoice 506
March 27	Jack Daniels invested an additional $2,000 in the business
March 28	sold cabinets to Creative Cookery on account, $1,290 plus 7 percent GST, invoice 111
March 29	received a cheque from Krafty Kitchens in full payment of the March 12 invoice 108
March 31	paid semimonthly salaries in the amount of $1,080, cheque 1105
March 31	received a cheque from Creative Cookery in full payment of the March 22 invoice 110, less the March 23 allowance
March 31	issued cheque 1106 to Allistar Supplies in full payment of its March 18 invoice 6042
March 31	Jack Daniels withdrew $300 for personal use, cheque 1107

Instructions

1. Record all transactions in a combined journal, page 9.
2. As a transaction is entered to accounts receivable or accounts payable, post it immediately to the appropriate subsidiary ledger.
3. As a transaction is entered in a sundry column, post immediately to the general ledger.
4. When all transactions are recorded, total, rule and crossfoot the journal. (Remember, when a figure is bracketed within a column, subtract that figure.)
5. Post the journal totals.

PROBLEM 9.6

The Surfside Company does not have to collect PST, but it must charge and pay 7 percent GST on all sales and purchases. Terms of sale are 2/10, n/30. Following are a partial chart of accounts, the names in the accounts receivable and accounts payable ledgers, and the transactions completed during February of the current year.

Partial Chart of Accounts	
101	Cash
110	Accounts Receivable
120	Office Equipment
210	Accounts Payable
220	GST Payable
230	GST Refundable
401	Sales
410	Sales Returns and Allowances
420	Sales Discounts
501	Purchases
510	Purchases Returns and Allowances
520	Purchases Discounts
620	Rent Expense
630	Advertising Expense

Accounts Receivable Subsidiary Ledger	Accounts Payable Subsidiary Ledger
Terry Long Geri Nash	Bestco Company Goode Company Western Company

February 1   purchased merchandise on an invoice dated January 30 from Goode Company; terms 2/10, n/60, $1,385 plus 7 percent GST

February 2   issued cheque 567 to *The Star* for advertising, $115 plus 7 percent GST

February 4   sold merchandise on account to Terry Long, invoice 862, $750 plus 7 percent GST, terms 2/10, n/30

February 5   returned for credit defective merchandise purchased from Goode Company on February 1, $135 plus 7 percent GST (note: the credit to GST refundable will be recorded by placing $9.45 in parentheses in the GST refundable *debit* column)

February 7   cash sales for the week ended February 7, $1,045 plus 7 percent GST

February 8   issued cheque 568 to Goode Company in payment of its invoice of January 30 less the return of February 5 and the discount

February 9   sold merchandise on account to Geri Nash, invoice 863, $570 plus 7 percent GST, terms 2/10, n/30

February 10   purchased office equipment on account from Western Company, terms n/10, EOM, $345 plus 7 percent GST

February 11   issued a credit memorandum to Geri Nash for defective merchandise sold to her on February 9 and returned by her, $70 plus 7 percent GST (note: the debit to GST payable will be recorded by placing $4.90 in parentheses in the GST payable credit column)

February 13   received a cheque from Terry Long in full payment of the February 4 invoice 862 less the discount

February 14   cash sales for the week ended February 14, $990 plus 7 percent GST

February 15   issued cheque 569 to Lakeland Realty for one month's rent, $850

February 16   issued a debit memorandum in the amount of $75 plus 7 percent GST to Western Company for defective office equipment purchased on February 10 (note: the credit to GST refundable will be recorded by placing $5.25 in parentheses in the GST refundable *debit* column)

February 17   purchased merchandise from Bestco Company on an invoice dated February 15; terms 2/10, n/60; $1,000 plus 7 percent GST

February 19   received a cheque from Geri Nash in full payment of the February 9 invoice 863 less the return of February 11 and the discount

February 21   cash sales for the week ended February 21, $1,120 plus 7 percent GST

February 23   purchased merchandise from Goode Company on an invoice dated February 21; terms 1/10, n/60; $785 plus 7 percent GST

February 24   sold merchandise on account to Geri Nash; invoice 864; $635 plus 7 percent GST; terms 2/10, n/30

February 25   issued cheque 570 to Bestco Company in payment of its invoice of February 15 less the discount

February 28   cash sales for the week ended February 28, $1,015 plus 7 percent GST

Instructions

1. Record all transactions in a combined journal, page 4.

2. As a transaction is entered to accounts receivable or accounts payable, post it immediately to the appropriate subsidiary ledger.

3. As a transaction is entered in a sundry column, post immediately to the general ledger.

4. When all transactions are recorded, total, rule and crossfoot the journal. (Remember, when a figure is bracketed within a column, subtract that figure.)

5. Post the journal totals.

CHAPTER 10

The Bank Account and Cash Funds

LEARNING OBJECTIVES

When you have completed this chapter, you should

1. have an increased understanding of accounting terminology.
2. have a basic understanding of bank accounts.
3. be able to reconcile a bank statement.
4. be able to prepare the journal entries necessary to bring the books up to date after bank statement reconciliation is complete.
5. be able to prepare the journal entries to establish and replenish a petty cash fund.
6. be able to prepare the journal entries required to establish a change fund.

VOCABULARY

accessible	easily obtained
automated	automatically controlled or operated
cancelled cheque	a cheque that has been paid by the bank and that is no longer negotiable
change fund	a certain amount of cash that is kept on hand for use in cash registers
denomination	a unit in a system of money (for example, a $10 bill, a $1 coin, a nickel, a dime)
deposit in transit	a deposit that has been made but that does not appear on this period's bank statement
endorsement	a signature or a company stamp on the back of a cheque; required before cashing or depositing the cheque
non-sufficient funds/ NSF cheque	a cheque previously deposited but debited back to the payee's account because there were not sufficient funds in the maker's account to cover it
outstanding cheque	a cheque that has been written but that has not yet been presented to the bank for payment
petty cash	a cash fund that is kept on hand from which small cash payments may be made
reconcile	to bring into agreement
restrictive endorsement	an endorsement that prohibits further circulation of a cheque
serial	arranged in a series; for example, 1001, 1002, 1003, 1004 ...

Introduction

Most businesses pay their bills by cheque and the accompanying cheque stubs provide information for the accountant. Entries are made in the cash payments journal from the stubs. Paying bills by serially numbered cheques provides an important element of internal control over cash; only certain persons will be authorized to write the cheques. It is easy to see whether any cheques are missing and whether the information recorded in the cash payments journal agrees with the information on the cheque itself.

Opening a Bank Account

Before a bank account may be opened, personal information (social insurance number, name, address, and so on) must be provided to the bank. A signature card is filled out and signed by each person who is authorized to sign cheques on the account. If there is any doubt about the validity of a signature on an incoming cheque, the bank employee will use the signature card to verify that the signature on the cheque is an authorized one.

Cheques with **serial** numbers are obtained from the bank with the depositor's name, address, and phone number printed on each. The numbered cheques allow the business owner to easily discover any missing cheques and thus help maintain the system of internal control over cash. In addition to the serial numbers at the top of each cheque, each depositor is assigned an account number that is printed on the cheque in magnetic ink so that cheques may be processed by computer.

Deposits

It is recommended business practice to make daily deposits of all cash received. Deposit slips contain a space to list currency, coins, and cheques. The following illustrates a deposit slip for Robert's Pastries:

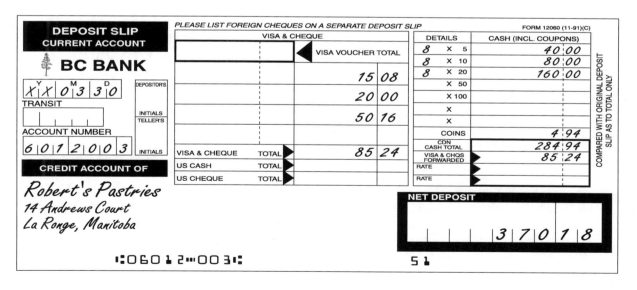

Most banks also provide deposit slips in book form with space to record the name of the person or the company paying by cheque. The carbon copy duplicate of the deposit slip is retained on file by the depositor and used as the source document for recording in the cash receipts journal.

Restrictive Endorsements

Deposits may be made by mail or in person. In either case, an **endorsement** in the form of a signature or company stamp is required. Cash deposits should not be sent through the mail because of the possibility of theft. Cheques, however, may be protected from theft by a **restrictive endorsement**, which stops any further circulation. The restrictive endorsement shown should be stamped or handwritten on the back of the cheques as soon as they are received.

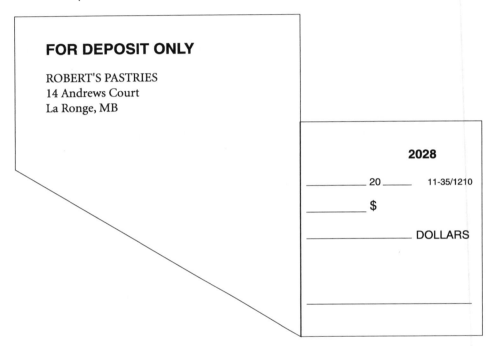

Automated Teller Machines

Deposits may be made at an **automated** teller machine (ATM), which makes the bank **accessible** for deposits and withdrawals 24 hours a day. The ATMs are convenient and easy to use. A plastic card, similar to an ordinary credit card, and a code number (known only to the depositor) are all that are required for their use. The ATM communicates with the depositor on a computer screen, processes the deposit or withdrawal, and dispenses a record of the transaction.

It is good business practice to use the services of an ATM. Because they may be used at any hour of the day or night, cash may conveniently be deposited after banking hours. When an automated teller machine is not available, the proprietor may wish to use a night depository so that large sums of cash are not lying around. The bank will provide deposit bags and a key to the night depository if the depositor wishes to take advantage of this service.

Cheque Stubs

Before a cheque is written, the accompanying cheque stub should be carefully filled in. The cheque stub should show the date the cheque was written, to whom, for what amount, and for what reason. In addition, it will show the balance in the cash account before and after the cheque is written.

The cheque stubs are used as the source documents for entries in the cash payments journal.

NO. 1843	
March 1 20 XX	
PREVIOUS BALANCE $ 2,330.80	
TO Peninsula Realty	
FOR March rent	
DEPOSITS 475.80	
TOTAL $ 2,806.60	
GST AMOUNT $ AMOUNT OF THIS CHEQUE $ 547.00	
BALANCE $ 2,259.60	

Robert's Pastries
14 Andrews Court
La Ronge, MB

NO. 1843

March 1 20 XX

PAY TO THE ORDER OF _____ *Peninsula Realty* _____

Five hundred and forty-seven—————————00⁄₁₀₀ $ 547.00

DOLLARS

🌲 **BC BANK**

FOR March rent

PER Robert Cumming

⑈060⑈2⑈003⑈

Stop Payment Orders

Once a cheque has been written and presented to someone as payment, it is the issuer's order to the bank to make payment. If the issuer changes her or his mind, a stop payment order may be issued that instructs the bank not to make the payment. The bank will charge the issuer a fee for the stop payment order, which is most effective if issued soon after the cheque is written. Obviously the bank cannot stop payment if the cheque has already been paid.

The Bank Statement

Once a month the bank sends a statement to the depositor showing all the transactions that occurred in that account. Each deposit and each cheque presented to the bank for payment is listed on the statement as well as the miscellaneous transactions which are usually accompanied by a code letter or a prepared list. Miscellaneous transactions are referred to as debits or credits to the account. Debit entries (such as cheques) are deductions from the account and credit entries (such as deposits) are additions to the account. On the accounting records of the bank, each depositor's account is handled like an account payable. A **cancelled cheque** is a cheque that has been paid by the bank and that is in some way marked paid or cancelled.

Bank Statement Reconciliation

When the bank statement is received, it will show the cash balance at the beginning and at the end of the period. In most cases, the ending cash balance will not agree with the depositor's general ledger balance. There are many reasons for this difference. The depositor must **reconcile** the bank statement, or bring it and the general ledger balance into agreement. Once reconciliation is complete, the depositor knows the correct cash balance. If reconciliation is completed at the end of the month, the reconciled cash balance will appear on the balance sheet as well as in the general ledger.

Some causes for the discrepancy between the ending bank balance and the general ledger balance follow:

1. **Outstanding cheques** have not yet been presented to the bank for payment, but have been deducted from the cheque stubs and the cash payments journal. They must be subtracted from the bank statement balance when reconciling.

2. **Deposits in transit** have been entered in the cash receipts journal and the cheque stubs but do not yet appear on the bank statement. All such deposits must be added to the bank balance when reconciling.

3. Service charges are made by the bank for handling the account. The service charge is usually based on the amount of the average daily balance in the account and the number of transactions that occur each month. A service charge will show on the bank statement as a debit entry (reducing the depositor's balance) and must be subtracted from the general ledger balance when reconciling.

4. Special collections are made by the bank for the depositor and will appear on the bank statement as miscellaneous credits (increasing the depositor's balance). Often, a depositor will designate the bank as payee on an outstanding note receivable. When the note becomes due, the maker will pay the face amount of the note plus the interest to the lender's bank, which will in turn deposit the money into the lender's account. Special collections will be added to the general ledger balance when reconciling.

5. Miscellaneous charges are made by the bank and will appear on the bank statement as miscellaneous debits reducing the depositor's balance. Such charges might include: (a) safe deposit box rental fee; (b) cheque printing charge; (c) fee for a stop payment order; and (d) charges for **NSF cheques** (non-sufficient funds in the bank to cover the amount of the cheque). In addition to bank charges, the depositor might authorize another firm to deduct money from the account on a regular basis. Such deductions might be for a loan payment, an insurance premium or a savings account. They will appear on the bank statement as debits (or deductions) from the depositor's balance. Miscellaneous charges, service charges, and special collections are subtracted from the chequebook balance when reconciling, and will be journalized and posted.

6. Errors may be made either by the bank or by the depositor and will, of course, cause a discrepancy when reconciling. When a bank error is discovered, the depositor should notify the bank immediately. Errors on the depositor's books should be corrected when reconciling

Steps in Preparing a Bank Statement Reconciliation

Before reconciliation can take place, the depositor needs the bank statement, cheque stubs, cash receipts and cash payments journal, and a calculator. Most bank statements provide a reconciliation form on the back of the statement. When reconciliation is complete, all the additions and subtractions to cash made by the bank and made on the company's books must be the same. Basically, the depositor must do the following:

1. Check to make sure that all deposits recorded in the cash receipts journal and in the cheque stubs are entered on the bank statement. Deposits that have been made but that do not appear on the bank statement are called deposits in transit and are added to the bank balance during reconciliation. It is possible, too, that a deposit might appear on the bank statement but not appear in the cash receipts journal or the cheque stubs because the bookkeeper forgot to record it. If this happens, the depositor must add the deposit to the cheque stubs. A correcting journal entry will be made to enter the amount in the cash receipts journal.

2. Compare the amounts of the cancelled cheques with the amounts written in the cash payments journal and the cheque stubs to make sure they are the same.

3. Check the miscellaneous debits and credits (subtractions and additions) on the bank statement. The debit entries will be substracted from the cheque stubs when

reconciling and the credit entries will be added. Journal entries are required to correct the general ledger.

Illustration of a Bank Statement Reconciliation

When Robert Cummings received the bank statement for Robert's Pastries, it showed a balance on March 31 of $5,571.39. The general ledger balance on this date was $5,975.88.

Robert took the following steps to reconcile the bank statement:

1. He compared the deposits in the cash receipts journal with those on the bank statement. There was one deposit in transit on March 31 for $371.50.

2. He compared the amounts of the cancelled cheques with the amounts entered in the cash payments journal. Robert noticed that cheque number 1872 written for $60 in payment of the electricity bill was recorded incorrectly in the cash payments journal as $90.

3. He compared the amounts of the cancelled cheques with the cash payments journal and found that there were five outstanding cheques:

1885	$ 20.00	1894	$10.00
1888	$ 32.14	1896	$48.50
1893	$150.16		

4. Robert noted the debit entries listed on the bank statement.

    a. March 10—an NSF cheque from Customer M for $150 and a debit memo from the bank for $20 representing the bank's charge for the NSF cheque.

    b. March 12—Robert's cheque to Provincial Life insurance for $137.79 cleared the bank. This is a pre-authorized cheque that comes directly from the insurance company to the bank and is automatically deducted from Robert's account for an insurance policy on the manager's life. Robert entered into the agreement and signed the necessary papers some time ago.

    c. Bank service charge—$16.

None of these debit entries were recorded on Robert's books before reconciliation.

To reconcile the bank statement, Robert must do the following:

Step 1.	Write in the ending bank balance	$5,571.39	
Step 2.	Add deposit in transit, March 31	+ 371.50	
	Subtotal	$5,942.89	
Step 3.	Subtract outstanding cheques:		
	1885	$ 20.00	
	1888	32.14	
	1893	150.16	
	1894	10.00	
	1896	48.50	
	Total	−260.80	
Step 4:	Determine adjusted bank balance		$5,682.09
Step 5:	Write in the ending general ledger balance		$5,975.88
Step 6:	*Add* the amount of the error in recording cheque number 1872		
	$90.00 − $60.00 = $30.00		+ 30.00
	Subtotal		$6,005.88

BC BANK

Robert's Pastries
14 Andrews Court
La Ronge, MB

Account Statement

Account No.	
6012003	

Period	
From	To
02/28	03/31/XX

Enclosures	Page
0	1

Date	Transaction Description	Cheques & Debits	Deposits & Credits	Balance
02 28				2669 80
03 01		321 00	475 80	
		547 00		2277 60
03 02		92 17	340 18	2225 61
03 03		50 00	353 06	
		113 06		2715 61
03 04		40 00	321 17	
		91 34		2905 44
03 05		20 00	350 60	3236 04
03 08		150 00	482 10	3568 14
03 09		51 00	330 18	
		57 26		
		30 00		3760 06
03 10	NSF Cheque—DM	150 00DM		
	NSF Charge—DM	20 00DM		
		59 68	340 79	3871 17
03 11		150 00	320 18	
		52 59		3988 76
03 12	Provincial Life	137 79DM	356 01	4206 98
03 15		124 82	403 50	
		60 00		4425 66
03 16		20 00	351 07	4756 73
03 17		86 96	348 32	5018 09
03 18		30 16	360 24	5348 17
03 19		120 00	366 80	
		54 84		5540 13
03 22		113 77	490 14	5916 50
02 23		330 00	340 06	5926 56
03 24		19 95	350 64	
		547 00		5710 25
03 25		503 57	353 90	5560 58
03 26		324 15	360 08	5596 51
03 29		50 00	365 20	5911 71
03 30		549 00	370 18	
		145 50		5587 39
03 31	SC	16 00		5571 39

DM = Debit memo   CM = Credit memo   SC = Service charge

Step 7: Subtract the bank statement debits:

    a. NSF cheque (Customer M) plus
       Service charge (debit memo) $170.00

    b. Insurance premium   137.79

    c. Bank service charge   16.00

    Total deductions   − 323.79

Step 8. Determine adjusted general ledger
    balance $5,682.09

Required Journal Entries

When reconciliation is complete and the correct cash account balance has been determined, certain journal entries must be made to bring the books up to date. Normally, a journal entry will be required for every correction made on the general ledger portion of the reconciliation. For Robert's Pastries, the general journal entries are:

GENERAL JOURNAL					PAGE 8
DATE	DESCRIPTION	POST REF.	DEBIT		CREDIT
20XX					
Mar. 31	Cash		30 00		
	Utilities Expense				30 00
	To Correct Incorrect Amount Recorded for				
	Cheque Number 1872 (Bank				
	Reconciliation, March 31, 20XX)				
31	Accounts Receivable, Customer "M"		170 00		
	Insurance Expense		137 79		
	Bank Charges Expense		16 00		
	Cash				323 79
	To Record Amounts Necessary after Bank				
	Statement Reconciliation, March 31, 20XX				

The first entry debiting Cash and crediting Utilities Expense was made because $30 *too much* was subtracted from the cash account in the cash payments journal (a $60 cheque was recorded as $90). Therefore, $30 has to be added back to the cheque stubs and to the cash account, and the Utilities Expense account must, too, be corrected.

The entry debiting Accounts Receivable for $170 places Customer M back on the books, because there were insufficient funds in M's account to cover the cheque given to Robert's Pastries. Notice that the $20 service charge is also debited to M's account in the hope that both the amount of the cheque and the service charge will be recovered from the customer.

The other entries record the debits to Insurance Expense and Bank Charges Expense and the corresponding credits to Cash.

After these entries have been posted, the books will be up to date. The ledger account for Cash will be equal to the corrected bank statement balance. The corrections must also be recorded in the cheque stubs so that they will agree with the ledger account for Cash.

T Account Bank Statement Reconciliation

A simple form may be used when reconciling the bank statement if a printed form is not available. The form simply lists the ending bank balance and any additions and subtractions on the left-hand side of the page and the ending general ledger balance and any additions or subtractions on the right-hand side of the page.

For Robert's Pastries, a T account reconciliation looks like this:

Robert's Pastries Bank Reconciliation March 31, 20XX				
Bank balance, 3/31		$5,571.39	General ledger balance, 3/31	$5,975.88
Add: Deposit in transit, 3/31		+ 371.50	Add: Error in recording cheque 1872	+ 30.00
		$5,942.89		$6,005.88
Deduct:			Deduct:	
Outstanding cheques			a. NSF cheque (DM) plus service	
#1885—	$ 20.00		charge (DM) $170.00	
#1888—	32.14		b. Insurance premium	
#1893—	150.16		(manager's life) 137.79	
#1894—	10.00		c. Service charge 16.00	
#1896—	48.50	− 260.80		323.79
Adjusted bank balance		$5,682.09	Adjusted general ledger balance	$5,682.09

The Petty Cash Fund

While business owners are advised to pay most bills by cheque, there are some payments that may be made in cash because it is so much more convenient. For example, payments to the mail carrier for postage due, payments for packages delivered, or small payments for supplies would best be made with cash. For such expenditures, a special cash fund called **petty cash** is established.

The amount of money put into the petty cash fund depends on the needs of the business. If there is danger of theft, the petty cash fund should be kept small and should be reimbursed often. If there is little danger of theft, the proprietor may choose to establish a fund that will last through the month.

Establishing the Fund

To establish the petty cash fund, a cheque is written in favour of the petty cashier. It is cashed and the money is put in a safe place. The entry will be recorded in the cash payments journal.

The entry simply takes money from one cash account and puts it into another. The petty cash account is an asset and will be listed on the balance sheet along with the cash account.

After the original entry to establish the fund, the account for petty cash will not be debited again unless it is decided to increase or decrease the amount of money kept in the fund.

CASH PAYMENTS JOURNAL					PAGE 10				
DATE	CHQ. NO.	PAID TO	ACCOUNT DEBITED	POST. REF.	SUNDRY ACCOUNTS DEBIT	ACCOUNTS PAYABLE DEBIT	PURCHASES DISCOUNT CREDIT	CASH CREDIT	
20XX									
Oct. 1	1075	Petty Cashier	Petty Cash		75 00			75 00	

Making Petty Cash Payments

Vouchers are kept with the petty cash for a record of all payments made out of the fund. If, for example, $6 is paid out of petty cash for the monthly charge for a local newspaper, a voucher would be filled out as follows:

```
PETTY CASH VOUCHER

No. ___1___                                    Date ___Oct. 3, 20XX___

PAID TO ___Bay Area Press___

AMOUNT PAID ___$6.00___

ACCOUNT DEBITED ___Miscellaneous Expense___

APPROVED BY                          PAYMENT RECEIVED BY
___R.C.___                           ___Sandy Odette___
```

Usually one or two persons will be given access to the petty cash fund and will make cash payments from it. The person(s) so designated should initial each voucher and have the one who is receiving the cash sign the voucher. Making one or two persons responsible for the fund and having the payee sign each voucher gives some internal control over the cash.

The Petty Cash Disbursements Register

While some companies prefer simply to put the vouchers into their various categories and find totals for each category, many firms require that petty cash disbursements be recorded in a register similar to the cash payments journal. On the next page is a petty cash disbursements register for the month of March.

Note that the amount of the fund, $75, is entered on the first line of the register. Each expenditure is recorded in the payments column and also is recorded under its appropriate column heading. When petty cash is replenished at the end of the month or sooner, each column is totalled. Crossfooting ensures that no errors have been made before the journal entry is prepared.

Distribution of Payments	Amount	Total of Payments Column
Supplies	$ 7.65	
Delivery Expense	15.65	
Miscellaneous Expense	17.00	
Sundry	30.00	
Total	$70.30	= $70.30

Reimbursing the Petty Cash Fund

The petty cash fund may be reimbursed at any time, and is usually done when the funds are low. Even if the fund is not particularly low at the end of the month (or at the end of the accounting period), petty cash should be reimbursed so that the proper expense accounts may be debited before the trial balance is prepared.

The entry to reimburse the petty cash fund will appear in the cash payments journal. The accountant will debit the accounts for which expenditures from the fund have been made and will credit cash for the total. The information for the entry is taken from the

DATE	VOUCHER NO.	EXPLANATION	RECEIPTS	PAYMENTS	DISTRIBUTION OF PAYMENTS				
					SUPPLIES 140	DELIVERY EXP. 640	MISC. EXP. 680	SUNDRY DEBITS ACCT. NO.	AMOUNT
20XX									
March 1		To Establish Fund	75 00						
3	1	Bay Area Press		6 00			6 00		
5	2	Sam Strauss—Cleaning		10 00				615	10 00
6	3	E & L Stationery		4 50	4 50				
9	4	United Delivery		8 40		8 40			
12	5	Sam Strauss—Cleaning		10 00				615	10 00
18	6	Burke's Drug Store		3 15	3 15				
20	7	Bay Area Press		6 00			6 00		
20	8	Postage		5 00			5 00		
25	9	Belmont Delivery		7 25		7 25			
30	10	R. Cummings, Drawing		10 00				360	10 00
		Totals	75 00	70 30	7 65	15 65	17 00		30 00
				4 70					
			75 00	75 00					
March 31		Balance	4 70						
		To Replenish, March 31	70 30						
April 1		Balance	75 00						

petty cash disbursements register where each column total and the entries in the sundry column represent cash spent for a particular expense during the period. Remember, the petty cash disbursements record is not a formal journal. It is similar to a worksheet; it is a place where the accountant summarizes the information about petty cash. Until the entry to reimburse petty cash is made in the cash disbursements journal, no formal record has been made of the petty cash expenditures.

The information for the following entry was taken from the petty cash disbursements register for the month of March.

CASH PAYMENTS JOURNAL							PAGE 10
DATE	CHQ. NO.	ACCOUNT DEBITED	POST. REF.	SUNDRY ACCOUNTS DEBIT	ACCOUNTS PAYABLE DEBIT	PURCHASES DISCOUNT CREDIT	CASH CREDIT
20XX							
Mar. 31	1104	Supplies		7 65			
		Delivery Expense		15 65			
		Miscellaneous Expense		17 00			
		R. Cummings, Drawing		10 00			
		Cleaning Expense		20 00			70 30

Notice that when the petty cash fund is reimbursed, the column totals and the individual amounts in the sundry column are debited. The Petty Cash account is not debited again. The ledger account for petty cash will contain the same balance that it had originally (in this case $75) unless it is decided to make the fund either larger or smaller.

The credit to cash, $70.30, represents a cheque written and cashed for that amount. The sum of $70.30 will be put back into the petty cash fund for use in the next period.

The Change Fund

Most businesses have on hand a **change fund**, which is cash that is used in the cash registers so that change may be made for customers. The journal entry to establish the change fund is as follows:

						SUNDRY ACCOUNTS DEBIT	ACCOUNTS PAYABLE DEBIT	PURCHASES DISCOUNT CREDIT	CASH CREDIT
DATE	CHQ. NO.	PAID TO	ACCOUNT DEBITED	POST. REF.					
20XX									
Oct. 1	1076	Cashier	Change Fund			20000			20000

CASH PAYMENTS JOURNAL — PAGE 10

The $200 will be obtained from the bank and will be in various **denominations**—that is, in nickels, dimes, $1 coins, $20 bills, and so on. The money will be placed in the cash register to be used for making change for customers. Assume that at the end of the day on October 7 the cash register tape shows total sales of $450. The amount of money that should be in the cash register is $717.50 which includes 7 percent GST, 8 percent PST, and the $200 change fund. The actual cash when counted, however, is $712.50; the register is $5 short. In general journal form, the entry to record the day's sales will be:

GENERAL JOURNAL — PAGE 29

DATE	DESCRIPTION	POST REF.	DEBIT	CREDIT
20XX				
Oct. 7	Cash		512 50	
	Cash Short and Over		5 00	
	Sales			450 00
	PST Payable			36 00
	GST Payable			31 50
	To Record Cash Sales and $5.00 Shortage			

The same entry recorded in the cash receipts journal looks like this:

CASH RECEIPTS JOURNAL — PAGE 10

DATE	RECEIVED FROM	ACCOUNT CREDITED	POST. REF.	SUNDRY ACCOUNTS CREDIT	ACCOUNTS RECEIVABLE CREDIT	SALES CREDIT	GST PAYABLE CREDIT	PST PAYABLE CREDIT	CASH SHORT AND OVER DR./(CR.)	CASH DEBIT
20XX										
Oct. 7	Cash Sales					45000	3150	3600	500	51250

Notice that the cash receipts journal has a special column for recording shortages and overages. The cash short and over account may have either a debit or a credit balance because it is debited for shortages and credited for overages. The column head is titled Cash Short and Over—Dr./(Cr.). Credit entries in the column will be enclosed in parentheses to indicate that they are credits. At the end of the accounting period, when the column is totalled, the accountant will determine whether the account has a debit or a credit balance.

After the day's receipts are accounted for, the $200 change fund is put back into the cash register. The accountant may need to make a trip to the bank to ensure that enough change is on hand for the following day's business.

The T accounts for the three cash accounts appear as follows:

Cash	101		Change Fund	110
10/31 Balance 3,588			10/31 Balance 200	

Petty Cash	105
10/31 Balance 75	

Each of these accounts appears on the partial balance sheet for Super Cookies on October 31, 20XX as follows:

Super Cookies
Balance Sheet
October 31, 20XX

Assets					
Cash	$ 3 5 8 8 00		
Petty Cash	7 5 00		
Change Fund	2 0 0 00		
Accounts Receivable	7 8 0 00		
Notes Receivable	4 3 0 0 00		
Total Assets		$ 3 7 6 4 1 00	

Summary

It is common business practice to pay bills by cheque and the cheque stubs and the cancelled cheques provide valuable information to the accountant. The stubs are used when preparing the journal entries for cash payments; the journals and cancelled cheques are used when reconciling the bank statement; and the cancelled cheques provide proof of payment.

Once a bank account has been opened, deposits of cash should be made daily. The depositor may wish to use an automated teller machine or a night depository so that she or he will not be restricted to regular banking hours. Daily bank deposits of cash help reduce the possibility of theft.

A restrictive endorsement should be placed on incoming cheques as soon as they are received. Again, this helps to safeguard against theft because the restrictive endorsement prohibits further circulation.

The bank will send the depositor a bank statement once a month. This provides the depositor with the opportunity to reconcile her or his cash records with the bank's records. Once reconciliation is complete, the depositor may be relatively sure that the cash balance obtained is the correct one.

In addition to a bank account, many businesses will establish a cash fund out of which small cash payments may be made. Payments from this fund, called petty cash, are recorded on a voucher and in a petty cash disbursements register.

If sales are made in the store, a change fund is necessary. This fund provides small cash denominations so that change may be given to customers.

Cash, petty cash, and the change fund are current assets and usually appear on the balance sheet as three separate accounts.

Vocabulary Review

Here is a list of the words and terms for this chapter:

accessible	non-sufficient funds/NSF
automated	outstanding cheque
cancelled cheque	petty cash
change fund	reconcile
denomination	restrictive endorsement
deposit in transit	serial
endorsement	

Fill in the blank with the correct word or term from the list.

1. A signature is sometimes referred to as a/an _____.
2. A fund that is kept on hand for making small cash payments is called _____.
3. An endorsement that prohibits further circulation of a cheque is a/an _____.
4. A word that means easily obtained is _____.
5. A cheque that has been paid by the bank is called a/an _____.
6. An automatically controlled banking machine is called a/an _____ teller.
7. Units in a system of money, such as a dime or a quarter, are referred to as a _____ of money.
8. A cheque that has not yet been presented to the bank for payment is called a/an _____.
9. To bring into agreement is to _____.
10. Numbers arranged in a series (1, 2, 3, 4, 5 …) are _____ numbers.
11. A deposit that has been made but that does not appear on the bank statement is referred to as a/an _____.
12. Cash that is kept on hand for use in the cash register is the _____.
13. A customer's cheque previously deposited but debited back to her or his account because of a lack of funds is a/an _____ cheque.

Match the words and terms on the left with the definitions on the right.

14. accessible	**a.**	a signature
15. automated	**b.**	a cheque paid by the bank
16. cancelled cheque	**c.**	a cheque not yet presented to the bank for payment
17. change fund		
18. denominations	**d.**	easily obtained
19. deposit in transit	**e.**	cash kept on hand for use in the cash register
20. endorsement	**f.**	automatically controlled
21. non-sufficient funds/NSF	**g.**	units in a money system
22. outstanding cheque	**h.**	in a series
23. petty cash	**i.**	an endorsement that prohibits further circulation
24. reconcile	**j.**	a deposit that does not yet appear on the bank statement

25. restrictive endorsement

26. serial

k. to bring into agreement

l. cash fund out of which small cash payments may be made

m. not enough money in a chequing account to cover a cheque

Exercises

EXERCISE 10.1

On May 22, at the end of the business day, the cash register for Mom's Auto Parts showed total sales of $472.18. The actual cash on hand was $682.18, which included a $200 change fund that would be placed back in the cash register. The daily deposit included the following: $2.18 in coins; $150.00 in currency; and three cheques: $96.14, $83.04, and $150.82. In the cash receipts journal, prepare the entry to record the day's sales and prepare a deposit slip for the daily deposit of cash. Use journal page 5.

EXERCISE 10.2

Following is the cash receipts journal for the first week in October showing the total cash sales and the cash short and over for each day. Assuming that cash short and over had a zero balance on October 1, what is the balance of the account on October 7? Is it a debit or a credit balance?

CASH RECEIPTS JOURNAL							PAGE 10
DATE	RECEIVED FROM	ACCOUNT CREDITED	POST. REF.	SALES CREDIT	PST PAYABLE CREDIT	CASH SHORT AND OVER DR./(CR.)	CASH DEBIT
20XX							
Oct. 1	Cash Sales			300 00	15 00	50	314 50
2	Cash Sales			320 00	16 00	(10 00)	346 00
3	Cash Sales			480 00	24 00	4 00	500 00
4	Cash Sales			518 00	25 90	1 00	542 90
5	Cash Sales			590 00	29 50	(5 00)	624 50
6	Cash Sales			502 00	25 10		527 10
7	Cash Sales			417 20	20 86	20 00	418 06

EXERCISE 10.3

Marcy Lennon sells accessories for pets in her small specialty store called "Pets 'n' People." In the past, she has had one cash register in the store with a change fund of $150 in it. On July 1, however, Marcy enlarged her store and bought a second cash register. She also wants to put $150 in this register. Answer the following questions:

a. To establish a change fund for the second cash register, what accounts should be debited and credited, and for how much?

b. What will be the balance in the Change Fund account after the journal entry in Step a has been made?

c. On which financial statement will the Change Fund account appear?

EXERCISE 10.4

Prepare general journal entries if necessary to record the following bank statement reconciliation adjustments. Use journal page 7.

a. Collection of a note by the bank for $6,000 plus interest of $910.

b. A deposit in transit of $1,215.

c. Four cheques were found to be outstanding: cheque number 604, $1,204.06; cheque number 609, $475.18; cheque number 614, $22.40; and cheque number 623, $573.20.

d. A service charge of $8.50 was deducted by the bank.

e. An NSF cheque in the amount of $372.18 from Jim Butler was returned by the bank. The bank charged a $30 fee.

f. A debit memo in the amount of $15, which represented the charge for a safe deposit box rental, was included with the bank statement.

EXERCISE 10.5

When the bank statement was received on March 2, it showed a balance of $4,116.80 on February 28 before reconciliation. After reconciliation, the adjusted general ledger balance is $4,120.02. If there was one deposit in transit of $520.50, what was the total amount of the outstanding cheques, assuming that there were no other adjustments to be made to the bank statement?

EXERCISE 10.6

After the bank statement was reconciled, the adjusted bank balance was $2,792.58. The general ledger balance before reconciliation was $2,286.58. The bank collected a note for $500 plus $10 in interest for the depositor. If there were no other adjustments to be made to the general ledger, what was the amount of the bank service charge?

EXERCISE 10.7

When reconciling the bank statement, tell whether the following would be additions to the bank statement, subtractions from the bank statement, additions to the general ledger, or subtractions from the general ledger.

	Add to Bank Statement	Subtract from Bank Statement	Add to General Ledger	Subtract from General Ledger
a. Outstanding cheques	_____	_____	_____	_____
b. Cheque-printing charge	_____	_____	_____	_____
c. A collection made by the bank for the depositor	_____	_____	_____	_____
d. A cheque written for $72.98 was recorded in the cash payments journal as $79.28	_____	_____	_____	_____
e. A deposit in transit	_____	_____	_____	_____
f. Bank service charges	_____	_____	_____	_____
g. A cheque written for $543.56 was recorded in the cash payments journal as $534.56	_____	_____	_____	_____
h. An automatic cheque for an insurance premium is included with the cancelled cheques	_____	_____	_____	_____

EXERCISE 10.8

Heinrich Zimler owns Heinrich's Foreign Auto Sales. On August 1, he decides to establish a petty cash fund of $150. On August 31, after the petty cash vouchers have been categorized and totalled for the month, the expenditures are found to be: $18 for postage; $30.75 for owner's drawing; $10.80 for delivery expense; $16.42 for supplies; $12 for a magazine subscription for customers' use; and $6.00 for a newspaper subscription for the waiting room. The amount of cash on hand on August 31 is $56.03. Prepare the entry in the cash payments journal, page 8, to (a) establish the petty cash fund on August 1 (cheque 1075) and (b) replenish the fund on August 31 (cheque 1146). Account titles are: Cash, 101; Petty Cash, 105; Supplies, 140; Heinrich Zimler, Drawing, 320; Postage Expense, 640; Miscellaneous Expense, 650; and Delivery Expense, 660.

EXERCISE 10.9

The petty cash fund for Betty's Barber Shop had a balance of $25 on September 1, 20XX. On September 9, Betty noticed that the fund was nearly used up. The cash on hand on September 9 was 35 cents. The totals of the petty cash payments register showed the following: Postage Expense, 640, $4.20; Miscellaneous Expense, 650, $5; and Entertainment Expense, 690, $15.45. Betty decided to make the fund $50 larger so that it would not have to be replenished so often. Prepare an entry in the cash payments journal, page 9, on September 9 that will both replenish the petty cash fund and enlarge the fund by $50. Use cheque 1902. The account number for Petty Cash is 135.

Problems

PROBLEM 10.1

Zorba's Delicatessen received a bank statement on November 2, 20XX. The bank balance for October 31 was $4,982.02. The general ledger balance at the time of reconciliation was $4,566.64. When reconciling, the following were found: four outstanding cheques, 1742, $462.81; 1745, $198.40; 1746, $42.69; and 1747, $51.08; two deposits in transit, October 30, $300 and October 31, $119.60; a bank service charge, $12; a cheque-printing charge, $18; a $90 automatic cheque for an insurance premium; and a $200 note receivable left with the bank for collection had been paid in full at the bank.

Instructions

1. Prepare a bank statement reconciliation on October 31 for Zorba's Delicatessen.

2. Prepare the necessary entries in general journal form to bring the books up to date after reconciliation. Use journal page 11. A partial chart of accounts includes the following: Cash, 101; Notes Receivable, 120; Insurance Expense, 650; and Bank Charges Expense, 670.

PROBLEM 10.2

Geri Speir owns Fillie's Frocks, a western wear store. On June 2, Geri received the bank statement. It showed a balance on May 31 of $6,420.95. The general ledger balance at the time of reconciliation was $6,446.11. When reconciling, Geri found one deposit in transit of $645.80. There were five outstanding cheques: 2016, $29.40; 2020, $150; 2025, $490; 2026, $10.50; and 2027, $65.04. The bank service charge was $10.50, and there was a cheque-printing charge of $16.50. When comparing the cancelled cheques with the cash payments journal, Geri noticed that cheque 1998, written on May 15 to Western Wear in payment of an account payable, was actually written for $75.87 but was recorded in the cash payments journal as $78.57. Geri also noticed that she forgot to record a $100 cash withdrawal from an automated teller on May 27 (the cash was for personal use).

Instructions

1. Prepare a bank statement reconciliation on May 31 for Fillie's Frocks.
2. Prepare the necessary entries in general journal form to bring the books up to date after reconciliation. Use journal page 27. A partial chart of accounts includes the following: Cash, 101; Accounts Payable, 210; Geri Speir, Drawing, 310; and Bank Charges Expense, 640.

PROBLEM 10.3

Marie Bouchard, owner of A–Z Novelties, received her bank statement on February 2. The January 31 bank balance was $3,240.60. The general ledger balance at the time of reconciliation was $3,223.59. During reconciliation, Marie noted that the bank service charge was $15. Also, a note receivable left at the bank for collection had been paid in full, $600 plus $60 interest. There were two deposits in transit: January 30, $649.28 and January 31, $596.81. The bank charge for cheque printing was $18. There were three outstanding cheques: 972, $450; 973, $95.40; and 974, $150. When comparing the cancelled cheques with the cash payments journal, Marie noticed that two errors had been made. Cheque 952, written on January 10 in payment of the electric bill, was actually written for $98.20 but was recorded in the cash payments journal as $89.20. Cheque 965, written on January 19 in payment for a desk for the office, was actually written for $370.32 but was recorded in the cash payments journal as $390.32. An automatic cheque for $70.30 in payment of an insurance premium was included with the cancelled cheques.

Instructions

1. Prepare a bank statement reconciliation on January 31 for A–Z Novelties.
2. Prepare the necessary entries in general journal form to bring the books up to date after reconciliation. Use journal page 33. A partial chart of accounts includes the following: Cash, 101; Notes Receivable, 110; Office Furniture, 170; Interest Income, 420; Utilities Expense 650; Insurance Expense, 660; and Bank Charges Expense, 670.

PROBLEM 10.4

The following information was available to reconcile Holiday Handicrafts' general ledger balance and the bank statement balance as of December 31, 20XX.

a. The December 31 cash balance according to the accounting records was $7,063.50, and the bank statement balance for that date was $10,362.50.

b. Cheque 124 for $178 and cheque 129 for $200, both written and entered in the accounting records in December, were not among the cancelled cheques. Two cheques, 117 for $587 and 119 for $95, were outstanding on November 30 when the bank and general ledger balances were reconciled. Cheque 119 was returned with the December cancelled cheques, but cheque 117 was not.

c. When the December cheques were compared with entries in the accounting records, it was found that cheque 121 in payment for office supplies had been correctly written for $654 but was erroneously entered in the accounting records as $645.

d. Two debit memoranda and a credit memorandum were included with the bank statement. The credit memorandum indicated that the bank had collected a $5,900 note receivable for Holiday Handicrafts, and had deducted a $25 service charge for the collection. One of the debit memoranda was for $215 for an NSF cheque from J. Warren in the amount of $205. The bank charged a $10 fee for the NSF cheque. The second debit memorandum was for $72 to cover interest on an outstanding bank loan.

e. The December 31 deposit in the amount of $3,245 had been placed in the bank's night depository after banking hours and did not appear on the bank statement.

Instructions

1. Prepare a T account bank statement reconciliation for Holiday Handicrafts on December 31, 20XX.

2. Prepare the necessary general journal entries (page 24) to bring the books up to date after the bank statement reconciliation. A partial chart of accounts includes the following: Cash, 101; Accounts Receivable, 110; Notes Receivable, 120; Office Supplies, 130; Bank Charges Expense, 630; and Interest Expense, 650.

PROBLEM 10.5

Shown below are the cash columns of the cash receipts and cash payments journals for Okanagan Valley Ski Resort for the month of October 20XX.

Cash Receipts Journal			Cash Payments Journal	
October 4	$ 3,174		Cheque 113	$ 1,930
7	1,407		114	1,472
10	1,559		115	2,413
15	187		116	689
17	2,130		117	230
22	1,404		118	118
23	721		119	307
25	4,208		120	1,326
29	5,105		121	640
Total	$19,895		122	3,016
			123	741
			Total	$12,882

The cash account in the general ledger shows the following:

Cash							ACCOUNT NO. 101	
DATE	EXPLANATION	POST. REF.	DEBIT		CREDIT		BALANCE	
20XX								
Oct. 1	Balance						13 542 00	
31		CR4	19 895 00				33 437 00	
31		CP8			12 882 00		20 555 00	

Okanagan Valley Ski Resort received the following bank statement:

DATE		EXPLANATION	CHEQUES	DEPOSITS	BALANCE
Okanagan Valley Ski Resort **321 Spring Road** **Peace River, B.C.**					
20XX					
Oct.	1				13 542 00
	3	113	1 930 00		
		115	2 413 00		9 199 00
	4			3 174 00	12 373 00
	5	116	689 00		11 684 00
	7			1 407 00	
		118	118 00		12 973 00
	9	119	307 00		12 666 00
	10			1 559 00	14 225 00
	15			187 00	14 412 00
	16	CM*		4 225 00	18 637 00
	17	120	1 326 00		
				2 130 00	19 441 00
	22			1 404 00	20 845 00
	24	122	3 016 00		
				721 00	18 550 00
	26			4 208 00	22 758 00
	31	SC**	10 00		22 748 00
	31	DM***	285 00		22 463 00
	31	123	714 00		21 749 00

*CM = Credit Memo   **SC = Service Charge   ***DM = Debit Memo

The credit memorandum from the bank indicated that the bank had collected a note receivable in the amount of $4,000 plus interest for Okanagan Valley Ski Resort. The debit memorandum indicated that a cheque in the amount of $260 from R. Walters had been returned because of non-sufficient funds. The bank assessed a service charge of $25 for the NSF cheque. Cheque 123 had been written in payment of the utilities bill.

Instructions

1. Prepare a T account bank statement reconciliation for Okanagan Valley Ski Resort as of October 31, 20XX.
2. Prepare the necessary general journal entries (page 19) to bring the books up to date after bank statement reconciliation. A partial chart of accounts includes the following: Cash, 101; Accounts Receivable, 110; Notes Receivable, 120; Interest Revenue, 420; Utilities Expense, 640; and Bank Charges Expense, 670.

PROBLEM 10.6

The following petty cash transactions occurred in October for the Jackson House of Guitars:

October 1   established a petty cash fund of $100; cheque I716

October 3   paid $5 for delivery charges; voucher 1

October 4   Herb Jackson took $20 cash for his personal use: voucher 2

October 7   paid $7.50 for newspaper subscription for customers' use, voucher 3

October 10   paid $15 to have windows washed; voucher 4

October 12   paid $5 for postage stamps; voucher 5

October 15   paid $9.50 for express mail charges; voucher 6

October 18   Herb Jackson took a customer to lunch, $17.80: voucher 7

October 21   paid $3.60 for office supplies, voucher 8

October 25   mailed a package to a customer, $3.70; voucher 9

October 27   paid $8 for an ad in a shoppers' newspaper: voucher 10

Instructions

1. Record the entry in the cash payments journal to establish the petty cash fund on October 1. Use page 18 for the journal.

2. Record in a petty cash register (page 10) the initial $100 deposit into the fund and the disbursements for the month. Column headings in the register should include postage expense, delivery expense, and entertainment expense. A partial chart of accounts includes: Cash, 101; Petty Cash, 110; Office Supplies, 120; Herb Jackson, Drawing, 310; Advertising Expense. 610; Delivery Expense, 620; Cleaning Expense, 630; Postage Expense, 640; Entertainment Expense, 650; and Subscription Expense, 660.

3. Total and rule the petty cash register.

4. Prepare the October 31 entry in the cash disbursements journal, cheque 1762, to replenish the petty cash fund.

5. Complete the petty cash register by indicating the October 31 balance, the deposit into the fund, and the balance on November 1.

PROBLEM 10.7

The following petty cash transactions occurred in January for Cowhide Products:

January 1   established a petty cash fund of $50; cheque 2640

January 2   paid $4.60 for office supplies; voucher 100

January 5   paid $12 for a magazine subscription for customers' use; voucher 101

January 6   owner Marge Wade took a customer to lunch, $15.20; voucher 102

January 7   paid $3.20 for office supplies; voucher 103

January 9   bought postage stamps, $6; voucher 104

January 14   Marge Wade withdrew $5 for personal use; voucher 105

January 15   bookkeeper replenished the petty cash fund and made it $50 larger; cheque 2682

January 17   Marge Wade took a client to lunch, $16.40; voucher 106

January 19   paid $15 postage to have parcels sent to a customer; voucher 107

January 20   bought $6.40 in office supplies; voucher 108

January 24   Marge Wade withdrew $10 for personal use; voucher 109

January 25   took packages to the post office for mailing; cost, $8.70; voucher 110

January 26   bought a fern for the store, $17.50 (debit Miscellaneous Expense); voucher 111

January 27   bought plant food for the fern, $3.90 (debit Miscellaneous Expense); voucher 112

January 31   sent flowers to a customer in the hospital, $19.70 (debit Miscellaneous Expense); voucher 113

Instructions

1. Record the entry in the cash payments journal (page 131 to establish the petty cash fund on January 1.

2. Record in a petty cash register (page 12) the initial $50 deposit into the fund and the disbursements from January 1 to January 14. Column headings for the register should include Office Supplies, Postage Expense, and Miscellaneous Expense. A partial chart of accounts includes: Cash, 101; Petty Cash, 110; Office Supplies, 120; Marge Wade, Drawing, 310; Advertising Expense, 610; Postage Expense, 640; Entertainment Expense, 650; Subscription Expense, 660; and Miscellaneous Expense, 670.

3. Total and rule the petty cash register.

4. Prepare the January 15 entry in the cash disbursements journal to replenish the petty cash fund and to make the fund $50 larger. Use page 14 for the journal and cheque 2682.

5. Complete the petty cash register for the January 1–14 time period by writing in the amounts required to replenish the fund and to make the fund $50 larger. The new balance on January 15 will be $100.

6. Continuing on with the month's transactions in a new petty cash register (page 13), record the disbursements from January 15 to January 31. Total and rule the register again.

7. Prepare the entry in the cash disbursements journal on January 31 (cheque 2731), to replenish the petty cash fund and restore it to a $100 balance.

8. Record in the petty cash register, page 13, the balance on January 31, the deposit into the fund, and the balance on February 1.

CHAPTER 11

Worksheets, Financial Statements, and Closing Entries for a Merchandising Business

LEARNING OBJECTIVES

When you have completed this chapter, you should

1. have a better understanding of accounting terminology.
2. be able to prepare a ten-column worksheet for a merchandising business.
3. have a basic understanding of cost of goods sold.
4. be able to prepare an income statement for a merchandising business.
5. be able to prepare a classified balance sheet.
6. be able to calculate current ratio and working capital.
7. be able to journalize and post the adjusting and closing entries for a merchandising business.

VOCABULARY

capital asset	an asset that is held for use in producing other assets
classified	separated into categories
current ratio	one of the indicators of short-term debt-paying ability; obtained by dividing current assets by current liabilities
gross profit	net sales minus cost of goods sold
liquid asset	an asset that is cash or easily converted into cash
working capital	one of the indicators of short-term debt-paying ability; obtained by subtracting current liabilities from current assets

Introduction

The material presented in this chapter completes the accounting cycle for a merchandising business. The accounting cycle, remember, refers to the sequence of accounting procedures that are performed during an accounting period. The cycle begins when a transaction occurs and is journalized and ends with the closing of the books. The steps in the accounting cycle, from beginning to end, are as follows:

1. Journalize transactions.
2. Post transactions.
3. Prepare a worksheet that includes:
   a. a trial balance,
   b. adjustments,
   c. an adjusted trial balance,
   d. income statement calculations, and
   e. balance sheet calculations.
4. Prepare an income statement.
5. Prepare a balance sheet.
6. Prepare schedules of accounts receivable and accounts payable.
7. Journalize and post the adjusting entries.
8. Journalize and post the closing entries.
9. Prepare a post-closing trial balance.

This chapter will concentrate on preparing the worksheet and financial statements and journalizing and posting the closing entries for a merchandising business. The worksheet for Ron's Appliances for the month ended June 30, 20XX is on pages 286–287. The trial balance is prepared directly from the ledger on June 30. Once it is complete and in balance, it should be double ruled. Look over the worksheet and then read the discussion material about merchandise inventory and the adjustments.

The Merchandise Inventory Account on the Worksheet

The merchandise inventory figure that appears on the trial balance represents the balance in the account on June 1 and is referred to as the beginning inventory. The beginning inventory appears on the worksheet as a debit in three places: on the original trial balance, on the adjusted trial balance, and on the income statement, where it will be used in calculating the cost of goods sold.

At the end of the period, June 30 in this case, the periodic inventory was taken, and the value of the actual merchandise on hand was $45,100. This is referred to as the ending inventory and is the current value of the asset. It appears on the worksheet in two places: as a credit on the income statement, where it will be used in the cost of goods sold calculation, and as a debit on the balance sheet, where it represents the actual value of merchandise on hand.

The merchandise inventory appears five times on the worksheet: four times as a debit and one time as a credit.

Beginning Inventory Appears	Ending Inventory Appears
As a **debit** on the trial balance	As a **debit** on the balance sheet
As a **debit** on the adjusted trial balance	As a **credit** on the income statement
As a **debit** on the income statement	

ACCT. NO.	ACCOUNT TITLES	UNADJUSTED TRIAL BALANCE		ADJUSTMENTS	
		DEBIT	CREDIT	DEBIT	CREDIT
	Ron's Appliances				
	Worksheet				
	For Month Ended June 30, 20XX				
101	Cash	11 600 00			
110	Accounts Receivable	13 600 00			
120	Notes Receivable	7 200 00			
130	Merchandise Inventory	46 000 00			
140	Supplies	1 960 00			a. 640 00
150	Prepaid Insurance	3 100 00			b. 100 00
160	Office Equipment	28 000 00			
161	Accumulated Amort.: OE		5 500 00		c. 500 00
170	Delivery Equipment	57 000 00			
171	Accumulated Amort.: DE		11 250 00		c. 750 00
180	Building	130 000 00			
181	Accumulated Amort.: Bldg.		7 500 00		c. 500 00
210	Accounts Payable		5 150 00		
220	Notes Payable		25 000 00		
240	Unearned Revenue		3 500 00	d. 900 00	
250	Mortgage Payable		90 000 00		
310	Ron Renner, Capital		124 390 00		
320	Ron Renner, Drawing	6 000 00			
410	Sales		104 100 00		d. 900 00
420	Sales Returns and Allow.	2 100 00			
430	Sales Discounts	2 900 00			
501	Purchases	58 000 00			
520	Purchases Rets. & Allow.		620 00		
530	Purchases Discounts		240 00		
540	Freight In	2 000 00			
610	Rent Expense	3 500 00			
620	Utilities Expense	750 00			
630	Wages Expense	5 700 00		e. 200 00	
	Totals	379 410 00	379 410 00		
650	Supplies Expense			a. 640 00	
660	Insurance Expense			b. 100 00	
670	Amortization Expense			c. 1 750 00	
230	Wages Payable				e. 200 00
				3 590 00	3 590 00
	Net Income				

	ADJUSTED TRIAL BALANCE		INCOME STATEMENT		BALANCE SHEET	
	DEBIT	CREDIT	DEBIT	CREDIT	DEBIT	CREDIT
	11600 00				11600 00	
	13600 00				13600 00	
	7200 00				7200 00	
	46000 00		46000 00	45100 00	45100 00	
	1320 00				1320 00	
	3000 00				3000 00	
	28000 00				28000 00	
		6000 00				6000 00
	57000 00				57000 00	
		12000 00				12000 00
	130000 00				130000 00	
		8000 00				8000 00
		5150 00				5150 00
		25000 00				25000 00
		2600 00				2600 00
		9000 00				9000 00
		124390 00				124390 00
	6000 00				6000 00	
		105000 00		105000 00		
	2100 00		2100 00			
	2900 00		2900 00			
	58000 00		58000 00			
		620 00		620 00		
		2400 00		2400 00		
	2000 00		2000 00			
	3500 00		3500 00			
	750 00		750 00			
	5900 00		5900 00			
	640 00		640 00			
	100 00		100 00			
	1750 00		1750 00			
		200 00				200 00
	381360 00	381360 00	123640 00	153120 00	302820 00	273340 00
			29480 00			29480 00
			153120 00	153120 00	302820 00	302820 00

Adjustments on the Worksheet

Adjustments are made at the end of the accounting period to bring certain accounts up to date. Each adjustment involves both an income statement account and a balance sheet account. Following is a brief explanation of the adjustments on the worksheet for Ron's Appliances.

a.   This adjustment records the amount of supplies used during June by debiting Supplies Expense and crediting Supplies for $640. The value of the ending inventory of supplies is the figure that should appear on the adjusted trial balance and on the balance sheet.

b.   This adjustment records the insurance expense for June by debiting Insurance Expense and crediting Prepaid Insurance for $100.

c.   This adjustment records amortization expense for June on assets that are to be amortized (office equipment, delivery, equipment, and the building). The debit in each case is to Amortization Expense and the credit is to the contra-asset account, Accumulated Amortization. The three debits to Amortization Expense may be added together and shown as one figure — $1,750 — on the worksheet, but the credits must be made individually to the Accumulated Amortization accounts ($500, $750, and $500).

d.   At some point in the past, Ron received cash in advance of actually delivering the merchandise. This transaction was recorded at the time as a debit to Cash and as a credit to the liability account, Unearned Revenue. This adjusting entry is to transfer a portion ($900) of the balance in Unearned Revenue to Sales, an earned revenue account.

e.   This adjustment records wages expense that have accrued at the end of the accounting period by debiting Wages Expense and crediting Wages Payable for $200.

Once all the adjustments are entered on the worksheet, the adjustments column should be totalled and ruled.

Completing the Worksheet

The next step involves combining the original trial balance with the adjustments for the adjusted trial balance. (If necessary, you may wish to review Chapter Five for details on preparing the worksheet.) Once the adjusted trial balance is complete and in balance, extensions may be made to the balance sheet and income statement columns of the worksheet. Extensions include entering the beginning merchandise inventory as a debit on the income statement and entering the ending inventory as a credit on the income statement and a debit on the balance sheet.

When extensions are complete, the income statement columns are totalled and the net income (or net loss) is determined. A net income figure is entered as a debit on the income statement and as a credit on the balance sheet. Finally, the remaining parts of the worksheet are totalled and ruled.

Cost of Goods Sold

After the worksheet is complete, the accountant may prepare the financial statements. Before discussing the income statement for a merchandising business, however, a discussion about the cost of goods sold is in order. When an item is sold by a retail store, several things have to be taken into consideration before a net income or loss figure can be determined. In addition to determining the related expenses, the *cost of the merchandise sold* must be calculated.

For example, assume that you buy a used car from a friend for $1,200. You pay $800 to have it painted, $150 for repairs, and $350 for new tires. Then you place a $50 ad in the newspaper offering to sell the car for $3,500. After a week's time, you sell the car for $3,400. To calculate your net income, you would do the following:

Revenue from Sale of Car		$3,400
Minus Cost of Purchase of Car		1,200
Gross Profit		$2,200
Minus Expenses		
Painting	$800	
Repairs	150	
Tires	350	
Ad in Paper	50	
Total Expenses		1,350
Net Income from Sale		$ 850

The **gross profit** is profit *before* expenses have been deducted; it is simply the revenue minus the cost of the item sold. When a large item such as an automobile is sold, the direct cost of the merchandise sold is relatively easy to figure. When a store sells smaller items that are difficult to identify individually, a different procedure is used to calculate the cost of goods sold.

Calculation for Cost of Goods Sold

Before the cost of goods sold can be calculated, three things must be known: (1) the cost of the beginning inventory, (2) the cost of purchases, and (3) the cost of the ending inventory.

Cost of Goods Sold		
Beginning Inventory	$21,500	The cost of merchandise on hand at the beginning of the period
Add: Cost of Purchases	46,200	Add the cost of purchases during the period
Total Goods Available for Sale	$67,700	Merchandise that was available for sale during the period
Minus: Ending Inventory	19,600	Minus the cost of merchandise at the end of the period
Cost of Goods Sold	$48,100	Equals the cost of merchandise sold

Goods Available for Sale

When the cost of purchases for the period is added to beginning inventory, the result is the total goods available for sale. The total goods available for sale does not equal the cost of goods sold, however, because not every item that was available for sale was sold. Some items remain in the store at the end of the accounting period; these items represent ending inventory, or the remaining goods. When the ending inventory is subtracted from all the goods available for sale, the result is the goods sold, or the cost of goods sold. The goods available for sale represents both the goods sold and the goods not sold, because it represents *everything that was available for sale in the store during the entire accounting period.*

The Merchandising Income Statement

The income statement for a merchandising business contains three main sections: (1) the revenue section, (2) the cost of goods sold section, and (3) the expense section. The three sections appear in this order:

1. Sales
2. —Cost of Goods Sold
   Gross Profit
3. —Expenses
   Net Income (or Net Loss)

The **gross profit**, remember, is profit before related expenses are deducted; it is the net sales minus cost of goods sold. The income statement is prepared directly from the worksheet, where many of the calculations have already been made. A partial worksheet showing the income statement columns for Ron's Appliances appears on page 291.

The net income has already been calculated. The accountant can now prepare the formal income statement for Ron's Appliances directly from the worksheet.

The following income statement for Ron's Appliances contains the three main elements: (1) revenue, (2) cost of goods sold, and (3) expenses.

Ron's Appliances			
Income Statement			
For Month Ended June 30, 20XX			
Revenue from Sales			
Sales			$105,000
Less: Sales Returns and Allowances		$ 2,100	
Sales Discounts		2,900	5,000
Net Sales			$100,000
Cost of Goods Sold			
Merchandise Inventory, June 1, 20XX		46,000	
Purchases		58,000	
Less: Purchases Returns and Allowances	$ 620		
Purchases Discounts	2,400	3,020	
Net Purchases		54,980	
Add: Freight In		2,000	
Cost of Purchases		56,980	
Cost of Merchandise Available for Sale		102,980	
Less: Merchandise Inventory, June 30, 20XX		45,100	
Cost of Goods Sold			57,880
Gross Profit			42,120
Expenses			
Rent Expense		3,500	
Utilities Expense		750	
Wages Expense		5,900	
Supplies Expense		640	
Insurance Expense		100	
Amortization Expense		1,750	
Total Expenses			12,640
Net Income			$ 29,480

Ron's Appliances
Worksheet (Partial)
For Month Ended June 30, 20XX

ACCT. NO.	ACCOUNT TITLES	ADJUSTED TRIAL BALANCE DEBIT	ADJUSTED TRIAL BALANCE CREDIT	INCOME STATEMENT DEBIT	INCOME STATEMENT CREDIT
101	Cash	11600 00			
110	Accounts Receivable	13600 00			
120	Notes Receivable	7200 00			
130	Merchandise Inventory	46000 00		46000 00	45100 00
140	Supplies	1320 00			
150	Prepaid Insurance	300 00			
160	Office Equipment	28000 00			
161	Accumulated Amort.: OE		600 00		
170	Delivery Equipment	57000 00			
171	Accumulated Amort.: DE		12000 00		
180	Building	130000 00			
181	Accumulated Amort.: Bldg.		8000 00		
210	Accounts Payable		5150 00		
220	Notes Payable		25000 00		
240	Unearned Revenue		2600 00		
250	Mortgage Payable		90000 00		
310	Ron Renner, Capital		124390 00		
320	Ron Renner, Drawing	6000 00			
410	Sales		105000 00		105000 00
420	Sales Returns and Allow.	2100 00		2100 00	
430	Sales Discounts	2900 00		2900 00	
501	Purchases	58000 00		58000 00	
520	Purchases Rets. & Allow.		620 00		620 00
530	Purchases Discounts		2400 00		2400 00
540	Freight In	2000 00		2000 00	
610	Rent Expense	3500 00		3500 00	
620	Utilities Expense	750 00		750 00	
630	Wages Expense	5900 00		5900 00	
	Totals				
650	Supplies Expense	640 00		640 00	
660	Insurance Expense	100 00		100 00	
670	Amortization Expense	1750 00		1750 00	
230	Wages Payable		200 00		
		381360 00	381360 00	123640 00	153120 00
	Net Income			29480 00	
				153120 00	153120 00

The cost of goods sold section of the income statement contains the calculation for cost of purchases, which makes the income statement appear to be more complicated than it really is. The following shows the three main elements of the cost of goods sold section: (1) beginning inventory, (2) cost of purchases, and (3) closing inventory.

Cost of Goods Sold			
1. Merchandise Inventory, June 1, 20XX			**$ 46,000**
Purchases		$58,000	
Less: Purchases Returns and Allowances	$ 620		
Purchases Discounts	2,400	3,020	
Net Purchases		54,980	
Add: Freight In		2,000	
2. Cost of Purchases			**56,980**
Total Cost of Merchandise Available for Sale			102,980
3. Less: Merchandise Inventory, June 30, 20XX			**45,100**
Cost of Goods Sold			$57,880

The Classified Balance Sheet

The balance sheet, too, is prepared directly from the worksheet. The accounts have already been adjusted, and the net income (or net loss) has already been calculated. The balance sheet portion of the worksheet for Ron's Appliances follows on page 000.

Assets and liabilities are **classified** on the balance sheet. That is, assets and liabilities are separated into categories: for assets, the categories are (1) current assets and (2) capital assets; for liabilities, the categories are (1) current liabilities and (2) long-term liabilities.

Current Assets

Current assets are listed on the balance sheet in their order of liquidity. A **liquid asset** is cash or an asset that can easily be converted into cash. Therefore Cash is always listed first, followed by Accounts Receivable, Notes Receivable, and Merchandise Inventory. The other current assets may be listed in any order.

Capital Assets

Capital assets are held for use in producing other assets. Following are those capital assets that are to be amortized shown with their Accumulated Amortization accounts as illustrated on page 293.

Capital Assets		
Office Equipment	$28,000	
Less: Accumulated Amortization: Office Equipment	6,000	$ 22,000
Delivery Equipment	57,000	
Less: Accumulated Amortization: Delivery Equipment	12,000	45,000
Building	130,000	
Less: Accumulated Amortization: Building	8,000	122,000
Total Plant and Equipment		$189,000

Ron's Appliances
Worksheet (Partial)
For Month Ended June 30, 20XX

ACCT. NO.	ACCOUNT TITLES	ADJUSTED TRIAL BALANCE DEBIT	CREDIT	DEBIT	CREDIT
101	Cash	11600 00		11600 00	
110	Accounts Receivable	13600 00		13600 00	
120	Notes Receivable	7200 00		7200 00	
130	Merchandise Inventory	46000 00		45100 00	
140	Supplies	1320 00		1320 00	
150	Prepaid Insurance	300 00		300 00	
160	Office Equipment	2800 00		2800 00	
161	Accumulated Amort.: OE		600 00		600 00
170	Delivery Equipment	5700 00		5700 00	
171	Accumulated Amort.: DE		1200 00		1200 00
180	Building	130000 00		130000 00	
181	Accumulated Amort.: Bldg.		8000 00		8000 00
210	Accounts Payable		5150 00		5150 00
220	Notes Payable		25000 00		25000 00
240	Unearned Revenue		2600 00		2600 00
250	Mortgage Payable		90000 00		90000 00
310	Ron Renner, Capital		124390 00		124390 00
320	Ron Renner, Drawing	6000 00		6000 00	
410	Sales		105000 00		
420	Sales Returns and Allow.	2100 00			
430	Sales Discounts	2900 00			
501	Purchases	58000 00			
520	Purchases Rets. & Allow.		620 00		
530	Purchases Discounts		2400 00		
540	Freight In	2000 00			
610	Rent Expense	3500 00			
620	Utilities Expense	750 00			
630	Wages Expense	5900 00			
	Totals				
650	Supplies Expense	640 00			
660	Insurance Expense	100 00			
670	Amortization Expense	1750 00			
230	Wages Payable		200 00		200 00
		381360 00	381360 00	302820 00	273340 00
	Net Income				29480 00
				302820 00	302820 00

Capital assets are recorded originally at their historic cost. The balance sheet shows the historic cost, the accumulated amortization, and the book value. If a firm owns land, it will be the first capital asset listed.

Current and Long-Term Liabilities

Current liabilities are those that are due within a relatively short period of time, usually one year. Current liabilities are paid out of current assets. On the balance sheet, Accounts Payable is listed first, followed by Notes Payable (that portion that is due within one year). The other current liabilities are listed in no particular order. A portion of the Mortgage Payable is usually listed as a current liability, but only the amount that is due and payable within one year.

Long-term liabilities are those that are due after one year's time. Mortgage Payable and Notes Payable (those portions due after one year's time) usually fall into this category.

Owner's Equity

There are no changes in presentation of owner's equity on the balance sheet. However, as you know, many business owners prepare a separate statement of owner's equity and show only the ending capital on the balance sheet. The balance sheet for Ron's Appliances follows.

Ron's Appliances			
Balance Sheet			
June 30, 20XX			
Assets			
Current Assets			
Cash		$ 11,600	
Accounts Receivable		13,600	
Notes Receivable		7,200	
Merchandise Inventory		45,100	
Supplies		1,320	
Prepaid Insurance		3,000	
Total Current Assets			$ 81,820
Capital Assets			
Office Equipment	$ 28,000		
Less: Accumulated Amortization: Office Equipment	6,000	22,000	
Delivery Equipment	57,000		
Less: Accumulated Amortization: Delivery Equipment	12,000	45,000	
Building	130,000		
Less: Accumulated Amortization: Building	8,000	122,000	
Total Plant and Equipment			189,000
Total Assets			$270,820
Liabilities			
Current Liabilities			
Accounts Payable	$ 5,150		
Notes Payable	25,000		
Wages Payable	200		
Unearned Revenue	2,600		
Mortgage Payable (current portion)	12,000		
Total Current Liabilities		44,950	
Long-Term Liabilities			
Mortgage Payable		78,000	
Total Liabilities		$122,950	
Owner's Equity			
Ron Renner, Capital, June 1, 20XX	$ 124,390		
Add: Net Income	29,480		
Subtotal	153,870		
Less: Ron Renner, Drawing	6,000		
Ron Renner, Capital, June 30, 20XX			147,870
Total Liabilities and Owner's Equity			$270,820

Current Ratio

The **current ratio** is a good indicator of a firm's ability to pay its short-term debts when they are due; it is determined by dividing total current assets by total current liabilities. For Ron's Appliances, the current ratio is:

$$\frac{\text{Current Assets} \ = \$81,820}{\text{Current Liabilities} = \$44,950} = 1.82:1.$$

The 1.82:1 figure (rounded to the nearest hundredth) indicates that current assets are 1.82 times as much as current liabilities. Most lenders and other readers of financial statements are very interested in the current ratio and would like to see it be at least 2:1 (twice as many current assets as current liabilities), because the current liabilities must be paid out of the current assets. Although a 2:1 ratio may be desirable, in reality the average in Canadian industry is around 1.7:1 or 1.8:1. A current ratio of 3:1 would be a strong current position, while a ratio of 1:1 would be weak. A 1:1 ratio indicates that every dollar of current assets is targeted for payment of short-term debt and nothing would be left over for emergencies or working capital.

Working Capital

The excess of current assets over current liabilities is **working capital**. For Ron's Appliances, it is:

Current Assets	–	Current Liabilities	=	Working Capital
$81,820	–	$44,950	=	$36,870

The working capital figure is, like the current ratio, an indication of a firm's short-term financial strength. It represents an amount of cash that a firm may put into, for example, volume buying, inventories, advertising, or favourable credit terms to customers.

Closing Entries

The discussion of closing entries in chapter 6 showed that there are four entries to be made for a service business. They are entries to (1) close all revenue accounts, (2) close all expense accounts, (3) transfer net income or loss to the capital account, and (4) transfer the balance of drawing to the capital account.

The first two closing entries are a little different for a merchandising business, because all of the cost of goods sold accounts must be closed in addition to the revenue and expense accounts. However, there are still four general journal entries required to close the books of a merchandising business, and they are made directly from the worksheet as before:

1. Close each account that appears in the credit column of the income statement.
2. Close each account that appears in the debit column of the income statement.
3. Transfer the net income or loss to the capital account.
4. Transfer the balance of the drawing account to the capital account.

Only the first two entries are different from those of a service business; the last two are exactly the same. The following shows the income statement columns of the worksheet for Ron's Appliances.

Ron's Appliances
Worksheet (Partial)
For Month Ended June 30, 20XX

ACCT. NO.	ACCOUNT TITLES	ADJUSTED TRIAL BALANCE DEBIT	CREDIT	INCOME STATEMENT DEBIT	CREDIT	
101	Cash	11600 00				
110	Accounts Receivable	13600 00				
120	Notes Receivable	7200 00				✓
130	Merchandise Inventory	46000 00		46000 00	45100 00	
140	Supplies	1320 00				
150	Prepaid Insurance	3000 00				
160	Office Equipment	28000 00				
161	Accumulated Amort.: OE		6000 00			
170	Delivery Equipment	57000 00				
171	Accumulated Amort.: DE		12000 00			
180	Building	130000 00				
181	Accumulated Amort.: Bldg.		8000 00			
210	Accounts Payable		5150 00			
220	Notes Payable		25000 00			
240	Unearned Revenue		2600 00			
250	Mortgage Payable		90000 00			
310	Ron Renner, Capital		124390 00			
320	Ron Renner, Drawing	6000 00				
410	Sales		105000 00		105000 00	✓
420	Sales Returns and Allow.	2100 00		2100 00		
430	Sales Discounts	2900 00		2900 00		
501	Purchases	58000 00		58000 00		
520	Purchases Rets. & Allow.		620 00		620 00	✓
530	Purchases Discounts		2400 00		2400 00	
540	Freight In	2000 00		2000 00		
610	Rent Expense	3500 00		3500 00		
620	Utilities Expense	750 00		750 00		
630	Wages Expense	5900 00		5900 00		
	Totals					
650	Supplies Expense	640 00		640 00		
660	Insurance Expense	100 00		100 00		
670	Amortization Expense	1750 00		1750 00		
230	Wages Payable		200 00			✓
		381360 00	381360 00	123640 00	153120 00	
	Net Income			29480 00		
				153120 00	153120 00	

The First Closing Entry

The first closing entry debits each account that appears in the credit column of the income statement; the total is credited to Income Summary. Add check marks to the worksheet next to the amounts as they are journalized.

GENERAL JOURNAL				PAGE 6	
DATE	DESCRIPTION	POST REF.	DEBIT	CREDIT	
20XX	Closing Entries				
June 30	Merchandise Inventory	130	4 5 1 0 0 00		
	Sales	410	10 5 0 0 0 00		
	Purchases Returns and Allowances	520	6 2 0 00		
	Purchases Discounts	530	2 4 0 0 00		
	Income Summary	360		15 3 1 2 0 00	
	To Close Income Statement Accounts with				
	Credit Balances and to Enter the Ending				
	Inventory on the Books				

After this first closing entry has been posted, the Merchandise Inventory account will look like this:

Merchandise Inventory   **130**

6/1	Balance	46,000	
6/30	Closing GJ6	45,100	

The effect of the first closing entry on the Merchandise Inventory account is to transfer the value of the ending inventory to the account. The beginning inventory figure is closed out in the second closing entry.

The Second Closing Entry

The second closing entry credits every account that appears on the debit side of the income statement and debits Income Summary. The following shows the income statement columns of the worksheet. Check marks have been placed opposite the accounts in the worksheet debit and credit columns for which closing entries have been made.

ACCT. NO.	ACCOUNT TITLES	ADJUSTED TRIAL BALANCE		INCOME STATEMENT	
		DEBIT	CREDIT	DEBIT	CREDIT
101	Cash	11 600 00			
110	Accounts Receivable	13 600 00			
120	Notes Receivable	7 200 00			
130	Merchandise Inventory	46 000 00		46 000 00 ✓	45 100 00 ✓
140	Supplies	1 320 00			
150	Prepaid Insurance	3 000 00			
160	Office Equipment	28 000 00			
161	Accumulated Amort.: OE		6 000 00		
170	Delivery Equipment	57 000 00			
171	Accumulated Amort.: DE		12 000 00		
180	Building	130 000 00			
181	Accumulated Amort.: Bldg.		8 000 00		
210	Accounts Payable		5 150 00		
220	Notes Payable		25 000 00		
240	Unearned Revenue		2 600 00		
250	Mortgage Payable		900 00		
310	Ron Renner, Capital		124 390 00		
320	Ron Renner, Drawing	6 000 00			
410	Sales		105 000 00		105 000 00 ✓
420	Sales Returns and Allow's.	2 100 00		2 100 00 ✓	
430	Sales Discounts	2 900 00		2 900 00 ✓	
501	Purchases	58 000 00		58 000 00 ✓	
520	Purchases Rets. & Allow's		620 00		620 00 ✓
530	Purchases Discounts		240 00		240 00 ✓
540	Freight In	2 000 00		2 000 00 ✓	
6610	Rent Expense	3 500 00		3 500 00 ✓	
620	Utilities Expense	750 00`		750 00 ✓	
630	Wages Expense	5 900 00		5 900 00 ✓	
	Totals				
650	Supplies Expense	640 00		640 00 ✓	
660	Insurance Expense	100 00		100 00 ✓	
670	Amortization Expense	1 750 00		1 750 00 ✓	
230	Wages Payable				
		381 360 00	381 360 00	123 640 00	153 120 00
	Net Income			29 480 00	
				153 120 00	153 120 00

Heading:
Ron's Appliances
Worksheet (Partial)
For Month Ended June 30, 20XX

		GENERAL JOURNAL										PAGE 6						
DATE		**DESCRIPTION**	**POST REF.**				**DEBIT**							**CREDIT**				
20XX		Closing Entries																
	30	Income Summary	360	1	2	3	6	4	0	00								
		Merchandise Inventory	130									4	6	0	0	0	00
		Sales Returns and Allowances	420										2	1	0	0	00
		Sales Discounts	430										2	9	0	0	00
		Purchases	501									5	8	0	0	0	00
		Freight In	540										2	0	0	0	00
		Rent Expense	610										3	5	0	0	00
		Utilities Expense	620											7	5	0	00
		Wages Expense	630										5	9	0	0	00
		Supplies Expense	650											6	4	0	00
		Insurance Expense	660											1	0	0	00
		Amortization Expense	670										1	7	5	0	00
		To Close Income Statement Accounts with															
		Debit Balances and to Close Out Beginning															
		Merchandise Inventory															

After the second closing entry has been posted, the Merchandise Inventory account appears as follows.

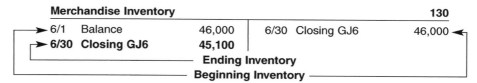

The account now reflects the value of the ending inventory. The ending inventory for this period becomes the beginning inventory of the next period.

The Third and Fourth Closing Entries

The third closing entry transfers the profit (or loss) to the owner's capital account, and the fourth transfers the balance of the drawing account to the owner's capital account.

GENERAL JOURNAL				PAGE 6	
DATE	DESCRIPTION	POST REF.	DEBIT	CREDIT	
20XX	Closing Entries				
30	Income Summary	360	29 480 00		
	Ron Renner, Capital	310		29 480 00	
	To Transfer Net Income to Capital				
30	Ron Renner, Capital	310	6 000 00		
	Ron Renner, Drawing	320		6 000 00	
	To Transfer Balance of Drawing to Capital				

After the third closing entry is posted, the income Summary account is closed as follows:

Income Summary   **360**

6/30	Closing GJ6	123,640	6/30	Closing GJ6	153,120
6/30	Closing GJ6	29,480			

The General Ledger after the Adjusting and Closing Entries Are Posted

The adjusting and closing entries are shown now, followed by T accounts representing the general ledger after they have been posted.

DATE		DESCRIPTION	POST REF.	DEBIT	CREDIT
		GENERAL JOURNAL			**PAGE 5**
20XX		Adjusting Entries			
June	30	Supplies Expense	650	6 4 0 00	
		Supplies	140		6 4 0 00
		To Record Supplies Used for June			
	30	Insurance Expense	660	1 0 0 00	
		Prepaid Insurance	150		1 0 0 00
		To Record Insurance Expense for June			
	30	Amortization Expense	670	1 7 5 0 00	
		Accumulated Amortization: OE	161		5 0 0 00
		Accumulated Amortization: DE	171		7 5 0 00
		Accumulated Amortization: Building	181		5 0 0 00
		To Record Amortization Expense			
	30	Unearned Revenue	240	9 0 0 00	
		Sales	410		9 0 0 00
		To Transfer a Portion of Unearned Revenue			
		to Sales			
	30	Wages Expense	630	2 0 0 00	
		Wages Payable	230		2 0 0 00
		To Record Accrued Wages			

		GENERAL JOURNAL										PAGE 6					
DATE		DESCRIPTION	POST REF.	DEBIT							CREDIT						
20XX		Closing Entries															
June	30	Merchandise Inventory	130		4	5	1	0	0	00							
		Sales	410	1	0	5	0	0	0	00							
		Purchases Returns and Allowances	520				6	2	0	00							
		Purchases Discounts	530			2	4	0	0	00							
		Income Summary	360								1	5	3	1	2	0	00
		To Close Income Statement Accounts with															
		Credit Balances and to Enter the Ending															
		Inventory on the Books															
	30	Income Summary	360	1	2	3	6	4	0	00							
		Merchandise Inventory	130									4	6	0	0	0	00
		Sales Returns and Allowances	420										2	1	0	0	00
		Sales Discounts	430										2	9	0	0	00
		Purchases	501									5	8	0	0	0	00
		Freight In	540										2	0	0	0	00
		Rent Expense	610										3	5	0	0	00
		Utilities Expense	620											7	5	0	00
		Wages Expense	630										5	9	0	0	00
		Supplies Expense	650											6	4	0	00
		Insurance Expense	660											1	0	0	00
		Amortization Expense	670										1	7	5	0	00
		To Close Income Statement Accounts with															
		Debit Balances and to Close Out Beginning															
		Merchandise Inventory															
	30	Income Summary	360		2	9	4	8	0	00							
		Ron Renner, Capital	310									2	9	4	8	0	00
		To Transfer Net Income to Capital															
	30	Ron Renner, Capital	310			6	0	0	0	00							
		Ron Renner, Drawing	320										6	0	0	0	00
		To Transfer Balance of Drawing to Capital															

Cash 101

6/30 Balance	11,600		

Accounts Receivable 110

6/30 Balance	13,600		

Notes Receivable 120

6/30 Balance	7,200		

Merchandise Inventory 130

6/1 Balance	46,000	6/30 Closing GJ6	46,000
6/30 Closing GJ6	45,100		

Supplies 140

6/1 Balance	1,960	6/30 Adjusting GJ5	640
	1,320		

Prepaid Insurance 150

6/1 Balance	3,100	6/30 Adjusting GJ5	100
	3,000		

Office Equipment 160

6/30 Balance	28,000		

Accumulated Amortization: Office Equipment 161

		6/1 Balance	5,500
		6/30 Adjusting GJ5	500
			6,000

Delivery Equipment 170

6/30 Balance	57,000		

Accumulated Amortization: Delivery Equipment 171

		6/1 Balance	11,250
		6/30 Adjusting GJ5	750
			12,000

Building 180

6/30 Balance	130,000		

Accumulated Amortization: Building 181

		6/1 Balance	7,500
		6/30 Adjusting GJ5	500
			8,000

Accounts Payable 210

		6/30 Balance	5,150

Notes Payable 220

		6/30 Balance	25,000

Wages Payable 230

		6/30 Adjusting GJ5	200

Unearned Revenue 240

6/30 Adjusting GJ5	900	6/1 Balance	3,500
			2,600

Mortgage Payable 250

		6/30 Balance	90,000

Ron Renner, Capital 310

6/30 Closing GJ6	6,000	6/1 Balance	124,390
		6/30 Closing GJ6	29,480
			153,870
			147,870

Ron Renner, Drawing 320

6/30 Balance	6,000	6/30 Closing GJ6	6,000

Income Summary 360

6/30 Closing GJ6	123,640	6/30 Closing GJ6	153,120
6/30 Closing GJ6	29,480		

Sales 410

6/30 Closing GJ6	105,000	6/30 Balance	104,100
		6/30 Adjusting GJ5	900

Sales Returns and Allowances 420

6/30 Balance	2,100	6/30 Closing GJ6	2,100

Sales Discounts 430

6/30 Balance	2,900	6/30 Closing GJ6	2,900

Purchases 501

6/30 Balance	58,000	6/30 Closing GJ6	58,000

Purchases Returns and Allowances 520

6/30 Closing GJ6	620	6/30 Balance	620

Purchase Discounts 530

6/30 Closing GJ6	2,400	6/30 Balance	2,400

Freight In 540

6/30 Balance	2,000	6/30 Closing GJ6	2,000

Rent Expense 610

6/30 Balance	3,500	6/30 Closing GJ6	3,500

Utilities Expense 620

6/30 Balance	750	6/30 Closing GJ6	750

Wages Expense 630

6/30 Balance	5,700	6/30 Closing GJ6	5,900
6/30 Adjusting GJ5	200		

Supplies Expense 650

6/30 Adjusting GJ5	640	6/30 Closing GJ6	640

Insurance Expense 660

6/30 Adjusting GJ5	100	6/30 Closing GJ6	100

Amortization Expense 670

6/30 Adjusting GJ5	1,750	6/30 Closing GJ6	1,750

The Post-Closing Trial Balance

All the revenue, cost of goods sold, and expense accounts have zero balances after the closing entries are posted. In addition, the capital account has been brought up to date (by adding the net income and subtracting the drawing), and the drawing account has been closed. The only accounts that remain open are the assets, liabilities, and owner's capital accounts.

The post-closing trial balance is prepared to ensure that debits equal credits in the accounts that remain open—the balance sheet accounts—before work is started for the next accounting period. It should be prepared directly from the ledger after the closing entries are posted. Following is the post-closing trial balance for Ron's Appliances.

Ron's Appliances Post-Closing Trial Balance June 30, 20XX		
Cash	$ 11 6 0 0 00	
Accounts Receivable	1 3 6 0 0 00	
Notes Receivable	7 2 0 0 00	
Merchandise Inventory	4 5 1 0 0 00	
Supplies	1 3 2 0 00	
Prepaid Insurance	3 0 0 0 00	
Office Equipment	2 8 0 0 0 00	
Accumulated Amortization: OE		$ 6 0 0 0 00
Delivery Equipment	5 7 0 0 0 00	
Accumulated Amortization: DE		1 2 0 0 0 00
Building	1 3 0 0 0 0 00	
Accumulated Amortization: Building		8 0 0 0 00
Accounts Payable		5 1 5 0 00
Notes Payable		2 5 0 0 0 00
Wages Payable		2 0 0 00
Unearned Revenue		2 6 0 0 00
Mortgage Payable		9 0 0 0 0 00
Ron Renner, Capital		1 4 7 8 7 0 00
Totals	$ 2 9 6 8 2 0 00	$ 2 9 6 8 2 0 00

Summary

The complete accounting cycle includes (1) journalizing, (2) posting, (3) preparing a worksheet with adjustments, (4) preparing all income statement, (5) preparing a balance sheet, (6) preparing schedules of accounts receivable and accounts payable, (7) journalizing and posting adjusting entries, (8) journalizing and posting closing entries, and (9) preparing a post-closing trial balance.

The worksheet for a merchandising business contains both the beginning and ending merchandise inventories. The beginning inventory figure is obtained from the general ledger and appears on the worksheet as a debit on the trial balance, the adjusted trial balance, and the income statement. The ending inventory figure, obtained by a physical count or an estimate, appears on the worksheet in two places: as a credit on the income statement and as a debit on the balance sheet. The inventory figures are used when calculating cost of goods sold on the income statement.

The income statement for a merchandising business contains three major sections: (1) revenue, (2) cost of goods sold, and (3) expenses. Revenue minus cost of goods sold produces the gross profit figure, and expenses subtracted from gross profit produces the net profit figure. The cost of goods sold is calculated as follows:

Beginning Inventory
+ Cost of Purchases
Cost of Merchandise Available for Sale
− Ending Inventory
Cost of Goods Sold

The income statement is prepared directly from the income statement columns of the worksheet, and the balance sheet is prepared from the balance sheet columns. The asset section of the balance sheet is classified into current assets and capital assets. Current assets are cash, items that can easily be converted into cash, or items that will be used up within one year's time. Capital assets include assets that are used in the production of other assets; such items might be furniture, office equipment, delivery vehicles, or land. Capital assets are shown on the balance sheet at their historical cost. Accumulated amortization is subtracted from cost, and the book value is calculated on the balance sheet.

Liabilities are also classified into two categories: current and long-term. Current liabilities must be paid within one year's time, and long-term liabilities are due after one year.

The current ratio is an indicator of a firm's short-term debt-paying ability and is calculated by dividing current assets by current liabilities. A ratio of 2:1 is considered to be adequate; a ratio of 3:1 is considered to be strong. Another indicator of short-term debt-paying ability is the working capital figure, which is obtained by subtracting current liabilities from current assets. Working capital represents the portion of current assets that is not targeted for paying current liabilities.

The closing entries, prepared directly from the income statement columns of the worksheet, accomplish the following:

1. All the revenue and contra-revenue accounts are closed.

2. All the cost of goods sold accounts (including purchases and contra-purchases accounts) are closed.

3. All the expense accounts are closed.

4. The merchandise inventory account is brought up to date by closing out the beginning inventory and entering the ending inventory figure on the books.

5. The drawing account is closed.

6. The capital account is brought up to date by adding the net income, or deducting the net loss, and by deducting drawing.

Once the closing entries are posted, the only remaining step in the accounting cycle is to prepare a post-closing trial balance. It ensures the equality of debits and credits in the ledger accounts that remain open—all of the balance sheet accounts except drawing.

Vocabulary Review

Here is a list of the words and terms for this chapter:

capital asset   gross profit

classified   liquid asset

current ratio   working capital

Fill in the blank with the correct word or term from the list.

1. The _____ is obtained by dividing current assets by current liabilities and is an indicator of short-term debt-paying ability.

2. Net sales minus cost of goods sold equals _____.

3. Current assets minus current liabilities is called _____ and is an indicator of a firm's short-term debt-paying ability.

4. When items are separated into categories, they are said to be _____.

5. A/an _____ is cash or is easily converted to cash.

6. A/an _____ is used to produce other assets.

Match the words and terms on the left with the definitions on the right.

 7. capital asset   **a.** separated into categories

 8. classified   **b.** net sales minus cost of goods sold

 9. current ratio   **c.** cash or easily converted into cash

10. gross profit   **d.** current assets minus current liabilities

11. liquid asset   **e.** current assets divided by current liabilities

12. working capital   **f.** used in production of other assets

Exercises

EXERCISE 11.1

Record the adjusting entries in a general journal (page 6) for the month of September 20XX for Ma and Pa Grocery. Use the following account titles: Supplies, Prepaid Insurance, Prepaid Advertising, Accumulated Amortization: Computer, Unearned Revenue, Wages Payable, Grocery Revenue, Amortization Expense, Insurance Expense, Advertising Expense, Supplies Expense, and Wages Expense.

a. The computer, purchased on January 2 of this year for $8,000, is expected to be useful for four years and will have a salvage value of $2,000.

b. On September 1 of this year, Ma and Pa Grocery received a cheque for $2,000 from a local orphanage. The money was for supplies and groceries to be delivered after September 1 and was credited to Unearned Revenue. During September, $800 worth of groceries were delivered to the orphanage.

c. On January 2 of this year, $1,800 was paid for a two-year insurance policy.

d. On September 1 of this year, $900 was paid for three months of advertising.

e. Three days' wages of $210 per day had accrued at the end of September.

f. The balance in the Supplies account on September 1 was $440. Additional supplies were purchased on September 18 for $120 and on September 24 for $70. The value of the supplies on hand on September 30 was $310.

EXERCISE 11.2

Tell on which section of the balance sheet each of the following accounts appears. The sections should be identified as current assets(CA), capital assets (CAP/A), current liabilities (CL), long-term liabilities (LTL), or owner's equity (OE). Also tell what the normal account balance is for each account listed.

Account Titles	Which Section of the Balance Sheet?	Normal Account Balance?
a. Prepaid Insurance		
b. Owner's Drawing		
c. Accounts Payable		
d. Building		
e. Cash		
f. Unearned Revenue		
g. Accumulated Amortization		
h. Office Furniture		
i. Mortgage Payable (all due in 10 years)		
j. Merchandise Inventory		

Now tell on which section of the income statement each of the following accounts appears. Sections should be identified as revenue (R), cost of goods sold (CGS), or expense (E). Also tell the normal account balance for each.

Account Titles	Which Section of the Income Statement?	Normal Account Balance?
k. Sales Discounts		
l. Purchases Discounts		
m. Wages Expense		
n. Sales Returns and Allowances		
o. Merchandise Inventory		
p. Sales		
q. Supplies Expense		
r. Freight In		
s. Purchases		
t. Purchases Returns and Allowances		

EXERCISE 11.3

The Merchandise Inventory account for Sam's Glass Shop shows a debit balance on February 1 of $17,640. Answer the following questions about this account:

a. What is the account classification for merchandise inventory?

b. How is the dollar value of the ending merchandise inventory determined?

c. The beginning merchandise inventory figure appears on the ten-column worksheet in three different places. What are those three places?

d. Assuming that the value of Sam's merchandise inventory on February 28 is $16,500, on which two worksheet columns will this ending inventory figure appear?

e. Where will the merchandise inventory figure appear on the financial statements?

EXERCISE 11.4

Following are the steps in the accounting cycle. Rearrange them in correct order, numbering each. As an example, the first is "(1) Journalize period's regular transactions."

Prepare trial balance, calculate adjustments, and complete worksheet.
Prepare a balance sheet.
Prepare a post-closing trial balance.
Journalize period's regular transactions.
Journalize and post closing entries.
Post regular transactions to ledger.
Prepare an income statement.
Journalize and post adjusting entries.
Prepare schedules of accounts receivable and payable.

EXERCISE 11.5

Given the following account balances, calculate (1) net sales and (2) cost of purchases.

Cash	$10,550
Sales Discounts	1,470
Purchases Discounts	3,880
Sales	94,000
Freight In	3,190
Merchandise Inventory	31,000
Purchases	49,600
Sales Returns and Allowances	2,630
Purchases Returns and Allowances	4,020

EXERCISE 11.6

From the following account balances, prepare the cost of goods sold section of an income statement for the month of August 20XX.

Purchases	$29,400
Merchandise Inventory, August 31	12,300
Purchases Returns and Allowances	410
Freight In	1,100
Purchases Discounts	290
Merchandise Inventory, August 1	11,400

EXERCISE 11.7

Following are the asset and liability accounts and their balances as of May 31, 20XX for Carlo's Italian Restaurant after the adjusting entries have been posted. Determine (1) the dollar amount of current assets, (2) the dollar amount of current liabilities, (3) the current ratio rounded to the nearest tenth, (4) the working capital, and (5) the total dollar value of capital assets as it would appear on the balance sheet.

Cash	$ 9,120
Accounts Payable	2,500
Merchandise Inventory	9,235
Equipment	15,000
Accumulated Amortization: Equipment	2,300
Payroll Taxes Payable	320
Supplies	940
Accounts Receivable	3,630
Wages Payable	550
Prepaid Insurance	500
Furniture	7,500
Accumulated Amortization: Furniture	1,800
Mortgage Payable ($6,000 due within 12 months)	50,000
Land	75,000
Unearned Revenue	3,500

EXERCISE 11.8

Following are the income statement columns of the May 20XX worksheet for Goodlife Vitamins, owned by Nancy Swanson. The balance of the owner's drawing account on May 31, 20XX was $3,600. Prepare the closing entries to: (1) close all accounts with credit balances and enter the ending merchandise inventory on the books, (2) close all accounts with debit balances and remove the beginning inventory from the books, (3) transfer the net income to the owner's capital account, and (4) transfer the balance of drawing to capital. Use general journal page 31.

	Income Statement	
	Debit	**Credit**
Merchandise Inventory	13,700	14,100
Sales		47,000
Sales Returns and Allowances	410	
Sales Discounts	520	
Purchases	29,000	
Purchases Returns and Allowances		330
Purchases Discounts		260
Freight In	1,100	
Rent Expense	1,800	
Advertising Expense	2,010	
Salary Expense	2,740	
Supplies Expense	390	
Amortization Expense	1,740	
Utilities Expense	330	
Totals	53,740	61,690
Net Income	7,950	
	61,690	61,690

EXERCISE 11.9

Following are the income statement columns of the March 20XX worksheet for Puffy Pastries, owned by Sam Yee. The balance of the owner's drawing account on March 31 was $1,500. Prepare the closing entries to: (1) close all accounts with credit balances and enter the ending inventory figure on the books, (2) close all accounts with debit balances and remove the beginning inventory figure from the books, (3) transfer the net loss to the owner's capital account, and (4) transfer the balance of drawing to capital. Use general journal page 56.

	Income Statement	
	Debit	Credit
Merchandise Inventory	3,000	2,100

Sales		14,300
Sales Returns and Allowances	390	
Purchases	8,000	
Purchases Discounts		740
Rent Expense	1,100	
Utilities Expense	310	
Salary Expense	1,200	
Supplies Expense	140	
Amortization Expense	3,500	
	17,640	17,140
Net Loss		500
	17,640	17,640

Problems

PROBLEM 11.1

Following are the T accounts and the related closing entries for Higgins' Grocery on January 31, 20XX.

Merchandise Inventory		130
1/31 Balance 13,400		

Henry Higgins, Capital		310
	1/31 Balance	15,200

Henry Higgins, Drawing		320
1/31 Balance 2,200		

Income Summary		330

Sales		410
	1/31 Balance	25,000

Sales Returns and Allowances		420
1/31 Balance 1,400		

Sales Discounts		430
1/31 Balance 900		

Purchases		510
1/31 Balance 16,500		

Purchases Returns and Allowances		520
	1/31 Balance	480

Purchases Discounts		530
	1/31 Balance	165

Rent Expense		610
1/31 Balance 900		

Utilities Expense		620
1/31 Balance 380		

Advertising Expense		630
1/31 Balance 520		

Insurance Expense		640
1/31 Balance 210		

Instructions

1. Post the closing entries to the T accounts provided. As posting is completed, be sure to place account numbers in the journal and the journal page number (GJ13) in the T accounts.

		GENERAL JOURNAL			PAGE 13	
DATE		**DESCRIPTION**	**POST REF.**	**DEBIT**	**CREDIT**	
20XX		Closing Entries				
Jan.	31	Merchandise Inventory		1 2 1 0 0 00		
		Sales		2 5 0 0 0 00		
		Purchases Returns and Allowances		4 8 0 00		
		Purchases Discounts		1 6 5 00		
		Income Summary			3 7 7 4 5 00	
		To Close Income Statement Accounts with				
		Credit Balances and to Enter the Ending				
		Inventory on the Books				
	31	Income Summary		3 4 2 1 0 00		
		Merchandise Inventory			1 3 4 0 0 00	
		Sales Returns and Allowances			1 4 0 0 00	
		Sales Discounts			9 0 0 00	
		Purchases			1 6 5 0 0 00	
		Rent Expense			9 0 0 00	
		Utilities Expense			3 8 0 00	
		Advertising Expense			5 2 0 00	
		Insurance Expense			2 1 0 00	
		To Close Income Statement Accounts with				
		Debit Balances and to Close Out the				
		Beginning Merchandise Inventory				
	31	Income Summary		3 5 3 5 00		
		Henry Higgins, Capital			3 5 3 5 00	
		To Transfer Net Income to Capital				
	31	Henry Higgins, Capital		2 2 0 0 00		
		Henry Higgins, Drawing			2 2 0 0 00	
		To Transfer Balance of Drawing to Capital				

Instructions (continued)

2. After posting has been completed, answer the following questions:

   a. What is the balance of the Income Summary account after posting has been completed?

   b. What is the balance of the Merchandise Inventory account after posting has been completed?

   c. Which income statement accounts remain open after posting has been completed?

   d. What is the balance of the drawing account after posting has been completed?

   e. What is the balance of the capital account on January 31, 20XX?

   f. What is the dollar amount of the net income for January?

PROBLEM 11.2

Following are the income statement columns of the worksheet for Koffee Kitchen, owned by Raymond White, for the month of February 20XX.

		Income Statement	
		Debit	**Credit**
130	Merchandise Inventory	11,400	10,600
410	Sales		27,400
420	Sales Returns and Allowances	600	
430	Sales Discounts	730	
501	Purchases	14,200	
520	Purchases Returns and Allowances		190
530	Purchases Discounts		510
540	Freight In	540	
610	Rent Expense	850	
620	Utilities Expense	240	
630	Wages Expense	1,500	
640	Advertising Expense	1,000	
650	Supplies Expense	190	
660	Insurance Expense	70	
670	Amortization Expense	850	
		32,170	38,700
	Net Income	6,530	
		38,700	38,700

Instructions

1. Journalize the four required closing entries. Use general journal page 6. The balance of the owner's drawing account on February 28 is $3,400.

2. Prepare an income statement for the month.

PROBLEM 11.3

On the following page are the balance sheet columns of the worksheet for Special Effects, a retail store owned by Betsy Rawlings, on September 30, 20XX.

Instructions

1. Prepare a classified balance sheet as of September 30, 20XX. The balance in Notes Payable is due in 6 months and $12,000 of the balance in Mortgage Payable is due within the next 12 months. Include a complete statement of owner's equity on the balance sheet.

2. Determine the current ratio. (Round to the nearest tenth of a percent.) Does it indicate a strong or a weak current position?

3. Determine the dollar amount of working capital.

		Income Statement Debit	Income Statement Credit
101	Cash	9,350	
110	Accounts Receivable	5,120	
120	Notes Receivable	5,700	
130	Merchandise Inventory	24,600	
140	Supplies	730	
150	Prepaid Insurance	1,500	
160	Office Equipment	14,000	
161	Accumulated Amortization: OE		5,000
170	Store Equipment	21,000	
171	Accumulated Amortization: SE		6,000
180	Building	55,000	
181	Accumulated Amortization: Bldg.		16,400
210	Accounts Payable		6,200
220	Notes Payable		14,600
230	Wages Payable		470
240	Unearned Revenue		1,370
250	Mortgage Payable		42,000
310	Betsy Rawlings, Capital		43,980
320	Betsy Rawlings, Drawing	3,650	
		140,650	136,020
	Net Income		4,630
		140,650	140,650

PROBLEM 11.4

Following on the next page are the trial balance columns of the worksheet for the month of April 20XX for Gail Greenwood, owner of Woman Source, a bookstore.

Instructions

1. Enter the account names, numbers, and balances into T accounts representing a general ledger and onto the trial balance columns of a worksheet. In addition to the accounts listed on the trial balance, add the following: Supplies Expense, 650; Insurance Expense, 660; Amortization Expense, 670: Wages Payable, 260; and Income Summary, 330.

2. Calculate the adjustments for April and enter the amounts in the adjustments columns of the worksheet. The necessary information is:

    a. The supplies inventory on April 30 is $310.

    b. A two-year insurance policy was purchased on March 1 of this year for $2,400.

    c. Office equipment was purchased on January 2 of last year; cost, $27,000; life, five years; salvage value, 0.

    d. Delivery equipment was purchased on January 4 of last year; cost, $40,000; life, four years; salvage value, $10,000.

    e. A building was purchased on January 2 of last year; cost, $35,000; life, 20 years; salvage value, $11,000.

    f. Wages payable on April 30 are $760.

    g. $800 of the unearned revenue has been earned during April

3. The value of the merchandise inventory on April 30 is $34,000. Enter the inventory figures in their appropriate places on the worksheet.

4. Complete the worksheet.

5. Prepare an income statement for Woman Source for the month of April 20XX.

6. Prepare a statement of owner's equity for Woman Source for the month of April 20XX.

7. Prepare a classified balance sheet for Woman Source as of April 30, 20XX. Include only the ending capital figure in the owner's equity section. $12,000 of the balance in Notes Payable is due within 12 months, and the mortgage is all due and payable in 10 years.

8. Journalize and post the adjusting entries. Use general journal page 48.

9. Journalize and post the closing entries. Use general journal page 49.

10. Prepare a post-closing trial balance.

| | | Income Statement | |
		Debit	Credit
101	Cash	10,400	
110	Accounts Receivable	3,300	
120	Notes Receivable	9,600	
130	Merchandise Inventory	31,000	
140	Supplies	760	
150	Prepaid Insurance	2,300	
160	Office Equipment	27,000	
161	Accumulated Amortization: OE		6,750
170	Delivery Equipment	40,000	
171	Accumulated Amortization: DE		9,375
180	Building	35,000	
181	Accumulated Amortization: Bldg.		1,500
210	Accounts Payable		5,100
220	Notes Payable		40,000
240	Unearned Revenue		1,800
250	Mortgage Payable		30,000
310	Gail Greenwood, Capital		67,265
320	Gall Greenwood, Drawing	4,400	
410	Sales		60,000
420	Sales Returns and Allowances	690	
430	Sales Discounts	1,600	
501	Purchases	49,000	
520	Purchases Returns and Allowances		1,110
530	Purchases Discounts		980
540	Freight In	2,500	
610	Rent Expense	1,400	
620	Utilities Expense	370	
630	Wages Expense	3,160	
640	Advertising Expense	1,400	
		223,880	223,880

PROBLEM 11.5

Following are the income statement and balance sheet columns of the worksheet for Pete Stavros, owner of Stavros Imports, for the month of August 20XX.

	Income Statement		Balance Sheet	
	Debit	Credit	Debit	Credit
Cash			15,340	
Accounts Receivable			6,050	
Notes Receivable			14,290	
Merchandise Inventory	12,290	15,450	15,450	
Supplies			1,020	
Prepaid Insurance			1,900	
Office Equipment			24,000	
Accumulated Amortization: OE				7,400
Store Equipment			34,000	
Accumulated Amortization: SE				17,500
Building			42,000	
Accumulated Amortization: Bldg.				20,600
Accounts Payable				3,030
Notes Payable				36,200
Wages Payable				1,420
Unearned Revenue				1,140
Mortgage Payable				25,700
Pete Stavros, Capital				44,420
Pete Stavros, Drawing			2,490	
Sales		49,740		
Sales Returns and Allowances	600			
Sales Discounts	500			
Purchases	35,000			
Purchases Returns and Allowances		1,610		
Purchases Discounts		700		
Freight In	1,960			
Rent Expense	1,500			
Utilities Expense	590			
Wages Expense	5,640			
Amortization Expense	4,470			
Advertising Expense	1,940			
Insurance Expense	160			
Repairs Expense	3,120			
Supplies Expense	600			
Totals	68,370	67,500	156,540	157,410
Net Loss		870	870	
	68,370	68,370	157,410	157,410

Instructions

1. Prepare an income statement for Stavros Imports for the month of August 20XX.
2. Prepare a classified balance sheet for Stavros Imports on August 31, 20XX, assuming that $12,000 of the balance in Notes Payable is due within a year's time and that $6,000 of the balance in Mortgage Payable is due within a year's time.
3. Journalize the closing entries on August 31. Use general journal page 29.
4. Determine the current ratio. (Round to the nearest tenth of a percent.)
5. Determine the dollar amount of working capital.

Comprehensive Problem 2 for Review of Chapters Seven–Eleven

Holly Harris owns a business called "Hobby House." It is a novelty store that sells model kits for cars, planes, and railroad equipment, accessories for model kits, miniature furniture and houses, unusual games and puzzles, and other novelty items. The chart of accounts and account balances for Hobby House on January 1, 20XX follow. The schedules of accounts receivable and payable showing the balances owed on January 1 appear below. The bank statement that Hobby House received from the New Brunswick Bank follows the transactions. Read all of the instructions (which follow the bank statement) before you begin work on the problem.

Hobby House Schedule of Accounts Receivable January 1, 20XX	
Dave Culver	$275.15
Jill Goode	291.05
Lynda Morrison	143.50
Peter Vermont	214.60
Total	$924.30

Hobby House Schedule of Accounts Payable January 1, 20XX	
Total Toys	$900.94
Model Supplies	714.76
The Toy Place	462.24
Total	$2,077.94

Chart of Accounts			
101	Cash	$15,399.63	
105	Petty Cash	–0–	
110	Change Fund	300.00	
120	Accounts Receivable	924.30	
130	Prepaid Insurance	–0–	
140	Office Supplies	642.50	
145	Merchandise Inventory	17,895.00	
150	Office Equipment	12,400.00	
151	Accumulated Amortization: Office Equipment		$4,800.00
160	Store Equipment	18,600.00	
161	Accumulated Amortization: Store Equipment		4,500.00

170	Office Furniture	2,790.00	
171	Accumulated Amortization: Office Furniture		1,395.00
180	Van	21,800.00	
181	Accumulated Amortization: Van		7,200.00
210	Accounts Payable		2,077.94
220	Notes Payable		30,620.00
230	PST Payable		605.40
240	GST Payable		529.73
242	GST Refundable	306.25	
244	GST Owing (Refund)		–0–
301	Holly Harris, Capital		39,329.61
310	Holly Harris, Drawing		
320	Income Summary		
410	Revenue from Sales		
420	Sales Returns and Allowances		
510	Purchases		
520	Purchases Returns and Allowances		
530	Purchases Discounts		
540	Freight In		
610	Rent Expense		
620	Utilities Expense		
625	Office Supplies Expense		
630	Interest Expense		
635	Insurance Expense		
640	Wages Expense		
650	Advertising Expense		
655	Amortization Expense		
660	Delivery Expense		
670	Subscription Expense		
680	Postage Expense		
690	Entertainment Expense		
695	Bank Charges Expense		

Transactions

January 1   issued cheque 405 for $360 to Business Insurance Company in payment for a two-year fire insurance policy

January 1   sold merchandise on account to Lynda Morrison on sales invoice 320; $52 plus PST and GST

January 1   received a cheque from Jill Goode for $291.05 in full payment of her account

January 1   issued cheque 406 for $100 to establish a petty cash fund (enter the receipt of the $100 into the petty Cash register after the cheque is recorded)

January 2   purchased merchandise for resale from Adult Toys for $408 plus GST on invoice 2982 dated January 2; terms 2/10, n/30

January 2   issued cheque 407 for $50 plus GST to Mercury's Trucking Company for delivering the purchase from Adult Toys

January 3   issued cheque 408 to Olympic Realty for $1,400 for January rent

January 4   issued cheque 409 to Model Supplies for $701.40 in full payment of December 29 purchase of $668 plus GST, less a 2 percent discount

January 5   issued cheque 410 to Adult Toys for $884.10 in full payment of December 30 purchase of $842 plus GST, less a 2 percent discount

January 5	sold merchandise on account to Dave Culver .on sales invoice 321, $76 plus PST and GST
January 6	record petty cash voucher 1 for $6.45 plus GST, payment for monthly subscription for the local newspaper
January 7	cash sales for the week are $3,642 plus PST and GST
January 8	issued cheque 411 for $275.60 to Ontario Hydro for electricity for the month
January 9	received a cheque from Peter Vermont for $100 in partial payment of his account
January 9	issued cheque 412 for $30.90 plus GST to Grand & Toy for office supplies
January 9	issued cheque 413 to The Toy Place for $462.24 in full payment of January 1 balance (no discount granted)
January 10	sold merchandise on account to Jill Goode on sales invoice 322; $125 plus PST and GST
January 10	record petty cash voucher 2 for $8.30 plus GST; spent for postage
January 11	issued credit memorandum 60-A to Jill Goode for $20 plus PST and GST relating to invoice 322 dated January 10
January 11	received a cheque from Dave Culver for $150 in partial payment of his account
January 12	issued cheque 414 for $428.40 to Adult Toys in full payment of January 2 invoice 2982 less the discount
January 12	purchased merchandise for resale from Model Supplies for $1,540 plus GST on invoice 333 dated January 12; terms 2/10, n/30
January 13	received a cheque from Lynda Morrison for $143.50 in partial payment of her account
January 14	issued debit memorandum 321-13 to Model Supplies for $120 plus GST for merchandise returned to them
January 14	record petty cash voucher 3 for $18.90 plus GST; Holly took a customer to lunch
January 15	cash sales for the week are $4,016 plus PST and GST
January 15	issued cheque 415 for $970 to Royal Trust for monthly payment on the outstanding note; $459 is for interest expense and the rest is for principal
January 15	issued cheque 416 for $1,250 plus GST to Total Toys for purchase of merchandise for resale
January 16	issued cheque 417 to Grant Tudor for $700 in payment of semi-monthly wages
January 17	issued cheque 418 to Treasurer of Ontario for $605.40 in payment of balance owed for provincial sales tax payable on January 1
January 17	issued cheque 419 to Holly Harris for $1,600 for personal use
January 18	sold merchandise on account to Peter Vermont on sales invoice 323; $70 plus PST and GST
January 19	purchased merchandise for resale from The Toy Place for $622 plus GST on invoice 78-32 dated January 19; terms n/30
January 21	cash sales for the week are $4,906 plus PST and GST
January 21	record petty cash voucher 4 for $17.30 plus GST; Holly took a customer to lunch

January 22   issued credit memorandum 61-A to Peter Vermont for $10 plus PST and GST relating to invoice 323 dated January 18

January 22   issued cheque 420 to Model Supplies for $1,491 in full payment of invoice 333-A dated January 12, less the return on January 14. Note: Calculate the discount on the original purchase price minus the return.

January 22   Holly purchased a computer and printer from Computerland for use in the office at a total cost of $10,700 plus GST; she paid no cash down, but signed a three-year, 9 percent note for the purchase

January 23   issued cheque 421 to The *Toronto Star* for $150 plus GST for advertising in January

January 23   issued cheque 422 for $2,070 plus GST to Adult Toys, for purchase of merchandise for resale

January 24   record petty cash voucher 5 for $8.45 plus GST for delivery expense

January 24   purchased merchandise for resale from Adult Toys for $750 plus GST on invoice 3053 dated January 24; terms 2/10, n/30

January 24   issued cheque 423 to Mercury's Trucking Company for $50 plus GST for delivering the purchase from Adult Toys

January 26   sold merchandise on account to Lynda Morrison on sales invoice 324; $190 plus PST and GST

January 27   received a cheque from Lynda Morrison for $59.80 in full payment of invoice 320 dated January 1

January 28   record petty cash voucher 6 for $30 plus GST for a magazine subscription

January 28   issued cheque 424 to Grant Tudor for $775 in payment of semimonthly wages

January 28   cash sales for the week are $3,760 plus PST and GST

January 29   received a cheque from Peter Vermont for $100 in partial payment of his account

January 30   purchased merchandise for resale from Model Supplies for $1,250 plus GST on invoice 461 dated January 30; terms 2/10 n/30

January 31   received a cheque from Dave Culver for $50 in partial payment of his account

January 31   issued cheque 425 for $95.65 to replenish the petty cash fund. Stop now and total and rule the petty cash register. (See instruction 9.)

January 31   issued cheque 426 to the Receiver General of Canada in full payment of the GST owing. Before recording the cheque in the cash payments journal, prepare the general journal entry to close the GST Payable and GST Refundable accounts to GST Owing (Refund) The balance in GST Owing (Refund) after these closing entries are posted will show the amount owed to the Receiver General. These entries will require: (1) a debit to GST Payable (to close the account) and a credit to GST Owing, and (2) a debit to GST Owing and a credit to GST Refundable (to close it). Again, the balance in GST Owing is the amount due the Receiver General.

New Brunswick Bank
327 South Street
St. Stephen, NB E3L 3C4

ACCOUNT STATEMENT

Date	Transaction Description	Cheques & Debits	Deposits & Credits	Balance
01 01	Balance			15,399.63
01 01			291.05	15,690.68
01 01	406	100.00		15,590.68
01 03	405	360.00		15,230.68
01 03	407	53.50		15,177.18
01 05	408	1,400.00		13,777.18
01 05	409	701.40		13,075.78
01 07	410	884.10		12,191.68
01 07			4,188.30	16,379.98
01 09			100.00	16,479.98
01 10	411	275.60		16,204.38
01 10	413	462.24		15,742.14
01 11	412	33.06		15,709.08
01 11			150.00	15,859.08
01 13			143.50	16,002.58
01 14	414	428.40		15,574.18
01 15			4,618.40	20,192.58
01 15	415	970.00		19,222.58
01 15	Cheque Printing	32.50		19,190.08
01 17	417	700.00		18,490.08
01 17	419	1,600.00		16,890.08
01 19	418	605.40		16,284.68
01 21			5,641.90	21,926.58
01 24	420	1,491.00		20,435.58
01 27	422	2,214.90		18,220.68
01 27	416	1,337.50		16,883.18
01 27			59.80	16,942.98
01 28			4,324.00	21,266.98
01 29	424	775.00		20,491.98
01 29			100.00	20,591.98
01 31	425	95.65		20,496.33
01 31	Service Charge	18.50		20,477.83

Instructions

1. Copy the account names, numbers, and balances into the general ledger and the names and balances into the accounts receivable and accounts payable ledgers. Post to the subsidiary ledgers immediately after each transaction.

2. Record sales on account in a sales journal (page 11) with the following column headings: sales credit, PST payable credit, GST payable credit, and accounts receivable debit. Hobby House is required to collect 8 percent provincial sales tax and 7 percent GST on all sales. Terms of sale are n/30.

3. Record credit purchases of merchandise for resale in a purchases journal (page 10) with the following column headings: purchases debit, GST refundable debit, and accounts payable credit. Holly always pays within the discount period when terms are offered.

4. Record all cash receipts in a cash receipts journal (page 12) with the following column headings: sundry credits, accounts receivable credit, sales credit, PST payable credit, GST payable credit, and cash debit:.

5. Record all cash payments in a cash payments journal (page 13) with the following column headings: sundry debits, accounts payable debit, purchases debit, purchases discounts credit, and cash credit.

6. Record all transactions that do not belong in a special journal in a general journal (page 24). Post after each transaction.

7. Record all petty cash payments in the petty cash register (page 14). Use the following column headings: receipts, payments, subscription expense, postage expense, entertainment expense, GST refundable, and sundry debits.

8. On January 31, total and rule the petty cash register, and then record cheque 425 for $95.65 to replenish the fund.

9. Total, crossfoot, and rule the sales, purchases, cash receipts, and cash payments journals.

10. Perform all the required summary and individual posting from the special journals.

11. Check the general journal to make sure all posting has been completed.

12. Prepare a bank statement reconciliation on January 31. The general ledger balance on January 31 is $20,283.67. Compare deposits in the cash receipts journal with the deposits on the bank statement to see if any are in transit. Compare the cheques in the cash payments journal with those on the bank statement to determine if any are outstanding.

13. Journalize any general journal entries necessary to bring the books up to date after reconciliation. After journalizing, post the transactions. The general ledger cash balance and the reconciled cash balance should be the same.

14. Prepare a trial balance of the general ledger on January 31 in the trial balance columns of the worksheet.

15. Calculate the data for adjustments for the month of January and enter the amounts in the adjustments columns of the worksheet.
    a. The supplies inventory on January 31 is $453.50.
    b. A two-year insurance policy was purchased on January 1 of this year for $360.
    c. Office equipment was purchased two years ago; cost, $12,400; life, 5 years; salvage value, $400.
    d. Store equipment was purchased one year ago; cost, $18,600; life, 4 years; salvage value, $600.
    e. Office furniture was purchased one year ago; cost, $2,790; life, 2 years; salvage value, zero.
    f. The van was purchased two years ago; cost, $21,800; life, 5 years; salvage value, $3,800.

16. The value of the merchandise inventory on January 31 is $16,695. Enter the inventory figures in their appropriate places on the worksheet and complete the worksheet.

17. Prepare schedules of accounts receivable and accounts payable. Compare the totals with the balances in the control accounts in the general ledger.

18. Prepare an income statement for Hobby House for the month of January 20XX.

19. Prepare a separate statement of owner's equity as of January 31, 20XX.

20. Prepare a classified balance sheet as of January 31, 20XX. $6,132 of the balance in notes payable is due within the next 12 months.

21. Journalize and post the adjusting entries on general journal page 26.

22. Journalize and post the closing entries on general journal page 27.

23. Prepare a post-closing trial balance as of January 31, 20XX.

CHAPTER 12

Payroll—Employee Deductions

LEARNING OBJECTIVES

When you have completed this chapter, you should

1. **have an increased understanding of accounting terminology.**
2. **have a basic understanding of the employer-employee relationship.**
3. **be able to calculate regular, overtime, and total earnings.**
4. **be able to determine Canada Pension Plan (CPP) and employment insurance (EI) premiums.**
5. **be able to determine federal and provincial income tax deductions.**
6. **be able to complete a payroll register.**
7. **be able to prepare the journal entry to record the payroll.**

VOCABULARY

Canada Customs and Revenue Agency (CCRA)	the federal government agency that is responsible for collecting the compulsory payroll deductions
claim codes	codes that are used to determine the amount of either federal or provincial income tax to be withheld from earnings
compulsory deductions	amounts required by law that must be withheld from gross earnings
employee	one who performs services for an employer and whose work may be directed by the employer
employer	an organization or a person who receives the services of an employee; the employer may provide the working place of, direct the activities of, and hire or fire the employee
employer health tax (EHT)	a tax imposed on employees or employers by the provincial government to provide health-care coverage for all citizens of the province
gross earnings	total earnings before deductions
independent contractor	one whose services may be hired for a fee, but whose work is not directed by the person or organization doing the hiring; the independent contractor is not considered to be an employee and therefore no payroll deductions are withheld
net earnings	gross earnings minus deductions
overtime	referred to in this text as hours worked over a weekly total of 40 hours

overtime earnings	referred to in this text as wages earned for hours worked over a weekly total of 40 hours; paid at time and a half or double the rate of regular earnings
regular earnings	referred to in this text as earnings for hours worked up to a weekly total of 40
salary	referred to in this text as earnings stated in annual, monthly, or weekly terms
tax credits	various personal amounts that exempt a portion of gross earnings from either federal or provincial income tax
TD1; also called personal tax credits return	federal government form completed by an employee and indicating various personal credits; each province and territory has its own TD1 form also indicating personal credits
tax on income (TONI) method	the method now used to determine personal provincial income tax
wages	referred to in this text as earnings stated in hourly terms
withhold	to refrain, or hold back, from giving

Introduction

Nearly everyone will receive or has received a paycheque at one time or another. The stub or pay slip that accompanies the paycheque shows the **gross earnings** (or total earnings) for the pay period, all deductions, and the **net earnings**, which are calculated by subtracting total deductions from gross earnings. The net or take-home pay is usually for much less than the actual amount earned because of the compulsory and voluntary deductions from gross earnings.

The **Canada Customs and Revenue Agency (CCRA)** is the federal government agency that collects payroll taxes. Employers must **withhold** (hold back) certain payroll taxes and remit to CCRA the amounts collected at regular intervals.

The Employer-Employee Relationship

An **employer** is a person or an organization that receives the services of an employee. The employer usually provides the place to work and the required tools. The employer may also discharge an employee and tell the employee when, where, and how a job is to be done.

An **employee** performs services for an employer and his or her work may be controlled by the employer.

An **independent contractor**, in contrast, is hired to do a specific job but may decide how the job is to be completed. Plumbers, doctors, tutors, and repair persons, for example, fall into this category.

It is important to make the distinction between employees and independent contractors because employers are required by law to withhold the compulsory deductions from wages paid to employees, while these deductions are not withheld on fees paid to independent contractors.

Laws Affecting Payroll

Both the federal and provincial governments have laws which affect payroll.

The *Income Tax Act, Canada Pension Act, Employment Insurance Act,* and the *Workers' Compensation Act* are federal laws. In the province of Quebec, the Canada

Pension Act is replaced by the *Quebec Pension Act* and is a responsibility of the provincial government.

Each province has an *Employment Standards Act* which governs minimum wages, maximum hours of work, statutory holidays, vacation pay, and other employment issues. While there are differences among the provinces, normally, employers are required to pay overtime to employees for any hours worked over 40 in a week. Overtime pay would include the employee's regular pay plus a premium of at least one-half the regular pay rate for the overtime hours. This means that the employee receives at least 1½ times the regular rate of pay for overtime hours. If employees belong to a union, the union contract may provide for a higher overtime premium than required by law. For example, a union contract may require double time for hours worked on Saturday or Sunday. If the union contract has terms better than the ones required by law, the union contract takes precedence. In addition to overtime rates, the union contract may specify that the employer withhold union dues from employees and remit them in a timely fashion to the union.

Each province also has a *Provincial Health Insurance Plan* ensuring everyone can receive hospital insurance. In some provinces, such as Ontario, this plan is completely paid for by the employer and is called the **Employer Health Tax (EHT)**. In other provinces, employees may pay for part or all of the health insurance premiums through payroll deductions or directly to the provincial government.

Because of the number of laws affecting payroll, it is necessary for employers to keep accurate payroll records and prepare the necessary reports required by the federal and provincial governments.

Compulsory Payroll Deductions

The Canada Customs and Revenue Agency (CCRA), formerly known as Revenue Canada, provides employers with all the necessary information for the withholding of payroll taxes. Every year CCRA publishes a booklet for each province, *Payroll Deductions Tables*, for registered employers or anyone else who requests it. These tables are also available on diskette and on the Internet.

As of January 1, 2001, there are four **compulsory deductions** (required by law) for payroll. They are: (1) Federal income tax: (2) Provincial income tax; (3) Canada Pension Plan contributions (CPP), or Quebec Pension Plan contributions; and (4) Employment Insurance premiums (EI).

Federal Income Tax

Every employee is required to fill out a **TD1** form, a *Personal Tax Credits Return*. This form is shown as Figure 12-1 on pages 340–41. **Tax credits** are amounts that are not subject to either federal or provincial income tax. The TD1 will show the employee's name, address, and social insurance number. In addition, it will also show the total tax credits claimed by the individual. The basic amount of the personal credit as of January 1, 2001, for all residents of Canada is $7,412.

Once employees list all personal tax credits to which they are entitled, they will arrive at the total claim amount which the employer uses to determine the claim code. The **claim code** is used to calculate the amount of federal income tax that must be deducted from the taxable earnings of the employee.

If an employee does not complete and sign a TD1 form the employer is required to withhold income tax from that employee as if she or he were single with no tax credits.

Provincial and Territorial Income Tax

As of January 1, 2001, the provinces of Canada, with the exception of Quebec, changed to the **tax on income method (TONI)** for calculating provincial income tax. (Quebec administers its own provincial personal income tax system.) Prior to January 1, 2001, the tax-on-tax method was used for determining the provincial tax; this method calculated provincial income tax as a percentage of federal income tax. On January 1, 2002, the territories, too, switched to the TONI method of income tax withholding.

If a province or territory has personal tax credit amounts that are different from the federal tax credit amounts, then employees will have to fill out both federal and provincial or territorial TD1 forms. For example, if an individual claims more than $7,634 on the federal TD1 in 2002, he or she will complete in addition a provincial or territorial personal tax credits form. Figure 12-2 on pages 342–43 shows the 2002 British Columbia TD1BC form. Note that the basic personal claim amount is $8,168, somewhat higher than the amount on the federal TD1. The total claim amount shown on the provincial or territorial TD1 will determine the claim code used for the calculation of provincial or territorial income tax.

Employers will have to determine employees' income tax deductions by referring to both federal and provincial or territorial tax tables.

Canada Pension Plan Contributions

The CPP applies to all employees between the ages of 18 and 70, with few exceptions. You should consult the CCRA's booklet *Payroll Deductions Tables* to find out what employment may not be subject to these contributions.

The contributions to be deducted are based on maximum pensionable earnings of $38,300 for 2001, with a basic exemption of $3,500. The rate for 2001 is 4.3 percent of pensionable earnings, for a maximum contribution of $1,496.40 per year. When an employee reaches the maximum contributions, an employer stops deducting CPP. The rates are subject to change each year.

The rates are subject to change regularly; for 2002, for example, the rate is 4.7 percent of $39,100 for a maximum contribution of $1,673.20. The rate for self-employed contributors is 9.4 percent.

The CPP tables in this text are 2001 tables. Again, the method for calculating does not change, even though the rates do.

Employment Insurance Premiums

In 1940, the Unemployment Insurance Act created a federal agency to administer a plan that would alleviate the hardships caused by unemployment. In 1971, this plan was revised, making employment insurance coverage compulsory for all Canadian workers under the age of 65 who are not self-employed. There are exceptions to this compulsory coverage, and one should consult the CCRA's publication *Payroll Deductions Tables* for further information.

Effective January 1, 2001, the employer is required to deduct an amount equal to 2.25 percent of the insurable earnings. The maximum 2001 insurable earnings are $39,000 per year, resulting in a maximum annual premium payable of $877.50. The employer will stop deducting the premiums when the employee's maximum annual insurable earnings are reached. The rates are subject to change each year; for 2002, the rate is 2.2 percent. In this text, we will use 2001 tables.

Voluntary Payroll Deductions

In addition to the compulsory deductions, employees may authorize other deductions. Among many possible voluntary deductions are registered pension plans; Canada Savings Bonds; hospital, health, accident, or life insurance; union or professional dues; contributions to a charity; and loan payments.

Salaries and Hourly Wages

Although the terms salary and wages are often used interchangeably, in this text **salary** normally refers to earnings that are stated in weekly, monthly, or annual terms. Among the many employees who might earn salaries are teachers, engineers, supervisory personnel, and administrators. **Wages** normally refers to earnings stated on an hourly basis; employees paid an hourly wage are often non-management personnel.

Calculating the Gross Payroll

Gross payroll is the total amount earned by all employees before any deductions are taken. It is determined by calculating the gross earnings for employees who earn salaries and for those who earn hourly wages.

Assume that the Credit Valley Accounting Service in North Bay, Ontario, has five employees: two are management and are paid annual salaries, and three are accounting clerks who are paid hourly wages, with time and a half for all hours worked over 40 in a week. The gross payroll calculations for the last week in May follow:

Management Personnel

Janine Dubeau	$34,320 per year
	$34,320/52 = $660 per week
David Jennings	$31,200 per year
	$31,200/52 = $600 per week

As you can see, the annual salary is divided by the number of weeks in a year to determine the weekly salary. Once the weekly salary has been calculated, it need not be recalculated for each new pay period.

The three hourly employees for the Credit Valley Accounting Service and their wages per hour are as follows:

Wage-Earning Personnel (Non-management)

James Austin	$12.00 per hour, worked 48 hours
Shahnez Wong	$11.00 per hour, worked 50 hours
Antonio Lasorda	$14.00 per hour, worked 39 hours

Each hourly employee is paid time and a half for hours worked over 40 in a week. To calculate each employee's weekly gross wage, determine: (1) the regular wage, which is the hourly rate times 40 hours (or less, if the employee worked fewer than 40 hours during the week); (2) the overtime premium, which is the hourly overtime rate times the number of hours worked overtime; and (3) the total of the regular wage and the overtime wage.

Austin

Step 1.   Determine regular wage

$12.00 x 40 hours = $480.00

Step 2. Determine overtime wage
$12.00 x 1.5 = $18.00
$18.00 x 8 hours = $144.00

Step 3. Determine gross wage
Add the results of Steps 1 and 2. **$624.00**

Wong

Step 1. Determine regular wage
$11.00 x 40 hours = $440.00

Step 2. Determine overtime wage
$11.00 x 1.5 = $16.50
$16.50 x 10 hours = $165.00

Step 3. Determine gross wage
Add the results of Steps 1 and 2. **$605.00**

Lasorda

Step 1. Determine regular wage
$14.00 x 39 hours =   **$546.00**

The total gross payroll for The Credit Valley Accounting Service for the last week of May is as follows:

Employee	Gross Earnings
Janine Dubeau	$ 660.00
David Jennings	600.00
James Austin	624.00
Shahnez Wong	605.00
Antonio Lasorda	546.00
Total	**$3,035.00**

Calculating the gross payroll is just the first step in the process. Once the gross earnings have been calculated, the payroll administrator must calculate each employee's deductions.

To simplify this example, we will assume the only deductions that the employees of The Credit Valley Accounting Service have are the compulsory ones, which means that their gross earnings are also their taxable earnings.

Federal Income Tax Deductions

The federal TD1 form, Figure 12-1, is shown on pages 340–41 at the end of this chapter. From the TD1, each of the five employees has determined his or her total claim amounts. And, by referring to *Chart 1, Federal Claim Codes*, that immediately follows, the claim codes for each employee can be determined.

Chart 1 – Federal Claim Codes			
Total Claim Amount	**Claim Code**	**Total Claim Amount**	**Claim Code**
No claim amount	0	17,276.01 – 18,920.00	8
Minimum – 7,412.00	1	18,920.01 – 20,564.00	9
7,412.01 – 9,056.00	2	20,564.01 – 22,208.00	10
9,056.01 – 10,700.00	3	22,208.01 – and over	X
10,700.01 – 12,344.00	4	Manual calculation required by employer	
12,344.01 – 13,988.00	5		
13,988.01 – 15,632.00	6	No withholding	E
15,632.01 – 17,276.00	7		

Employee	Claim Amount	Federal Claim Code
Dubeau	$ 7,412	1
Jennings	13,706	5
Austin	10,912	4
Wong	8,912	2
Lasorda	7,412	1

The actual amount of federal income tax to be withheld may be determined by referring to the wage bracket tables in the CCRA's *Payroll Deductions Tables*. The tables are separated into varying pay periods. Refer to the two pages of these tables for a weekly payroll period in Figure 12-3 on pages 344 and 345.

Starting with Janine Dubeau, find the amount of Janine's earnings in the left-hand column of the federal wage-bracket income tax table. The appropriate income bracket is $653–$661. With your finger, follow across the column until you reach the amount listed under federal claim code 1. The amount of federal income tax to be withheld for Janine is $79.85.

Continue this process to determine the federal income tax to be withheld from each employee.

Employee	Federal Claim Code	Gross Earnings	Federal Income Tax Payable
Dubeau	1	$ 660.00	$ 79.85
Jennings	5	$ 600.00	50.40
Austin	4	$ 624.00	65.55
Wong	2	$ 605.00	67.25
Lasorda	1	$ 546.00	59.15
Totals		$3,035.00	$322.20

Provincial Income Tax Deductions

The employees' total claim amounts from the provincial TD1ON form are not the same as their federal claim amounts. When this occurs, their claim codes for provincial income tax may be different than their claim codes for federal income tax. The following table shows the provincial claim amounts and the provincial claim codes.

Chart 2 – Ontario Claim Codes			
Total Claim Amount	**Claim Code**	**Total Claim Amount**	**Claim Code**
No claim amount	0	17,026.01 – 18,626.00	8
Minimum – 7,426.00	1	18,626.01 – 20,226.00	9
7,426.01 – 9,026.00	2	20,226.01 – 21,826.00	10
9,026.01 – 10,626.00	3	21,826.01 – and over	X
10,626.01 – 12,226.00	4	Manual calculation required by employer	
12,226.01 – 13,826.00	5		
13,826.01 – 15,426.00	6	No withholding	E
15,426.01 – 17,026.00	7		

Following the same procedure that we used to determine the federal income tax payable, we can find the amount of provincial income tax payable by referring to the wage bracket tables prepared by CCRA, *Payroll Deductions Table*. You can find two pages of Ontario's tables reproduced in this text as Figure 12-4 on pages 346 and 347.

Employee	Provincial Claim Amounts	Provincial Claim Code	Gross Earnings	Provincial Income Tax Payable
Dubeau	$ 7,426	1	$660.00	$31.70
Jennings	13,732	5	600.00	19.35
Austin	9,876	3	624.00	25.30
Wong	8,926	2	605.00	25.80
Lasorda	7,426	1	546.00	23.15
Totals			$3,035.00	$125.30

Deductions for Canada Pension Plan and Employment Insurance

The CPP and EI deductions may be determined by referring to the appropriate columns in the *Payroll Deductions Tables*. Figure 12-5 on pages 348–351 shows four pages of Canada Pension Plan contributions for weekly pay periods and Figure 12-6 on pages 352–353 shows two pages of Employment Insurance premiums. To calculate the CPP contribution, you may not multiply the wage times the rate (4.7 percent) because the $3,500 exemption is built into the tables. You may, however, for EI, multiply the gross wage by the current rate up to the maximum taxable earnings.

Employee	Gross Earnings	CPP Contributions	EI Premiums
Dubeau	$ 660.00	$ 25.49	$14.85
Jennings	$ 600.00	$ 22.91	$13.50
Austin	$ 624.00	$ 23.94	$14.04
Wong	$ 605.00	$ 23.12	$13.61
Lasorda	$ 546.00	$ 20.58	$12.29
Totals	$3,035.00	$116.04	$68.29

The Payroll Register

The payroll administrator uses the payroll register much as a worksheet, summarizing all the information necessary to calculate the **net earnings** (take home pay), and record salaries and wages expense, the payroll tax liabilities, and salaries and wages payable. The payroll register for the last week in May for the Credit Valley Accounting Service is shown on page 330. Note that a column has been added for the voluntary deduction, charitable contributions.

Steps in Completing the Payroll Register

The payroll administrator will complete the payroll register in this order:

Step 1. Calculate each employee's regular, overtime, and total earnings. Total each of these columns before determining payroll deductions.

Step 2. Prove the accuracy of work so far by adding the total **regular earnings** to the total **overtime earnings**. Your answer must be the total earnings. For the Credit Valley Accounting Service, the calculations are as follows:

Total regular earnings	$2,726.00
Total overtime earnings	+ 309.00
Total earnings	$3,035.00

Employee	Total Hrs.	Hourly Rate	Regular Earnings	Overtime Earnings	Total Earnings	Fed. Claim Code	Fed. Income Taxes	Prov. Claim Code	Prov. Income Taxes	CPP Cont.	EI Prem.	Char. Cont.	Total Ded.	Net Pay
Dubeau	Mgmt		660.00		660.00	1	79.85	1	31.70	25.49	14.85	10.00	161.89	498.11
Jennings	Mgmt		600.00		600.00	5	50.40	5	19.35	22.91	13.50	10.00	116.16	483.84
Austin	48	12.00	480.00	144.00	624.00	4	65.55	3	25.30	23.94	14.04	10.00	138.83	485.17
Wong	50	11.00	440.00	165.00	605.00	2	67.25	2	25.80	23.12	13.61	10.00	139.78	465.22
Lasorda	39	14.00	546.00		546.00	1	59.15	1	23.15	20.58	12.29	10.00	125.17	420.83
Totals			2,726.00	309.00	3,035.00		322.20		125.30	116.04	68.29	50.00	681.83	2,353.17

Step 3.   Determine the payroll deductions for each individual employee and total each individual deductions column.

Step 4.   Calculate the total deductions for each employee and determine the column total.

Step 5.   Before continuing, add the totals of the individual deductions columns. The sum must equal the total of the total deductions column, or else an error has been made and must be found before continuing. For the Credit Valley Accounting Service, this calculation is:

Total federal tax	$322.20
Total provincial tax	125.30
Total CPP	116.04
Total EI	68.29
Total charitable contributions	50.00
Total deductions	$681.83

Step 6.   Calculate the net earnings for each employee by subtracting her or his total deductions from total earnings, then find the column total.

Step 7.   Prove that the column total is accurate by subtracting the total of the total deductions column from the total of the total earnings column.

Total earnings	$3,035.00
Total deductions	− 681.83
Net earnings	$2,353.17

The payroll administrator should check the accuracy of the work at each step in the preparation of the payroll as mistakes are easier to find and are not carried forward.

The Journal Entry to Record the Payroll

Once the payroll register has been completed, the payroll administrator has all the necessary information for the journal entry. The total gross earnings represent the employer's total salaries and wages expense for the week. The amounts withheld by the employer represent liabilities, because the employer must submit each amount to a government agency, an insurance company, an employee union, and so on.

Usually, salaries expense and wages expense are kept separate in the ledgers. In this example, salaries expense refers to management salaries. The entry to record the week's payroll for the Credit Valley Accounting Service is as follows:

GENERAL JOURNAL						
DATE	DESCRIPTION	POST REF.	DEBIT		CREDIT	
20XX						
May 31	Salaries Expense		1 2 6 0 00			
	Wages Expense		1 7 7 5 00			
	Federal Income Tax Payable				3 2 2 20	
	Provincial Income Tax Payable				1 2 5 30	
	Canada Pension Plan Payable				1 1 6 04	
	Employment Insurance Payable				6 8 29	
	Charitable Contributions Payable				5 0 00	
	Salaries Payable				9 8 1 95	
	Wages Payable				1 3 7 1 22	
	To Record the Week's Salaries and Wages					
	Expense and the Related Payroll Liabilities					

The Payroll Bank Account

Many firms have a separate payroll bank account. After the payroll administrator records the gross earnings, the deductions, and net salaries and wages, she or he will make the following entry:

GENERAL JOURNAL						
DATE	DESCRIPTION	POST REF.	DEBIT		CREDIT	
20XX						
May 31	Salaries Payable		9 8 1 95			
	Wages Payable		1 3 7 1 22			
	Cash				2 3 5 3 17	
	To Record Payment of Salaries and Wages					

A cheque may now be written for the net amount of the payroll, $2,353.17, and deposited in a special cash account for payroll. Individual cheques can then be written and after employees have cashed their cheques, the payroll cash account will have a zero balance.

Summary

Employers must be familiar with the laws as they relate to payroll. They are required, for example, to withhold from the gross earnings of most employees, CPP contributions, EI premiums, and both federal and provincial income taxes, and they must remit these amounts to the proper government agency within a certain period of time. For the employer to deduct the correct amounts, each employee must file with the employer a federal TD1, a Personal Tax Credits Return that shows the employee's marital status, social insurance number, and amount of tax credits claimed. If the employer does not have a TD1 form on hand for an employee, deductions must be taken as though the employee were single with no tax credits. In addition, employees may be required to fill out a provincial TD1 form.

Most of the information that an employer needs concerning payroll and payroll deductions is found in the CCRA booklet *Payroll Deductions Tables*, which may be obtained free of charge from the Canada Customs and Revenue Agency.

The entire payroll may be calculated on a payroll register, after which time the cheques may be written and the journal entry recorded. The gross payroll is debited to salaries and/or wages expense, and amounts withheld from employees' earnings are credited to liability accounts.

Vocabulary Review

Here is a list of the words and terms for this chapter.

Canada Customs and Revenue Agency (CCRA)

claim codes	overtime
compulsory deductions	overtime earnings
employee	regular earnings
employer	salary
Employer Health Tax (EHT)	tax on income (TONI) method
gross earnings	TD1, personal tax credits return
independent contractor	wages
net earnings	withhold

Fill in the blank with the correct word or term from the list.

1. A word that means to refrain or hold back from giving is _____.
2. Earnings for the first 40 hours in a week are referred to as _____.
3. Earnings for hours worked over a weekly total of 40 are referred to as _____.
4. The federal government department responsible for collecting CPP, EI, and income taxes is _____.
5. A/An _____ may have her or his work directed by the employer.
6. Codes used to determine the amount of federal or provincial income tax to be withheld from earnings are called _____.
7. _____ refers to earnings before any deductions are taken.
8. _____ refers to gross earnings minus all deductions for the period.
9. Hours worked over a weekly total of 40 are referred to as _____.
10. A/An _____ may direct the activities of an employee and may hire and fire the employee.

11. Earnings stated in terms of a month or a year are referred to as _____.

12. Earnings stated hourly are referred to as _____.

13. An employer may hire a/an _____ to perform services for a fee, but the employer will probably not direct the activities of this person, nor will the employer withhold payroll taxes from earnings.

14. A government form completed by an employee indicating various tax credits for federal income tax purposes is the _____

15. Amounts that are required by law to be withheld from earnings are _____.

16. The current method for determining provincial income tax is called the _____.

17. The provincial tax on employers and employees to provide health care for citizens of the province is called _____.

Match the words and terms on the left with the definitions on the right.

18. Canada Customs and Revenue Agency (CCRA)
19. claim codes
20. compulsory deductions
21. employee
22. employer
23. Employer Health Tax (EHT)
24. gross earnings
25. independent contractor
26. net earnings
27. overtime
28. overtime earnings
29. regular earnings
30. salary
31. tax on income (TONI) method
32. TD1, personal tax credits return
33. wages
34. withhold

a. gross earnings minus deductions
b. earnings for the first 40 hours worked in a week
c. one who may direct the activities of an employee
d. hours worked over a weekly total of 40 paid at time and a half
e. a provincial tax for providing health care for citizens
f. one who performs services for an employer but who is not an employee
g. earnings stated in yearly or monthly terms
h. total earnings before any deductions are taken
i. to hold back from giving
j. federal government department that collects income taxes
k. one who performs services for and is under the direction of an employer
l. earnings stated on an hourly basis
m. earnings for hours worked over a weekly total of 40
n. a government form completed by an employee indicating various tax credits for income tax purposes
o. current method for determining provincial income tax
p. amounts required by law to be withheld from earnings
q. codes for determining amount of federal or provincial income tax to be withheld

Exercises

EXERCISE 12.1

For each employee listed, determine the regular earnings, overtime earnings, and gross earnings and total each column. (Regular earnings plus overtime earnings equals gross earnings.) Overtime is paid at time and a half for all hours over a weekly total of 40.

Employee	Hours Worked	Hourly Wage	Regular Earnings	Overtime Earnings	Gross Earnings
Goldstein	48	$10.50	_____	_____	_____
McDonald	50	8.60	_____	_____	_____
Murray	42	9.60	_____	_____	_____
Huang	46	8.80	_____	_____	_____
Totals			_____	_____	_____

EXERCISE 12.2

For the first weekly payroll period of the year, determine the CPP contribution and EI premiums to be deducted for each employee; also determine the column totals. Refer to Figures 12-5 and 12-6.

Employee	Gross Pay	CPP Contribution	EI Premium
McGregor	$559.99	_____	_____
Mandela	602.70	_____	_____
Goodman	665.12	_____	_____
Chang	562.00	_____	_____
Chavez	642.60	_____	_____
Bartz	669.55	_____	_____
Totals		_____	_____

EXERCISE 12.3

Determine the federal and provincial (Ontario) claim codes for each of the following. Use Figures 12-3 and 12-5.

Employee	Total Exemptions	Federal Claim Code	Provincial Claim Code
Mandrake	$ 7,400.00	_____	_____
Graham	7,425.00	_____	_____
Williams	17,200.00	_____	_____
Deschutes	12,200.00	_____	_____
Cropier	9,030.00	_____	_____

EXERCISE 12.4

Glenda Cousteau earns $12.64 an hour and is paid time and a half for hours worked over a weekly total of 40. Calculate Glenda's net earnings for a week in which she works 47 hours. Use Charts 1 and 2 to determine federal and provincial claim codes (Glenda has total exemptions of $7,420). Use Figures 12-3 and 12-4 to determine income taxes. Tables 12-5 and 12-6 may be used to determine CPP contributions and EI premiums. Glenda has $15.00 per week withheld for savings.

EXERCISE 12.5

Auburn Company has a four-day work week. Time and a half is paid for hours worked over a daily total of 10. Calculate the regular earnings, overtime earnings, gross earnings, and column totals for each of the following.

Employee	Hours Worked				Hourly Wage	Regular Earnings	Overtime Earnings	Gross Earnings
	M	T	W	Th				
Habib	10	10	12	8	$14.20	_____	_____	_____
Wiggins	10	10	14	10	12.80	_____	_____	_____
Montoya	12	12	12	12	10.66	_____	_____	_____
Nanook	14	12	10	10	12.44	_____	_____	_____

EXERCISE 12.6

Calculate the federal and provincial income tax withholding for each of the following employees of Debrondan Industries. Use Figures 12-3 and 12-4.

Employee	Federal Claim Code	Provincial Claim Code	Earnings	Federal Income Tax	Provincial Income Tax
Samaan	1	1	$ 901.00	_____	_____
Thomson	3	3	1,217.00	_____	_____
Culver	2	3	1,557.00	_____	_____
Santana	4	5	685.00	_____	_____
Chow	6	6	641.00	_____	_____
Totals			_____	_____	_____

EXERCISE 12.7

Following are some figures from the payroll register of the North Bay Company. Determine the amounts of the missing figures.

Regular earnings	**$1,269.38**
Overtime earnings	a. _____
Gross earnings	1,737.70
CPP contributions	31.74
EI premiums	b. _____
Federal income tax withheld	301.69
Provincial income tax withheld	50.45
Charitable contributions withheld	89.00
Savings withheld	18.00
Total deductions	c. _____
Net earnings	$1,204.55

EXERCISE 12.8

Prepare the journal entry (page 50) to record the wages payable on March 28 from the information taken from the payroll register of East Coast Real Estate. Use the following payroll account titles: Wages Expense, CPP Payable, EI Payable, Federal Income Taxes Payable, Provincial Income Taxes Payable, Employee Savings Payable, and Wages Payable.

Regular earnings	**$2,368.50**
Overtime earnings	512.48
CPP contributions	49.38
EI premiums	54.19
Federal income tax withheld	201.67
Provincial income tax withheld	55.01
Savings withheld	64.00

Problems

PROBLEM 12.1

Atlantic Consultants has five employees: two are management and are not paid overtime, and three are office personnel who are paid double time for hours worked over a weekly total of 40. Following are the employees' names, the amounts they are paid, and the hours worked for the week.

Name	Salary/Wage	Hours Worked
Ann Suter, Management	$49,140 per year	50
Wayne Heintz, Management	$48,100 per year	48
Mae Wong, Office Personnel	$12.50 per hour	46
Robert Bracken, Office Personnel	$9.20 per hour	50
Ricardo Chicos, Office Personnel	$7.76 per hour	60

Instructions

Calculate for each employee (a) regular earnings, (b) overtime earnings, and (c) gross earnings for the week of August 9, 20xx. Also calculate the column totals for regular earnings, overtime earnings and gross earnings.

PROBLEM 12-2

The following information is available for Alberta Products for the week of May10, 20xx.

Employee	Federal Claim Code	Provincial Claim Code	Hours Worked	Hourly Wage
O'Shaunessy	4	5	40	$15.02
LeMonde	1	1	44	13.20
Johnstone	3	3	48	14.60
Kelly	5	5	40	16.80
Laurent	2	3	45	15.02

Instructions

1. Complete a payroll register for Alberta Products for the week of May 10, 20xx. Each employee is paid time and a half for hours worked over a weekly total of 40.
    a. Calculate regular earnings, overtime earnings, and gross earnings. At this point, check to make sure that total regular earnings plus total overtime earnings equals total gross earnings.
    b. Calculate the CPP contributions. No employee has earned over $38,300. Refer to Figure 12-5.
    c. Calculate the EI premiums. No employee has earned over $39,000. Refer to Figure 12-6.
    d. Determine the federal income tax deductions. Use Figure 12-3.
    e. Determine the provincial income tax deductions. Use Figure 12-4.
    f. Include in the deductions for each employee $18 for charitable contributions.
    g. Calculate total deductions. The total of each deduction column must equal the total of the total deductions column.
    h. Calculate net pay. Total gross earnings minus total deductions must equal total net earnings.

2. Prepare the general journal entry (page 33) to record wages expense and the payroll liabilities.

PROBLEM 12.3

The following payroll information is available on February 10, 20xx for Timeshare, a firm employing six people.

Employee	Federal Claim Amount	Provincial Claim Amount	Hours Worked	Hourly Wage	Charitable Contributions
Corbeil	$ 6,500	$ 6,500	45	$13.80	$12.50
Bergeron	7,427	7,427	46	14.20	12.50
Wellington	6,456	6,456	45	14.20	8.00
Da Vinci	10,626	10,800	36	16.40	8.00
MacKay	13,900	13,900	44	15.40	12.50
Weaver	10,420	10,420	40	18.00	18.00

Instructions

1. Complete a payroll register for Timeshare for the week of February 4, 20xx. Each employee is paid time and a half for hours worked over a weekly total of 40. Round calculations to the nearest penny.
    a. Calculate regular earnings, overtime earnings, and gross earnings. Total regular earnings plus total overtime earnings must equal total gross earnings.
    b. Calculate the CPP contributions. No employee has earned over $38,300. Refer to Figure 12-5.
    c. Calculate the EI premiums. No employee has earned over $39,000. Refer to Figure 12-6.
    d. Determine the federal and provincial claim codes for each employee, using Charts 1 and 2.
    e. Determine the amount of federal and provincial income taxes to be withheld using Figures 12-3 and 12-4.
    f. Include in your calculations for total deductions the amount withheld for charitable contributions.
    g. Calculate total deductions. The total of each deduction column must equal the total of the total deductions column.
    h. Calculate net earnings. Total gross earnings minus total deductions must equal total net earnings.
2. Prepare the general journal entry (page 19) to record the wages payable.

PROBLEM 12.4

The following payroll information is available for The Shirt House on March 31, 20xx.

Employee	Federal Claim Amount	Provincial Claim Amount	Hours Worked	Hourly Wage	Employee Savings
McIntosh	$ 6,456	$ 6,456	Mgmt.	_____	$40.00
Dinh	7,400	7,520	Mgmt.	_____	_____
Duclos	7,427	7,427	38	14.20	8.00
Martini	10,626	10,626	45	14.20	20.00
Ifrah	9,060	9,080	44	14.80	20.00
St. James	7,415	7,433	40	14.80	_____

Instructions

1. Complete a payroll register for The Shirt House for the week of March 25, 20xx. Employees, except management, are paid double time for hours worked over a weekly total of 40.

   a. Calculate regular earnings, overtime earnings, and gross earnings. The manager, McIntosh, earns $38,740 a year and Duclos earns $37,960.

   b. Calculate the CPP contributions. No employee has earned over $38,300. Refer to Figure 12-5.

   c. Calculate the EI premiums. No employee has earned over $39,000. Refer to Figure 12-6.

   d. Determine the federal and provincial claim codes for each employee, using Charts 1 and 2.

   e. Determine the amount of federal and provincial income taxes to be withheld using Figures 12-3 and 12-4.

   f. Include in your calculations for total deductions the amount withheld for employee savings.

   g. Calculate total deductions.

   h. Calculate net earnings.

2. Prepare the general journal entry (page 17) to record the wages payable and salaries payable (management salaries).

Figure 12–1(1) Federal TD1 Form

 Canada Customs and Revenue Agency — Agence des douanes et du revenu du Canada   **2001 PERSONAL TAX CREDITS RETURN**   TD1

Complete this TD1 form if you have a new employer or payer and you will receive salary, wages, commissions, pensions, Employment Insurance benefits, or any other remuneration. Be sure to sign and date it on the back page and give it to your employer or payer who will use it to determine the amount of your payroll tax deductions.

If you do not complete a TD1 form, your new employer or payer will deduct taxes after allowing the basic personal amount **only**.

You **do not** have to complete a new TD1 form every year unless there is a change in your personal tax credit amounts. Complete a new TD1 form no later than seven days after the change.

You can get the forms and publications mentioned on this form from our Internet site at **www.ccra-adrc.gc.ca** or by calling 1-800-959-2221.

Last name	First name and initial(s)	Date of birth (YYYY/MM/DD)	Employee number
Address including postal code		For non-residents only – Country of permanent residence	Social insurance number

1. Basic personal amount – Every resident of Canada can claim this amount. If you will have more than one employer or payer in 2001, see the section called "Income from other employers or payers" on the back page. If you are a non-resident, see the section called "Non-residents" on the back page.   **$7,412**

2. Age amount – If you will be 65 or older on December 31, 2001, and your net income for the year will be $26,941 or less, enter $3,619. If your net income will be between $26,941 and $51,068 and you want to calculate a partial claim, get the *Worksheet for the 2001 Personal Tax Credits Return* (TD1-WS) and complete the appropriate section.

3. Pension income amount – If you will receive regular pension payments from a pension plan or fund (excluding Canada or Quebec Pension Plans (CPP/QPP), Old Age Security and guaranteed income supplements), enter $1,000 or your estimated annual pension income, whichever is less.

4a. Tuition and education amounts (full-time) – If you are a student enrolled full-time at a university, college, or educational institution certified by Human Resources Development Canada, enter the total of the tuition fees you will pay, if more than $100 per institution, plus $400 for each month that you will be enrolled full-time.

4b. Tuition and education amounts (part-time) – If you are a student enrolled part-time at a university, college, or educational institution certified by Human Resources Development Canada, enter the total of the tuition fees you will pay, if more than $100 per institution, plus $120 for each month that you will be enrolled part-time.

5. Disability amount – If you will claim the disability amount on your income tax return by using Form T2201, *Disability Tax Credit Certificate*, enter $6,000.

6. Spousal amount – If you are supporting your spouse or common-law partner who lives with you, and his or her net income for the year will be $629 or less, enter $6,294. If his or her net income for the year will be between $629 and $6,923 and you want to calculate a partial claim, get the *Worksheet for the 2001 Personal Tax Credits Return* (TD1-WS) and complete the appropriate section.

7. Equivalent-to-spouse amount – If you do not have a spouse or common-law partner and you support a dependent relative who lives with you, and his or her net income for the year will be $629 or less, enter $6,294. If his or her net income for the year will be between $629 and $6,923 and you want to calculate a partial claim, get the *Worksheet for the 2001 Personal Tax Credits Return* (TD1-WS) and complete the appropriate section.

8. Caregiver amount – If you are taking care of a dependant who lives with you, whose net income for the year will be $11,953 or less, and who is either your or your spouse's or common-law partner's:
• parent or grandparent age 65 or older, **or**
• relative age 18 or older who is dependent on you because of an infirmity,
enter $3,500. If the dependant's net income for the year will be between $11,953 and $15,453 and you want to calculate a partial claim, get the *Worksheet for the 2001 Personal Tax Credits Return* (TD1-WS) and complete the appropriate section.

9. Amount for infirm dependant age 18 or older – If you are supporting an infirm dependant age 18 or older who is your or your spouse's or common-law partner's relative, who lives in Canada, and his or her net income for the year will be $4,966 or less, enter $3,500. You cannot claim an amount for a dependant claimed on line 8. If the dependant's net income for the year will be between $4,966 and $8,466 and you want to calculate a partial claim, get the *Worksheet for the 2001 Personal Tax Credits Return* (TD1-WS) and complete the appropriate section.

10. Amounts transferred from your spouse or common-law partner – If your spouse or common-law partner will not use all of his or her age amount, pension income amount, tuition and education amounts (maximum $5,000), or disability amount on his or her income tax return, enter the unused part.

11. Amounts transferred from your dependant – If your dependant will not use all of his or her tuition and education amounts (maximum $5,000) or disability amount on his or her income tax return, enter the unused part.

12. TOTAL CLAIM AMOUNT – Add lines 1 through line 11. Your employer or payer will use this amount to determine the amount of your payroll tax deductions.   **$**

Form continues on the back ⟶

Figure 12–1(2) Federal TD1 Form

Deduction for living in a prescribed zone

If you live in the Northwest Territories, Nunavut, Yukon, or another prescribed zone for more than six months in a row beginning or ending in 2001, you can claim:

- $7.50 for each day that you live in the prescribed zone; or
- $15 for each day that you live in the prescribed zone, if during that time you live in a dwelling that you maintain, and you are the only person living in that dwelling who is claiming this deduction.

$ _____

For more information, get Form T2222, *Northern Residents Deductions*, and the publication called *Northern Residents Deductions – Places in Prescribed Zones.*

Additional tax to be deducted

If you receive other income, including non-employment income such as CPP or QPP benefits, or Old Age Security pension, you may want to have more tax deducted from each pay. By doing this, you may not have to pay as much tax when you file your income tax return.

To choose this option, state the amount of additional tax you want to have deducted from each pay. To change this deduction later, you will have to complete a new *Personal Tax Credits Return.*

$ _____

Reduction in tax deductions

You can ask for a reduction in tax deductions if you are eligible for deductions or non-refundable tax credits that are not listed on this form (for example: periodic contributions to an RRSP, child care or employment expenses, charitable donations). To make this request, complete Form T1213, *Request to Reduce Tax Deductions at Source,* to get a letter of authority from your Tax Services Office.

Give the letter of authority to your employer or payer. You do not need a letter of authority if your employer deducts RRSP contributions from your salary.

Non-residents

If you are a non-resident of Canada, tick this box and answer the question below. If you are unsure of your residency status, call your tax services office at 1-800-959-8281 or the International Tax Services Office at 1-800-267-5177.

Non-resident ☐

Will you include 90% or more of your world income when determining your taxable income earned in Canada in 2001? If yes, complete the front page. If no, enter "0" on line 12 on the front page and do not complete lines 2 to 11 as you are not entitled to the personal tax credits.

Yes ☐ No ☐

Income from other employers or payers

Your earnings may not be subject to payroll tax deductions if your employment income from all employers for the year will be less than your total claim amount.

Will your total employment income for the year be less than your total claim amount on line 12 on the front page?

Yes ☐ No ☐

If you have more than one employer or payer and you have already claimed personal tax credit amounts on another Form TD1 for 2001, you can choose not to claim them again. By doing this, you may not have to pay as much tax when you file your income tax return. To choose this option, enter "0" on line 12 on the front page and do not complete lines 2 to 11.

Certification

I certify that the information given in this return is, to the best of my knowledge, correct and complete.

Signature _____ Date _____

It is a serious offence to make a false return.

Provincial Personal Tax Credits Return

In addition to this Form TD1, you may have to complete a *Provincial Personal Tax Credits Return.*

If your claim amount on line 12 on the front page is more than $7,412, complete a provincial TD1 form in addition to this form. If you are an employee, use the TD1 form for your province of employment. If you are a pensioner, use the TD1 form for your province of residence. Your employer or payer will use both forms to determine your tax deductions.

For 2001, there are no provincial TD1 forms for the Northwest Territories, Nunavut, and Yukon. If you work or reside in one of those places, your employer or payer will use this form only to determine your tax deductions.

If you are claiming the basic personal amount **only** (your claim amount on line 12 on the front page is $7,412), do not complete a provincial TD1 form. Your employer or payer will deduct provincial taxes after allowing the provincial basic personal amount.

NOTE: If you are a Saskatchewan resident with children under 18, you may claim the Child amount on the *2001 Saskatchewan Personal Tax Credits Return* (TD1SK). Therefore, you may want to complete the TD1SK form even if you are claiming the basic personal amount **only** on the front page of this form (your claim amount on line 12 is $7,412).

If you entered "0" on line 12 on the front page because you are a non-resident and you will not include 90% or more of your world income when determining your taxable income earned in Canada in 2001, do not complete a provincial TD1. You are not entitled to the provincial personal tax credits.

Printed in Canada

Figure 12–2(1) British Columbia TD1 Form

2002 BRITISH COLUMBIA PERSONAL TAX CREDITS RETURN   TD1BC

Do I have to complete this form?

Complete this British Columbia TD1 form if you completed a federal Form TD1, *2002 Personal Tax Credits Return*, and you are:

- an employee working in British Columbia; or
- a pensioner residing in British Columbia.

If you complete this form, be sure to sign and date it on the back page and give it to your employer or payer with your federal TD1 form. Your employer or payer will use both forms to determine the amount of your payroll tax deductions.

Last name	First name and initial(s)	Date of birth (YYYY/MM/DD)	Employee number
Address including postal code		For non-residents only – Country of permanent residence	Social insurance number

1. Basic personal amount – Every person employed in British Columbia and every pensioner residing in British Columbia can claim this amount. If you will have more than one employer or payer at the same time in 2002, see the section called "Income from other employers or payers" on the back page.   **$8,168**

2. Age amount – If you will be 65 or older on December 31, 2002, and your net income from all sources will be $27,265 or less, enter $3,663. If your net income will be between $27,265 and $51,685 and you want to calculate a partial claim, get the *Worksheet for the 2002 British Columbia Personal Tax Credits Return* (TD1BC-WS) and complete the appropriate section.

3. Pension income amount – If you will receive regular pension payments from a pension plan or fund (excluding Canada or Quebec Pension Plans (CPP/QPP), Old Age Security and guaranteed income supplements), enter $1,000 or your estimated annual pension income, whichever is less.

4a. Tuition and education amounts (full-time) – If you are a student enrolled full-time at a university, college, or educational institution certified by Human Resources Development Canada, enter the total of the tuition fees you will pay, if more than $100 per institution, plus $200 for each month that you will be enrolled full-time.

4b. Tuition and education amounts (part-time) – If you are a student enrolled part-time at a university, college, or educational institution certified by Human Resources Development Canada, enter the total of the tuition fees you will pay, if more than $100 per institution, plus $60 for each month that you will be enrolled part-time.

5. Disability amount – If you will claim the disability amount on your income tax return by using Form T2201, *Disability Tax Credit Certificate*, enter $4,453.

6. Spouse or common-law partner amount – If you are supporting your spouse or common-law partner who lives with you, and his or her net income for the year will be $699 or less, enter $6,994. If his or her net income for the year will be between $699 and $7,693 and you want to calculate a partial claim, get the *Worksheet for the 2002 British Columbia Personal Tax Credits Return* (TD1BC-WS) and complete the appropriate section.

7. Amount for an eligible dependant – If you do not have a spouse or common-law partner and support a dependent relative who lives with you, and his or her net income for the year will be $699 or less, enter $6,994. If his or her net income for the year will be between $699 and $7,693 and you want to calculate a partial claim, get the *Worksheet for the 2002 British Columbia Personal Tax Credits Return* (TD1BC-WS) and complete the appropriate section.

8. Caregiver amount – If you are taking care of a person who lives with you, whose net income for the year will be $12,096 or less, and who is **either** your or your spouse's or common-law partner's:

- parent or grandparent age 65 or older, **or**
- relative age 18 or older who is dependent on you because of an infirmity,

enter $2,475. If the dependant's net income for the year will be between $12,096 and $14,571 and you want to calculate a partial claim, get the *Worksheet for the 2002 British Columbia Personal Tax Credits Return* (TD1BC-WS) and complete the appropriate section.

9. Amount for infirm dependant age 18 or older – If you are supporting an infirm dependant age 18 or older who is your or your spouse's or common-law partner's relative, who lives in Canada, and his or her net income for the year will be $5,693 or less, enter $2,475. You cannot claim an amount for a dependant claimed on line 8. If the dependant's net income for the year will be between $5,693 and $8,168 and you want to calculate a partial claim, get the *Worksheet for the 2002 British Columbia Personal Tax Credits Return* (TD1BC-WS) and complete the appropriate section.

10. Amounts transferred from your spouse or common-law partner – If your spouse or common-law partner will not use all of his or her age amount, pension income amount, tuition and education amounts (maximum $5,000), or disability amount on his or her income tax return, enter the unused part.

11. Amounts transferred from a dependant – If your dependant will not use all of his or her tuition and education amounts (maximum $5,000) or disability amount on his or her income tax return, enter the unused part.

12. TOTAL CLAIM AMOUNT – Add lines 1 through line 11. Your employer or payer will use your claim amount to determine the amount of your provincial payroll tax deductions.   **$**

Form continues on the back ⟶

Figure 12–2(2) British Columbia TD1 Form

Forms and publications

You can get the forms and publications mentioned on this form from the Internet at **www.ccra.gc.ca/forms** or by calling 1-800-959-2221.

Why is there a British Columbia TD1 form?

British Columbia has its own tax rates and brackets, as well as its own non-refundable tax credits. Your provincial income tax is calculated directly on your taxable income.

Your employer or payer uses the personal tax credit amounts you claim on your TD1 form to calculate your federal payroll tax deductions. Similarly, your employer or the payer of your pension will now calculate the provincial tax to deduct from your pay or pension cheque using the personal tax credit amounts you claim on your TD1BC form.

If you wish to have more tax deducted, complete the section called "Additional tax to be deducted" on the federal TD1 form.

If you are eligible to have less tax deducted, see the section called "Reduction in tax deductions" on the federal TD1 form.

Income from other employers or payers

Your earnings may not be subject to payroll tax deductions if your total income from all employers and payers for the year will be less than your total claim amount.

Will your total income for the year be less than your total claim amount on line 12 on the front page?   Yes ☐   No ☐

If you have more than one employer or payer at the same time and you have already claimed personal tax credit amounts on another Form TD1BC for 2002, you can choose not to claim them again. By doing this, you may not have to pay as much tax when you file your income tax return. To choose this option, enter "0" on line 12 on the front page and do not complete lines 2 to 11.

Certification

I certify that the information given in this return is, to the best of my knowledge, correct and complete.

Signature _____   Date _____

It is a serious offence to make a false return.

Printed in Canada

Figure 12–3(1) Federal Wage Bracket Tables

| Ontario
Federal tax deductions only
Effective January 1, 2001
Weekly (52 pay periods a year) | | | | | | | | | | | Ontario
Retenues d'impôt fédéral seulement
En vigueur le 1er janvier 2001
Hebdomadaire (52 périodes de paie par année) |

Pay		Federal claim codes/Codes de demande fédéraux										
Rémunération		0	1	2	3	4	5	6	7	8	9	10
From De	Less than Moins de					Deduct from each pay Retenez sur chaque paie						
477. -	485	72.40	49.60	47.05	42.00	36.95	31.85	26.80	21.75	16.70	11.65	6.60
485. -	493	73.60	50.75	48.25	43.20	38.15	33.05	28.00	22.95	17.90	12.85	7.75
493. -	501	74.75	51.95	49.45	44.40	39.30	34.25	29.20	24.15	19.10	14.05	8.95
501. -	509	75.95	53.15	50.65	45.60	40.50	35.45	30.40	25.35	20.30	15.20	10.15
509. -	517	77.15	54.35	51.85	46.75	41.70	36.65	31.60	26.55	21.50	16.40	11.35
517. -	525	78.35	55.55	53.05	47.95	42.90	37.85	32.80	27.75	22.70	17.60	12.55
525. -	533	79.55	56.75	54.20	49.15	44.10	39.05	34.00	28.95	23.85	18.80	13.75
533. -	541	80.75	57.95	55.40	50.35	45.30	40.25	35.20	30.15	25.05	20.00	14.95
541. -	549	81.95	59.15	56.60	51.55	46.50	41.45	36.40	31.30	26.25	21.20	16.15
549. -	557	83.15	60.35	57.80	52.75	47.70	42.65	37.60	32.50	27.45	22.40	17.35
557. -	565	84.35	61.55	59.00	53.95	48.90	43.85	38.75	33.70	28.65	23.60	18.55
565. -	573	85.55	62.75	60.20	55.15	50.10	45.05	39.95	34.90	29.85	24.80	19.75
573. -	581	86.75	63.95	61.40	56.35	51.30	46.25	41.15	36.10	31.05	26.00	20.95
581. -	589	87.95	65.15	62.60	57.55	52.50	47.40	42.35	37.30	32.25	27.20	22.15
589. -	597	89.25	66.40	63.90	58.85	53.80	48.70	43.65	38.60	33.55	28.50	23.40
597. -	605	90.90	68.10	65.55	60.50	55.45	50.40	45.35	40.30	35.20	30.15	25.10
605. -	613	92.60	69.75	67.25	62.20	57.15	52.05	47.00	41.95	36.90	31.85	26.75
613. -	621	94.25	71.45	68.90	63.85	58.80	53.75	48.70	43.65	38.55	33.50	28.45
621. -	629	95.95	73.15	70.60	65.55	60.50	55.40	50.35	45.30	40.25	35.20	30.15
629. -	637	97.60	74.80	72.25	67.20	62.15	57.10	52.05	47.00	41.90	36.85	31.80
637. -	645	99.30	76.50	73.95	68.90	63.85	58.75	53.70	48.65	43.60	38.55	33.50
645. -	653	100.95	78.15	75.65	70.55	65.50	60.45	55.40	50.35	45.25	40.20	35.15
653. -	661	102.65	79.85	77.30	72.25	67.20	62.15	57.05	52.00	46.95	41.90	36.85
661. -	669	104.30	81.50	79.00	73.90	68.85	63.80	58.75	53.70	48.65	43.55	38.50
669. -	677	106.00	83.20	80.65	75.60	70.55	65.50	60.40	55.35	50.30	45.25	40.20
677. -	685	107.65	84.85	82.35	77.25	72.20	67.15	62.10	57.05	52.00	46.90	41.85
685. -	693	109.35	86.55	84.00	78.95	73.90	68.85	63.75	58.70	53.65	48.60	43.55
693. -	701	111.00	88.20	85.70	80.60	75.55	70.50	65.45	60.40	55.35	50.25	45.20
701. -	709	112.70	89.90	87.35	82.30	77.25	72.20	67.10	62.05	57.00	51.95	46.90
709. -	717	114.35	91.55	89.05	84.00	78.90	73.85	68.80	63.75	58.70	53.60	48.55
717. -	725	116.05	93.25	90.70	85.65	80.60	75.55	70.50	65.40	60.35	55.30	50.25
725. -	733	117.70	94.90	92.40	87.35	82.25	77.20	72.15	67.10	62.05	57.00	51.90
733. -	741	119.40	96.60	94.05	89.00	83.95	78.90	73.85	68.75	63.70	58.65	53.60
741. -	749	121.15	98.35	95.80	90.75	85.70	80.60	75.55	70.50	65.45	60.40	55.35
749. -	757	122.85	100.05	97.55	92.50	87.40	82.35	77.30	72.25	67.20	62.15	57.05
757. -	765	124.65	101.85	99.30	94.25	89.20	84.10	79.05	74.00	68.95	63.90	58.85
765. -	773	126.40	103.60	101.05	96.00	90.95	85.90	80.85	75.75	70.70	65.65	60.60
773. -	781	128.15	105.35	102.80	97.75	92.70	87.65	82.60	77.55	72.45	67.40	62.35
781. -	789	129.90	107.10	104.60	99.50	94.45	89.40	84.35	79.30	74.25	69.15	64.10
789. -	797	131.65	108.85	106.35	101.30	96.20	91.15	86.10	81.05	76.00	70.95	65.85
797. -	805	133.45	110.65	108.10	103.05	98.00	92.90	87.85	82.80	77.75	72.70	67.65
805. -	813	135.20	112.40	109.85	104.80	99.75	94.70	89.65	84.55	79.50	74.45	69.40
813. -	821	136.95	114.15	111.60	106.55	101.50	96.45	91.40	86.35	81.25	76.20	71.15
821. -	829	138.70	115.90	113.40	108.30	103.25	98.20	93.15	88.10	83.05	77.95	72.90
829. -	837	140.45	117.65	115.15	110.10	105.00	99.95	94.90	89.85	84.80	79.75	74.65
837. -	845	142.25	119.45	116.90	111.85	106.80	101.70	96.65	91.60	86.55	81.50	76.45
845. -	853	144.00	121.20	118.65	113.60	108.55	103.50	98.45	93.35	88.30	83.25	78.20
853. -	861	145.75	122.95	120.40	115.35	110.30	105.25	100.20	95.15	90.05	85.00	79.95
861. -	869	147.50	124.70	122.20	117.10	112.05	107.00	101.95	96.90	91.85	86.75	81.70
869. -	877	149.25	126.45	123.95	118.90	113.80	108.75	103.70	98.65	93.60	88.55	83.45
877. -	885	151.05	128.25	125.70	120.65	115.60	110.50	105.45	100.40	95.35	90.30	85.25
885. -	893	152.80	130.00	127.45	122.40	117.35	112.30	107.25	102.15	97.10	92.05	87.00
893. -	901	154.55	131.75	129.20	124.15	119.10	114.05	109.00	103.95	98.85	93.80	88.75
901. -	909	156.30	133.50	131.00	125.90	120.85	115.80	110.75	105.70	100.65	95.55	90.50
909. -	917	158.05	135.25	132.75	127.70	122.60	117.55	112.50	107.45	102.40	97.35	92.25

This table is available on diskette (TOD).   D-3   Vous pouvez obtenir cette table sur disquette (TSD).

Figure 12–3(2) Federal Wage Bracket Tables

Ontario
Federal tax deductions only
Effective January 1, 2001
Weekly (52 pay periods a year)

Ontario
Retenues d'impôt fédéral seulement
En vigueur le 1er janvier 2001
Hebdomadaire (52 périodes de paie par année)

Pay / Rémunération		Federal claim codes/Codes de demande fédéraux										
From / De	Less than / Moins de	0	1	2	3	4	5	6	7	8	9	10
						Deduct from each pay / Retenez sur chaque paie						
917. -	929	160.25	137.45	134.95	129.90	124.80	119.75	114.70	109.65	104.60	99.55	94.45
929. -	941	162.90	140.10	137.60	132.50	127.45	122.40	117.35	112.30	107.25	102.15	97.10
941. -	953	165.55	142.75	140.20	135.15	130.10	125.05	120.00	114.95	109.85	104.80	99.75
953. -	965	168.20	145.40	142.85	137.80	132.75	127.70	122.65	117.55	112.50	107.45	102.40
965. -	977	170.85	148.05	145.50	140.45	135.40	130.30	125.25	120.20	115.15	110.10	105.05
977. -	989	173.50	150.65	148.15	143.10	138.00	132.95	127.90	122.85	117.80	112.75	107.65
989. -	1001	176.10	153.30	150.80	145.70	140.65	135.60	130.55	125.50	120.45	115.35	110.30
1001. -	1013	178.75	155.95	153.40	148.35	143.30	138.25	133.20	128.15	123.05	118.00	112.95
1013. -	1025	181.40	158.60	156.05	151.00	145.95	140.90	135.85	130.75	125.70	120.65	115.60
1025. -	1037	184.05	161.25	158.70	153.65	148.60	143.50	138.45	133.40	128.35	123.30	118.25
1037. -	1049	186.65	163.85	161.35	156.30	151.20	146.15	141.10	136.05	131.00	125.95	120.85
1049. -	1061	189.30	166.50	164.00	158.90	153.85	148.80	143.75	138.70	133.65	128.55	123.50
1061. -	1073	191.95	169.15	166.60	161.55	156.50	151.45	146.40	141.35	136.25	131.20	126.15
1073. -	1085	194.60	171.80	169.25	164.20	159.15	154.10	149.05	143.95	138.90	133.85	128.80
1085. -	1097	197.25	174.45	171.90	166.85	161.80	156.70	151.65	146.60	141.55	136.50	131.45
1097. -	1109	199.85	177.05	174.55	169.50	164.40	159.35	154.30	149.25	144.20	139.15	134.05
1109. -	1121	202.50	179.70	177.20	172.10	167.05	162.00	156.95	151.90	146.85	141.75	136.70
1121. -	1133	205.15	182.35	179.80	174.75	169.70	164.65	159.60	154.55	149.45	144.40	139.35
1133. -	1145	207.80	185.00	182.45	177.40	172.35	167.30	162.25	157.15	152.10	147.05	142.00
1145. -	1157	210.45	187.65	185.10	180.05	175.00	169.90	164.85	159.80	154.75	149.70	144.65
1157. -	1169	213.05	190.25	187.75	182.70	177.60	172.55	167.50	162.45	157.40	152.35	147.25
1169. -	1181	215.70	192.90	190.40	185.30	180.25	175.20	170.15	165.10	160.05	154.95	149.90
1181. -	1193	218.50	195.70	193.15	188.10	183.05	178.00	172.95	167.90	162.80	157.75	152.70
1193. -	1205	221.65	198.80	196.30	191.25	186.20	181.10	176.05	171.00	165.95	160.90	155.80
1205. -	1217	224.75	201.95	199.40	194.35	189.30	184.25	179.20	174.10	169.05	164.00	158.95
1217. -	1229	227.85	205.05	202.55	197.45	192.40	187.35	182.30	177.25	172.20	167.10	162.05
1229. -	1241	231.00	208.20	205.65	200.60	195.55	190.50	185.40	180.35	175.30	170.25	165.20
1241. -	1253	234.10	211.30	208.75	203.70	198.65	193.60	188.55	183.50	178.40	173.35	168.30
1253. -	1265	237.25	214.40	211.90	206.85	201.80	196.70	191.65	186.60	181.55	176.50	171.40
1265. -	1277	240.35	217.55	215.00	209.95	204.90	199.85	194.80	189.70	184.65	179.60	174.55
1277. -	1289	243.45	220.65	218.15	213.05	208.00	202.95	197.90	192.85	187.80	182.70	177.65
1289. -	1301	246.60	223.80	221.25	216.20	211.15	206.10	201.00	195.95	190.90	185.85	180.80
1301. -	1313	249.70	226.90	224.35	219.30	214.25	209.20	204.15	199.10	194.00	188.95	183.90
1313. -	1325	252.85	230.00	227.50	222.45	217.40	212.30	207.25	202.20	197.15	192.10	187.00
1325. -	1337	255.95	233.15	230.60	225.55	220.50	215.45	210.40	205.30	200.25	195.20	190.15
1337. -	1349	259.05	236.25	233.75	228.65	223.60	218.55	213.50	208.45	203.40	198.30	193.25
1349. -	1361	262.20	239.40	236.85	231.80	226.75	221.70	216.60	211.55	206.50	201.45	196.40
1361. -	1373	265.30	242.50	239.95	234.90	229.85	224.80	219.75	214.70	209.60	204.55	199.50
1373. -	1385	268.45	245.60	243.10	238.05	233.00	227.90	222.85	217.80	212.75	207.70	202.60
1385. -	1397	271.55	248.75	246.20	241.15	236.10	231.05	226.00	220.90	215.85	210.80	205.75
1397. -	1409	274.65	251.85	249.35	244.25	239.20	234.15	229.10	224.05	219.00	213.90	208.85
1409. -	1421	277.80	255.00	252.45	247.40	242.35	237.30	232.20	227.15	222.10	217.05	212.00
1421. -	1433	280.90	258.10	255.55	250.50	245.45	240.40	235.35	230.30	225.20	220.15	215.10
1433. -	1445	284.05	261.20	258.70	253.65	248.60	243.50	238.45	233.40	228.35	223.30	218.20
1445. -	1457	287.15	264.35	261.80	256.75	251.70	246.65	241.60	236.50	231.45	226.40	221.35
1457. -	1469	290.25	267.45	264.95	259.85	254.80	249.75	244.70	239.65	234.60	229.50	224.45
1469. -	1481	293.40	270.60	268.05	263.00	257.95	252.90	247.80	242.75	237.70	232.65	227.60
1481. -	1493	296.50	273.70	271.15	266.10	261.05	256.00	250.95	245.90	240.80	235.75	230.70
1493. -	1505	299.65	276.80	274.30	269.25	264.20	259.10	254.05	249.00	243.95	238.90	233.80
1505. -	1517	302.75	279.95	277.40	272.35	267.30	262.25	257.20	252.10	247.05	242.00	236.95
1517. -	1529	305.85	283.05	280.55	275.45	270.40	265.35	260.30	255.25	250.20	245.10	240.05
1529. -	1541	309.00	286.20	283.65	278.60	273.55	268.50	263.40	258.35	253.30	248.25	243.20
1541. -	1553	312.10	289.30	286.75	281.70	276.65	271.60	266.55	261.50	256.40	251.35	246.30
1553. -	1565	315.25	292.40	289.90	284.85	279.80	274.70	269.65	264.60	259.55	254.50	249.40
1565. -	1577	318.35	295.55	293.00	287.95	282.90	277.85	272.80	267.70	262.65	257.60	252.55

This table is available on diskette (TOD).   D-4   **Vous pouvez obtenir cette table sur disquette (TSD).**

Figure 12–4(1) Ontario Wage Bracket Tables

| **Ontario** Provincial tax deductions only Effective January 1, 2001 Weekly (52 pay periods a year) | | | | | | | | | | | **Ontario** Retenues d'impôt provincial seulement En vigueur le 1er janvier 2001 Hebdomadaire (52 périodes de paie par année) |

Pay Rémunération		Provincial claim codes/Codes de demande provinciaux										
From De	Less than Moins de	0	1	2	3	4	5	6	7	8	9	10
							Deduct from each pay Retenez sur chaque paie					
529. -	537	31.05	22.20	21.25	19.35	17.45	15.55	13.60	11.70	9.80	7.90	6.00
537. -	545	31.50	22.65	21.70	19.80	17.90	16.00	14.10	12.20	10.25	8.35	6.45
545. -	553	32.00	23.15	22.20	20.25	18.35	16.45	14.55	12.65	10.75	8.85	6.90
553. -	561	32.45	23.60	22.65	20.75	18.85	16.90	15.00	13.10	11.20	9.30	7.40
561. -	569	32.90	24.05	23.10	21.20	19.30	17.40	15.50	13.55	11.65	9.75	7.85
569. -	577	33.40	24.50	23.55	21.65	19.75	17.85	15.95	14.05	12.10	10.20	8.30
577. -	585	33.85	25.00	24.05	22.15	20.20	18.30	16.40	14.50	12.60	10.70	8.75
585. -	593	34.30	25.45	24.50	22.60	20.70	18.75	16.85	14.95	13.05	11.15	9.25
593. -	601	34.90	26.05	25.10	23.20	21.30	19.35	17.45	15.55	13.65	11.75	9.85
601. -	609	35.60	26.75	25.80	23.90	22.00	20.05	18.15	16.25	14.35	12.45	10.55
609. -	617	36.30	27.45	26.50	24.60	22.70	20.80	18.85	16.95	15.05	13.15	11.25
617. -	625	37.00	28.15	27.20	25.30	23.40	21.50	19.60	17.65	15.75	13.85	11.95
625. -	633	37.75	28.85	27.90	26.00	24.10	22.20	20.30	18.40	16.45	14.55	12.65
633. -	641	38.45	29.60	28.60	26.70	24.80	22.90	21.00	19.10	17.20	15.25	13.35
641. -	649	39.15	30.30	29.35	27.40	25.50	23.60	21.70	19.80	17.90	16.00	14.05
649. -	657	39.85	31.00	30.05	28.15	26.20	24.30	22.40	20.50	18.60	16.70	14.80
657. -	665	40.55	31.70	30.75	28.85	26.95	25.00	23.10	21.20	19.30	17.40	15.50
665. -	673	41.25	32.40	31.45	29.55	27.65	25.75	23.80	21.90	20.00	18.10	16.20
673. -	681	41.95	33.10	32.15	30.25	28.35	26.45	24.55	22.60	20.70	18.80	16.90
681. -	689	42.65	33.80	32.85	30.95	29.05	27.15	25.25	23.35	21.40	19.50	17.60
689. -	697	43.40	34.55	33.55	31.65	29.75	27.85	25.95	24.05	22.15	20.20	18.30
697. -	705	44.10	35.25	34.30	32.35	30.45	28.55	26.65	24.75	22.85	20.90	19.00
705. -	713	44.80	35.95	35.00	33.10	31.15	29.25	27.35	25.45	23.55	21.65	19.70
713. -	721	45.50	36.65	35.70	33.80	31.90	29.95	28.05	26.15	24.25	22.35	20.45
721. -	729	46.20	37.35	36.40	34.50	32.60	30.65	28.75	26.85	24.95	23.05	21.15
729. -	737	46.90	38.05	37.10	35.20	33.30	31.40	29.45	27.55	25.65	23.75	21.85
737. -	745	47.65	38.80	37.80	35.90	34.00	32.10	30.20	28.30	26.40	24.45	22.55
745. -	753	48.35	39.50	38.55	36.65	34.75	32.85	30.90	29.00	27.10	25.20	23.30
753. -	761	49.10	40.25	39.30	37.40	35.45	33.55	31.65	29.75	27.85	25.95	24.05
761. -	769	49.85	41.00	40.05	38.10	36.20	34.30	32.40	30.50	28.60	26.65	24.75
769. -	777	50.60	41.70	40.75	38.85	36.95	35.05	33.15	31.25	29.30	27.40	25.50
777. -	785	51.30	42.45	41.50	39.60	37.70	35.80	33.90	31.95	30.05	28.15	26.25
785. -	793	52.05	43.20	42.25	40.35	38.45	36.50	34.60	32.70	30.80	28.90	27.00
793. -	801	52.80	43.95	43.00	41.10	39.15	37.25	35.35	33.45	31.55	29.65	27.70
801. -	809	53.55	44.70	43.70	41.80	39.90	38.00	36.10	34.20	32.30	30.35	28.45
809. -	817	54.25	45.40	44.45	42.55	40.65	38.75	36.85	34.95	33.00	31.10	29.20
817. -	825	55.00	46.15	45.20	43.30	41.40	39.50	37.55	35.65	33.75	31.85	29.95
825. -	833	55.75	46.90	45.95	44.05	42.15	40.20	38.30	36.40	34.50	32.60	30.70
833. -	841	56.50	47.65	46.70	44.75	42.85	40.95	39.05	37.15	35.25	33.35	31.40
841. -	849	57.25	48.35	47.40	45.50	43.60	41.70	39.80	37.90	35.95	34.05	32.15
849. -	857	57.95	49.10	48.15	46.25	44.35	42.45	40.55	38.60	36.70	34.80	32.90
857. -	865	58.70	49.85	48.90	47.00	45.10	43.20	41.25	39.35	37.45	35.55	33.65
865. -	873	59.45	50.60	49.65	47.75	45.80	43.90	42.00	40.10	38.20	36.30	34.40
873. -	881	60.20	51.35	50.40	48.45	46.55	44.65	42.75	40.85	38.95	37.00	35.10
881. -	889	60.90	52.05	51.10	49.20	47.30	45.40	43.50	41.60	39.65	37.75	35.85
889. -	897	61.65	52.80	51.85	49.95	48.05	46.15	44.20	42.30	40.40	38.50	36.60
897. -	905	62.40	53.55	52.60	50.70	48.80	46.85	44.95	43.05	41.15	39.25	37.35
905. -	913	63.15	54.30	53.35	51.45	49.50	47.60	45.70	43.80	41.90	40.00	38.05
913. -	921	63.90	55.05	54.05	52.15	50.25	48.35	46.45	44.55	42.65	40.70	38.80
921. -	929	64.60	55.75	54.80	52.90	51.00	49.10	47.20	45.25	43.35	41.45	39.55
929. -	937	65.35	56.50	55.55	53.65	51.75	49.85	47.90	46.00	44.10	42.20	40.30
937. -	945	66.10	57.25	56.30	54.40	52.50	50.55	48.65	46.75	44.85	42.95	41.05
945. -	953	66.85	58.00	57.05	55.10	53.20	51.30	49.40	47.50	45.60	43.70	41.75
953. -	961	67.60	58.70	57.75	55.85	53.95	52.05	50.15	48.25	46.30	44.40	42.50
961. -	969	68.30	59.45	58.50	56.60	54.70	52.80	50.90	48.95	47.05	45.15	43.25

This table is available on diskette (TOD).   E-3   Vous pouvez obtenir cette table sur disquette (TSD).

Figure 12–4(2) Ontario Wage Bracket Tables

Ontario
Provincial tax deductions only
Effective January 1, 2001
Weekly (52 pay periods a year)

Ontario
Retenues d'impôt provincial seulement
En vigueur le 1er janvier 2001
Hebdomadaire (52 périodes de paie par année)

Pay Rémunération		Provincial claim codes/Codes de demande provinciaux										
		0	1	2	3	4	5	6	7	8	9	10
From De	Less than Moins de					Deduct from each pay Retenez sur chaque paie							
969. -	981	69.40	60.40	59.45	57.50	55.60	53.70	51.80	49.90	48.00	46.10	44.15
981. -	993	70.75	61.50	60.55	58.65	56.75	54.80	52.90	51.00	49.10	47.20	45.30
993. -	1005	72.05	62.60	61.65	59.75	57.85	55.95	54.00	52.10	50.20	48.30	46.40
1005. -	1017	73.40	63.70	62.75	60.85	58.95	57.05	55.15	53.20	51.30	49.40	47.50
1017. -	1029	74.70	64.80	63.85	61.95	60.05	58.15	56.25	54.35	52.40	50.50	48.60
1029. -	1041	76.05	65.95	65.00	63.05	61.15	59.25	57.35	55.45	53.55	51.60	49.70
1041. -	1053	77.40	67.05	66.10	64.20	62.25	60.35	58.45	56.55	54.65	52.75	50.80
1053. -	1065	78.70	68.15	67.20	65.30	63.40	61.45	59.55	57.65	55.75	53.85	51.95
1065. -	1077	80.05	69.40	68.30	66.40	64.50	62.60	60.65	58.75	56.85	54.95	53.05
1077. -	1089	81.35	70.75	69.60	67.50	65.60	63.70	61.80	59.85	57.95	56.05	54.15
1089. -	1101	82.70	72.10	70.95	68.65	66.70	64.80	62.90	61.00	59.05	57.15	55.25
1101. -	1113	84.05	73.40	72.25	69.95	67.80	65.90	64.00	62.10	60.20	58.30	56.35
1113. -	1125	85.35	74.75	73.60	71.30	69.00	67.00	65.10	63.20	61.30	59.40	57.50
1125. -	1137	86.70	76.05	74.90	72.65	70.35	68.10	66.20	64.30	62.40	60.50	58.60
1137. -	1149	88.00	77.40	76.25	73.95	71.70	69.40	67.30	65.40	63.50	61.60	59.70
1149. -	1161	89.35	78.75	77.60	75.30	73.00	70.70	68.45	66.55	64.60	62.70	60.80
1161. -	1173	90.90	80.05	78.90	76.65	74.35	72.05	69.75	67.65	65.75	63.80	61.90
1173. -	1185	92.65	81.40	80.25	77.95	75.65	73.40	71.10	68.80	66.85	64.95	63.00
1185. -	1197	94.55	82.85	81.70	79.45	77.15	74.85	72.55	70.25	68.05	66.15	64.25
1197. -	1209	96.65	84.45	83.30	81.05	78.75	76.45	74.15	71.90	69.60	67.50	65.60
1209. -	1221	98.75	86.10	84.95	82.65	80.35	78.05	75.75	73.50	71.20	68.90	66.90
1221. -	1233	100.80	87.70	86.55	84.25	81.95	79.65	77.40	75.10	72.80	70.50	68.25
1233. -	1245	102.90	89.30	88.15	85.85	83.55	81.30	79.00	76.70	74.40	72.10	69.85
1245. -	1257	105.00	91.20	89.75	87.45	85.15	82.90	80.60	78.30	76.00	73.75	71.45
1257. -	1269	107.10	93.25	91.80	89.05	86.80	84.50	82.20	79.90	77.60	75.35	73.05
1269. -	1281	109.15	95.35	93.85	90.90	88.40	86.10	83.80	81.50	79.25	76.95	74.65
1281. -	1293	111.25	97.45	95.95	93.00	90.00	87.70	85.40	83.15	80.85	78.55	76.25
1293. -	1305	113.35	99.55	98.05	95.10	92.10	89.30	87.00	84.75	82.45	80.15	77.85
1305. -	1317	115.45	101.65	100.15	97.15	94.20	91.20	88.65	86.35	84.05	81.75	79.45
1317. -	1329	117.55	103.70	102.25	99.25	96.30	93.30	90.35	87.95	85.65	83.35	81.10
1329. -	1341	119.60	105.80	104.30	101.35	98.35	95.40	92.40	89.55	87.25	85.00	82.70
1341. -	1353	121.70	107.90	106.40	103.45	100.45	97.50	94.50	91.55	88.85	86.60	84.30
1353. -	1365	123.80	110.00	108.50	105.50	102.55	99.55	96.60	93.60	90.65	88.20	85.90
1365. -	1377	125.90	112.05	110.60	107.60	104.65	101.65	98.70	95.70	92.75	89.80	87.50
1377. -	1389	128.00	114.15	112.70	109.70	106.70	103.75	100.75	97.80	94.80	91.85	89.10
1389. -	1401	130.05	116.25	114.75	111.80	108.80	105.85	102.85	99.90	96.90	93.95	90.95
1401. -	1413	132.15	118.35	116.85	113.90	110.90	107.95	104.95	101.95	99.00	96.00	93.05
1413. -	1425	134.25	120.45	118.95	115.95	113.00	110.00	107.05	104.05	101.10	98.10	95.15
1425. -	1437	136.35	122.50	121.05	118.05	115.10	112.10	109.15	106.15	103.20	100.20	97.20
1437. -	1449	138.40	124.60	123.10	120.15	117.15	114.20	111.20	108.25	105.25	102.30	99.30
1449. -	1461	140.50	126.70	125.20	122.25	119.25	116.30	113.30	110.35	107.35	104.40	101.40
1461. -	1473	142.60	128.80	127.30	124.30	121.35	118.35	115.40	112.40	109.45	106.45	103.50
1473. -	1485	144.70	130.90	129.40	126.40	123.45	120.45	117.50	114.50	111.55	108.55	105.60
1485. -	1497	146.80	132.95	131.50	128.50	125.55	122.55	119.55	116.60	113.60	110.65	107.65
1497. -	1509	148.85	135.05	133.55	130.60	127.60	124.65	121.65	118.70	115.70	112.75	109.75
1509. -	1521	150.95	137.15	135.65	132.70	129.70	126.75	123.75	120.80	117.80	114.80	111.85
1521. -	1533	153.05	139.25	137.75	134.75	131.80	128.80	125.85	122.85	119.90	116.90	113.95
1533. -	1545	155.15	141.30	139.85	136.85	133.90	130.90	127.95	124.95	122.00	119.00	116.05
1545. -	1557	157.20	143.40	141.90	138.95	135.95	133.00	130.00	127.05	124.05	121.10	118.10
1557. -	1569	159.30	145.50	144.00	141.05	138.05	135.10	132.10	129.15	126.15	123.20	120.20
1569. -	1581	161.40	147.60	146.10	143.15	140.15	137.15	134.20	131.20	128.25	125.25	122.30
1581. -	1593	163.50	149.70	148.20	145.20	142.25	139.25	136.30	133.30	130.35	127.35	124.40
1593. -	1605	165.60	151.75	150.30	147.30	144.35	141.35	138.40	135.40	132.40	129.45	126.45
1605. -	1617	167.65	153.85	152.35	149.40	146.40	143.45	140.45	137.50	134.50	131.55	128.55
1617. -	1629	169.75	155.95	154.45	151.50	148.50	145.55	142.55	139.60	136.60	133.65	130.65

This table is available on diskette (TOD).   E-4   Vous pouvez obtenir cette table sur disquette (TSD).

Figure 12–5(1) CPP Contributions

Canada Pension Plan Contributions
Weekly (52 pay periods a year)

Cotisations au Régime de pensions du Canada
Hebdomadaire (52 périodes de paie par année)

Pay Rémunération From - De	To - À		Pay Rémunération From - De	To - À		Pay Rémunération From - De	To - À		Pay Rémunération From - De	To - À	
536.03 -	536.25	20.16	552.77 -	552.99	20.88	569.51 -	569.74	21.60	586.26 -	586.48	22.32
536.26 -	536.48	20.17	553.00 -	553.23	20.89	569.75 -	569.97	21.61	586.49 -	586.71	22.33
536.49 -	536.71	20.18	553.24 -	553.46	20.90	569.98 -	570.20	21.62	586.72 -	586.95	22.34
536.72 -	536.95	20.19	553.47 -	553.69	20.91	570.21 -	570.43	21.63	586.96 -	587.18	22.35
536.96 -	537.18	20.20	553.70 -	553.92	20.92	570.44 -	570.67	21.64	587.19 -	587.41	22.36
537.19 -	537.41	20.21	553.93 -	554.16	20.93	570.68 -	570.90	21.65	587.42 -	587.64	22.37
537.42 -	537.64	20.22	554.17 -	554.39	20.94	570.91 -	571.13	21.66	587.65 -	587.88	22.38
537.65 -	537.88	20.23	554.40 -	554.62	20.95	571.14 -	571.37	21.67	587.89 -	588.11	22.39
537.89 -	538.11	20.24	554.63 -	554.85	20.96	571.38 -	571.60	21.68	588.12 -	588.34	22.40
538.12 -	538.34	20.25	554.86 -	555.09	20.97	571.61 -	571.83	21.69	588.35 -	588.57	22.41
538.35 -	538.57	20.26	555.10 -	555.32	20.98	571.84 -	572.06	21.70	588.58 -	588.81	22.42
538.58 -	538.81	20.27	555.33 -	555.55	20.99	572.07 -	572.30	21.71	588.82 -	589.04	22.43
538.82 -	539.04	20.28	555.56 -	555.78	21.00	572.31 -	572.53	21.72	589.05 -	589.27	22.44
539.05 -	539.27	20.29	555.79 -	556.02	21.01	572.54 -	572.76	21.73	589.28 -	589.50	22.45
539.28 -	539.50	20.30	556.03 -	556.25	21.02	572.77 -	572.99	21.74	589.51 -	589.74	22.46
539.51 -	539.74	20.31	556.26 -	556.48	21.03	573.00 -	573.23	21.75	589.75 -	589.97	22.47
539.75 -	539.97	20.32	556.49 -	556.71	21.04	573.24 -	573.46	21.76	589.98 -	590.20	22.48
539.98 -	540.20	20.33	556.72 -	556.95	21.05	573.47 -	573.69	21.77	590.21 -	590.43	22.49
540.21 -	540.43	20.34	556.96 -	557.18	21.06	573.70 -	573.92	21.78	590.44 -	590.67	22.50
540.44 -	540.67	20.35	557.19 -	557.41	21.07	573.93 -	574.16	21.79	590.68 -	590.90	22.51
540.68 -	540.90	20.36	557.42 -	557.64	21.08	574.17 -	574.39	21.80	590.91 -	591.13	22.52
540.91 -	541.13	20.37	557.65 -	557.88	21.09	574.40 -	574.62	21.81	591.14 -	591.37	22.53
541.14 -	541.37	20.38	557.89 -	558.11	21.10	574.63 -	574.85	21.82	591.38 -	591.60	22.54
541.38 -	541.60	20.39	558.12 -	558.34	21.11	574.86 -	575.09	21.83	591.61 -	591.83	22.55
541.61 -	541.83	20.40	558.35 -	558.57	21.12	575.10 -	575.32	21.84	591.84 -	592.06	22.56
541.84 -	542.06	20.41	558.58 -	558.81	21.13	575.33 -	575.55	21.85	592.07 -	592.30	22.57
542.07 -	542.30	20.42	558.82 -	559.04	21.14	575.56 -	575.78	21.86	592.31 -	592.53	22.58
542.31 -	542.53	20.43	559.05 -	559.27	21.15	575.79 -	576.02	21.87	592.54 -	592.76	22.59
542.54 -	542.76	20.44	559.28 -	559.50	21.16	576.03 -	576.25	21.88	592.77 -	592.99	22.60
542.77 -	542.99	20.45	559.51 -	559.74	21.17	576.26 -	576.48	21.89	593.00 -	593.23	22.61
543.00 -	543.23	20.46	559.75 -	559.97	21.18	576.49 -	576.71	21.90	593.24 -	593.46	22.62
543.24 -	543.46	20.47	559.98 -	560.20	21.19	576.72 -	576.95	21.91	593.47 -	593.69	22.63
543.47 -	543.69	20.48	560.21 -	560.43	21.20	576.96 -	577.18	21.92	593.70 -	593.92	22.64
543.70 -	543.92	20.49	560.44 -	560.67	21.21	577.19 -	577.41	21.93	593.93 -	594.16	22.65
543.93 -	544.16	20.50	560.68 -	560.90	21.22	577.42 -	577.64	21.94	594.17 -	594.39	22.66
544.17 -	544.39	20.51	560.91 -	561.13	21.23	577.65 -	577.88	21.95	594.40 -	594.62	22.67
544.40 -	544.62	20.52	561.14 -	561.37	21.24	577.89 -	578.11	21.96	594.63 -	594.85	22.68
544.63 -	544.85	20.53	561.38 -	561.60	21.25	578.12 -	578.34	21.97	594.86 -	595.09	22.69
544.86 -	545.09	20.54	561.61 -	561.83	21.26	578.35 -	578.57	21.98	595.10 -	595.32	22.70
545.10 -	545.32	20.55	561.84 -	562.06	21.27	578.58 -	578.81	21.99	595.33 -	595.55	22.71
545.33 -	545.55	20.56	562.07 -	562.30	21.28	578.82 -	579.04	22.00	595.56 -	595.78	22.72
545.56 -	545.78	20.57	562.31 -	562.53	21.29	579.05 -	579.27	22.01	595.79 -	596.02	22.73
545.79 -	546.02	20.58	562.54 -	562.76	21.30	579.28 -	579.50	22.02	596.03 -	596.25	22.74
546.03 -	546.25	20.59	562.77 -	562.99	21.31	579.51 -	579.74	22.03	596.26 -	596.48	22.75
546.26 -	546.48	20.60	563.00 -	563.23	21.32	579.75 -	579.97	22.04	596.49 -	596.71	22.76
546.49 -	546.71	20.61	563.24 -	563.46	21.33	579.98 -	580.20	22.05	596.72 -	596.95	22.77
546.72 -	546.95	20.62	563.47 -	563.69	21.34	580.21 -	580.43	22.06	596.96 -	597.18	22.78
546.96 -	547.18	20.63	563.70 -	563.92	21.35	580.44 -	580.67	22.07	597.19 -	597.41	22.79
547.19 -	547.41	20.64	563.93 -	564.16	21.36	580.68 -	580.90	22.08	597.42 -	597.64	22.80
547.42 -	547.64	20.65	564.17 -	564.39	21.37	580.91 -	581.13	22.09	597.65 -	597.88	22.81
547.65 -	547.88	20.66	564.40 -	564.62	21.38	581.14 -	581.37	22.10	597.89 -	598.11	22.82
547.89 -	548.11	20.67	564.63 -	564.85	21.39	581.38 -	581.60	22.11	598.12 -	598.34	22.83
548.12 -	548.34	20.68	564.86 -	565.09	21.40	581.61 -	581.83	22.12	598.35 -	598.57	22.84
548.35 -	548.57	20.69	565.10 -	565.32	21.41	581.84 -	582.06	22.13	598.58 -	598.81	22.85
548.58 -	548.81	20.70	565.33 -	565.55	21.42	582.07 -	582.30	22.14	598.82 -	599.04	22.86
548.82 -	549.04	20.71	565.56 -	565.78	21.43	582.31 -	582.53	22.15	599.05 -	599.27	22.87
549.05 -	549.27	20.72	565.79 -	566.02	21.44	582.54 -	582.76	22.16	599.28 -	599.50	22.88
549.28 -	549.50	20.73	566.03 -	566.25	21.45	582.77 -	582.99	22.17	599.51 -	599.74	22.89
549.51 -	549.74	20.74	566.26 -	566.48	21.46	583.00 -	583.23	22.18	599.75 -	599.97	22.90
549.75 -	549.97	20.75	566.49 -	566.71	21.47	583.24 -	583.46	22.19	599.98 -	600.20	22.91
549.98 -	550.20	20.76	566.72 -	566.95	21.48	583.47 -	583.69	22.20	600.21 -	600.43	22.92
550.21 -	550.43	20.77	566.96 -	567.18	21.49	583.70 -	583.92	22.21	600.44 -	600.67	22.93
550.44 -	550.67	20.78	567.19 -	567.41	21.50	583.93 -	584.16	22.22	600.68 -	600.90	22.94
550.68 -	550.90	20.79	567.42 -	567.64	21.51	584.17 -	584.39	22.23	600.91 -	601.13	22.95
550.91 -	551.13	20.80	567.65 -	567.88	21.52	584.40 -	584.62	22.24	601.14 -	601.37	22.96
551.14 -	551.37	20.81	567.89 -	568.11	21.53	584.63 -	584.85	22.25	601.38 -	601.60	22.97
551.38 -	551.60	20.82	568.12 -	568.34	21.54	584.86 -	585.09	22.26	601.61 -	601.83	22.98
551.61 -	551.83	20.83	568.35 -	568.57	21.55	585.10 -	585.32	22.27	601.84 -	602.06	22.99
551.84 -	552.06	20.84	568.58 -	568.81	21.56	585.33 -	585.55	22.28	602.07 -	602.30	23.00
552.07 -	552.30	20.85	568.82 -	569.04	21.57	585.56 -	585.78	22.29	602.31 -	602.53	23.01
552.31 -	552.53	20.86	569.05 -	569.27	21.58	585.79 -	586.02	22.30	602.54 -	602.76	23.02
552.54 -	552.76	20.87	569.28 -	569.50	21.59	586.03 -	586.25	22.31	602.77 -	602.99	23.03

B-8   Employee's maximum CPP contribution for the year 2001 is $1496.40   La cotisation maximale de l'employé au RPC pour l'année 2001 est de 1496,40 $

Figure 12–5(2) CPP Contributions

Canada Pension Plan Contributions
Weekly (52 pay periods a year)

Cotisations au Régime de pensions du Canada
Hebdomadaire (52 périodes de paie par année)

Pay Rémunération From - De	To - À		Pay Rémunération From - De	To - À		Pay Rémunération From - De	To - À		Pay Rémunération From - De	To - À	
603.00	603.23	23.04	619.75	619.97	23.76	636.49	636.71	24.48	653.24	653.46	25.20
603.24	603.46	23.05	619.98	620.20	23.77	636.72	636.95	24.49	653.47	653.69	25.21
603.47	603.69	23.06	620.21	620.43	23.78	636.96	637.18	24.50	653.70	653.92	25.22
603.70	603.92	23.07	620.44	620.67	23.79	637.19	637.41	24.51	653.93	654.16	25.23
603.93	604.16	23.08	620.68	620.90	23.80	637.42	637.64	24.52	654.17	654.39	25.24
604.17	604.39	23.09	620.91	621.13	23.81	637.65	637.88	24.53	654.40	654.62	25.25
604.40	604.62	23.10	621.14	621.37	23.82	637.89	638.11	24.54	654.63	654.85	25.26
604.63	604.85	23.11	621.38	621.60	23.83	638.12	638.34	24.55	654.86	655.09	25.27
604.86	605.09	23.12	621.61	621.83	23.84	638.35	638.57	24.56	655.10	655.32	25.28
605.10	605.32	23.13	621.84	622.06	23.85	638.58	638.81	24.57	655.33	655.55	25.29
605.33	605.55	23.14	622.07	622.30	23.86	638.82	639.04	24.58	655.56	655.78	25.30
605.56	605.78	23.15	622.31	622.53	23.87	639.05	639.27	24.59	655.79	656.02	25.31
605.79	606.02	23.16	622.54	622.76	23.88	639.28	639.50	24.60	656.03	656.25	25.32
606.03	606.25	23.17	622.77	622.99	23.89	639.51	639.74	24.61	656.26	656.48	25.33
606.26	606.48	23.18	623.00	623.23	23.90	639.75	639.97	24.62	656.49	656.71	25.34
606.49	606.71	23.19	623.24	623.46	23.91	639.98	640.20	24.63	656.72	656.95	25.35
606.72	606.95	23.20	623.47	623.69	23.92	640.21	640.43	24.64	656.96	657.18	25.36
606.96	607.18	23.21	623.70	623.92	23.93	640.44	640.67	24.65	657.19	657.41	25.37
607.19	607.41	23.22	623.93	624.16	23.94	640.68	640.90	24.66	657.42	657.64	25.38
607.42	607.64	23.23	624.17	624.39	23.95	640.91	641.13	24.67	657.65	657.88	25.39
607.65	607.88	23.24	624.40	624.62	23.96	641.14	641.37	24.68	657.89	658.11	25.40
607.89	608.11	23.25	624.63	624.85	23.97	641.38	641.60	24.69	658.12	658.34	25.41
608.12	608.34	23.26	624.86	625.09	23.98	641.61	641.83	24.70	658.35	658.57	25.42
608.35	608.57	23.27	625.10	625.32	23.99	641.84	642.06	24.71	658.58	658.81	25.43
608.58	608.81	23.28	625.33	625.55	24.00	642.07	642.30	24.72	658.82	659.04	25.44
608.82	609.04	23.29	625.56	625.78	24.01	642.31	642.53	24.73	659.05	659.27	25.45
609.05	609.27	23.30	625.79	626.02	24.02	642.54	642.76	24.74	659.28	659.50	25.46
609.28	609.50	23.31	626.03	626.25	24.03	642.77	642.99	24.75	659.51	659.74	25.47
609.51	609.74	23.32	626.26	626.48	24.04	643.00	643.23	24.76	659.75	659.97	25.48
609.75	609.97	23.33	626.49	626.71	24.05	643.24	643.46	24.77	659.98	660.20	25.49
609.98	610.20	23.34	626.72	626.95	24.06	643.47	643.69	24.78	660.21	660.43	25.50
610.21	610.43	23.35	626.96	627.18	24.07	643.70	643.92	24.79	660.44	660.67	25.51
610.44	610.67	23.36	627.19	627.41	24.08	643.93	644.16	24.80	660.68	660.90	25.52
610.68	610.90	23.37	627.42	627.64	24.09	644.17	644.39	24.81	660.91	661.13	25.53
610.91	611.13	23.38	627.65	627.88	24.10	644.40	644.62	24.82	661.14	661.37	25.54
611.14	611.37	23.39	627.89	628.11	24.11	644.63	644.85	24.83	661.38	661.60	25.55
611.38	611.60	23.40	628.12	628.34	24.12	644.86	645.09	24.84	661.61	661.83	25.56
611.61	611.83	23.41	628.35	628.57	24.13	645.10	645.32	24.85	661.84	662.06	25.57
611.84	612.06	23.42	628.58	628.81	24.14	645.33	645.55	24.86	662.07	662.30	25.58
612.07	612.30	23.43	628.82	629.04	24.15	645.56	645.78	24.87	662.31	662.53	25.59
612.31	612.53	23.44	629.05	629.27	24.16	645.79	646.02	24.88	662.54	662.76	25.60
612.54	612.76	23.45	629.28	629.50	24.17	646.03	646.25	24.89	662.77	662.99	25.61
612.77	612.99	23.46	629.51	629.74	24.18	646.26	646.48	24.90	663.00	663.23	25.62
613.00	613.23	23.47	629.75	629.97	24.19	646.49	646.71	24.91	663.24	663.46	25.63
613.24	613.46	23.48	629.98	630.20	24.20	646.72	646.95	24.92	663.47	663.69	25.64
613.47	613.69	23.49	630.21	630.43	24.21	646.96	647.18	24.93	663.70	663.92	25.65
613.70	613.92	23.50	630.44	630.67	24.22	647.19	647.41	24.94	663.93	664.16	25.66
613.93	614.16	23.51	630.68	630.90	24.23	647.42	647.64	24.95	664.17	664.39	25.67
614.17	614.39	23.52	630.91	631.13	24.24	647.65	647.88	24.96	664.40	664.62	25.68
614.40	614.62	23.53	631.14	631.37	24.25	647.89	648.11	24.97	664.63	664.85	25.69
614.63	614.85	23.54	631.38	631.60	24.26	648.12	648.34	24.98	664.86	665.09	25.70
614.86	615.09	23.55	631.61	631.83	24.27	648.35	648.57	24.99	665.10	665.32	25.71
615.10	615.32	23.56	631.84	632.06	24.28	648.58	648.81	25.00	665.33	665.55	25.72
615.33	615.55	23.57	632.07	632.30	24.29	648.82	649.04	25.01	665.56	665.78	25.73
615.56	615.78	23.58	632.31	632.53	24.30	649.05	649.27	25.02	665.79	666.02	25.74
615.79	616.02	23.59	632.54	632.76	24.31	649.28	649.50	25.03	666.03	666.25	25.75
616.03	616.25	23.60	632.77	632.99	24.32	649.51	649.74	25.04	666.26	666.48	25.76
616.26	616.48	23.61	633.00	633.23	24.33	649.75	649.97	25.05	666.49	666.71	25.77
616.49	616.71	23.62	633.24	633.46	24.34	649.98	650.20	25.06	666.72	666.95	25.78
616.72	616.95	23.63	633.47	633.69	24.35	650.21	650.43	25.07	666.96	667.18	25.79
616.96	617.18	23.64	633.70	633.92	24.36	650.44	650.67	25.08	667.19	667.41	25.80
617.19	617.41	23.65	633.93	634.16	24.37	650.68	650.90	25.09	667.42	667.64	25.81
617.42	617.64	23.66	634.17	634.39	24.38	650.91	651.13	25.10	667.65	667.88	25.82
617.65	617.88	23.67	634.40	634.62	24.39	651.14	651.37	25.11	667.89	668.11	25.83
617.89	618.11	23.68	634.63	634.85	24.40	651.38	651.60	25.12	668.12	668.34	25.84
618.12	618.34	23.69	634.86	635.09	24.41	651.61	651.83	25.13	668.35	668.57	25.85
618.35	618.57	23.70	635.10	635.32	24.42	651.84	652.06	25.14	668.58	668.81	25.86
618.58	618.81	23.71	635.33	635.55	24.43	652.07	652.30	25.15	668.82	669.04	25.87
618.82	619.04	23.72	635.56	635.78	24.44	652.31	652.53	25.16	669.05	669.27	25.88
619.05	619.27	23.73	635.79	636.02	24.45	652.54	652.76	25.17	669.28	669.50	25.89
619.28	619.50	23.74	636.03	636.25	24.46	652.77	652.99	25.18	669.51	669.74	25.90
619.51	619.74	23.75	636.26	636.48	24.47	653.00	653.23	25.19	669.75	669.97	25.91

Employee's maximum CPP contribution for the year 2001 is $1496.40   La cotisation maximale de l'employé au RPC pour l'année 2001 est de 1496,40 $ **B-9**

Figure 12–5(3) CPP Contributions

Canada Pension Plan Contributions
Weekly (52 pay periods a year)

Cotisations au Régime de pensions du Canada
Hebdomadaire (52 périodes de paie par année)

Pay Rémunération From - De	To - À		Pay Rémunération From - De	To - À		Pay Rémunération From - De	To - À		Pay Rémunération From - De	To - À	
669.98 -	670.20	25.92	686.72 -	686.95	26.64	703.47 -	703.69	27.36	720.21 -	720.43	28.08
670.21 -	670.43	25.93	686.96 -	687.18	26.65	703.70 -	703.92	27.37	720.44 -	720.67	28.09
670.44 -	670.67	25.94	687.19 -	687.41	26.66	703.93 -	704.16	27.38	720.68 -	720.90	28.10
670.68 -	670.90	25.95	687.42 -	687.64	26.67	704.17 -	704.39	27.39	720.91 -	721.13	28.11
670.91 -	671.13	25.96	687.65 -	687.88	26.68	704.40 -	704.62	27.40	721.14 -	721.37	28.12
671.14 -	671.37	25.97	687.89 -	688.11	26.69	704.63 -	704.85	27.41	721.38 -	721.60	28.13
671.38 -	671.60	25.98	688.12 -	688.34	26.70	704.86 -	705.09	27.42	721.61 -	721.83	28.14
671.61 -	671.83	25.99	688.35 -	688.57	26.71	705.10 -	705.32	27.43	721.84 -	722.06	28.15
671.84 -	672.06	26.00	688.58 -	688.81	26.72	705.33 -	705.55	27.44	722.07 -	722.30	28.16
672.07 -	672.30	26.01	688.82 -	689.04	26.73	705.56 -	705.78	27.45	722.31 -	722.53	28.17
672.31 -	672.53	26.02	689.05 -	689.27	26.74	705.79 -	706.02	27.46	722.54 -	722.76	28.18
672.54 -	672.76	26.03	689.28 -	689.50	26.75	706.03 -	706.25	27.47	722.77 -	722.99	28.19
672.77 -	672.99	26.04	689.51 -	689.74	26.76	706.26 -	706.48	27.48	723.00 -	723.23	28.20
673.00 -	673.23	26.05	689.75 -	689.97	26.77	706.49 -	706.71	27.49	723.24 -	723.46	28.21
673.24 -	673.46	26.06	689.98 -	690.20	26.78	706.72 -	706.95	27.50	723.47 -	723.69	28.22
673.47 -	673.69	26.07	690.21 -	690.43	26.79	706.96 -	707.18	27.51	723.70 -	723.92	28.23
673.70 -	673.92	26.08	690.44 -	690.67	26.80	707.19 -	707.41	27.52	723.93 -	724.16	28.24
673.93 -	674.16	26.09	690.68 -	690.90	26.81	707.42 -	707.64	27.53	724.17 -	724.39	28.25
674.17 -	674.39	26.10	690.91 -	691.13	26.82	707.65 -	707.88	27.54	724.40 -	724.62	28.26
674.40 -	674.62	26.11	691.14 -	691.37	26.83	707.89 -	708.11	27.55	724.63 -	724.85	28.27
674.63 -	674.85	26.12	691.38 -	691.60	26.84	708.12 -	708.34	27.56	724.86 -	725.09	28.28
674.86 -	675.09	26.13	691.61 -	691.83	26.85	708.35 -	708.57	27.57	725.10 -	725.32	28.29
675.10 -	675.32	26.14	691.84 -	692.06	26.86	708.58 -	708.81	27.58	725.33 -	725.55	28.30
675.33 -	675.55	26.15	692.07 -	692.30	26.87	708.82 -	709.04	27.59	725.56 -	725.78	28.31
675.56 -	675.78	26.16	692.31 -	692.53	26.88	709.05 -	709.27	27.60	725.79 -	726.02	28.32
675.79 -	676.02	26.17	692.54 -	692.76	26.89	709.28 -	709.50	27.61	726.03 -	726.25	28.33
676.03 -	676.25	26.18	692.77 -	692.99	26.90	709.51 -	709.74	27.62	726.26 -	726.48	28.34
676.26 -	676.48	26.19	693.00 -	693.23	26.91	709.75 -	709.97	27.63	726.49 -	726.71	28.35
676.49 -	676.71	26.20	693.24 -	693.46	26.92	709.98 -	710.20	27.64	726.72 -	726.95	28.36
676.72 -	676.95	26.21	693.47 -	693.69	26.93	710.21 -	710.43	27.65	726.96 -	727.18	28.37
676.96 -	677.18	26.22	693.70 -	693.92	26.94	710.44 -	710.67	27.66	727.19 -	727.41	28.38
677.19 -	677.41	26.23	693.93 -	694.16	26.95	710.68 -	710.90	27.67	727.42 -	727.64	28.39
677.42 -	677.64	26.24	694.17 -	694.39	26.96	710.91 -	711.13	27.68	727.65 -	727.88	28.40
677.65 -	677.88	26.25	694.40 -	694.62	26.97	711.14 -	711.37	27.69	727.89 -	728.11	28.41
677.89 -	678.11	26.26	694.63 -	694.85	26.98	711.38 -	711.60	27.70	728.12 -	728.34	28.42
678.12 -	678.34	26.27	694.86 -	695.09	26.99	711.61 -	711.83	27.71	728.35 -	728.57	28.43
678.35 -	678.57	26.28	695.10 -	695.32	27.00	711.84 -	712.06	27.72	728.58 -	728.81	28.44
678.58 -	678.81	26.29	695.33 -	695.55	27.01	712.07 -	712.30	27.73	728.82 -	729.04	28.45
678.82 -	679.04	26.30	695.56 -	695.78	27.02	712.31 -	712.53	27.74	729.05 -	729.27	28.46
679.05 -	679.27	26.31	695.79 -	696.02	27.03	712.54 -	712.76	27.75	729.28 -	729.50	28.47
679.28 -	679.50	26.32	696.03 -	696.25	27.04	712.77 -	712.99	27.76	729.51 -	729.74	28.48
679.51 -	679.74	26.33	696.26 -	696.48	27.05	713.00 -	713.23	27.77	729.75 -	729.97	28.49
679.75 -	679.97	26.34	696.49 -	696.71	27.06	713.24 -	713.46	27.78	729.98 -	730.20	28.50
679.98 -	680.20	26.35	696.72 -	696.95	27.07	713.47 -	713.69	27.79	730.21 -	730.43	28.51
680.21 -	680.43	26.36	696.96 -	697.18	27.08	713.70 -	713.92	27.80	730.44 -	730.67	28.52
680.44 -	680.67	26.37	697.19 -	697.41	27.09	713.93 -	714.16	27.81	730.68 -	730.90	28.53
680.68 -	680.90	26.38	697.42 -	697.64	27.10	714.17 -	714.39	27.82	730.91 -	731.13	28.54
680.91 -	681.13	26.39	697.65 -	697.88	27.11	714.40 -	714.62	27.83	731.14 -	731.37	28.55
681.14 -	681.37	26.40	697.89 -	698.11	27.12	714.63 -	714.85	27.84	731.38 -	731.60	28.56
681.38 -	681.60	26.41	698.12 -	698.34	27.13	714.86 -	715.09	27.85	731.61 -	731.83	28.57
681.61 -	681.83	26.42	698.35 -	698.57	27.14	715.10 -	715.32	27.86	731.84 -	732.06	28.58
681.84 -	682.06	26.43	698.58 -	698.81	27.15	715.33 -	715.55	27.87	732.07 -	732.30	28.59
682.07 -	682.30	26.44	698.82 -	699.04	27.16	715.56 -	715.78	27.88	732.31 -	732.53	28.60
682.31 -	682.53	26.45	699.05 -	699.27	27.17	715.79 -	716.02	27.89	732.54 -	732.76	28.61
682.54 -	682.76	26.46	699.28 -	699.50	27.18	716.03 -	716.25	27.90	732.77 -	732.99	28.62
682.77 -	682.99	26.47	699.51 -	699.74	27.19	716.26 -	716.48	27.91	733.00 -	733.23	28.63
683.00 -	683.23	26.48	699.75 -	699.97	27.20	716.49 -	716.71	27.92	733.24 -	733.46	28.64
683.24 -	683.46	26.49	699.98 -	700.20	27.21	716.72 -	716.95	27.93	733.47 -	733.69	28.65
683.47 -	683.69	26.50	700.21 -	700.43	27.22	716.96 -	717.18	27.94	733.70 -	733.92	28.66
683.70 -	683.92	26.51	700.44 -	700.67	27.23	717.19 -	717.41	27.95	733.93 -	734.16	28.67
683.93 -	684.16	26.52	700.68 -	700.90	27.24	717.42 -	717.64	27.96	734.17 -	734.39	28.68
684.17 -	684.39	26.53	700.91 -	701.13	27.25	717.65 -	717.88	27.97	734.40 -	734.62	28.69
684.40 -	684.62	26.54	701.14 -	701.37	27.26	717.89 -	718.11	27.98	734.63 -	734.85	28.70
684.63 -	684.85	26.55	701.38 -	701.60	27.27	718.12 -	718.34	27.99	734.86 -	735.09	28.71
684.86 -	685.09	26.56	701.61 -	701.83	27.28	718.35 -	718.57	28.00	735.10 -	735.32	28.72
685.10 -	685.32	26.57	701.84 -	702.06	27.29	718.58 -	718.81	28.01	735.33 -	735.55	28.73
685.33 -	685.55	26.58	702.07 -	702.30	27.30	718.82 -	719.04	28.02	735.56 -	735.78	28.74
685.56 -	685.78	26.59	702.31 -	702.53	27.31	719.05 -	719.27	28.03	735.79 -	736.02	28.75
685.79 -	686.02	26.60	702.54 -	702.76	27.32	719.28 -	719.50	28.04	736.03 -	736.25	28.76
686.03 -	686.25	26.61	702.77 -	702.99	27.33	719.51 -	719.74	28.05	736.26 -	736.48	28.77
686.26 -	686.48	26.62	703.00 -	703.23	27.34	719.75 -	719.97	28.06	736.49 -	736.71	28.78
686.49 -	686.71	26.63	703.24 -	703.46	27.35	719.98 -	720.20	28.07	736.72 -	746.71	29.00

B-10 Employee's maximum CPP contribution for the year 2001 is $1496.40   La cotisation maximale de l'employé au RPC pour l'année 2001 est de 1496,40 $

Figure 12–5(4) CPP Contributions

Canada Pension Plan Contributions
Weekly (52 pay periods a year)

Cotisations au Régime de pensions du Canada
Hebdomadaire (52 périodes de paie par année)

Pay Rémunération From - De	To - À		Pay Rémunération From - De	To - À		Pay Rémunération From - De	To - À		Pay Rémunération From - De	To - À	
746.72	756.71	29.43	1466.72	1476.71	60.39	2186.72	2196.71	91.35	2906.72	2916.71	122.31
756.72	766.71	29.86	1476.72	1486.71	60.82	2196.72	2206.71	91.78	2916.72	2926.71	122.74
766.72	776.71	30.29	1486.72	1496.71	61.25	2206.72	2216.71	92.21	2926.72	2936.71	123.17
776.72	786.71	30.72	1496.72	1506.71	61.68	2216.72	2226.71	92.64	2936.72	2946.71	123.60
786.72	796.71	31.15	1506.72	1516.71	62.11	2226.72	2236.71	93.07	2946.72	2956.71	124.03
796.72	806.71	31.58	1516.72	1526.71	62.54	2236.72	2246.71	93.50	2956.72	2966.71	124.46
806.72	816.71	32.01	1526.72	1536.71	62.97	2246.72	2256.71	93.93	2966.72	2976.71	124.89
816.72	826.71	32.44	1536.72	1546.71	63.40	2256.72	2266.71	94.36	2976.72	2986.71	125.32
826.72	836.71	32.87	1546.72	1556.71	63.83	2266.72	2276.71	94.79	2986.72	2996.71	125.75
836.72	846.71	33.30	1556.72	1566.71	64.26	2276.72	2286.71	95.22	2996.72	3006.71	126.18
846.72	856.71	33.73	1566.72	1576.71	64.69	2286.72	2296.71	95.65	3006.72	3016.71	126.61
856.72	866.71	34.16	1576.72	1586.71	65.12	2296.72	2306.71	96.08	3016.72	3026.71	127.04
866.72	876.71	34.59	1586.72	1596.71	65.55	2306.72	2316.71	96.51	3026.72	3036.71	127.47
876.72	886.71	35.02	1596.72	1606.71	65.98	2316.72	2326.71	96.94	3036.72	3046.71	127.90
886.72	896.71	35.45	1606.72	1616.71	66.41	2326.72	2336.71	97.37	3046.72	3056.71	128.33
896.72	906.71	35.88	1616.72	1626.71	66.84	2336.72	2346.71	97.80	3056.72	3066.71	128.76
906.72	916.71	36.31	1626.72	1636.71	67.27	2346.72	2356.71	98.23	3066.72	3076.71	129.19
916.72	926.71	36.74	1636.72	1646.71	67.70	2356.72	2366.71	98.66	3076.72	3086.71	129.62
926.72	936.71	37.17	1646.72	1656.71	68.13	2366.72	2376.71	99.09	3086.72	3096.71	130.05
936.72	946.71	37.60	1656.72	1666.71	68.56	2376.72	2386.71	99.52	3096.72	3106.71	130.48
946.72	956.71	38.03	1666.72	1676.71	68.99	2386.72	2396.71	99.95	3106.72	3116.71	130.91
956.72	966.71	38.46	1676.72	1686.71	69.42	2396.72	2406.71	100.38	3116.72	3126.71	131.34
966.72	976.71	38.89	1686.72	1696.71	69.85	2406.72	2416.71	100.81	3126.72	3136.71	131.77
976.72	986.71	39.32	1696.72	1706.71	70.28	2416.72	2426.71	101.24	3136.72	3146.71	132.20
986.72	996.71	39.75	1706.72	1716.71	70.71	2426.72	2436.71	101.67	3146.72	3156.71	132.63
996.72	1006.71	40.18	1716.72	1726.71	71.14	2436.72	2446.71	102.10	3156.72	3166.71	133.06
1006.72	1016.71	40.61	1726.72	1736.71	71.57	2446.72	2456.71	102.53	3166.72	3176.71	133.49
1016.72	1026.71	41.04	1736.72	1746.71	72.00	2456.72	2466.71	102.96	3176.72	3186.71	133.92
1026.72	1036.71	41.47	1746.72	1756.71	72.43	2466.72	2476.71	103.39	3186.72	3196.71	134.35
1036.72	1046.71	41.90	1756.72	1766.71	72.86	2476.72	2486.71	103.82	3196.72	3206.71	134.78
1046.72	1056.71	42.33	1766.72	1776.71	73.29	2486.72	2496.71	104.25	3206.72	3216.71	135.21
1056.72	1066.71	42.76	1776.72	1786.71	73.72	2496.72	2506.71	104.68	3216.72	3226.71	135.64
1066.72	1076.71	43.19	1786.72	1796.71	74.15	2506.72	2516.71	105.11	3226.72	3236.71	136.07
1076.72	1086.71	43.62	1796.72	1806.71	74.58	2516.72	2526.71	105.54	3236.72	3246.71	136.50
1086.72	1096.71	44.05	1806.72	1816.71	75.01	2526.72	2536.71	105.97	3246.72	3256.71	136.93
1096.72	1106.71	44.48	1816.72	1826.71	75.44	2536.72	2546.71	106.40	3256.72	3266.71	137.36
1106.72	1116.71	44.91	1826.72	1836.71	75.87	2546.72	2556.71	106.83	3266.72	3276.71	137.79
1116.72	1126.71	45.34	1836.72	1846.71	76.30	2556.72	2566.71	107.26	3276.72	3286.71	138.22
1126.72	1136.71	45.77	1846.72	1856.71	76.73	2566.72	2576.71	107.69	3286.72	3296.71	138.65
1136.72	1146.71	46.20	1856.72	1866.71	77.16	2576.72	2586.71	108.12	3296.72	3306.71	139.08
1146.72	1156.71	46.63	1866.72	1876.71	77.59	2586.72	2596.71	108.55	3306.72	3316.71	139.51
1156.72	1166.71	47.06	1876.72	1886.71	78.02	2596.72	2606.71	108.98	3316.72	3326.71	139.94
1166.72	1176.71	47.49	1886.72	1896.71	78.45	2606.72	2616.71	109.41	3326.72	3336.71	140.37
1176.72	1186.71	47.92	1896.72	1906.71	78.88	2616.72	2626.71	109.84	3336.72	3346.71	140.80
1186.72	1196.71	48.35	1906.72	1916.71	79.31	2626.72	2636.71	110.27	3346.72	3356.71	141.23
1196.72	1206.71	48.78	1916.72	1926.71	79.74	2636.72	2646.71	110.70	3356.72	3366.71	141.66
1206.72	1216.71	49.21	1926.72	1936.71	80.17	2646.72	2656.71	111.13	3366.72	3376.71	142.09
1216.72	1226.71	49.64	1936.72	1946.71	80.60	2656.72	2666.71	111.56	3376.72	3386.71	142.52
1226.72	1236.71	50.07	1946.72	1956.71	81.03	2666.72	2676.71	111.99	3386.72	3396.71	142.95
1236.72	1246.71	50.50	1956.72	1966.71	81.46	2676.72	2686.71	112.42	3396.72	3406.71	143.38
1246.72	1256.71	50.93	1966.72	1976.71	81.89	2686.72	2696.71	112.85	3406.72	3416.71	143.81
1256.72	1266.71	51.36	1976.72	1986.71	82.32	2696.72	2706.71	113.28	3416.72	3426.71	144.24
1266.72	1276.71	51.79	1986.72	1996.71	82.75	2706.72	2716.71	113.71	3426.72	3436.71	144.67
1276.72	1286.71	52.22	1996.72	2006.71	83.18	2716.72	2726.71	114.14	3436.72	3446.71	145.10
1286.72	1296.71	52.65	2006.72	2016.71	83.61	2726.72	2736.71	114.57	3446.72	3456.71	145.53
1296.72	1306.71	53.08	2016.72	2026.71	84.04	2736.72	2746.71	115.00	3456.72	3466.71	145.96
1306.72	1316.71	53.51	2026.72	2036.71	84.47	2746.72	2756.71	115.43	3466.72	3476.71	146.39
1316.72	1326.71	53.94	2036.72	2046.71	84.90	2756.72	2766.71	115.86	3476.72	3486.71	146.82
1326.72	1336.71	54.37	2046.72	2056.71	85.33	2766.72	2776.71	116.29	3486.72	3496.71	147.25
1336.72	1346.71	54.80	2056.72	2066.71	85.76	2776.72	2786.71	116.72	3496.72	3506.71	147.68
1346.72	1356.71	55.23	2066.72	2076.71	86.19	2786.72	2796.71	117.15	3506.72	3516.71	148.11
1356.72	1366.71	55.66	2076.72	2086.71	86.62	2796.72	2806.71	117.58	3516.72	3526.71	148.54
1366.72	1376.71	56.09	2086.72	2096.71	87.05	2806.72	2816.71	118.01	3526.72	3536.71	148.97
1376.72	1386.71	56.52	2096.72	2106.71	87.48	2816.72	2826.71	118.44	3536.72	3546.71	149.40
1386.72	1396.71	56.95	2106.72	2116.71	87.91	2826.72	2836.71	118.87	3546.72	3556.71	149.83
1396.72	1406.71	57.38	2116.72	2126.71	88.34	2836.72	2846.71	119.30	3556.72	3566.71	150.26
1406.72	1416.71	57.81	2126.72	2136.71	88.77	2846.72	2856.71	119.73	3566.72	3576.71	150.69
1416.72	1426.71	58.24	2136.72	2146.71	89.20	2856.72	2866.71	120.16	3576.72	3586.71	151.12
1426.72	1436.71	58.67	2146.72	2156.71	89.63	2866.72	2876.71	120.59	3586.72	3596.71	151.55
1436.72	1446.71	59.10	2156.72	2166.71	90.06	2876.72	2886.71	121.02	3596.72	3606.71	151.98
1446.72	1456.71	59.53	2166.72	2176.71	90.49	2886.72	2896.71	121.45	3606.72	3616.71	152.41
1456.72	1466.71	59.96	2176.72	2186.71	90.92	2896.72	2906.71	121.88	3616.72	3626.71 *	152.84

Employee's maximum CPP contribution for the year 2001 is $1496.40
* If the earnings are above this amount, follow the calculation method shown in publication T4001, *Payroll Deductions - Basic Information.*

La cotisation maximale de l'employé au RPC pour l'année 2001 est de 1496,40 $ **B-11**
* Si la rémunération dépasse ce montant, consultez la méthode de calcul qui se trouve dans la publication T4001, *Renseignements de base sur les retenues sur la paie.*

Figure 12–6(1) EI Premiums

Employment Insurance Premiums   ## Cotisations à l'assurance-emploi

From - De	To - À	Premium	From - De	To - À	Premium	From - De	To - À	Premium	From - De	To - À	Premium
512.23 -	512.66	11.53	544.23 -	544.66	12.25	576.23 -	576.66	12.97	608.23 -	608.66	13.69
512.67 -	513.11	11.54	544.67 -	545.11	12.26	576.67 -	577.11	12.98	608.67 -	609.11	13.70
513.12 -	513.55	11.55	545.12 -	545.55	12.27	577.12 -	577.55	12.99	609.12 -	609.55	13.71
513.56 -	513.99	11.56	545.56 -	545.99	12.28	577.56 -	577.99	13.00	609.56 -	609.99	13.72
514.00 -	514.44	11.57	546.00 -	546.44	12.29	578.00 -	578.44	13.01	610.00 -	610.44	13.73
514.45 -	514.88	11.58	546.45 -	546.88	12.30	578.45 -	578.88	13.02	610.45 -	610.88	13.74
514.89 -	515.33	11.59	546.89 -	547.33	12.31	578.89 -	579.33	13.03	610.89 -	611.33	13.75
515.34 -	515.77	11.60	547.34 -	547.77	12.32	579.34 -	579.77	13.04	611.34 -	611.77	13.76
515.78 -	516.22	11.61	547.78 -	548.22	12.33	579.78 -	580.22	13.05	611.78 -	612.22	13.77
516.23 -	516.66	11.62	548.23 -	548.66	12.34	580.23 -	580.66	13.06	612.23 -	612.66	13.78
516.67 -	517.11	11.63	548.67 -	549.11	12.35	580.67 -	581.11	13.07	612.67 -	613.11	13.79
517.12 -	517.55	11.64	549.12 -	549.55	12.36	581.12 -	581.55	13.08	613.12 -	613.55	13.80
517.56 -	517.99	11.65	549.56 -	549.99	12.37	581.56 -	581.99	13.09	613.56 -	613.99	13.81
518.00 -	518.44	11.66	550.00 -	550.44	12.38	582.00 -	582.44	13.10	614.00 -	614.44	13.82
518.45 -	518.88	11.67	550.45 -	550.88	12.39	582.45 -	582.88	13.11	614.45 -	614.88	13.83
518.89 -	519.33	11.68	550.89 -	551.33	12.40	582.89 -	583.33	13.12	614.89 -	615.33	13.84
519.34 -	519.77	11.69	551.34 -	551.77	12.41	583.34 -	583.77	13.13	615.34 -	615.77	13.85
519.78 -	520.22	11.70	551.78 -	552.22	12.42	583.78 -	584.22	13.14	615.78 -	616.22	13.86
520.23 -	520.66	11.71	552.23 -	552.66	12.43	584.23 -	584.66	13.15	616.23 -	616.66	13.87
520.67 -	521.11	11.72	552.67 -	553.11	12.44	584.67 -	585.11	13.16	616.67 -	617.11	13.88
521.12 -	521.55	11.73	553.12 -	553.55	12.45	585.12 -	585.55	13.17	617.12 -	617.55	13.89
521.56 -	521.99	11.74	553.56 -	553.99	12.46	585.56 -	585.99	13.18	617.56 -	617.99	13.90
522.00 -	522.44	11.75	554.00 -	554.44	12.47	586.00 -	586.44	13.19	618.00 -	618.44	13.91
522.45 -	522.88	11.76	554.45 -	554.88	12.48	586.45 -	586.88	13.20	618.45 -	618.88	13.92
522.89 -	523.33	11.77	554.89 -	555.33	12.49	586.89 -	587.33	13.21	618.89 -	619.33	13.93
523.34 -	523.77	11.78	555.34 -	555.77	12.50	587.34 -	587.77	13.22	619.34 -	619.77	13.94
523.78 -	524.22	11.79	555.78 -	556.22	12.51	587.78 -	588.22	13.23	619.78 -	620.22	13.95
524.23 -	524.66	11.80	556.23 -	556.66	12.52	588.23 -	588.66	13.24	620.23 -	620.66	13.96
524.67 -	525.11	11.81	556.67 -	557.11	12.53	588.67 -	589.11	13.25	620.67 -	621.11	13.97
525.12 -	525.55	11.82	557.12 -	557.55	12.54	589.12 -	589.55	13.26	621.12 -	621.55	13.98
525.56 -	525.99	11.83	557.56 -	557.99	12.55	589.56 -	589.99	13.27	621.56 -	621.99	13.99
526.00 -	526.44	11.84	558.00 -	558.44	12.56	590.00 -	590.44	13.28	622.00 -	622.44	14.00
526.45 -	526.88	11.85	558.45 -	558.88	12.57	590.45 -	590.88	13.29	622.45 -	622.88	14.01
526.89 -	527.33	11.86	558.89 -	559.33	12.58	590.89 -	591.33	13.30	622.89 -	623.33	14.02
527.34 -	527.77	11.87	559.34 -	559.77	12.59	591.34 -	591.77	13.31	623.34 -	623.77	14.03
527.78 -	528.22	11.88	559.78 -	560.22	12.60	591.78 -	592.22	13.32	623.78 -	624.22	14.04
528.23 -	528.66	11.89	560.23 -	560.66	12.61	592.23 -	592.66	13.33	624.23 -	624.66	14.05
528.67 -	529.11	11.90	560.67 -	561.11	12.62	592.67 -	593.11	13.34	624.67 -	625.11	14.06
529.12 -	529.55	11.91	561.12 -	561.55	12.63	593.12 -	593.55	13.35	625.12 -	625.55	14.07
529.56 -	529.99	11.92	561.56 -	561.99	12.64	593.56 -	593.99	13.36	625.56 -	625.99	14.08
530.00 -	530.44	11.93	562.00 -	562.44	12.65	594.00 -	594.44	13.37	626.00 -	626.44	14.09
530.45 -	530.88	11.94	562.45 -	562.88	12.66	594.45 -	594.88	13.38	626.45 -	626.88	14.10
530.89 -	531.33	11.95	562.89 -	563.33	12.67	594.89 -	595.33	13.39	626.89 -	627.33	14.11
531.34 -	531.77	11.96	563.34 -	563.77	12.68	595.34 -	595.77	13.40	627.34 -	627.77	14.12
531.78 -	532.22	11.97	563.78 -	564.22	12.69	595.78 -	596.22	13.41	627.78 -	628.22	14.13
532.23 -	532.66	11.98	564.23 -	564.66	12.70	596.23 -	596.66	13.42	628.23 -	628.66	14.14
532.67 -	533.11	11.99	564.67 -	565.11	12.71	596.67 -	597.11	13.43	628.67 -	629.11	14.15
533.12 -	533.55	12.00	565.12 -	565.55	12.72	597.12 -	597.55	13.44	629.12 -	629.55	14.16
533.56 -	533.99	12.01	565.56 -	565.99	12.73	597.56 -	597.99	13.45	629.56 -	629.99	14.17
534.00 -	534.44	12.02	566.00 -	566.44	12.74	598.00 -	598.44	13.46	630.00 -	630.44	14.18
534.45 -	534.88	12.03	566.45 -	566.88	12.75	598.45 -	598.88	13.47	630.45 -	630.88	14.19
534.89 -	535.33	12.04	566.89 -	567.33	12.76	598.89 -	599.33	13.48	630.89 -	631.33	14.20
535.34 -	535.77	12.05	567.34 -	567.77	12.77	599.34 -	599.77	13.49	631.34 -	631.77	14.21
535.78 -	536.22	12.06	567.78 -	568.22	12.78	599.78 -	600.22	13.50	631.78 -	632.22	14.22
536.23 -	536.66	12.07	568.23 -	568.66	12.79	600.23 -	600.66	13.51	632.23 -	632.66	14.23
536.67 -	537.11	12.08	568.67 -	569.11	12.80	600.67 -	601.11	13.52	632.67 -	633.11	14.24
537.12 -	537.55	12.09	569.12 -	569.55	12.81	601.12 -	601.55	13.53	633.12 -	633.55	14.25
537.56 -	537.99	12.10	569.56 -	569.99	12.82	601.56 -	601.99	13.54	633.56 -	633.99	14.26
538.00 -	538.44	12.11	570.00 -	570.44	12.83	602.00 -	602.44	13.55	634.00 -	634.44	14.27
538.45 -	538.88	12.12	570.45 -	570.88	12.84	602.45 -	602.88	13.56	634.45 -	634.88	14.28
538.89 -	539.33	12.13	570.89 -	571.33	12.85	602.89 -	603.33	13.57	634.89 -	635.33	14.29
539.34 -	539.77	12.14	571.34 -	571.77	12.86	603.34 -	603.77	13.58	635.34 -	635.77	14.30
539.78 -	540.22	12.15	571.78 -	572.22	12.87	603.78 -	604.22	13.59	635.78 -	636.22	14.31
540.23 -	540.66	12.16	572.23 -	572.66	12.88	604.23 -	604.66	13.60	636.23 -	636.66	14.32
540.67 -	541.11	12.17	572.67 -	573.11	12.89	604.67 -	605.11	13.61	636.67 -	637.11	14.33
541.12 -	541.55	12.18	573.12 -	573.55	12.90	605.12 -	605.55	13.62	637.12 -	637.55	14.34
541.56 -	541.99	12.19	573.56 -	573.99	12.91	605.56 -	605.99	13.63	637.56 -	637.99	14.35
542.00 -	542.44	12.20	574.00 -	574.44	12.92	606.00 -	606.44	13.64	638.00 -	638.44	14.36
542.45 -	542.88	12.21	574.45 -	574.88	12.93	606.45 -	606.88	13.65	638.45 -	638.88	14.37
542.89 -	543.33	12.22	574.89 -	575.33	12.94	606.89 -	607.33	13.66	638.89 -	639.33	14.38
543.34 -	543.77	12.23	575.34 -	575.77	12.95	607.34 -	607.77	13.67	639.34 -	639.77	14.39
543.78 -	544.22	12.24	575.78 -	576.22	12.96	607.78 -	608.22	13.68	639.78 -	640.22	14.40

Yearly maximum insurable earnings are $39,000   Le maximum annuel de la rémunération assurable est de 39 000 $
Yearly maximum employee premiums are $877.50   La cotisation maximale annuelle de l'employé est de 877.50 $ C-5

Figure 12–6(2) EI Premiums

Employment Insurance Premiums   Cotisations à l'assurance-emploi

Insurable Earnings Rémunération assurable			Insurable Earnings Rémunération assurable			Insurable Earnings Rémunération assurable			Insurable Earnings Rémunération assurable		
From - De	To - À		From - De	To - À		From - De	To - À		From - De	To - À	
640.23	640.66	14.41	672.23	672.66	15.13	704.23	704.66	15.85	736.23	736.66	16.57
640.67	641.11	14.42	672.67	673.11	15.14	704.67	705.11	15.86	736.67	737.11	16.58
641.12	641.55	14.43	673.12	673.55	15.15	705.12	705.55	15.87	737.12	737.55	16.59
641.56	641.99	14.44	673.56	673.99	15.16	705.56	705.99	15.88	737.56	737.99	16.60
642.00	642.44	14.45	674.00	674.44	15.17	706.00	706.44	15.89	738.00	738.44	16.61
642.45	642.88	14.46	674.45	674.88	15.18	706.45	706.88	15.90	738.45	738.88	16.62
642.89	643.33	14.47	674.89	675.33	15.19	706.89	707.33	15.91	738.89	739.33	16.63
643.34	643.77	14.48	675.34	675.77	15.20	707.34	707.77	15.92	739.34	739.77	16.64
643.78	644.22	14.49	675.78	676.22	15.21	707.78	708.22	15.93	739.78	740.22	16.65
644.23	644.66	14.50	676.23	676.66	15.22	708.23	708.66	15.94	740.23	740.66	16.66
644.67	645.11	14.51	676.67	677.11	15.23	708.67	709.11	15.95	740.67	741.11	16.67
645.12	645.55	14.52	677.12	677.55	15.24	709.12	709.55	15.96	741.12	741.55	16.68
645.56	645.99	14.53	677.56	677.99	15.25	709.56	709.99	15.97	741.56	741.99	16.69
646.00	646.44	14.54	678.00	678.44	15.26	710.00	710.44	15.98	742.00	742.44	16.70
646.45	646.88	14.55	678.45	678.88	15.27	710.45	710.88	15.99	742.45	742.88	16.71
646.89	647.33	14.56	678.89	679.33	15.28	710.89	711.33	16.00	742.89	743.33	16.72
647.34	647.77	14.57	679.34	679.77	15.29	711.34	711.77	16.01	743.34	743.77	16.73
647.78	648.22	14.58	679.78	680.22	15.30	711.78	712.22	16.02	743.78	744.22	16.74
648.23	648.66	14.59	680.23	680.66	15.31	712.23	712.66	16.03	744.23	744.66	16.75
648.67	649.11	14.60	680.67	681.11	15.32	712.67	713.11	16.04	744.67	745.11	16.76
649.12	649.55	14.61	681.12	681.55	15.33	713.12	713.55	16.05	745.12	745.55	16.77
649.56	649.99	14.62	681.56	681.99	15.34	713.56	713.99	16.06	745.56	745.99	16.78
650.00	650.44	14.63	682.00	682.44	15.35	714.00	714.44	16.07	746.00	746.44	16.79
650.45	650.88	14.64	682.45	682.88	15.36	714.45	714.88	16.08	746.45	746.88	16.80
650.89	651.33	14.65	682.89	683.33	15.37	714.89	715.33	16.09	746.89	747.33	16.81
651.34	651.77	14.66	683.34	683.77	15.38	715.34	715.77	16.10	747.34	747.77	16.82
651.78	652.22	14.67	683.78	684.22	15.39	715.78	716.22	16.11	747.78	748.22	16.83
652.23	652.66	14.68	684.23	684.66	15.40	716.23	716.66	16.12	748.23	748.66	16.84
652.67	653.11	14.69	684.67	685.11	15.41	716.67	717.11	16.13	748.67	749.11	16.85
653.12	653.55	14.70	685.12	685.55	15.42	717.12	717.55	16.14	749.12	749.55	16.86
653.56	653.99	14.71	685.56	685.99	15.43	717.56	717.99	16.15	749.56	749.99	16.87
654.00	654.44	14.72	686.00	686.44	15.44	718.00	718.44	16.16	750.00	750.44	16.88
654.45	654.88	14.73	686.45	686.88	15.45	718.45	718.88	16.17	750.45	750.88	16.89
654.89	655.33	14.74	686.89	687.33	15.46	718.89	719.33	16.18	750.89	751.33	16.90
655.34	655.77	14.75	687.34	687.77	15.47	719.34	719.77	16.19	751.34	751.77	16.91
655.78	656.22	14.76	687.78	688.22	15.48	719.78	720.22	16.20	751.78	752.22	16.92
656.23	656.66	14.77	688.23	688.66	15.49	720.23	720.66	16.21	752.23	752.66	16.93
656.67	657.11	14.78	688.67	689.11	15.50	720.67	721.11	16.22	752.67	753.11	16.94
657.12	657.55	14.79	689.12	689.55	15.51	721.12	721.55	16.23	753.12	753.55	16.95
657.56	657.99	14.80	689.56	689.99	15.52	721.56	721.99	16.24	753.56	753.99	16.96
658.00	658.44	14.81	690.00	690.44	15.53	722.00	722.44	16.25	754.00	754.44	16.97
658.45	658.88	14.82	690.45	690.88	15.54	722.45	722.88	16.26	754.45	754.88	16.98
658.89	659.33	14.83	690.89	691.33	15.55	722.89	723.33	16.27	754.89	755.33	16.99
659.34	659.77	14.84	691.34	691.77	15.56	723.34	723.77	16.28	755.34	755.77	17.00
659.78	660.22	14.85	691.78	692.22	15.57	723.78	724.22	16.29	755.78	756.22	17.01
660.23	660.66	14.86	692.23	692.66	15.58	724.23	724.66	16.30	756.23	756.66	17.02
660.67	661.11	14.87	692.67	693.11	15.59	724.67	725.11	16.31	756.67	757.11	17.03
661.12	661.55	14.88	693.12	693.55	15.60	725.12	725.55	16.32	757.12	757.55	17.04
661.56	661.99	14.89	693.56	693.99	15.61	725.56	725.99	16.33	757.56	757.99	17.05
662.00	662.44	14.90	694.00	694.44	15.62	726.00	726.44	16.34	758.00	758.44	17.06
662.45	662.88	14.91	694.45	694.88	15.63	726.45	726.88	16.35	758.45	758.88	17.07
662.89	663.33	14.92	694.89	695.33	15.64	726.89	727.33	16.36	758.89	759.33	17.08
663.34	663.77	14.93	695.34	695.77	15.65	727.34	727.77	16.37	759.34	759.77	17.09
663.78	664.22	14.94	695.78	696.22	15.66	727.78	728.22	16.38	759.78	760.22	17.10
664.23	664.66	14.95	696.23	696.66	15.67	728.23	728.66	16.39	760.23	760.66	17.11
664.67	665.11	14.96	696.67	697.11	15.68	728.67	729.11	16.40	760.67	761.11	17.12
665.12	665.55	14.97	697.12	697.55	15.69	729.12	729.55	16.41	761.12	761.55	17.13
665.56	665.99	14.98	697.56	697.99	15.70	729.56	729.99	16.42	761.56	761.99	17.14
666.00	666.44	14.99	698.00	698.44	15.71	730.00	730.44	16.43	762.00	762.44	17.15
666.45	666.88	15.00	698.45	698.88	15.72	730.45	730.88	16.44	762.45	762.88	17.16
666.89	667.33	15.01	698.89	699.33	15.73	730.89	731.33	16.45	762.89	763.33	17.17
667.34	667.77	15.02	699.34	699.77	15.74	731.34	731.77	16.46	763.34	763.77	17.18
667.78	668.22	15.03	699.78	700.22	15.75	731.78	732.22	16.47	763.78	764.22	17.19
668.23	668.66	15.04	700.23	700.66	15.76	732.23	732.66	16.48	764.23	764.66	17.20
668.67	669.11	15.05	700.67	701.11	15.77	732.67	733.11	16.49	764.67	765.11	17.21
669.12	669.55	15.06	701.12	701.55	15.78	733.12	733.55	16.50	765.12	765.55	17.22
669.56	669.99	15.07	701.56	701.99	15.79	733.56	733.99	16.51	765.56	765.99	17.23
670.00	670.44	15.08	702.00	702.44	15.80	734.00	734.44	16.52	766.00	766.44	17.24
670.45	670.88	15.09	702.45	702.88	15.81	734.45	734.88	16.53	766.45	766.88	17.25
670.89	671.33	15.10	702.89	703.33	15.82	734.89	735.33	16.54	766.89	767.33	17.26
671.34	671.77	15.11	703.34	703.77	15.83	735.34	735.77	16.55	767.34	767.77	17.27
671.78	672.22	15.12	703.78	704.22	15.84	735.78	736.22	16.56	767.78	768.22	17.28

C-6   Yearly maximum insurable earnings are $39,000   Le maximum annuel de la rémunération assurable est de 39 000 $
Yearly maximum employee premiums are $877.50   La cotisation maximale annuelle de l'employé est de 877.50 $

CHAPTER 13

Payroll—Employer Taxes and Other Obligations

LEARNING OBJECTIVES

When you have completed this chapter, you should

1. have an increased understanding of accounting terminology.
2. have a basic understanding of the employer's obligation for payroll taxes.
3. be able to calculate the employer's tax liability for Canada pension plan (CPP) and for employment insurance (EI).
4. be able to prepare the journal entry to record the employer's payroll tax expense.
5. be able to calculate the monthly remittance to the Canada Customs and Revenue Agency (CCRA) for employees' federal and provincial income tax, Canada pension plan, and employment insurance.
6. be able to complete a T4 statement and a T4 summary.
7. be able to calculate workers' compensation insurance expense.
8. be able to calculate the employer's health tax expense.

VOCABULARY

cumulative	acquired by or resulting from accumulation
form PD7A	a form provided by the CCRA that is used by employers who are making remittances of employee income taxes, CPP, and EI
T4 statement	a form provided by the CCRA that the employer must complete and give to each employee on or before the last day of February each year showing the employee's total earnings from the employer for the calendar year just ended, taxable benefits received from the employer, and all payroll deductions; a copy of each T4 must also be remitted to the Canada Customs and Revenue Agency
T4 summary	a form that summarizes the information shown on each employee's T4 statement and which must be sent to the CCRA on or before the last day of February each year, together with the individual T4 statement copies
remuneration	payment for
workers' compensation insurance	a provincial insurance program that is paid for by the employer and that will provide payments to employees who are absent from work because of job-related injury or illness

Introduction

Employers, as well as employees, are liable for the payment of certain payroll obligations. The amounts withheld from employees' earnings are liabilities of the employer, while taxes levied on the employer are expenses and will appear on the income statement as a reduction in net income.

The employer is responsible for keeping accurate payroll records and for filing forms with the Canada Customs and Revenue Agency at regular intervals. If an employer does not comply with CCRA rules, he or she will face penalties and interest. For example, a 10 percent or 20 percent penalty will be applied if remittances are sent after the due date; if the required amount of income tax, CPP contributions, or EI premiums is not deducted from employees' salaries; and if the amounts were withheld but not remitted. In addition, if the employer does not deduct CPP contributions or EI insurance, then that employer will be responsible for paying the employee's share of these taxes as well as the employer's share.

Employer's Payroll Taxes

The employer's payroll taxes are based on the earnings of employees. The two main categories of employer taxes are (1) Canada pension plan, and (2) employment insurance.

Canada Pension Plan (CPP)

Each month, the employer matches the amount deducted from an employee's salary or wages for CPP. The contribution rate used in this text for employers and employees is the 2001 rate of 4.3 percent based on maximum pensionable (taxable) earnings of $38,300. The basic exemption is $3,500; thus, the maximum employee contribution for 2001 is $1,496.40 ($38,300 − $3,500 = $34,800 x .043). Employers will stop deducting CPP contributions when the maximum employee contribution of $1,496.40 has been reached. The $3,500 exemption is built into the tables, so CPP contributions are deducted until an employee has earned $38,300 in any year. Also, as a result of the exemption being built into the tables, it is not possible to multiply the gross wages by the rate, as it is with EI.

Employment Insurance (EI)

Employers and employees must pay employment insurance premiums on the EI insurable earnings. The premium rate for 2001 is 2.25 percent based on insurable earnings of $39,000. Employers will stop deducting EI premiums once the maximum amount of $877.50 has been withheld ($39,000 × .0225 = $877.50). The employer must contribute each month an amount equal to 1.4 times the amount deducted from an employee's salary or wages for employment insurance.

The Calculation of Employer's Payroll Taxes

When the payroll register has been completed, calculations can be made to determine the amount of the employer's payroll taxes. Using the information from the payroll register for the Credit Valley Accounting Service on May 31, 2002, the calculation of the employer's payroll taxes and the journal entry to record them are as follows:

Canada Pension Plan	1	× 116.04	=	$116.04
Employment Insurance	1.4	× 68.29	=	95.61
Total payroll tax expense for the week				$211.65

GENERAL JOURNAL					
DATE	DESCRIPTION	POST REF.	DEBIT	CREDIT	
20XX					
May 31	Payroll Tax Expense		2 1 1 65		
	Canada Pension Plan Payable			1 1 6 04	
	Employment Insurance Payable			9 5 61	
	To Record Payroll Tax Expense and Related				
	Liabilities For Week Ending May 31				

The employer will record this payroll tax expense at the time the salaries and wages are recorded. However, the CPP contributions and EI premiums will not be paid at the same time that the salaries and wages are paid. The payroll taxes will be recorded and carried on the books as liabilities until they are paid at the appropriate intervals.

Remitting Income Tax Deductions, Canada Pension Plan Contributions, and Employment Insurance Premiums

An employer who has not previously remitted federal or provincial income tax deductions, CPP contributions, and EI premiums should contact her or his tax centre by telephoning a toll-free number found in the blue pages of the telephone directory under Canada Customs and Revenue Agency. The employer will be provided with a business number (BN), other relevant information, and a preprinted **Form PD7**A which will be completed when remitting taxes. This form is reproduced as Figure 13-1 on page 357.

Under a new system introduced in 1998 that simplifies and streamlines the way businesses deal with government, the business number (BN) is used for four major business accounts which include corporate income tax, import/export duties, payroll deductions, and goods and services tax/harmonized sales tax (GST/HST).

Depending on the average monthly remittance in the previous calendar year, an employer will be classified as a regular, quarterly, accelerated threshold 1, or accelerated threshold 2 remitter, and must remit these amounts at the appropriate due dates for their classification.

If the employer is classified as a regular remitter, the remittances must be made to the CCRA by the fifteenth day of the month following the month the deductions were made. Payment can be made by cheque or money order (made payable to the Receiver General for Canada) to a Canadian financial institution, tax centre or local tax services office. The employer's financial institution may also have electronic payment options. Any payment made to a Canadian financial institution must be accompanied by the form provided by CCRA. An automatic penalty will result if a cheque is returned because of nonsufficient funds. Also, if the remittance form has not been received in the mail, or if it has been lost, the employer should send a cheque or money order to the tax centre giving the account number and the month for which the payment is being made. The

Figure 13–1 Form PD7A

Canada Customs and Revenue Agency   **Agence des douanes et du revenu du Canada**

ACCOUNTING ENTRIES - EXPLANATIONS

AMOUNT PAID: payments of Canada Pension Plan contributions, Employment Insurance premiums and income tax (net of adjustments) for the year indicated.

GROSS PAYROLL IN REMITTING PERIOD (dollars only): all remuneration before any deductions. It includes regular wages, commissions, overtime pay, paid leave, taxable benefits and allowances, piecework payments, and special payments. It is equivalent to the monthly total of all amounts that would appear in Box 14, "Employment income" on the T4 slip. For quarterly remitters, it is the total of these amounts for the last month of the quarter.

NUMBER OF EMPLOYEES IN LAST PAY PERIOD: the number of people who drew pay during the last pay period in the month or quarter. Include anyone for whom you will complete a T4 slip, such as part-time and temporary employees, employees absent with pay, etc. Do not include persons for whom you will not complete a T4 slip, such as occasional employees not part of your payroll, and persons who did not draw pay in the last pay period in the month or quarter such as those on unpaid leave.

REMITTING PROCEDURES

We must receive deductions made during the month or quarter by the due date. For more information see the *Employer's Guide*. The date of receipt is the date the payment is delivered to the Receiver General (i.e., tax services office, tax centre, or a financial institution) and not the date you mailed the payment. Please include your share of Canada Pension Plan contributions and Employment Insurance premiums when you remit your employees' deductions.

We will apply penalties for late or deficient remittances on amounts over $500 unless the failure is made knowingly or under circumstances amounting to gross negligence, in which case the minimum $500 will not apply.

If you make your payment at an Automated Teller Machine, check with your financial institution to make sure your payment will be processed and credited to the Receiver General account by the due date.

ENQUIRIES

If you need more information, or help in completing the form or using the Payroll Deductions Tables, contact your tax services office. Please quote your account number on all correspondence.

Form authorized by the Minister of National Revenue

AMOUNT OF PAYMENT ▶

CPP contributions	EI premiums	Tax deductions	Current payment	Gross payroll	No. of employees in last pay period

RC107 E (01) *Tear off here and return lower portion with your payment.*

Canada Customs and Revenue Agency **Agence des douanes et du revenu du Canada** **CURRENT SOURCE DEDUCTIONS REMITTANCE VOUCHER** 002022 **RC107 E (01)**

YOU MUST COMPLETE THIS AREA

6

Do not use this area

Business Number

Legal Name

Address

City   Province   Postal Code

Gross payroll in remitting period (dollars only) 0,0

Number of employees in last pay period

End of remitting period for which deductions were withheld   Year   Month

Amount paid

002022 0006 0000 00 000000000000000 000000 0000000000000 7

employer is responsible for timely remittance of taxes even if the remittance form has not been received.

Accelerated threshold 1 and accelerated threshold 2 remitters are categorized based upon how much money they remit each month. Businesses that collect between $15,000 and $50,000 in a month must remit two times a month. Businesses who collect $50,000 or more must remit four times a month.

For more information regarding forms, instructions, information or the remittance of payroll taxes, look on the web at http://www.ccra-adrc.gc.ca/tax/business

The Journal Entries To Record Remittances To The Receiver General

Assuming the Credit Valley Accounting Service is classified as a regular remitter, their remittance must be made in time to reach the CCRA by the fifteenth day of the month following the payment of wages. Let us further assume that their general ledger showed the following amounts as of May 31.

Federal Income Tax Payable		**Provincial Income Tax Payable**	
5/31	2,730.80	5/31	715.89

CPP Payable		**EI Payable**	
5/31	1,174.29	5/31	741.80

The journal entry required when the federal and provincial income tax, CPP, and EI obligations are paid is:

GENERAL JOURNAL				
DATE	DESCRIPTION	POST REF.	DEBIT	CREDIT
20XX				
June 14	Federal Income Tax Payable		2 7 3 0 80	
	Provincial Income Tax Payable		7 1 5 89	
	Canada Pension Plan Payable		1 1 7 4 29	
	Employment Insurance Payable		7 4 1 80	
	Cash			5 3 6 2 78
	To Record Monthly Remittance To The			
	Receiver General for Payroll Liabilities			

Employees' Individual Earnings Record

For each employee, an individual earnings record must be kept. It contains important personal information; gross and net earnings and all deductions for each payroll period; and **cumulative** monthly (for weekly payroll periods), quarterly, and annual totals for gross and net earnings and all deductions.

Cumulative totals are very useful to the payroll administrator because once an employee has contributed the maximum annual amount to CPP ($1,496.40) or EI ($877.50), no further deductions for either of these are required for the remainder of the calendar year.

Employee's Individual Earnings Record									

Name Farenz, Gerald   **Employee No.** 9806-2   **Date Employed** Feb. 14, 1998

Address 12 Addison Cr, Brampton, ON   **Social Insurance No.** 123 456 789

Female _____ **Male** X   **Federal Net Claim Code** 3   **Provincial Net Claim Code** 4

Married _____ **Single** X   **Pay Rate** $4,300 Per Month

Phone No. 905 681-2705   **Date of Birth** 8/14/1967

Period Ending	Gross Earnings	CPP Contri- butions	EI Premiums	Federal Income Tax	Provincial Income Tax	Union Dues	Charitable Contri- butions	Total Deduc- tions	Net Pay
Cumulative to									
Aug. 31	37,800	1,377.76	774.00	4,985.20	1,977.60			9,114.56	29,685.44
Sept. 30	4,300	118.64	96.75	623.15	247.20			1,085.74	3,214.26
Cumulative to									
Sept. 30	42,100	1,496.40	870.75	5,608.35	2,224.80			10,200.30	32,899.70
Oct. 31	4,300	—	6.75	623.15	247.20			877.10	3,422.90
Cumulative to									
Oct. 31	$46,400	1,496.40	877.50	6,231.50	2,472.00	——	——	11,077.40	36,322.60

You will notice in the individual earnings record of Gerald Farenz that the contribution for CPP in September was $118.64. This amount was determined by subtracting the cumulative total from August 31 of $1,377.76 from the annual maximum payable for CPP, $1,496.40. No more CPP deductions will be taken from Gerald's salary for the remainder of the year. Note also that in October only $6.75 was deducted for EI premiums. This represents the maximum payable of $877.50 minus the cumulative amount from the previous September pay period, $870.75.

Form T4 – Statement of Remuneration Paid

Employers must give a **T4 statement** annually to each employee to whom **remuneration** was paid. The T4 will show, among other things, total earnings, any tips or benefits reported, and amounts deducted for income tax, CPP, EI, registered pension plans, and union dues. Figure 13-2 on page 360 shows a T4 for 2001.

The information for the preparation of the T4 is obtained from the employee's individual earnings record. The T4 shows earnings for the previous calendar year and all deductions. A copy must be given to each employee and to the CCRA by the last day of February of the year following the payment of salary or wages. The CCRA must also be given a summary of total amounts reported on all T4 slips issued for the year on a form known as the **T4 summary**, which is reproduced as Figure 13-3 on page 361. Federal and provincial income taxes are combined on the T4 and T4 summary.

It is unlawful for an employer to willfully fail to supply an employee with a T4 statement. It is also unlawful to willfully supply false information on the form.

Workers' Compensation Insurance

Most employers are required to pay **workers' compensation insurance**, which provides certain payments to employees who are injured on the job or who become ill as a result of something that is job-related. The workers' compensation insurance rates are based on the degree of risk involved in various job categories. For example, restaurant kitchen

Figure 13.2   T4 Statement

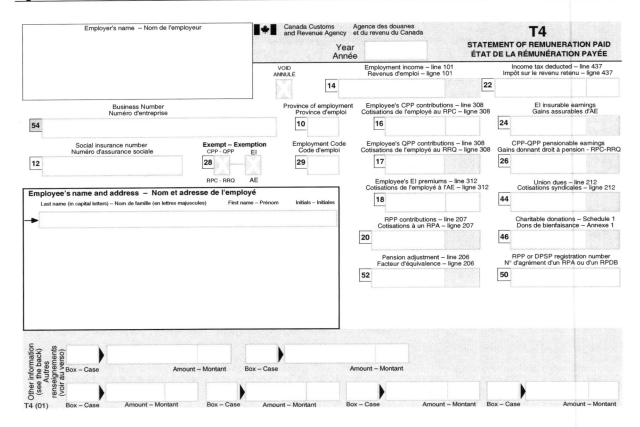

workers (because of possible cuts, burns, etc.) have a higher risk of becoming injured on the job than an usher in a theatre; therefore, the restaurant owner would pay a higher workers' compensation insurance premium per kitchen worker than the theatre owner would pay per usher.

The premium is normally paid a year in advance and is based on the year's estimated gross payroll.

Assume that the estimated payroll for the Credit Valley Accounting Service is $154,280 and that the workers' compensation insurance rate is .15 percent (or 15 cents on every $100). The premium for the year would be determined as follows:

a. Move decimal point two places to the left before multiplying   .15% = .0015

b. Multiply rate by estimated payroll   .0015 × $154,280 = $231.42

The general journal entry at the beginning of the year to record the insurance premium would be:

GENERAL JOURNAL					
DATE	DESCRIPTION	POST REF.	DEBIT		CREDIT
20XX					
Jan. 12	Workers' Compensation Insurance Expense		2 3 1 42		
	Cash				2 3 1 42
	To Record Payment of Annual Premium				
	For Workers' Compensation Insurance				

Figure 13.2   T4 Summary

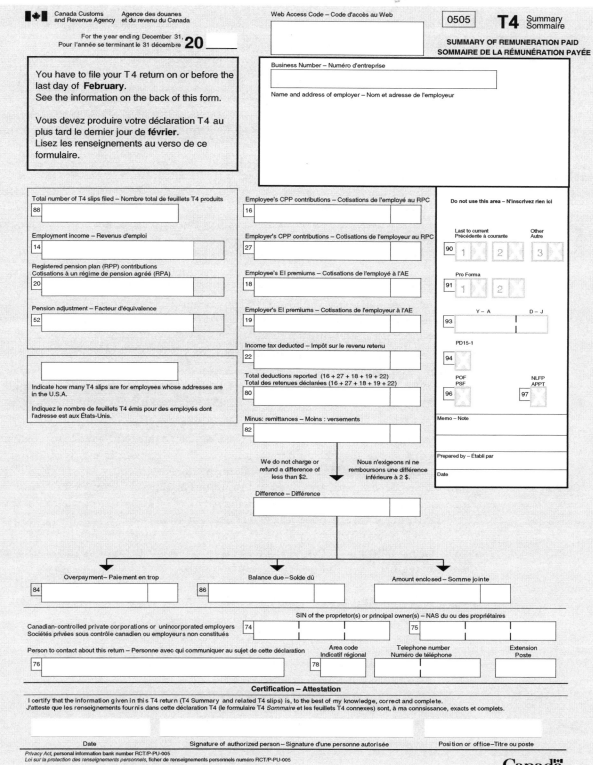

At the end of the year, the accounting records show total payroll for the Credit Valley Accounting Service to be $160,450. An additional premium is required because the original premium was based on $154,280. The additional premium is calculated as follows:

a. Figure extra amount on which premium is to be calculated by subtracting estimated payroll from actual payroll. $160,450 − 154,280 = $ 6,170

b. Multiply the extra amount by .0015   .0015 x $6,170 = $ 9.26

The additional premium is $9.26. The journal entry to record the additional premium payment for workers' compensation insurance requires a debit to Workers' Compensation Insurance Expense and a credit to Cash for $9.26. Of course, if the actual payroll is less than the amount estimated, the company would be entitled to a refund.

Employer's Health Tax

In all provinces, there is now a legislated provincial health insurance plan, which is intended to provide health-care coverage to all of the citizens of that province. As mentioned previously, in some provinces employees may pay for part or all of the health insurance premiums through payroll deductions.

In the province of Ontario this provincial insurance is called the employer's health tax (EHT) and is completely paid for by the employer. For 2001, the rate is 1.95 percent for payrolls over $400,000. The first $400,000 is exempt.

In the province of Manitoba, the EHT is paid for completely by general provincial revenues and federal subsidies and is based on the following rates:

Total Annual Manitoba Remuneration	Rate (%)
Less than $1,000,000	exempt
Between $1,000,000 and $2,000,000	4.3% on the amount in excess of $1 million
Over $2,000,000	2.15% on total payroll (no $1 million exemption

In the province of Quebec, the EHT is calculated on a rate which varies from 2.7 percent on payrolls less than $1 million to 4.26 percent for payrolls in excess of $5 million per year, and is once again completely paid for by the employer.

In Ontario all employers are required to submit an annual return to the Ministry of Finance by March 15 of the year following the payment of wages stating their total annual gross payroll for the calendar year just ended.

If the total annual gross payroll is up to and including $400,000, only the EHT return is due. If the total annual gross payroll is in excess of $400,000, monthly installment payments are required, in addition to the annual return.

The general journal entry to record the payment of the health tax requires a debit to Employers' Health Tax Expense and a credit to Cash.

SUMMARY

Employers must be familiar with all the laws relating to payroll, keep accurate payroll records, and submit the correct amounts to the various government agencies at the appropriate intervals.

Amounts actually paid by employers, as opposed to amounts withheld from employees' wages, are expenses and are deducted from revenue when determining net income.

Employers are required to pay payroll taxes in addition to deducting certain amounts from employees' wages. For Canada pension plan, the employer matches the amount paid by employees up to the maximum amount of $1,496.40 for each employee. For employment insurance, the employer pays 1.4 times the amount deducted from employees' wages, up to the maximum amount of $877.50 for each employee each year. Rates and maximum amounts on which they are based change frequently; however, the method for calculating deductions and payroll taxes does not change.

In addition to these payroll taxes, employers are usually required to pay a workers' compensation insurance premium based on the total annual gross payroll and the degree of risk involved in that type of employment. This insurance is designed to provide payments to employees who are injured on the job or who contract a job-related illness.

In some provinces, employers must also pay an employer's health tax which is intended to provide health-care coverage to all citizens of that province.

Employers must also supply all employees with a T4 statement showing gross annual salary or wages and all deductions during the year. This statement must be given to all employees by February 28 of the year following the payment of wages. On this same date, the employer must send copies of the T4 statements to the Canada Customs and Revenue Agency along with a T4 summary.

Vocabulary Review

Here is a list of the words and terms for this chapter.

cumulative	T4 statement
Form PD7A	T4 summary
remuneration	workers' compensation insurance

Fill in the blank with the correct word or term from the list.

1. _____ is a form provided by CCRA that is used by employers making monthly remitances of income taxes, CPP, and EI.
2. The form that summarizes the information shown on a T4 statement is called a/an _____.
3. A word that means resulting from accumulation is _____.
4. _____ is a form provided by CCRA that the employer must complete to show the employees' total earnings and deductions for the previous year.
5. _____ provides insurance for employees who incur job-related injuries.
6. Another word for payment is _____.

Match the words and terms on the left with the definitions on the right.

7. cumulative
8. Form PD7A
9. remuneration
10. T4 statement
11. T4 summary
12. workers' compensation insurance

a. acquired by or resulting from accumulation
b. a provincial government insurance program paid for by the employer
c. payment for
d. the form that must be completed and given to each employee on or before the last day of February
e. the form that must be forwarded to CCRA on or before the last day in February
f. the form that employers use to remit monthly employee deductions

Exercises

EXERCISE 13.1

Dorothy London, owner of London's Tax Service, employs six people. Their gross wages for the year are:

Employee	Gross Wages
1	$47,000
2	38,600
3	38,900
4	38,750
5	54,000
6	38,460

Calculate the following. Round answers to the nearest penny where required.

a. Calculate the employees' total CPP contributions for the year. Remember, when an employee has earned the maximum taxable amount of $38,300, no more CPP contribution is deducted for the year. The maximum amount deducted is $1,496.40 ($38,300 − $3,500 x .043).

b. Calculate the total EI premiums for the year if the rate is 2.25 percent of each employee's gross wages up to $39,000. Round to the nearest cent where necessary.

c. Calculate the employer's total wages expense for the year.

d. Calculate the employer's total payroll tax expense for the year. The employer's EI premium is 1.4 times the amount paid by employees.

EXERCISE 13.2

Wanda St. James lives in Ontario and earns $16.00 an hour as an electrician. She receives double time for working more than 40 hours in a week. For the week ended January 30, Wanda worked 50 hours. Her payroll deductions for the week include CPP, EI, federal income tax (claim code 3) , provincial income tax (claim code 3), union dues of $18.00, and health insurance of $8.40.

a. Prepare the general journal entry (page 25) to record Wanda's gross earnings, her deductions, and the wages payable. Use the federal and provincial income tax tables and the tables for CPP in Chapter 12. Calculate EI premiums at 2.25 percent of Wanda's gross earnings.

b. Prepare the general journal entry to record the employer's payroll tax expense. The employer's EI premium is 1.4 times the amount withheld from the employee's wages. Round to the nearest penny where required.

EXERCISE 13.3

On April 30, the general ledger for Rayco had the following balances: Canada Pension Plan Payable, $398.66; Employment Insurance Payable, $175.62; Federal Income Taxes Payable, 708.15; and Provincial Income Taxes Payable, $207.60.

a. Prepare a general journal entry (page 34) on May 10 to record the payment to CCRA due on or before May 15.

b. Calculate the total payroll tax expense for the employer. Round to the nearest penny where required.

EXERCISE 13.4

Payroll data for Bay Area Home Cleaning include the following for the month of January: Gross wages, $45,200; CPP contributions, $3,887.20; EI premiums, $2,440.80; Federal Income Tax withheld, $8,714; and Provincial Income Tax withheld, $2,198.16.

a. Prepare a general journal entry (page 44) dated January 31 to record the gross wages, employee deductions, and wages payable.

b. Prepare a general journal entry on January 31 to record the employer's payroll tax expense.

c. Prepare a general journal entry on January 31 to record payment of the Employer's Health Tax expense of 1.95 percent of gross wages. (Note: When wages are over $400,000 annually, monthly installment payments are required.) Assume that the $400,000 salary exemption has already been used up.

EXERCISE 13.5

On January 3, Year 1, the bookkeeper for Hudson River Lines estimated that the annual payroll would be $98,620 and, on the basis of this estimate, paid a workers' compensation insurance premium of .3 percent of the gross payroll. On January 4, Year 2, the bookkeeper figured the actual payroll for Year 1 to have been $110,700.

a. Prepare a general journal entry (page 39) on January 3, Year 1, to pay the estimated premium for Year 1.

b. Prepare a general journal entry (page 84) on January 4, Year 2, to pay the additional amount due for Year 1.

EXERCISE 13.6

The weekly salary and cumulative wages through November are listed for the employees of The Queen's Realty. Determine for each the taxable wages for Canada Pension Plan contributions and Employment Insurance premiums for the first week in December, and determine the amount of the CPP contribution and EI premium for the first week in December. Remember, CPP is based on maximum pensionable earnings of $38,300 and a maximum contribution of $1,496.40 per year. EI is 2.25 percent of the first $39,000 earned. Use the tables in Chapter 12 to determine CPP contributions.

Employee	Weekly Pay	Cumulative Through November	Dec. 1-7 Taxable Wages for CPP	CPP Contribution	Dec. 1-7 Taxable Wages for EI	EI Premium
A	$910.00	$43,680	_____	_____	_____	_____
B	700.00	38,000	_____	_____	_____	_____
C	800.00	38,800	_____	_____	_____	_____
D	675.00	32,400	_____	_____	_____	_____
E	760.00	37,900	_____	_____	_____	_____
	TOTALS		_____	_____	_____	_____

EXERCISE 13.7

Carlos Pietro owns Pietro's Travel Agency. The agency's business number is 377620491. The business address is 496 West Main Street, Hinsdale, N.S. He employs Nathaniel Joseph Emerson whose address is 420 North Oak Street, Hinsdale, N.S. L4Y 2G4. The employee's individual earnings record shows Emerson's social insurance number to be 321324321. His salary for the year was $52,000; federal and provincial income tax withheld was $11,047.40; CPP contributions were $1,496.40; and EI premiums, $877.50. Complete Emerson's T4 statement.

Problems

PROBLEM 13.1

Tuan Bui is single and has no dependants. His address is 97 Sylvan Avenue, Englewood, Ontario. His phone number is 321-0685; his birthdate is 03/24/65; and his social insurance number is 987654321. Tuan works for M & M Storage Company. He was hired on January 2, 2000. His employee number is M-7432-6. His weekly wages are $1,000. His net claim code for federal and provincial income taxes is 1. Weekly union dues are $10. Tuan's gross pay and deductions are the same for each pay period.

Instructions

Prepare an individual earnings record for Tuan Bui for the first four pay periods of the year. Wages are paid on January 8, 15, 22 and 29. January 31 falls on a Sunday. Prepare monthly totals. Round all calculations where required. Use cheque numbers 109, 328, 407, and 515. Determine federal and provincial income tax withholding and CPP contributions from the tables in Chapter 12. EI is 2.25 percent of the first $39,000 earned.

PROBLEM 13.2

B.C. Travel Agency employs eight people. The accounts that relate to payroll and their June 1 balances are as follows:

Cash	$17,900.00	Wages Payable	0
CPP Payable	736.16	Wages Expense	0
EI Payable	462.24	Payroll Tax Expense	0
Federal Income Tax Payable	1,874.40		
Provincial Income Tax Payable	462.25		

The following transactions relating to payroll occurred in June and July.

June 15   issued a cheque for monthly payment of amounts owed for Canada Pension Plan, employment insurance, and employees' income taxes. Use the balances in the ledger.

June 15   recorded semimonthly wages expense and amounts withheld from employees' wages.

Gross wages	$4,280.00
CPP contributions	184.04
EI premiums	96.30
Federal income tax withheld	848.00
Provincial income tax withheld	170.00

June 15   recorded the employer's payroll tax expense

June 15   issued a cheque for the net pay made payable to the payroll bank account (debit Wages Payable and credit Cash)

June 30   recorded semimonthly wages expense and amounts withheld from employees' wages

Gross wages	$4,392.00
CPP contributions	188.86
EI premiums	98.82
Federal income tax withheld	852.98
Provincial income tax withheld	173.26

June 30   recorded the employer's payroll tax expense

June 30   issued a cheque payable to the payroll bank account for the net pay

July 15   issued a cheque for the amount due CCRA for payroll taxes for June

Instructions

1. Enter the account names and June 1 balances into the general ledger.

2. Journalize each transaction in a general journal (page 86). Post to the general ledger immediately after each transaction so that the amounts owed can be determined. Round calculations to the nearest penny where required.

3. Answer the following questions about the accounts after all the entries have been journalized and posted.

    a. What was the total wages expense for June?

    b. What was the total payroll tax expense for June?

PROBLEM 13.3

The payroll records for Sasha Records of 10 Prince Andrew Place, Don Mills, Ontario M3G 2T8, for the month of March show the following totals which represent the amounts withheld from nine employees' wages during March.

CPP contributions	$ 1,008.35
EI premiums	527.63
Federal income tax withheld	4,924.50
Provincial income tax withheld	988.76
Gross Payroll	23,450.00

Instructions

1. Calculate the amounts that will be shown on form PD7A and that will be remitted to CCRA by April 15. Sasha Records business number is 764982043-0021.

2. Complete the form PD7A. Combine federal and provincial income taxes, CPP contributions, and EI premiums on the form.

3. Prepare the journal entry (page 36) to record the payment to CCRA.

PROBLEM 13.4

On January 4, Year 1, the bookkeeper of Arco Metals estimated that the total annual gross payroll would be $178,760. On the basis of this estimate, he paid a workers' compensation insurance premium of .42 percent (.0042) of the gross payroll. One January 10, Year 2, the bookkeeper calculated the actual payroll for Year 1 to have been $198,520.

Instructions

1. Prepare a general journal entry on January 4, Year 1, to pay the estimated workers' compensation insurance premium. Round all calculations where required.

2. Prepare a general journal on January 6, Year 2, to pay the additional workers' compensation insurance premium owed for Year 1.

PROBLEM 13.5

Paul Nakamoto, SIN 987-654-321, owns Nakamoto, Inc., located at 543 High Street, Peterborough, Ontario L4S 1K0. Nakamoto's employer account number is 12345 and its telephone number is (613) 287-1589. Nakamoto, Inc. has a total of six employees and the following information is available from the end-of-year payrolls. Nakamoto, Inc. has weekly payroll periods.

Employee	Gross Salary	CPP Contri- bution	EI Premium	Fed. & Prov. Income Tax Deducted
Crozier	$ 42,190	$1,496.40	$ 877.50	$10,969.40
Culver	39,780	1,496.40	877.50	9,640.20
Graham	48,640	1,496.40	877.50	12,646.40
Mandrake	32,100	1,229.80	722.25	7,560.80
Reynolds	29,640	1,124.76	666.90	6,928.70
Weir	29,120	1,101.88	655.20	5,281.30
Totals	221,470	7,945.64	4,676.85	53,026.80

The CPP contributions deducted for each employee were 4.3 percent of maximum taxable earnings and the EI premiums withheld were 2.25 percent of insurable earnings. The employees' addresses and social insurance numbers are as follows:

Name	Address	Social Insurance Number
Crozier, James	294 First Street	
	Peterborough, Ontario L4S 1K0	321 654 832
Culver, David	74 Summerhill Avenue	
	Peterborough, Ontario L4S 2K0	204 368 215
Graham, Daniel	104 Forest Lane	
	Peterborough, Ontario L4S 2K0	123 456 789
Mandrake, Rodger	68 Queens Quay	
	Peterborough, Ontario L4S 2N0	237 822 069
Reynolds, Carl	2703 Burton Road	
	Peterborough, Ontario L4S 2R0	174 281 236
Weir, Terry	79 Cuthbert Drive	
	Peterborough, Ontario L4S 1R0	437 289 163

Instructions

1. Complete T4 statements for each employee. Federal and provincial income taxes are combined on the T4.

2. Complete a T4 summary for the year. All payments for the year to CCRA have been made on time.

PROBLEM 13.6

The monthly salary and cumulative wages through October are listed for the employees of Vancouver Delivery Service.

Employee	Weekly Pay	Wages Through October	Nov. 1-7 Taxable Wages for CPP	CPP Contribution	Nov. 1-7 Taxable Wages for EI	EI Premium
A	$880	$37,750				
B	700	37,040				
C	875	37,760				
D	860	36,895				
E	1,046	45,000				
F	744	32,000				
	TOTALS					

Employee	Weekly Pay	Cumulative Wages Through Nov. 7	Nov. 8-14 Taxable Wages for CPP	CPP Contribution	Nov. 8-14 Taxable Wages for EI	EI Premium
A	$880	$_____				
B	700					
C	875					
D	860					
E	1,046					
F	744					
	TOTALS					

Instructions

1. Determine for each employee the taxable wages for Canada Pension Plan contributions and Employment Insurance premiums for the first week in November. Use the tables in Chapter 12 to determine the amount of the CPP contribution. The maximum pensionable earnings for CPP are $38,300. EI is 2.25 percent of the first $39,000 earned. Round to the nearest cent where necessary. Calculate totals.

2. Determine for each employee the cumulative wages through November 7, the CPP contribution and the EI premium for the second week in November. Calculate totals.

Comprehensive Problem 3 for Review of Chapters Twelve–Thirteen

On Monday, December 4, 20xx, Jan Howard started a new position as the payroll clerk for Hillcrest Industries located at 307 Main Street, Owen Sound, Ontario L4R 3X2. The employer account number is 54321. Before Jan joined the firm, the owner, Malcolm Rhodes, had kept all the payroll records.

From the outset, Malcolm tells Jan that Hillcrest Industries is a sole proprietorship that has five employees including herself. The plant is open every week from Monday through Friday and never opens on weekends. A normal working day is eight hours and hourly employees are paid time and a half for hours worked in excess of 40 per week. Employees paid an annual salary do not receive overtime pay, but when they work more than 40 hours a week, they are given an equal number of hours off.

December 25 and December 26 are paid holidays for all employees regardless of the length of time they have been employed. December 30 and 31 fall on Saturday and Sunday; therefore, the books are closed for the year as of December 29.

Employees are paid weekly every Friday. All overtime hours are in December. Three employees are paid an hourly wage and have $20 deducted for union dues from their second and fourth cheques each month. Union dues deducted from employees' wages are paid to the union on the same date that they are deducted. Mathers has $15 deducted weekly; Tremblay, $10 weekly; and Howard, $6 weekly, for charitable contributions.

All payroll entries to date have been correctly journalized and posted and all December 1 ledger balances are correct.

When Malcolm estimated the gross payroll for the year, he estimated that it would be $167,500. Based on this estimate, he paid .29 percent of the gross payroll for workers' compensation insurance.

Malcolm gave Jan the payroll register and the employees' individual earnings records correctly completed through December 1. Malcolm had prepared an individual earnings record for Jan.

The remittances made during the year to CCRA, including the December remittance, are:

CPP employee deductions	$5,896.22
CPP employer contributions	5,896.22
EI employee premiums	3,415.50
EI employer contributions	4,781.70
Federal income tax withheld	21,297.60
Provincial income tax withheld	8,491.20

The payroll register headings used, employees' individual earnings records, and the general ledger follow.

Payroll Register

Employee	Total Hours	Hourly Rate	Reg. Earn.	OT Earn.	Total Earn.	Fed. Claim Code	Fed. Income Tax	Prov. Claim Code	Prov. Income Tax	CPP Contributions	EI Premiums	Union Dues	Charitable Contributions	Total Deductions	Net Pay

---

Employee's Individual Earnings Record

Name Mathers, Doug   **Employee No.** 1   **Date Employed** 11/3/19X1

Address 1702 Wellington Street   **Social Insurance No.** 304-628-917

Owen Sound, Ont. L4R 3X9

Female _____ **Male** X   **Federal Net Claim Code** 2   **Provincial Net Claim Code** 2

Married X **Single** _____   **Pay Rate** $46,800 per year

Phone No. 123-4556   **Date of Birth** 09/06/60

Period Ending	Gross Earnings	CPP Contributions	EI Premiums	Federal Income Tax	Provincial Income Tax	Union Dues	Charitable Contributions	Total Deductions	Net Pay
Cumulative to Dec. 1	$43,200	1,496.40	877.50	6,201.60	2,524.80	—	720.00	11,820.30	31,379.70

Employee's Individual Earnings Record

Name Livingston, Brenda   **Employee No.** 2   **Date Employed** 1/5/19X2

Address 42 Summerside Drive   **Social Insurance No.** 406-281-755

Owen Sound, Ont. L4R 3X9

Female X **Male** _____   **Federal Net Claim Code** 1   **Provincial Net Claim Code** 1

Married X **Single** _____   **Pay Rate** $20.00 per hour

Phone No. 123-7852   **Date of Birth** 10/06/69

Period Ending	Gross Earnings	CPP Contributions	EI Premiums	Federal Income Tax	Provincial Income Tax	Union Dues	Charitable Contributions	Total Deductions	Net Pay
Cumulative to Dec. 1	$38,400	1,496.40	864.00	5,311.20	2,109.60	480.00	—	10,261.20	28,138.80

Employee's Individual Earnings Record

Name Tomlin, Scott   **Employee No.** 3   **Date Employed** 2/7/19X3

Address 324 Queen Street East   **Social Insurance No.** 409-672-815

Owen Sound, Ont. L4R 3X7

Female _____ **Male** X   **Federal Net Claim Code** 2   **Provincial Net Claim Code** 3

Married _____ **Single** X   **Pay Rate** $19.50 per hour

Phone No. 123-9003   **Date of Birth** 07/28/74

Period Ending	Gross Earnings	CPP Contributions	EI Premiums	Federal Income Tax	Provincial Income Tax	Union Dues	Charitable Contributions	Total Deductions	Net Pay
Cumulative to Dec. 1	$37,440	1,462.24	842.39	4,934.40	1,900.80	480.00	—	9,619.83	27,820.17

Employee's Individual Earnings Record

Name Tremblay, Jill
Address 3275 Dunedin Road
 Meaford, Ont. L0L 1S4
Female X **Male** _____
Married X **Single** _____
Phone No. 532-0129

Employee No. 4
Social Insurance No. 503-287-152

Federal Net Claim Code 2
Pay Rate $19.25 per hour
Date of Birth 04/23/72

Date Employed 5/4/19X4

Provincial Net Claim Code 2

Period Ending	Gross Earnings	CPP Contributions	EI Premiums	Federal Income Tax	Provincial Income Tax	Union Dues	Charitable Contributions	Total Deductions	Net Pay
Cumulative to Dec. 1	$36,960	1,441.18	831.61	4,850.40	1,956.00	480.00	480.00	10,039.19	26,920.81

Employee's Individual Earnings Record

Name Howard, Jan
Address 193 Highview Drive
 Thornbury, Ont. L0L 2V0
Female X **Male** _____
Married _____ **Single** X
Phone No. 428-1702

Employee No. 5
Social Insurance No. 208-113-564

Federal Net Claim Code 1
Pay Rate $31,200 per year
Date of Birth 09/26/74

Date Employed 12/4/19X5

Provincial Net Claim Code 1

Period Ending	Gross Earnings	CPP Contributions	EI Premiums	Federal Income Tax	Provincial Income Tax	Union Dues	Charitable Contributions	Total Deductions	Net Pay
Cumulative to Dec. 1									

General Ledger Account Balances

Account Number	Account Title	Debit Balance	Credit Balance
101	Cash	$25,044.35	
205	Wages Payable		
210	Canada Pension Plan Payable		731.98
215	Employment Insurance Payable		444.96
220	Federal Income Tax Payable		1,764.60
222	Provincial Income Tax Payable		707.60
225	Union Dues Payable		
240	Charitable Contributions Payable		
610	Wages Expense		
615	Payroll Tax Expense		
620	Workers' Compensation Insurance Expense		

Payroll Transactions (Post immediately after each transaction.)

December 8   Complete the payroll register for the week using the following information. Refer to the individual earnings records for rates of pay.
Remember, employees paid an annual salary are not paid overtime.

Also remember that CPP contributions are not deducted after an employee earns $38,300 and EI premiums are no longer deducted after an employee earns $39,000.

Employee	Hours Worked
Mathers	44
Livingston	42
Tomlin	48
Tremblay	36
Howard	40

December 8 Record the employee earnings in their individual employee earnings records.

December 8 Calculate cumulative to-date totals in the individual earnings records.

December 8 Prepare the journal entry to record the wages payable for the week.

December 8 Prepare the journal entry to record employer's payroll tax expense for the week.

December 8 Issue a cheque for the net pay made payable to the payroll bank account (debit Wages Payable and credit Cash)

December 12 Prepare the journal entry to record the amount due to Canada Customs and Revenue Agency for payroll taxes for November. The general ledger contains the amounts due.

December 15 Complete the payroll register for the week using the following information. Be sure to check the individual earnings records to determine cumulative earnings before calculating CPP and EI deductions. Also, remember that union dues are deducted the second and fourth pay periods of the month for hourly workers.

Employee	Hours Worked
Mathers	50
Livingston	40
Tomlin	42
Tremblay	44
Howard	45

December 15 Record the employee earnings in the individual earnings records

December 15 Calculate cumulative to-date totals in the individual earnings records.

December 15 Prepare the journal entry to record the wages payable for the week.

December 15 Prepare the journal entry to record the employer's payroll tax expense.

December 15 Issue a cheque for the net pay made payable to the payroll bank account.

December 15 Prepare the journal entry to record payment of union dues deducted.

December 22 Complete the payroll register for the week using the following information.

Employee	Hours Worked
Mathers	40
Livingston	44
Tomlin	40
Tremblay	46
Howard	40

December 22   Record the employee earnings in the individual employee earnings records.

December 22   Calculate cumulative to-date totals in the individual earnings records.

December 22   Prepare the journal entry to record the wages payable for the week.

December 22   Prepare the journal entry to record the employer's payroll tax expense.

December 22   Issue a cheque for the net pay made payable to the payroll bank account.

December 29   Complete the payroll register for the week using the following information. Mathers and Howard will be paid their regular week's salary.

Employee	Hours Worked
Mathers	24
Livingston	24
Tomlin	24
Tremblay	24
Howard	24

December 29   Record the employee earnings in the individual employee earnings records.

December 29   Calculate cumulative-to-date totals in the employees' individual earnings records.

December 29   Prepare the journal entry to record the wages payable for the week.

December 29   Prepare the journal entry to record the employer's payroll tax expense.

December 29   Issue a cheque for the net pay made payable to the payroll bank account.

December 29   Prepare the journal entry to record payment of union dues deducted.

December 29   Prepare the journal entry to record the additional premium paid for workers' compensation insurance based on actual wages for the year.

January 10   Prepare the journal entry to record payment for the amount due to CCRA for December.

February 20   Prepare T4 statements for all employees.

February 20   Prepare a T4 summary for CCRA.

Instructions

1.   Assume that you are Jan Howard, the payroll clerk. Make sure that all balances have been correctly entered in the general ledger and in the individual earnings records before completing the work required for each transaction.

2.   When calculating the gross earnings for each employee in the payroll register, use the following rates:

   a.   For federal and provincial income taxes, use the tables in Chapter 12.

   b.   For CPP, use the tables in Chapter 12. Do not deduct CPP contributions once an employee has earned $38,300.

   c.   For EI, the rate is 2.25 percent of the first $39,000 earned for employees. For the employer, the rate is 1.4 times the amount deducted for employees.

3. Record all journal entries in the general journal beginning with page 9.

4. Post immediately following each transaction.

5. Prepare T4 statements for each employee using the information from the individual earnings records.

6. Prepare a T4 summary for CCRA using the information from the individual earnings records.

CHAPTER 14

Partnership Accounting

LEARNING OBJECTIVES

When you have completed this chapter, you should

1. have a better understanding of accounting terminology.
2. understand the general characteristics of a partnership and the importance of each one.
3. be able to calculate the division of profits, prepare the proper journal entries, and prepare the financial statements for a partnership.
4. be able to calculate and prepare the journal entries for the sale of a partnership interest, the withdrawal of a partner, and the addition of a partner.
5. be able to calculate and prepare the journal entries for a partnership that is going out of business.

VOCABULARY

account form balance sheet	a balance sheet that shows assets on the left-hand side and liabilities and owner's equity on the right-hand side
deficit	a deficiency in amount; i.e., in this chapter, a deficit balance in the capital account is an abnormal, or a debit, balance
liquidation	to settle the accounts and distribute the assets of a business
mutual agency	the legal ability of a partner to bind the partnership to contracts within the scope of the partnership
partnership	a voluntary association of two or more legally competent persons who agree to do business as co-owners for profit
profit-loss ratio	the method chosen by partners for dividing the profits or losses; also called the income and loss sharing ratio
realization	the conversion of noncash assets to cash
unlimited liability	each partner is *personally* liable for the business debts

Introduction

The three common types of business are the proprietorship, the corporation, and the partnership. It is important to note that corporations, though fewer in number than proprietorships or partnerships, transact at least 10 times the business of all other business forms combined. There are advantages and disadvantages to each type of business organization.

Accounting for a partnership is similar to accounting for a proprietorship except there is more than one owner.

General Partnership Characteristics

General partnerships and limited partnerships are recognized by Canadian law. In this chapter, we will concentrate on general partnerships, which are governed by provincial law and registration requirements, and which have certain characteristics. Following is a discussion of each.

Voluntary Association

A **partnership** is a voluntary association of two or more legally competent persons (persons who are of age and sound mental capacity) to carry on as co-owners a business for profit. Because a partnership is based on agreement, no person can be a partner against her or his will. Doctors, accountants, and lawyers frequently form partnerships, and this form of business organization is common in small service and retail businesses.

Partnership Agreement

Two or more legally competent people may form a partnership. It is best if their agreement is in writing, but it may be expressed verbally. The partnership contract is prepared by a lawyer, though an acccountant may review it. The contract will stipulate, among other things, how partnership income and losses are to be divided among the partners.

Taxation

A partnership is taxed like a proprietorship. In other words, the partners are taxed based upon the partnership's net income, not on their withdrawals from the business.

Limited Life

A partnership is a business carried on by individuals and can not exist separate and apart from those individuals. Should something happen to take away the ability of a partner to contract (death, bankruptcy or lack of legal capacity), the partnership may be terminated. Also, the life of a partnership may be limited by terms in the partnership contract, or it may be terminated by any one of the partners at will.

Mutual Agency

Mutual agency is the legal ability of each partner, acting as an agent of the business, to enter into and bind it to contracts within the scope of the partnership. For example, Alyce, Ben, and Charlie are partners in an accounting firm. Ben may bind the partnership by contracting to buy a computer for the business, even if the other two partners know nothing of the purchase. They are bound to the contract because a computer is an expected and necessary piece of equipment for an accounting firm. However, the firm would not be bound if Ben should contract to buy land with the expectation that its value would increase because this transaction is considered to be outside the purpose of an accounting business.

Partners may agree to limit the power of one or more of the partners to negotiate contracts for the business. Outsiders are bound by this agreement only if they are aware of it.

Unlimited Liability

Much like in a proprietorship, partners have unlimited liability for their business. **Unlimited liability** means that each partner is personally liable for the debts of the business. When a partnership business is unable to pay its debts, the creditors may satisfy their claims from the personal assets of any of the partners. If any one partner can not pay her or his share of the debt, creditors may make their claims against any of the other partners.

Advantages and Disadvantages of a Partnership

A partnership has advantages over other forms of business. By combining the abilities and capital of two or more persons, business potential may be greatly expanded. Also, a partnership is much easier to form than a corporation because an agreement between parties is all that is required. However, there are several disadvantages—limited life, unlimited liability, and mutual agency are among these and pose potential legal problems that must be considered when forming any new partnership.

The Drawing Account

Partnership accounting is the same as accounting for a proprietorship except there are separate capital and drawing accounts for each partner. The fundamental accounting equation (Assets = Liabilities + Owner's Equity) remains unchanged except that total owners' equity is the sum of the partners' capital accounts. Similar to a proprietorship, the partners (owners) do not receive salaries but withdraw assets from the business for their personal needs. Generally, the rules for withdrawals are decided beforehand by the partnership agreement. For example, assume that Partner Arnold withdraws $5,000 from a partnership firm of which he is a member. The journal entry to show this withdrawal is as follows:

GENERAL JOURNAL					Page	
DATE	DESCRIPTION	POST REF.	DEBIT		CREDIT	
20XX						
Jan. 15	Arnold, Drawing		5 0 0 0 00			
	Cash				5 0 0 0 00	
	To Record the Withdrawal of Cash					

At the end of the accounting period, the drawing accounts of each partner are closed to their individual capital accounts. Following is the journal entry to close the drawing account of Partner Arnold to his capital account.

GENERAL JOURNAL					Page	
DATE	DESCRIPTION	POST REF.	DEBIT		CREDIT	
20XX						
Jan. 31	Arnold, Capital		5 0 0 0 00			
	Arnold, Drawing				5 0 0 0 00	
	To Record the Closing of Arnold's Drawing					
	Account to Capital					

Accounting for a partnership requires calculations be made for the division of profits and losses and the preparation of journal entries for the addition or withdrawal of a partner. In addition, special problems must be solved when a partnership is going out of business. Each of these will be discussed in the following paragraphs.

Dividing the Net Income

Remember that partners are owners of the business, not employees, and as such, may divide their net income as they choose. The partnership contract, however, must state how the net income or loss is to be divided. If there is no contract, the law states that profits and losses will be divided equally. The method chosen by the partners for dividing the profits or losses is called the **profit-loss ratio**. This chapter will discuss a number of methods that may be used. Profits and losses:

1. may be divided equally
2. may be distributed on a fractional basis
3. may be distributed based on amounts invested
4. may be distributed using a fixed ratio
5. may be distributed using a salary allowance with any remaining profits divided equally or using a ratio

Dividing Net Income Equally

Partners may divide profits equally. For example, M. Saar, J. Loretto, and S. Abdullah are partners. Saar invested $50,000 in cash and other assets, Loretto invested $30,000 cash, and Abdullah invested $40,000 cash in their accounting firm. The following balance sheet was prepared on December 31 before adjusting and closing entries for the year had been prepared.

Saar, Loretto, and Abdullah, Accountants Balance Sheet December 31, 20XX		
Assets		
Cash	$80 000 00	
Other Assets	50 000 00	
Total Assets		$130 000 00
Liabilities		
Accounts Payable		$10 000 00
Owners' Equity		
Saar, Capital	50 000 00	
Loretto, Capital	30 000 00	
Abdullah, Capital	40 000 00	120 000 00
Total Liabilities and Owners' Equity		$130 000 00

Revenues were $96,000 and expenses were $60,000, leaving $36,000 net income to be distributed to the three partners' capital accounts. Once the amount to be allocated is determined, a closing entry crediting the capital accounts is required. If net income is to be divided equally, the Income Summary account is closed to the capital accounts as follows:

GENERAL JOURNAL					Page	
DATE	DESCRIPTION	POST REF.	DEBIT		CREDIT	
20XX						
Dec. 31	Income Summary		3 6 0 0 0 00			
	Saar, Capital				1 2 0 0 0 00	
	Loretto, Capital				1 2 0 0 0 00	
	Abdullah, Capital				1 2 0 0 0 00	
	To Close Income Summary to Capital					

Dividing Net Income Based on Amounts Invested

The partners may agree to divide net income using a fraction determined by using the amounts of the original capital investment. The following shows the steps involved in this calculation:

1. Determine the amounts originally invested.

Saar	$ 50,000
Loretto	30,000
Abdullah	40,000
Total	$120,000

2. Determine fractions. (The denominator is the total amount invested, $120,000, and each partner's individual investment becomes the numerator.)

	Ratio				Profits to be Divided		Total Allocated
Saar	$\dfrac{50,000}{120,000}$	=	$\dfrac{5}{12}$	$\times$	$36,000	=	$15,000
Loretto	$\dfrac{30,000}{120,000}$	=	$\dfrac{3}{12}$	$\times$	36,000	=	9,000
Abdullah	$\dfrac{40,000}{120,000}$	=	$\dfrac{4}{12}$	$\times$	36,000	=	12,000
Total to be allocated							$36,000

The general journal entry to close the Income Summary to the capital accounts is as follows:

GENERAL JOURNAL				Page	
DATE	**DESCRIPTION**	**POST REF.**	**DEBIT**	**CREDIT**	
20XX					
Dec. 31	Income Summary		36 0 0 0 00		
	Saar, Capital			15 0 0 0 00	
	Loretto, Capital			9 0 0 0 00	
	Abdullah, Capital			12 0 0 0 00	
	To Record the Closing of the Income				
	Summary to Capital				

Dividing Net Income Using a Fixed Ratio

In the partnership agreement, the contract may specify a fixed ratio to be used to divide the profits or losses. For example, Saar, Loretto, and Abdullah decide to use a ratio of 3:2:1, respectively. To use this ratio, convert the ratio into a fraction and multiply it by the net income or loss of the period. The steps for using the ratio to divide the profit are as follows:

1. Determine the fraction from the ratio. Add: 3 + 2 + 1 = 6. Thus, 6 becomes the denominator of the fraction. The numerators are the numbers in the ratio.

Saar	3/6 or 1/2
Loretto	2/6 or 1/3
Abdullah	1/6

2. Calculate the distribution amounts.

	Fraction		Profits to be Divided		Total Allocated
Saar	1/2	×	$36,000	=	$18,000
Loretto	1/3	×	$36,000	=	12,000
Abdullah	1/6	×	$36,000	=	6,000
Total					$36,000

The general journal entry to close the Income Summary to the capital accounts is as follows:

GENERAL JOURNAL				Page	
DATE	**DESCRIPTION**	**POST REF.**	**DEBIT**	**CREDIT**	
20XX					
Dec. 31	Income Summary		36 0 0 0 00		
	Saar, Capital			18 0 0 0 00	
	Loretto, Capital			12 0 0 0 00	
	Abdullah, Capital			6 0 0 0 00	
	To Record the Closing of the Income				
	Summary to Capital				

Dividing Net Income by Paying Interest on Investments and Salary Allowances

Another common way to divide profits is to pay interest on the original capital investments, give a salary allowance, and divide any remainder equally or according to a fixed ratio. The following example assumes 5 percent (.05) interest on the original investment, salary allowances of $10,000 to each partner, and any remainder to be divided equally. The following shows the calculations made to determine the distribution.

	Share to Saar	Share to Loretto	Share to Abdullah	Total
Total Amount to Be Divided				$36,000
Allocated as Interest:				
Saar (5% × $50,000)	$ 2,500			
Loretto (5%× $30,000)		$ 1,500		
Abdullah (5%× $40,000)			$ 2,000	
Total Interest				−6,000
Balance				$30,000
Salary Allowances	10,000	10,000	10,000	−30,000
Totals to Each	$12,500	$11,500	$12,000	0

There is no remainder to be divided in this instance. The following is the journal entry to close the Income Summary to the capital accounts.

GENERAL JOURNAL					Page	
DATE	DESCRIPTION	POST REF.	DEBIT		CREDIT	
20XX						
Dec. 31	Income Summary		36 000 00			
	Saar, Capital				12 500 00	
	Loretto, Capital				11 500 00	
	Abdullah, Capital				12 000 00	
	To Record the Closing of the Income					
	Summary to Capital					

Now assume the same facts except that Saar will receive $10,000 salary allowance, Loretto will receive $8,000, and Abdullah will receive $9,000. The remainder, if any, will be divided equally. The calculation to determine the distribution would then be as follows:

	Share to Saar	Share to Loretto	Share to Abdullah	Total
Total Amount to Be Divided				$36,000
5% Interest	$ 2,500	$ 1,500	$ 2,000	−6,000
Balance				$30,000
Salary Allowance	10,000	8,000	9,000	−27,000
Balance				3,000
Remainder Divided by 3	1,000	1,000	1,000	−3,000
Totals	$13,500	$10,500	$12,000	0

The general journal entry to close the Income Summary to the capital accounts is as follows:

DATE		DESCRIPTION	POST REF.	DEBIT	CREDIT
20XX					
Dec.	31	Income Summary		3 6 0 0 0 00	
		Saar, Capital			1 3 5 0 0 00
		Loretto, Capital			1 0 5 0 0 00
		Abdullah, Capital			1 2 0 0 0 00
		To Record the Closing of the Income			
		Summary to Capital			

GENERAL JOURNAL — Page

The methods illustrated thus far are used for calculating the proper allocation of profits to the partners. The use of the salary allowance method does not require the partners to withdraw a certain amount as salary. The salary allowances are used solely for calculating the distribution of net income. The closing of the Income Summary account to the capital accounts of the partners is the end result of the method used to share profits or losses.

Partnership Financial Statements

The financial statements of a partnership business are similar to those of a proprietorship. The income statement, statement of changes in partners' equity and the balance sheet follow. Assume that each partner has withdrawn $8,000 during the year.

Saar, Loretto, and Abdullah, Accountants Income Statement For Year Ended December 31, 20XX		
Professional Revenue	$96 000 00	
Operating Expenses	60 000 00	
Net Income		$36 000 00
Allocation of Net Income to the Partners:		
Saar		
Interest at 5% (.05 × $50,000)	$ 2 500 00	
Salary Allowance	10 000 00	
1/3 of Remaining Net Income	1 000 00	
Total		$13 500 00
Loretto		
Interest at 5% (.05 × $30,000)	$ 1 500 00	
Salary Allowance	8 000 00	
1/3 of Remaining Net Income	1 000 00	
Total		$10 500 00
Abdullah		
Interest at 5% (.05 × $40,000)	$ 2 000 00	
Salary Allowance	9 000 00	
1/3 of Remaining Net Income	1 000 00	
Total		$12 000 00
Net Income Allowed		$36 000 00

Saar, Loretto, and Abdullah, Accountants Statement of Changes in Partners' Equity For Year Ended December 31, 20XX	Saar	Loretto	Abdullah	Total
Capital, January 1	50 000 00	30 000 00	40 000 00	120 000 00
Add: Additional Invest.	0 00	0 00	0 00	0 00
Add: Net Income	13 500 00	10 500 00	12 000 00	36 000 00
Subtotals	63 500 00	40 500 00	52 000 00	156 000 00
Deduct: Withdrawals	8 000 00	8 000 00	8 000 00	24 000 00
Capital, December 31	55 500 00	32 500 00	44 000 00	132 000 00

Saar, Loretto, and Abdullah, Accountants Balance Sheet December 31, 20XX		
Assets		
Cash	$9 2 0 0 0 00	
Other Assets	5 0 0 0 0 00	
Total Assets		$1 4 2 0 0 0 00
Liabilities		
Accounts Payable		$1 0 0 0 0 00
Owners' Equity		
Saar, Capital	$5 5 5 0 0 00	
Loretto, Capital	3 2 5 0 0 00	
Abdullah, Capital	4 4 0 0 0 00	1 3 2 0 0 0 00
Total Liabilities and Owner's Equity		$1 4 2 0 0 0 00

Accounting for a Deficit When Distributing Net Income

In the event the method used for distribution of net income results in a deficit amount (negative) after interest and salary allowances, the deficit must be subtracted in the calculation rather than added. Assume for the partnership of Saar, Loretto, and Abdullah that the method for distributing net income or loss is to calculate interest at 5 percent of the original investment, give salary allowances of $10,000, $8,000, and $9,000, respectively, and divide any remainder equally. The following example will show the use of this method when profits are $24,000. The calculation to determine the distribution is as follows:

	Share to Saar	Share to Loretto	Share to Abdullah	Total
Total Amount to Be Divided				$24,000
5% Interest	$ 2,500	$ 1,500	$ 2,000	−6,000
Balance				$18,000
Salary Allowance	10,000	8,000	9,000	−27,000
Deficit Balance				$(9,000)
Deficit Distributed	(3,000)	(3,000)	(3,000)	9,000
Totals	$ 9,500	$ 6,500	$ 8,000	0

The general journal entry to close the Income Summary to the capital accounts will debit income summary for $24,000 and credit the individual capital accounts.

Distributing a Net Loss

The above examples cover only net income. Should a loss occur, the procedure for distributing the loss to the partners' capital accounts is the same as distributing net income unless the partners agree otherwise. Losses will reduce both assets and capital. Assuming that the partners share profits and losses equally, and assuming a $36,000 loss, the closing entry debits the individual partner's capital accounts $12,000 each and credits Income Summary for $36,000.

The Account Form Balance Sheet

An **account form balance sheet** shows the assets on the left-hand side and liabilities and owner's equity on the right-hand side. The account form balance sheet will be used in this chapter to demonstrate changes in the balance sheet as they occur from the withdrawal of a partner, the addition of a partner, or a partnership going out of business. The report form balance sheet has been used in previous chapters. Following are illustrations of various possibilities for changes in the composition of the partnership.

Withdrawing or Adding a New Partner

A partnership is based on a contractual agreement among individuals and ends when a partner withdraws from the firm or a new partner is added. The business, however, may continue with a new partnership agreement. A partner may withdraw by selling his or her interest or equity in cash or other assets. If all the partners agree, a new partner may join the firm either by buying the interest of a present partner, by contributing additional assets equal to the equity he or she is acquiring, or by investing either more or less than the equity he or she will receive.

The partnership agreement should outline the procedure governing a partner who wishes to withdraw from the business. Withdrawal may occur when a partner wants to retire or does not wish to continue under the present business arrangements. For example, assume that Abdullah, with an equity of $40,000, wants to retire. The partnership contract provides that an audit be performed which includes having all assets appraised to determine market value. In addition, a determination must be made of all liabilities of the partnership. Should the audit reveal that assets and liabilities are different than reflected on the books of the partnership, adjustments are made to the record to determine the true equities of the partners. Once this is accomplished, the contract may provide that assets be distributed to the retiring partner if it does not jeopardize the future profitability of the remaining partners.

Sale of Partnership Interest for More Than Partner's Equity

Assume that M. Saar wants to sell his interest to B. Knight. The balance sheet before this sale is as follows:

Saar, Loretto, and Abdullah, Accountants Balance Sheet December 31, 20XX				
Assets		**Liabilities and Owners' Equity**		
		Liabilities		
Cash	$ 5 0 0 0 0 00	Accounts Payable		$ 1 0 0 0 0 00
Other Assets	8 0 0 0 0 00			
		Owners' Equity		
		Saar, Capital	$ 5 0 0 0 0 00	
		Loretto, Capital	3 0 0 0 0 00	
		Abdullah, Capital	4 0 0 0 0 00	1 2 0 0 0 0 00
		Total Liabilities and		
Total Assets	$ 1 3 0 0 0 0 00	Owner's Equity		$ 1 3 0 0 0 0 00

Knight has agreed to pay Saar $60,000 for his equity in the business. Loretto and Abdullah agree to accept Knight as a partner. The general journal entry to record the transfer is as follows:

GENERAL JOURNAL					PAGE	
DATE	DESCRIPTION	POST REF.	DEBIT		CREDIT	
20XX						
Aug. 31	Saar, Capital		5 0 0 0 0 00			
	Knight, Capital				5 0 0 0 0 00	
	To Record the Transfer of Saar's Equity					
	in the Partnership to Knight					

After this entry, the old partnership is ended and a new partnership is formed. The only change in the balance sheet will be the substitution of Knight for Saar. After the new partnership is formed, a new contract is written.

Two points should be noted. First, the $60,000 Knight paid Saar was a personal transaction between the two and does not affect the partnership records. The $50,000 equity of Saar is transferred to Knight with the approval of the other two partners. Remember, the business entity concept requires that personal transactions be kept separate from business transactions. The second point to note is that Loretto and Abdullah must agree to have Knight as a partner since a partnership is based on agreement of all parties.

Partner Admitted with Investment Same as Equity

Assume that Knight is to invest $40,000 in cash to receive a one-fourth interest in the partnership. The following shows the equity of the present owners:

Saar	$ 50,000
Loretto	30,000
Abdullah	40,000
Total	$120,000

After Knight's investment of $40,000, the total equity is $160,000. One-fourth of $160,000 is $40,000, the equity of the new partner. The journal entry to illustrate the addition of Knight under this assumption is as follows:

GENERAL JOURNAL					PAGE	
DATE	DESCRIPTION	POST REF.	DEBIT		CREDIT	
20XX						
Aug. 31	Cash		4 0 0 0 0 00			
	Knight, Capital				4 0 0 0 0 00	
	To Record the Addition of Knight as a					
	Partner with a One-Fourth Interest					

After the entry is posted, the assets and equities of the new partnership will appear as follows:

Saar, Loretto, and Abdullah, Accountants					
Balance Sheet					
December 31, 20XX					
Assets			**Liabilities and Owners' Equity**		
			Liabilities		
Cash	$	9 0 0 0 0 00	Accounts Payable		$ 1 0 0 0 0 00
Other Assets		8 0 0 0 0 00			
			Owners' Equity		
			Saar, Capital	$ 5 0 0 0 0 00	
			Loretto, Capital	3 0 0 0 0 00	
			Abdullah, Capital	4 0 0 0 0 00	
			Knight, Capital	4 0 0 0 0 00	1 6 0 0 0 0 00
			Total Liabilities and		
Total Assets	$ 1 7 0 0 0 0 00		Owner's Equity		$ 1 7 0 0 0 0 00

Withdrawal of a Partner

Assume that Abdullah wants to retire and will accept cash equal to her equity. Assume further that assets and liabilities are the same as presented on the balance sheet on page 386 and that the withdrawal of cash by Abdullah will not jeopardize the firm's cash position. The general journal entry to record the withdrawal of Abdullah is as follows.

GENERAL JOURNAL					PAGE
DATE	DESCRIPTION	POST REF.	DEBIT	CREDIT	
20XX					
Aug. 31	Abdullah, Capital		4 0 0 0 0 00		
	Cash			4 0 0 0 0 00	
	To Record the Withdrawal of Rose who				
	Receives Cash Equal to Her Equity				

Sometimes when a partner retires, the remaining partners may not wish to give an amount equal to the retiring partner's equity. The retiring partner may then agree to take an amount less than the value of his or her capital account. If this is the situation, the profit-loss sharing ratio is used to adjust the capital accounts of the remaining partners. Assume that the profits and losses are to be divided equally, and Abdullah agrees to take $30,000 in cash for her $40,000 equity. The entry to show the withdrawal of Abdullah for $30,000 cash is as follows:

GENERAL JOURNAL				Page	
DATE	DESCRIPTION	POST REF.	DEBIT	CREDIT	
20XX					
Aug. 31	Abdullah, Capital		4 0 0 0 0 00		
	Cash			3 0 0 0 0 00	
	Saar, Capital			5 0 0 0 00	
	Loretto, Capital			5 0 0 0 00	
	To Record the Withdrawal of Abdullah who				
	Receives Cash Less Than Her Equity				

Bonus to Old Partners

A new partner may be expected to invest more assets than the equity he or she is to receive. This might occur because the equities of the present partners may not reflect the true worth of an already successful business. If this is the case, the partnership is worth more than the records indicate. For example, assume that the present equities are the same as previously indicated and that Knight is to invest cash of $36,000 for a one-fifth interest. The amount to be credited to Knight's capital account for a 1/5 interest is determined as follows:

Equities of the present partners	$120,000
Investment of the new partner	36,000
Total equities of the new partnership	156,000
Equity of Knight (1/5 × $156,000 = $31,200)	$ 31,200

Providing the present partners share equally, the bonus of $4,800 (the difference between the cash given, $36,000, and the equity received, $31,200) will be divided by 3 and the capital accounts of the present partners will each be increased by $1,600. The following is the journal entry to admit Knight as one-fifth partner.

GENERAL JOURNAL				Page	
DATE	DESCRIPTION	POST REF.	DEBIT	CREDIT	
20XX					
Aug. 31	Cash		3 6 0 0 0 00		
	Saar, Capital			1 6 0 0 00	
	Loretto, Capital			1 6 0 0 00	
	Abdullah, Capital			1 6 0 0 00	
	Knight, Capital			3 1 2 0 0 00	
	To Record the Addition of Knight as				
	Partner with a One-Fifth Interest				

After the entry is posted, the assets, liabilities, and owners' equity are as follows:

Saar, Loretto, and Abdullah, Accountants Balance Sheet December 31, 20XX				
Assets		**Liabilities and Owners' Equity**		
		Liabilities		
Cash	$ 86000 00	Accounts Payable		$ 10000 00
Other Assets	80000 00			
		Owners' Equity		
		Saar, Capital	$ 51600 00	
		Loretto, Capital	31600 00	
		Abdullah, Capital	41600 00	
		Knight, Capital	31200 00	156000 00
		Total Liabilities and		
Total Assets	$ 166000 00	Owner's Equity		$ 166000 00

Bonus to New Partner

A bonus may be given to a new partner when the new partner is given more equity than his or her current capital balance. Assume that Knight invests $20,000 for a one-fourth interest. The equity given to Knight in this case is greater than his equity. Thus Saar, Loretto, and Abdullah, who share net income and losses equally, must give up an equal-portion of their equity to Knight as determined below.

Equities of the present partners	$120,000
Add investment of new partner	20,000
Total equities of the new partnership	140,000
Equity of Knight (1/4 × $140,000 = $35,000)	$ 35,000

There is $15,000 difference between the $20,000 cash investment of Knight and total equity of $35,000 he received. The $15,000 is a bonus to Knight. However, the difference must be shared by the present partners as a reduction in their capital accounts. The reduction in the capital accounts is $5,000 each. The entry to record the addition of Knight under these circumstances is as follows.

	GENERAL JOURNAL			Page	
DATE	**DESCRIPTION**	**POST REF.**	**DEBIT**	**CREDIT**	
20XX					
Aug. 31	Cash		20000 00		
	Saar, Capital		5000 00		
	Loretto, Capital		5000 00		
	Abdullah, Capital		5000 00		
	Knight, Capital			35000 00	
	To Record the Addition of Knight as a				
	Partner with a One-Fourth Interest				

After the entry is posted, the assets, liabilities, and owners' equity appear as follows.

Saar, Loretto, and Abdullah, Accountants Balance Sheet December 31, 20XX					
Assets		**Liabilities and Owners' Equity**			
		Liabilities			
Cash	$ 7 0 0 0 0 00	Accounts Payable			$ 1 0 0 0 0 00
Other Assets	8 0 0 0 0 00				
		Owners' Equity			
		Saar, Capital	$ 4 5 0 0 0 00		
		Loretto, Capital	2 5 0 0 0 00		
		Abdullah, Capital	3 5 0 0 0 00		
		Knight, Capital	3 5 0 0 0 00	1 4 0 0 0 0 00	
		Total Liabilities and			
Total Assets	$ 1 5 0 0 0 0 00	Owner's Equity			$ 1 5 0 0 0 0 00

This type of situation might occur when a new partner has a special talent or business skill that will increase the profitability of the firm. However, there are times when a bonus is not recorded at all. Rather, goodwill is recorded and the old partners' capital accounts are increased. This method is seldom used; the bonus method is the preferred method.

In the event the two remaining partners are eager to see Abdullah retire, they may abe willing to give more than Abdullah's equity. Assume that they agree to give Abdullah $40,000 in cash and a note payable for $10,000 for her $40,000 equity. The entry to record this situation is as follows:

GENERAL JOURNAL				Page	
DATE	DESCRIPTION	POST REF.	DEBIT	CREDIT	
20XX					
Aug. 31	Abdullah, Capital		4 0 0 0 0 00		
	Saar, Capital		5 0 0 0 00		
	Loretto, Capital		5 0 0 0 00		
	Cash			4 0 0 0 0 00	
	Notes Payable			1 0 0 0 0 00	
	To Record the Withdrawal of Abdullah				
	Who Receives Cash and a Note Payable				
	for Her Equity				

The remaining partners share the additional equity given to Abdullah as a loss to themselves. Many other variations similar to these can be used. However, whatever method is used, assets must equal liabilities and owners' equity at all times.

Going Out of Business—Liquidation

Partners may determine that it is no longer possible to continue in business. This may occur if the partners have unsettled disputes or the business is no longer profitable and liquidation becomes necessary. **Liquidation** is the total process of going out of business, or the legal process of converting assets to cash, paying all creditors, and making final distribution of cash to the partners. This legal process also means that each partner is liable to pay the creditors whether or not there is sufficient cash remaining. Although many different circumstances occur in liquidation, only two are discussed here. In each case, there are four steps to be followed.

1. Convert all noncash assets to cash and record the gain or loss on liquidation.

2. Distribute the gains or losses to the partners' capital accounts according to the profit-loss ratio.

3. Pay the liabilities.

4. Distribute the remaining cash according to the equities (capital balances) of the partners.

A temporary account called Loss or Gain from Liquidation is opened to assemble the gains or losses that may occur when selling the assets. It is credited for a gain and debited for a loss. The conversion of noncash assets to cash is called **realization**. Partners will normally share losses and gains from liquidation using their income and loss sharing ratio.

Assets Sold for a Gain

The liquidation of a partnership may be illustrated using the following information. Saar, Loretto, and Abdullah, the partners in the accounting firm in previous illustrations, have had a bitter dispute over business policies. They decide to dissolve the partnership. To illustrate a liquidation where assets are sold for a gain, assume the following balance sheet before liquidation.

Saar, Loretto, and Abdullah, Accountants Balance Sheet December 31, 20XX				
Assets		**Liabilities and Owners' Equity**		
		Liabilities		
Cash	$ 30 000 00	Accounts Payable		$ 10 000 00
Other Assets	100 000 00			
		Owners' Equity		
		Saar, Capital	$ 50 000 00	
		Loretto, Capital	30 000 00	
		Abdullah, Capital	40 000 00	120 000 00
		Total Liabilities and		
Total Assets	$ 130 000 00	Owner's Equity		$ 130 000 00

Assume that the other assets are sold for $109,000 and the partners share profits and losses equally. The four steps necessary upon liquidation are shown as journal entries.

1. Convert all noncash assets to cash and record the gain or loss on liquidation.

GENERAL JOURNAL					PAGE	
DATE	**DESCRIPTION**	**POST REF.**	**DEBIT**		**CREDIT**	
20XX						
Dec. 31	Cash		1 0 9 0 0 0 00			
	Other Assets				1 0 0 0 0 0 00	
	Loss or Gain on Realization				9 0 0 0 00	
	To Record the Sale of Other Assets					

2. Distribute gains or losses to the partners' capital accounts according to the profit-loss ratio.

GENERAL JOURNAL					Page	
DATE	**DESCRIPTION**	**POST REF.**	**DEBIT**		**CREDIT**	
20XX						
Dec. 31	Loss or Gain on Realization		9 0 0 0 00			
	Saar, Capital				3 0 0 0 00	
	Loretto, Capital				3 0 0 0 00	
	Abdullah, Capital				3 0 0 0 00	
	To Record the Closing of the Loss or Gain					
	on Realization Account to the Partners'					
	Capital Accounts					

After posting these two entries, the balance sheet appears as follows.

Saar, Loretto, and Abdullah, Accountants Balance Sheet December 31, 20XX				
Assets		**Liabilities and Owners' Equity**		
		Liabilities		
Cash	$ 1 3 9 0 0 0 00	Accounts Payable		$ 1 0 0 0 0 00
		Owners' Equity		
		Saar, Capital	$ 5 3 0 0 0 00	
		Loretto, Capital	3 3 0 0 0 00	
		Abdullah, Capital	4 3 0 0 0 00	1 2 9 0 0 0 00
		Total Liabilities and		
Total Assets	$ 1 3 9 0 0 0 00	Owner's Equity		$ 1 3 9 0 0 0 00

3. Pay the liabilities.

GENERAL JOURNAL					PAGE
DATE	**DESCRIPTION**	**POST REF.**	**DEBIT**	**CREDIT**	
20XX					
Dec. 31	Accounts Payable		1 0 0 0 0 00		
	Cash			1 0 0 0 0 00	
	To Record Payment to the Creditors				

4. Distribute the remaining cash according to the equities of the partners.

GENERAL JOURNAL					Page
DATE	**DESCRIPTION**	**POST REF.**	**DEBIT**	**CREDIT**	
20XX					
Dec. 31	Saar, Capital		5 3 0 0 0 00		
	Loretto, Capital		3 3 0 0 0 00		
	Abdullah, Capital		4 3 0 0 0 00		
	Cash			1 2 9 0 0 0 00	
	To Record the Closing of the Partnership				
	Books				

Once the above entries are posted, every account in the partnership records will have a zero balance, signifying the termination of this business.

It is important to remember that cash remaining after liquidation is distributed to partners according to their capital balances while gains and losses from liquidation are allocated according to the income and loss sharing ratio.

Assets Sold for a Loss

Many times a business cannot sell its other assets at the amount carried in the records. Assets will deteriorate with age and therefore are not as marketable as when they were new. Assume that other assets are listed on the balance sheet at $100,000 and that they are sold for $91,000. This is a $9,000 loss to the partners and will result in reducing both their assets and capital accounts. Each of the four steps are presented as journal entries as follows.

1. Convert all noncash assets to cash and record the gain or loss on liquidation.

GENERAL JOURNAL					PAGE
DATE	**DESCRIPTION**	**POST REF.**	**DEBIT**	**CREDIT**	
20XX					
Dec. 31	Cash		9 1 0 0 0 00		
	Loss or Gain on Realization		9 0 0 0 00		
	Other Assets			1 0 0 0 0 0 00	
	To Record the Sale of Other Assets				

2. Distribute the gains or losses to the partners' capital accounts according to the profit-loss ratio.

		GENERAL JOURNAL					Page	
DATE		DESCRIPTION	POST REF.		DEBIT		CREDIT	
20XX								
Dec.	31	Saar, Capital			3 0 0 0 00			
		Loretto, Capital			3 0 0 0 00			
		Abdullah, Capital			3 0 0 0 00			
		Loss or Gain on Realization					9 0 0 0 00	
		To Record the Closing of the Loss to						
		Partners' Capital Accounts						

3. Pay the liabilities.

		GENERAL JOURNAL					PAGE	
DATE		DESCRIPTION	POST REF.		DEBIT		CREDIT	
20XX								
Dec.	31	Accounts Payable			1 0 0 0 0 00			
		Cash					1 0 0 0 0 00	
		To Record the Payment of the Creditors						

After the above entries are posted, the T-accounts will appear as follows:

Cash			Other Assets			Accounts Payable	
30,000	10,000		100,000	100,000		10,000	10,000
91,000							
111,000							

Saar, Capital			Loretto, Capital			Abdullah, Capital	
3,000	50,000		3,000	30,000		3,000	40,000
	47,000			**27,000**			**37,000**

Loss or Gain on Realization	
9,000	9,000

There is $111,000 left in the Cash account, and the total remaining capital account balances equal $111,000. In step four, the amount of cash to be distributed to each partner is determined by the balance in each partner's capital account.

4. Distribute the remaining cash according to the equities of the partners.

GENERAL JOURNAL																		Page						
DATE		DESCRIPTION	POST REF.		DEBIT									CREDIT										
20XX																								
Dec.	31	Saar, Capital			4	7	0	0	0	00														
		Loretto, Capital			2	7	0	0	0	00														
		Abdullah, Capital			3	7	0	0	0	00														
		Cash										1	1	1	0	0	0	00						
		To Record the Closing of the Partnership																						
		Books																						

After this entry is posted, all the accounts have a zero balance and the partnership is terminated.

A problem may occur if one partner's share of the loss is greater than the balance of his or her capital account. If this is the case, the partner must cover the deficit by paying cash into the partnership. In this situation, a **deficit** is a debit balance in a partner's capital account. This could occur from liquidation losses, losses from previous periods, or withdrawals before liquidation. For example, assume the partners Saar, Loretto, and Abdullah share profits and losses in a 2:2:1 ratio. If the other assets are shown at $100,000 on the balance sheet and sold for $20,000, a loss of $80,000 must be distributed. The four steps, presented as journal entries, will illustrate this problem and are as follows.

1. Convert all assets to cash.

GENERAL JOURNAL																		PAGE						
DATE		DESCRIPTION	POST REF.		DEBIT									CREDIT										
20XX																								
Dec.	31	Cash			2	0	0	0	0	00														
		Loss or Gain on Realization			8	0	0	0	0	00														
		Other Assets										1	0	0	0	0	0	00						
		To Record the Sale of the Other Assets																						

2. Distribute the gains or losses to the partners' capital accounts according to the profit-loss ratio.

GENERAL JOURNAL					Page	
DATE	DESCRIPTION	POST REF.	DEBIT		CREDIT	
20XX						
Dec. 31	Saar, Capital		*3 2 0 0 0 00			
	Loretto, Capital		3 2 0 0 0 00			
	Abdullah, Capital		1 6 0 0 0 00			
	Loss or Gain on Realization				8 0 0 0 0 00	
	To Record the Closing of the Loss to the					
	Partners' Capital Accounts on a 2:2:1 Ratio					

*Calculation of division of loss:
Saar   2/5 × $80,000 = $32,000
Bagwell 2/5 × $80,000 = 32,000
Abdullah 1/5 × $80,000 = 16,000

3.   Pay the creditors.

GENERAL JOURNAL					PAGE	
DATE	DESCRIPTION	POST REF.	DEBIT		CREDIT	
20XX						
Dec. 31	Accounts Payable		1 0 0 0 0 00			
	Cash				1 0 0 0 0 00	
	To Record the Payment of the Creditors					

After the above entries are posted, the T accounts will appear as follows:

Cash		Other Assets		Accounts Payable	
30,000	10,000	100,000	100,000	10,000	10,000
20,000					
40,000					

Saar, Capital		Loretto, Capital		Abdullah, Capital	
32,000	50,000	32,000	30,000	16,000	40,000
	18,000	**2,000**			**24,000**

Loss or Gain on Realization	
80,000	80,000

Loretto has a debit balance of $2,000 in his capital account and is liable to the partnership for his deficit. If Loretto has sufficient personal assets and contributes $2,000 to the firm to cover his debit balance, step four can be completed as follows:

4.   Distribute the remaining cash according to the equities of the partners.

    a.   Payment of cash by Loretto.

GENERAL JOURNAL				PAGE	
DATE	**DESCRIPTION**	**POST REF.**	**DEBIT**	**CREDIT**	
20XX					
Dec. 31	Cash		2 0 0 0 00		
	Loretto, Capital			2 0 0 0 00	
	To Record the Cash Contribution of Loretto				
	to Cover His Liability				

b. Distribute remaining cash.

GENERAL JOURNAL				Page	
DATE	**DESCRIPTION**	**POST REF.**	**DEBIT**	**CREDIT**	
20XX					
Dec. 31	Saar, Capital		1 8 0 0 0 00		
	Abdullah, Capital		2 4 0 0 0 00		
	Cash			4 2 0 0 0 00	
	To Record the Closing of the Partnership				
	Books				

After posting these two entries, all the accounts have a zero balance and the partnership is terminated. However, if Loretto has no personal assets and cannot pay his debt, because of unlimited liability Saar and Abdullah must share this additional loss according to their portion of the profit-loss ratio, without Loretto, which is 2:1. The journal entries for step four under these circumstances are as follows.

4. Distribute the remaining cash according to the equities of the partners.

a. Distribute the $2,000 loss.

GENERAL JOURNAL				Page	
DATE	**DESCRIPTION**	**POST REF.**	**DEBIT**	**CREDIT**	
20XX					
Dec. 31	Saar, Capital		* 1 3 3 3 00		
	Abdullah, Capital		6 6 7 00		
	Loretto, Capital			2 0 0 0 00	
	To Record Loretto's Liability as a Loss to				
	the Remaining Partners				

*Calculation of division of loss:
Saar   2/3 × $2,000 = $1,333
Abdullah   1/3 × $2,000 =   667

b. Distribute the remaining cash.

		GENERAL JOURNAL				Page	
DATE		DESCRIPTION	POST REF.	DEBIT		CREDIT	
20XX							
Dec.	31	Saar, Capital		1 6 6 6 7 00			
		Abdullah, Capital		2 3 3 3 3 00			
		Cash				4 0 0 0 0 00	
		To Record the Closing of the Partnership					
		Books					

After posting of the above entries, all the accounts have a zero balance and the partnership is terminated.

Even though the partner with the deficit cannot pay at the present time, the liability is not eliminated. If the deficit partner becomes able to pay at some time in the future, he or she must do so.

Summary

A partnership is a voluntary association of two or more legally competent persons to carry on as co-owners a business for profit. It is best if they have a written partnership agreement, but their contract may be a verbal one. Partnerships are characterized by limited life, which means that the partnership cannot exist separate from the individual partners, thus it may end when one partner becomes unable, through death, bankruptcy or lack of legal capacity, to contract. Partners, through mutual agency, have the legal ability to enter into contracts within the scope of the partnership. Such contracts are binding on the other partners. Unlimited liability, which also characterizes partnerships, refers to the fact that each partner is personally liable for the debts of the business. Though there are many advantages to forming a partnership, limited life, unlimited liability, and mutual agency are disadvantages that should be considered before forming a new partnership.

Partnership accounting is the same as proprietorship accounting, except that each partner has his or her own drawing account. Partners are owners of the business and do not receive salaries; rather, their drawing accounts are debited when cash is taken for personal use and income taxes are based on their share of the net income of the business.

Partners will decide upon a profit-loss ratio which will be used to determine how profits and losses are to be allocated. Profits and losses may be distributed: (1) equally; (2) on a fractional basis; (3) based on amounts invested; or (4) using a fixed ratio. Should there be a loss, it will be distributed to the partners' capital accounts the same way as a net income unless there is an agreement to the contrary.

A new partnership may be created when a new individual buys the interest of one of the existing partners, or if an additional person is admitted as a partner. In such a case, the old partnership is dissolved. In addition to adding a new partner, an existing partner may wish to withdraw from the partnership. In such a case, the value of all assets and liabilities of the partnership must be determined by an audit.

Partners may decide, because, for example, of unsettled disputes or lack of profitability, to liquidate. When this occurs: (1) all noncash assets must be converted to cash (called realization) and the gain or loss on liquidation recorded; (2) gains or losses must be distributed to the partners' capital accounts according to their profit-loss ratio; (3) liabilities must be paid; and (4) any remaining cash must be distributed to the partners according to their capital balances. Partners normally share gains and losses from liquidation according to their profit-loss sharing ratio.

Vocabulary Review

Here is a list of the words and terms for this chapter:

account form balance sheet	partnership
deficit	profit-loss ratio
liquidation	realization
mutual agency	unlimited liability

Fill in the blank with the correct word or term from the list.

1. The total process of going out of business is _____.

2. A/an _____ is an association of two or more competent persons who agree to do business as co-owners for profit.

3. The ability of each partner, acting as an agent of the business, to enter into and bind it to contracts within the apparent scope of the business is _____.

4. _____ is the conversion of noncash assets to cash.

5. The method used by the partners to divide profits or losses in the _____.

6. A/an _____ is an abnormal balance in a capital account.

7. The principle that each partner is personally liable for the debts of the business is called _____.

8. _____ shows the three major categories—assets, liabilities, and owner's equity—in a horizontal manner.

Match the words and terms on the left with the definitions on the right.

9. account form balance sheet

10. deficit

11. liquidation

12. mutual agency

13. partnership

14. profit-loss ratio

15. realization

16. unlimited liability

a. the method used by the partners to divide profits or losses

b. each partner is personally liable for the debts of the business

c. an association of two or more competent persons who agree to do business as co-owners for profit

d. an abnormal balance in a capital account

e. the conversion of noncash assets to cash

f. the total proces of going out of business

g. the ability of each partner, acting as an agent of the business, to enter into and bind it to contracts within the apparent scope of the partnership

h. the format of a balance sheet that shows the assets, liabilities, and owners' equity in a horizontal manner

Exercises

EXERCISE 14.1

Morton and Long plan to enter into a law partnership, investing $30,000 and $20,000, respectively. They have agreed on everything but how to divide the profits. Calculate each partner's share of the profit under each of the following independent assumptions.

a. If the first year's net income is $50,000 and they cannot agree, how should the profits be divided?

b. If the partners agree to share net income according to their investment ratio, how should the $50,000 be divided?

c. If the owners agree to share net income by granting 10 percent interest on their original investments, giving salary allowances of $10,000 each, and dividing the remainder equally, how should the $50,000 be divided?

EXERCISE 14.2

Assume Morton and Long from Exercise 14.1 use method c to divide profits and net income is $20,000. How should the income be divided?

EXERCISE 14.3

After a number of years, Long, from Exercise 14.1, decided to go with a large law firm and wishes to sell his interest to Brown. Long's equity at this time is $35,000. Morton agrees to take Brown as a partner, and Long sells his interest to Brown for $40,000. Prepare the general journal entry on December 31, 20XX to record the sale of Long's interest to Brown.

EXERCISE 14.4

Smith, White, and Saint are partners owning the Book Nook. The equities of the partners are $60,000, $50,000, and $40,000, respectively. They share profits and losses equally. White wishes to retire on May 31, 20XX. Prepare the general journal entries to record White's retirement under each independent assumption.

a.   White is paid $50,000 in partnership cash.

b.   White is paid $40,000 in partnership cash.

c.   White is paid $55,000 in partnership cash.

EXERCISE 14.5

Hall and Mason share profits and losses equally and have capital balances of $60,000 and $40,000, respectively. Taylor is to be admitted on January 2, 20XX, and is to receive a one-third interest in the firm. Prepare the general journal entries to record the addition of Taylor as a partner under the following unrelated circumstances.

a.   Taylor invests $50,000.

b.   Taylor invests $62,000.

c.   Taylor invests $47,000.

EXERCISE 14.6

Martin, Pearson, and Henderson are partners sharing profits and losses in a 2:1:1 ratio. Their capital balances are $30,000, $25,000, and $20,000, respectively. Because of an economic turndown, they have decided to liquidate. After all assets are sold and the creditors paid, $43,000 cash remains in the business chequing account.

a.   Determine the amount of their losses by using the accounting equation.

b.   Using the profit-loss ratio, determine the amount of loss to be distributed to each partner, and determine their new capital balances.

c.   Determine the amount of cash each partner will receive in the final distribution.

EXERCISE 14.7

Baker, Marshall, and Perryman share profits and losses equally and begin their business with investments of $20,000, $15,000, and $8,000, respectively. They have been unprofitable in their business venture and decide they must liquidate. After all the assets are sold and all debts paid, $16,000 cash remains in the business chequing account.

a.   Determine the amount of their losses by using the accounting equation.

b.   Using the profit-loss ratio, determine the amount of loss allocated to each partner, and determine their new capital balances.

c.   Calculate the amount of cash, if any, each partner will receive under the different assumptions below.

   (1) Perryman has personal assets and pays the amount she owes to the partnership.

   (2) Perryman has no personal assets and does not pay the amount she owes to the partnership.

Problems

PROBLEM 14.1

Jones, Brady, and Bell formed a partnership making investments of $40,000, $60,000, and $80,000, respectively. They believe the net income from their business for the first year will be $81,000. They are considering several alternative methods for sharing this expected profit, which are: (1) divide the profits equally; (2) divide the profits according to their investment ratio; (3) divide the profits by giving an interest allowance of 10 percent on original investments, granting $10,000 salary allowance to each partner, and dividing any remainder equally. Round to the nearest dollar where required.

Instructions

a. Prepare a schedule showing distribution of net income under methods 1, 2, and 3. It should have the following headings.

Plan	Calculations	Share to Jones	Share to Brady	Share to Bell	Total Allocated

b. Journalize the closing of the Income Summary account on December 31, 20XX using the information from b above.

PROBLEM 14.2

Abner, Black, and Cobb share profits and losses equally and have capital balances of $60,000, $50,000, and $50,000, respectively. Cobb wishes to sell his interest and leave the business on July 31 of this year. Cobb is to sell his interest to Williams with the approval of Abner and Black.

Instructions

Prepare the general journal entries, without explanations, to record the following independent assumptions.

a. Cobb sells his interest to Williams for $50,000.

b. Cobb sells his interest to Williams for $40,000.

c. Cobb decides to stay in the partnership but sell one-half of his interest to Williams for $30,000. (*Hint:* What is the value of half of Cobb's capital account?)

d. If Williams is admitted as a new partner, must a new partnership agreement be written? Why?

PROBLEM 14.3

Coleman and Simmons are partners and own the ABC Gift Shop. They formed their partnership on January 2, 20XX, with investments of $50,000 and $25,000. Simmons invested an additional $5,000 on July 7. They share profits giving 10 percent interest allowance on beginning investments and dividing the remainder on a 2:1 ratio. Following is their trial balance before closing.

Coleman and Simmons Trial Balance December 31, 20XX															
Cash	$	1	9	0	0	0	00								
Accounts Receivable			5	0	0	0	00								
Merchandise Inventory		6	0	0	0	0	00								
Equipment		2	0	0	0	0	00								
Accumulated Amortization: Equipment								$		1	0	0	0	0	00
Accounts Payable										1	0	0	0	0	00
Coleman, Drawing		1	0	0	0	0	00								
Simmons, Drawing		1	0	0	0	0	00								
Coleman, Capital										5	0	0	0	0	00
Simmons, Capital										3	0	0	0	0	00
Sales									1	0	0	0	0	0	00
Operating Expenses			7	6	0	0	0	00							
	$	2	0	0	0	0	0	00	$	2	0	0	0	0	0	00

a. Prepare the general journal entries, without explanations, to record the closing of all the nominal accounts (revenue and expense) using the Income Summary account.

b. Prepare a schedule showing the distribution of net income to the partners. It should have the following headings.

Calculations	Share to Coleman	Share to Simmons	Total Allocated

c. Prepare the general journal entries to record the closing of the Income Summary account to the capital accounts, and close the drawing accounts to the capital accounts.

d. Prepare the partnership income statement showing the allocation of net income.

e. Prepare the statement of owners' equity.

f. Prepare a balance sheet.

PROBLEM 14.4

Arnold, Cole, and Yamaguchi are partners, owning Pizza Plus and sharing profits and losses in a 3:2:1 ratio. The balance sheet, presented in account form format for this business, is as follows.

Arnold, Cole, and Yamaguchi Balance Sheet June 30, 20XX																	
Assets								**Liabilities and Owners' Equity**									
Cash						$	65000 00	Liabilities									
Delivery Truck #1		25000 00						Accounts Payable						$	3000 00		
Acc. Amort. Tr. #1		10000 00		15000 00													
Delivery Truck #2		35000 00						Owners' Equity									
Acc. Amort. Tr. #2		7000 00		28000 00				Arnold, Capital		60000 00							
								Cole, Capital		30000 00							
								Yamaguchi, Capital		15000 00		105000 00					
								Total Liabilities and									
Total Assets						$	108000 00	Owner's Equity						$	108000 00		

Arnold wishes to withdraw from the firm. Cole and Yamaguchi agree.

Prepare the general journal entries, without explanations, to record the June 30 withdrawal of Arnold under the following independent assumptions.

a. Arnold withdraws taking partnership cash of $60,000.

b. Arnold withdraws taking cash of $32,000 and truck #2 (debit Accumulated Amortization and credit Truck).

c. Arnold withdraws taking cash of $51,000

d. Arnold withdraws taking cash of $25,000 and a $44,000 note given by the partnership.

e. Arnold withdraws taking cash of $25,000, a $20,000 note, and truck #1.

PROBLEM 14.5

Garcia, Keller, and Henley are partners who share profits and losses in a 3:1:2 ratio. Their capital account balances are $60,000, $25,000, and $35,000, respectively. Watts is to be admitted to the firm on March 31, 20XX with a one-fourth interest.

Instructions

Prepare the general journal entries to record the following unrelated assumptions. Omit explanations.

a. Watts is to be admitted by investing cash of $40,000.

b. Watts is to be admitted by investing cash of $30,000.

c. Watts is to be admitted by investing cash of $50,000.

PROBLEM 14.6

Bentley, Colby, and Musharaf plan to liquidate their partnership. They share profits and losses on a 3:2:1 ratio. At the time of liquidation, the partnership balance sheet appears as follows:

Bentley, Colby, and Musharaf Balance Sheet June 30, 20XX			
Assets		**Liabilities and Owners' Equity**	
		Liabilities	
Cash	$ 23000000	Accounts Payable	$ 3000000
Other Assets	11500000		
		Owners' Equity	
		Bentley, Capital	4800000
		Colby, Capital	3600000
		Musharaf, Capital	2400000 10800000
		Total Liabilities and	
Total Assets	$13800000	Owner's Equity	$13800000

Prepare the general journal entries, without explanations, to record (1) the sale of the other assets; (2) the distribution of the loss or gain on realization; (3) the payment to the creditors; and (4) the final distribution of cash. Each of the following are unrelated assumptions.

a. The other assets are sold for $115,000.

b. The other assets are sold for $79,000.

c. The other assets are sold for $55,000.

PROBLEM 14.7

Irby, Jalisco, and Whitehorse are partners in a video rental business, sharing profits and losses in a 2:1:1 ratio. Business has decreased due to the number of other rental stores in their area. They decide it would be best to liquidate. Their December 31, 20XX balance sheet information is as follows.

Balance Sheet Information	
Cash	$15,000
Video Inventory	75,000
Accounts Payable	25,000
Irby, Capital	25,000
Jalisco, Capital	20,000
Whitehorse, Capital	20,000

Instructions

Prepare the general journal entries, without explanations, to show: (1) the sale of the noncash assets; (2) the distribution of the losses or gains; (3) the payment to the creditors; and (4) the final distribution of cash under each of the following independent assumptions.

a. The video inventory is sold for $63,000.

b. The video inventory is sold for $25,000

c. The video inventory is sold for $20,000 and the partner with the deficit can and does pay from personal assets.

d. The same assumption as c above, except the partner with the deficit cannot pay.

Appendix:
Check Figures for Problems

Problem Number	Check Figure
1.1	Total assets, $12,450
1.2	Total assets, $16,700
1.3	Total assets, $24,000
1.4	Total assets, $20,575
1.5	Total assets, $5,870
2.1	Total assets, $9,750
2.2	Net loss, $500
2.3	Total assets, $8,455
2.4	Net income, $7,560
2.5	Total assets, $19,860
2.6	a–Understated
3.1	Trial balance total, $27,300
3.2	Trial balance total, $135,577
3.3	Trial balance total, $69,065
3.4	Trial balance total, $38,695
3.5	Trial balance total, $39,870
3.6	a–Yes
4.1	Trial balance total, $359,983
4.2	Trial balance total, $120,575
4.3	Trial balance total, $19,475
4.4	Corrected net income, $3,970
5.1	Net income, $1,049
5.2	Net income, $1,645
5.3	Net income, $2,540
5.4	Net income, $7,710
5.5	Net income, $85
5.6	Corrected net income, $1,985
6.1	No check figure
6.2	Trial balance total, $27,625
6.3	Net loss, $8,575
6.4	Net Loss, $2,036
6.5	Net income, $104
6.6	Trial balance total, $37,115
CP#1	Trial balance total, $386,782.64
	Net income, $2,465.18
7.1	Schedule of accounts receivable, $5,852.10
7.2	Sales journal AR column total, $7,896.60
7.3	Sales journal, AR column total, $897.00
7.4	Sales journal, AR column total, $13,075.40
7.5	Sales journal, AR column total, $2,328.75
8.1	Purchases journal, AP column total, $8,051.75
8.2	Purchases journal, AP column total, $6,088.30
8.3	Purchases journal, AP column total, $33,250.25
8.4	Purchases journal, AP column total, $11,556.00
8.5	Purchases journal, AP column total, $8,035.70

Problem Number	Check Figure
9.1	CR journal, cash debit column total, $18,664.05
9.2	CP journal, cash credit column total, $8,641,19
9.3	CP journal, cash debit column total, $10,430.30
	CP journal, cash credit column total, $9,602.60
9.4	CR journal, cash debit column total, $7,940.95
	CP journal, cash credit column total, $6,241.04
9.5	Combined journal cash debit column total, $8,601.00
9.6	Combined journal cash debit column total, $5,774.40
10.1	Adjusted bank balance, $4,646.64
10.2	Adjusted bank balance, $6,321.81
10.3	Adjusted bank balance, $3,791.29
10.4	Adjusted bank balance, $12,642.50
10.5	Adjusted bank balance, $24,512.00
10.6	Total petty cash disbursements, $95.10
10.7	Total petty cash disbursements Jan. 16–31, $97.60
11.1	Net income, $3,535
11.2	Net income, $6,530
11.3	Total assets, $109,600
11.4	Net income, $3,285
11.5	Net loss, $870
CP#2	CR journal cash debit column total, $19,666.95
	CP journal cash credit column total, $14,782.91
	Adjusted Trial balance, $120,947.12
12.1	Gross earnings, $3,692.80
12.2	Net earnings, $2,508.13
12.3	Net earnings, $3,080.58
12.4	Net earnings, $3,023.18
13.1	Cumulative net pay, Jan. 31, $2,845.68
13.2	June wages expense, $8,672.00
13.3	Total remittance, $9,196.27
13.4	Workers' compensation insurance additional premium, $82.99
13.5	Total deductions, $80,142.52
13.6	Total taxable wages Nov. 1–7, $3,394
	Total taxable wages Nov. 8–14, $1,849
CP#3	Net earnings, Dec. 8, $3,098.33; Dec. 15, $3,068.70; Dec. 22, $3,258.11; Dec. 29, $2,547.89
14.1	Allocated to Jones, $25,000
14.2	No check figure
14.3	Share of net income to Coleman, $16,000
14.4	No check figure
14.5	(c) Credit Watts, capital, $42,500
14.6	(c) Debit Bentley, capital, $30,000 to distribute loss to him and debit Bentley, capital, $18,000 to distribute cash

Index